SANTALI BEAKO̱RO̱N

SAMAṄOK̇KANA

Alakjạ̃ṛĩ Murmutạkinren dulạṛiạ
Bạbu James J. Murmu

Ar
onko sanam so̠maj do̠ro̠diạko
o̠ko̠e do̠ ạḍi khicạ umạrrege
sermapuriko dukạn lahaen.

Kiạ Jharna So̠no̠do̠r Kạmiṭi,
Sahebgõ̠ñj, Santal Pargana, India

SANTALI BEAKO̱RO̱N
PART-I

Based on P. O. Bodding's
Materials for a Santali Grammar

Alakjãṛĩ Murmu
Rạghunath Hãsdak̓

GYAN

ISBN: 978-81-212-1960-0

Published, 2019

Published by

Gyan Publishing House
5, Ansari Road
Daryaganj, New Delhi-110002
Phone: 011-47034999, 9811692060
www.gyanbooks.com
E-mail: books@gyanbooks.com

Printed at: G. Print Process, Delhi.

ỌNỌLIẠKINAḰ ONOROM

Alakjā̤ṛī Murmu

Man Alakjā̤ṛī Murmu dọ noa dhuṛi dhạrti reaḱ pạhil marsal dọ 05.10.1955 hilạḱe ńẹlleda. Uniaḱ bukạ dọ topawakana-Ato Chọṭa Durgạpur (Jẹṭkẹ Durgạpur), (phẹḍ-Hirạnpur), Ḍak Oṛaḱ-Ạrjunpur, Jilạ Sahebgō̤ńj (S.P.), Jharkhaṇḍ. Nui ać babawaḱ ńutum dọ Jạdu Murmu ar gọgọ dọ Mạni Soren. Man Alakjā̤ṛī dọ Muṇḍli Misạn (Tinpahaṛ) khọn Miḍil khan Miṭris Biḍạu dọ Guihạjuṛi (Ḍumkạ) khọne pas oḍokleda. Inạ tayọm kọlẹj dọ Sahebgọńjreye paṛhaolena. Laha sẹć paṛhaoḱa mẹnte, nui dọ Bharọt reaḱ Rajdhạni Dilli sẹće dạṛ hẹćlena. Dillire paṛhao baṛakate, nui dọ nọṇḍẹge *Ministry of Defence*re miṭ *civilian* lekate sọrkari kạmireye bọlọena.

Man Alakjā̤ṛī Murmu dọ miṭ sọmaj susạriạge. Uni dọ Gọṭa Bharọt Santal Bhạlại ar Lẹgcar Bạisi (Nāwā Dilli) sāote hō̤ joṛaoe tahē̤kana. Kạṭić khọnge nui dọ Santali sāohẹṭre ạḍi mọn tahē̤ hẹćakantaea. Onatege nui dọ ạḍi lekan sọmaj ranakaḿ bisại cetan Santali ar Hindi sakamkore ạḍi lekan daman-daman ọnọlkoe ọl ạgueṭa.

Nit hạbićte Man Alakjā̤ṛī Murmu họṭẹte ọlakan noako puthi chapa sọdọrakana - *"Pạrsi dọ Sọmaj Reaḱ Ạrsi"*, *"Pạrsi dọ Ame Sāohāmea"* ar Hinditeaḱ *"Samae Ka Huṅkar"*.

Rạghunath Hãsdaḱ

Man Rạghunath Hãsdaḱaḱ bukạ topa dọ Ato Pạriạṛdaha, Ḍak Oṛaḱ–Bạliạḍaṅgal, (Phẹḍ-Mahespur), Jilạ-Pakọṛ, Jharkhaṇḍ-814 111. Uniaḱ janam dọ 06.03.1974 hilạḱ hoelena. Man Rạghunath Hãsdaḱ aċ babawaḱ ńutum dọ Mạńjhi Hãsdaḱ ar gọgọaḱ ńutum dọ Surujmuni Mạrḍi. Nuiaḱ ọl-paṛhao dọ ato iskul khọnge ẹhọp̣lena, Miḍil iskul dọ Bạliạḍaṅgal khọn, khan Miṭris Biḍạu dọ Amṛapaṛa *High School* khọne pas oḍokleda. *Inter* dọ S.P. College Dumka ar IGNOU khọn dọ BA (Hindi). Man Rạghunath Hãsdaḱ dọ teheń gapa miṫ ceceṫ mahasọege.

Rạghunath Hãsdaḱ dọ jọtọ lekan lipite Santali puthiko dọe paṛhao baṛaeṫkan tahẽkangea, mẹnkhan asọkaete onako reaḱ banan *(spelling)* ńẹlte dọ ạḍi kis-kise ạikạueṫkan tahẽkana.

Tinre Rạghunath mahasọe dọ P. O. Boḍiṅ sãoteye opromena, khane ńẹlkeda jẹ P. O. Boḍiṅma tis sedaere cọ ona Santali aṛaṅ ar urgạn gọṛhọn babọtmae ọl cukạuakaṫ. Mẹnkhan Rạghunath Mahasọeaḱ bhabna dọ niạge je cedaḱ ẹntere hõ Man P. O. Boḍiṅaḱ uduḱ ḍahar dọ baṅbon pańjaeṫkana. Nõḱõe noako uihạrkatege nẹ hạli Man Rạghunath Hãsdaḱ dọ Bhasa Bigyan cetanre kuṛpaṛe kạmikana.

Nẹ hạli Man Rạghunath Hãsdaḱ dọ Santali reaḱ Aṛaṅ ar Urgạn Gọṛhọn cetanreye kạmikana.

ONOṚ

Pạrsi dọ miṫ dinre baṅ sirjạuakana. Ona sirjạuḱre tinạḱ jug cọṅ hosọr parọmakana. Niạ laha noa hõ baḍae reaḱ ạḍi jạruṛ je ẹṇḍẹkhan manwawaḱ sirjọn dọ tọbẹ tis? Cedaḱje pạrsi dọ ẹkẹn manwageko beohara, manwa chaḍa noa dọ jãhãtinạḱ janwarko hotẹte hõ beoharoḱ, onkoaḱ ona aṛaṅ dọ pạrsi ọhọbon mẹn daṛekea, bickọm ona dọ ẹkẹn aṛaṅ mọtọgebo metaḱa.

Dhọrọm reaḱ Sọnọt Puthikore manwa sirjọn reaḱ ạḍi lekan lạnạiko menaḱ iạte, ona sẹċ jạsti baṅ galmaraokate, noa dọ sạri utạrgea je tis sedaere cọ Cando Baba dọ pạhil gọ-babaye sirjạuleṫkinạ. Bujhạu ocobon lạgiṫ, unkin dọ Pilcu Haṛam ar Pilcu Buḍhibon metakinkana. Pilcu Haṛam-Buḍhiren bõs-budạko saṅge idiena. Khan onko dọ duniạ reaḱ kona-konareko ạtiṅ pasnao idiena. Jọs katha dọ niạge je abo Hoṛ họpọnko hõ miṫ thọkrebon hạtiṅ begarente, jaga-jagare bẹrẹl baṛakate nahaḱ dọ Jharkhaṇḍ, Bihar, Uṛisa, Pạchim Baṅgal, Assam, Meghalay, Tripura eman rajọsṭi, khan Bharọt reaḱ lạṭu-lạṭu sọhọrko chaḍa bahre disạm Nepal, Mayanmar, Bhuṭan ar Baṅgladẹs emankore hõbon girạbạsiakana.

Ṭuṅ ghuṛire pạrsi dọ baṅ sirjạuakana, bickọm ẹtọhọp̣re manwa dọ guṅgṛạgebon tahẽkana. Miṫ eṭagiċ sāo gapalmarao lạgiṫ dọ uduḱ-unuduḱte kạmibon calaoleda. Bhorme-bhormete jinisko reaḱ jãhãn cinhạ, citạr, họṛmọ hạṭiṅko reaḱ laṛaona tayọm sẹsantire dọ aṛaṅko reaḱ lipi sirjạuena. Ọnẹbon baḍae leka; pạrsi dọ bar lekana - Rọṛteaḱ ar Ọlteaḱ. Ọnọl lạgiṫ oka citạr beoharoḱkan, onage lipi dọko metaḱkana.

Aboren hapṛamko dọ caḱ cọ *Puthi khọn thutige sọrọsaḱko* metawada. Mẹnkhan jug reaḱ tanaṛamre hapṛamkoaḱ noa hunudis dọ ekal bẹrtha utạrena. Nahaḱ jug dọ ạḍige bọdọl hẹċakana. Kạmpuṭar jug hẹċente sanamaḱ dọ cupuṫre hẹċ samṭaoena. Noa surikre Santali pạrsi reaḱ nagambon paṅjalekhan, ạḍi bhabnage aṭkaroḱkana. ẹnte jug hisạbte pạrsi dọ ceka cọye thiyạ thapeyentabona.

O̱no̱l rupre Santaliteak̓ pa̱hil puthi do̱ kana - *An Introduction to the Santal Language.* Noa puthi do̱ mit̓ Misa̱na̱ri *Rev. Jeremia Philips* ho̱te̱te 1852 salre chapa so̱do̱rlena. Uni do̱ Uṛisa reak̓ Jelasorre tahẽ̱kate noa puthi do̱e o̱lleda. Noa puthire 5000 Santali sabadko la̱git̓ do̱ Baṅgla haro̱p beoharakana. La̱ikak̓ do̱ nia̱ge je noa puthi do̱ Santali Beako̱ro̱n cetanre o̱lakan tahẽ̱kana. Nui tayo̱m a̱ḍi lekan misa̱na̱riko do̱ Santali pa̱rsiko susa̱r idileda. Onko modre ńum ńamo̱go̱k̓ bidesi sahebko do̱ – *Rev. E. L. Puxley, Dr. C. R. Lepsus, Rev. W. T. Stores, Rev. L. O. Skrefsrud, Rev. Edward C. Jonson, Rev. E. G. Man, Rev. H. P. Borresen, Rev. Edward Cornelius, R. Carstairs, Rev. C. H. Bompass, Rev. R. R. Rosenland, Rev. J. Gausdal, Sir, W. G. Archer, Andrew Campbell, Rev. W. T. Cole, R. M. Macphail, W. Martin, R. Carstairs* ar *Rev. P. O. Bodding* eman.

Bestebon baḍae leka; oka so̱do̱r samaṅ ro̱ṛkatebon galmaraok̓kan, ona do̱ ro̱ṛteak̓ pa̱rsi, khan oka o̱lkate la̱ia̱go̱k̓kan ona do̱ o̱lteak̓ pa̱rsiko metak̓kana. Noa hõ pusṭa̱uabonma je Beako̱ro̱n se̱ *Grammar* do̱ pa̱rsi kho̱n baṅge lahak̓a, bicko̱m Beako̱ro̱n do̱ pa̱rsirege so̱ge̱ mesalgea. E̱ṇḍe̱khan Beako̱ro̱n do̱ onage; oka do̱ pa̱rsi reak̓ ro̱ṛ ar o̱l babo̱t jo̱to̱ lekan a̱n-a̱riye la̱iet̓kan. Ona surikre la̱ikak̓ do̱ nia̱ge je Beako̱ro̱n do̱ aso̱kacte pa̱rsi reak̓ lipi ar ayat reak̓ jo̱to̱ lekateye chiṇḍa̱uet̓a.

Santali pa̱rsi cetan a̱ḍi kho̱nd ro̱ndket̓re baḍaena je Santali la̱git̓ P. O. Boḍiṅ okae ka̱mi oṭoakat̓, ona do̱ bigyanik dharate *(scientifically)* jo̱to̱ bo̱ḍo̱ jo̱to̱ kho̱n so̱ro̱s uta̱rgea. Boḍiṅ saheb do̱ Santali reak̓ lipiye sapṛao gula̱ṇḍkeda ar mimit̓ Santali sabadko do̱ Beako̱ro̱n dharateye ńum oṭokada. Pa̱rsi cetanre Boḍiṅ saheb jãhãn sa̱bik Beako̱ro̱n puthi do̱ bae o̱lakada, bicko̱m uni do̱ Beako̱ro̱n o̱l la̱git̓ mo̱so̱la se̱ jo̱to̱ lekan saj sapap̓koe do̱ho̱ oṭokada. Beako̱ro̱n o̱l la̱git̓ Boḍiṅ sahebak̓ noako saj sapap̓ do̱ a̱ḍi so̱ro̱sanak̓ge - *A Santali Grammar for Beginners-1929; Materials for A Santali Grammar, Part-I (Mostly Phonetics)-1930; Materials for A Santali Grammar, Part-II (Mostly Morphology)-1929; A Santal Dictionary (V vol)-1932-36* ar mit̓ o̱no̱l - *A Plea for a Standardized System of Writing the Muṇḍa or Kolarian Languages, Journal of the Asiatic Society of Bengal - 1925 (N.S.XXI).*

Nit hạbić asọkaete Beakọrọn cetanre ạḍi kọm puthikoge ọl baṛawakana. Jãhãtinạk̓ puthikoge ọlakan; mẹnkhan onako sanam dọ P. O. Boḍiṅ samaṅre ạḍi kọmjọrge sạbitok̓kana. Judi hutkạm onko ọnọliạko Boḍiṅ saheb bes lekako bujhạu tiạk̓lekhan, pasẹć onko họtẹte ọlak̓ Beakọrọn dọ ar bhage hoe daṛekok̓a. Mẹnkhan Boḍiṅ cetanre ạuṛi-pạthạuṛi sirạgaete, uni dọko chibaṅaekana. Jãhãtinạk̓ Boḍiṅ saheb Họṛ kukhi khọn bae ọmọnlen ar sẹ jãhãtinạk̓ uni dọ bidesi ar misạnạriye tahẹ̃kan, mẹnkhan Santali cetan uniak̓ banaḍae dọ unạk̓ge sọrọsa je tin din hạbić noa dhuṛi dhạrtire Santali tahẹ̃na, un din hạbić P. O. Boḍiṅ dọ jivẹt̓geye tahẹ̃na.

Sạrige Beakọrọn dọ pạrsi reak̓ mimit̓ gọṭẹć sabad ar sẹ ayatko ruti-rutiye chiṇḍạuet̓kana. Mẹnkhan pạrsi ar sẹ jãhã lekan Beakọrọn niạmạri kange, ona dọ sọmaj khọn dọ ọhọge marań daṛelena. Ạḍi hahaṛage aṭkarok̓kana; ẹnkathae aboren hapṛamko họ̃ dhọra bań dhọra noa Beakọrọn ạri cetanreko *"Citrighuṭulet̓a."* Ar unre Beakọrọn ạri dọko bạṭilket̓te sọmajạrige sọrọsak̓ko metawada ar sẹ sọmajiạ anaṅgọcge sanam họṛteko manaokeda.

Beakọrọnre mit̓ ạri menak̓a - Lekha *(Number).* Noa Lekha ạri lekate Santalire dọ pẹ lekan Lekha menak̓a; metak̓me - Mit̓ Lekha *(Singular),* Bar Lekha *(Dual Number)* ar Saṅge Lekha *(Plural).* Khaṭọte bujhạuabon lạgit̓; mit̓ *Present Indefinite* ayat reak̓ nạmunabon ńẹla :-

Kạjnum *(Verb)*	**Lekha** ***(Number)***		
	Mit̓ Lekha *(Singular*	Bar Lekha *(Dual Number)*	Saṅge Lekha *(Plural)*
Calak̓	*Iń dọń calak̓kana.*	*Ạliń dọliń calak̓kana.*	*Ale dọle calak̓kana.*

Noa ạri lekate, okare miṫ hoṛ (jivianaḱ) se̱ miṫṭe̱ć (be̱jivianaḱ) reaḱ bibro̱n babo̱tre galmaraoḱkan, o̱ṇḍe̱ do̱ Miṫ Lekha reaḱge laṛcaṛ hoyoḱa. Me̱nkhan Santal so̱maj reaḱ le̱gcar-ạricạli lekate miṫ jãwãe se̱ bạhu do̱ jãhãtinạḱe aċ mo̱to̱ge, e̱ntere hõ tinre sạgại lekate judi jãwãe ar se̱ye bạhu kankhan, tinre uni do̱ miṫ eṭagiċren maraṅ ho̱ṛko sãote metaḱme go̱-babaḱ lekanko - hõeharea, ajhnarea, bahõeharea sãote do̱ Beako̱ro̱n reaḱ niạm kãṛgokate, jãhãtinạḱe aċ mo̱to̱ge, uni do̱ aċaḱ galmaraore Bar Lekha reaḱe laṛcaṛa. Onkage balayako hõ. Balaya galmaraore jãhãtinạḱ bar ho̱ṛgekin galmarao, to̱be̱ unkin do̱ dene banar gharõńjrenko ńum halaṅkate Saṅge Lekha reaḱkin laṛcaṛa. Noa pạrtulte sanamaḱ do̱ pusṭạu uṭaroḱa :-

Bạhu se̱ jãwãe miṫ eṭagiċren baba/go̱go̱ se̱ maraṅ ho̱ṛko são galmaraore :-

Baba/Go̱go̱ - Tinre co̱ jãwãe/bạhuben he̱ċakan?

Jãwãe/Bạhu - Holaliń he̱ċakana ba/go̱.

Balayakin galmaraoḱre :-

Pạhiliċ - Ado̱, ce̱ṫ leka hộ sumdhi, napae baṛageabon tho̱?

Dosariċ - Hẽ hộ sumdhi, napae do̱bon napae baṛagea. Me̱nkhan Bala kuṛige thoṛa…

Cedaḱ e̱ṇḍe̱khan onka do̱? Noa do̱ noa iạte; tinre bapla hoyoḱkana, unre bạhu-jãwãe do̱ sanamaḱ lekatekin miṫ uṭaroḱkana. Metaḱme unkin do̱ jãhãtinạḱ eskargekin tahe̱n, me̱nkhan aso̱kaete maraṅ ho̱ṛko samaṅre do̱kin bana hoṛ kana. Bạhu se̱ jãwãe do̱ ạkin banar juri-pạri mesalkate galmarao hoyoḱtaea. Onkage unkinaḱ gharõńj hõ miṫ eṭaḱ gharõńj sãote to̱l midoḱkana. Ona iạtege bạhu/jãwãe do̱ maraṅ hoṛ sãotekin galmaraoḱre - *ạliń, aben* Bar Lekha reaḱkin laṛcaṛa ar balayako do̱ - *abo/abon* Saṅge Lekha reaḱko beohara.

Ạḍi bhabna se̱le̱ṫ lại so̱do̱ro̱ḱkana e̱nkathae Beako̱ro̱n se̱ *Grammar* lạgiṫ gulạṇḍ uṭạr sabadko reaḱ Ạḍi anaṭ aṭkaroḱkana. Sapha kathate mẹnlekhan, ninạḱge mẹnọgọḱkana je jageliń daṛeat́, onako sabad dọ Santalite tọrjọmae reaḱliń kurumuṭuakada. Boge-bạṛic̓ dọ jọtọkotebon ńẹl juta.

Sạrige Man P. O. Boḍiṅ dọ marań pạrsi budgạriạgeye *(linguist)* tahẽkana. Uni Santali lạgit́ okae kạmiakat́ dọ jugero jug hạbic̓ jiạrge tahẽ idiḱa. Mẹnkhan Boḍiṅ danańen unạḱ din parọmọḱkanre hõ uniaḱ lại ḍahar dọ caḱ cọ bhage sạhit́te bańbon pańjaet́a. Nõḱõe noako guni-bhạbikatege ạliń noa puthiren bạpuṛic̓ sasapṛaokin dọ uniaḱ gọyọn pańjae reaḱliń kurumuṭuakada. Saphate pusṭauabonma je ạliń dọ ạliń sẹc̓ khọn ar jãhãnaḱ lại reaḱ dọ bańliń uṭu cuṭu baṛaekana, bickọm Man Boḍiṅ saheb okae lạiakat́, onage ape disạm họṛko talare porcar-pasnao reaḱliń kurumuṭuakada. Hẽ, jẹmọn ar jãhãn bhul-bisạrko alo hoyoḱ, ona lạgit́ dọ Hindi ar Iṅgrạji reaḱ Beakọrọn puthiko reaḱ hõ gọṛọ hataoakana. Hoe daṛeaḱa, noa puthi sasapṛaore pasẹc̓ jãhãkore tar antar menaḱkhan, ona dọ ạliń sasapṛaokin ṭhen lạitabonpe, jẹmọn onako dọ darae sọnọdọrkore sudhạr daṛeaḱ.

Johar sẹlẹt́,

Santal Sọmajre ạliń dọ,

Tạrik : May 20, 2019
Pakọṛ (Santal Pargana)

Alakjãṛĩ Murmu
Rạghunath Hãsdaḱ

(An excerpt from "A Santal Dictionary", Vol. I, by P. O. Bodding)

Preface

The Santal language, or Santali, as it is usually called by Anglo-Indians, is spoken by about three million people living in a strip of country to the south of the Ganges, comprising districts belonging to Bengal and Bihar and Orissa in North-eastern India, and now also in northern Bengal districts up to Assam. The Santals are by far the most numerous of the aboriginal peoples and tribes known generally as Kols, Kolarians or Muṇḍas.

None of these names has been generally accepted. The designation Muṇḍã is perhaps now most commonly used, chiefly owing to the fact that it was adopted in Sir GEORGE GRIERSON'S monumental Linguistic Survey of India, because it was used by MAX MULLER, the first scholar to classify these vernaculars as a separate linguistic group. According to Santal traditions the ancestors of these peoples came as immigrants to Champa (possibly the country to the North-west of the present Chota Nagpur plateau), prior to which "we and the Muṇḍãs, the Birhoṛ, the Kuṛmbis, etc., were called by the name of Kharwar". This name apparently included all Muṇḍãs, except the Savaras and Gadabas in the South, peoples unknown to the present day Santals. For this reason, therefore, the Linguistic Survey used Kherwari as a common name for these languages, the Savaras and Gadabas excluded.

Now Santal is a name given to this people by foreigners. In Santal tradition it is told the name was given to them after they had been resident for some time in *Sat* or *Sãot*, a tract of the present Midnapur district. The Hindi form *Santal* and the Bengali form of the same word, *Sãotaṛ*, accordingly seem to describe them as a people belonging to Sat or Saot, Sat'ers as one might say. This is quite possible. Doublets such as *Santhal* or *Sonthal,* which are, even at the present day, occasionally used in official documents and publications, will, no doubt, gradually disappear.

It might be mentioned that *Sat* has been explained as derived from Sanskrit *sãmanta*, bordering, so that the same *Santal* might really mean "a man of the border", "a borderer".

Among themselves, the Santals use the designation *hoṛ,* i.e., "a man", "a human being", and their language is called *hoṛ roṛ,* "men's speech" or "talk".

How the Santals or their ancestors were known to other Indian peoples, is a question that cannot be discussed here. The description given of the *dasyus* in the Mahabharata seems to be adaptable to many a Santal. The Ramayaṇa tells us how Rama was assisted by Hanuman, the Monkey King. It is of interest in this connexion to remember that the Hindus, even to this day, occasionally call the Santals monkeys, and, further, that the Santal traditions state that their ancestors went to and assisted King Ram, as they call him when he conquered Ravaṇa, or *Rabon raj,* the Santals say, in Lanka or Ceylon. If their traditions are to be believed, their ancestors - or at all events, some of them - were at one time of a much higher civilization than the Santals of to-day and themselves administered a country of their own .

The Santals first came to the parts how known as the Santal Parganas district some 150 years ago, having been called in by Paharia landlords to clear the jungle. About one hundred years ago, Europeans began to come into contact with them, missionaries being the first to take an interest in, and to study their language.

The first to publish anything about, and also in, the Santal language, was, so far as the present writer knows, the Rev. J. Phillips, a Baptist missionary living in Orissa. In 1852, he published "An Introduction the Santal language." This work contains a grammar and a vocabulary. Mr. Phillips used the Bengali characters for Santali, and he has evidently to some degree been influenced by his knowledge of Bengali. As a first attempt it is a creditable piece of work.

Shortly afterwards, in 1855, came the Santal insurrection, in reality an attempt to get rid of the Hindu usurers and oppressors, and by no means an insurrection against the British administration, or the Honorable East India Company, then ruling the country. This event made the Santals more generally known and led to important results. A new district was formed, the present Santal Parganas, with separate administration rules, the object of which was to protect the Santals and other aborigines from their more cunning neighbors. Another result was that Christian missions took up work among the Santals in this new district. From this time dates the proper study of the Santal language.

In 1868, the Rev. E. L. PUXLEY, of the Church Missionary Society, edited "A Vocabulary of the Santali Language". Mr. PUXLEY discontinued the use of Bengali characters, and since then, except for a very few small books, practically only a few fragments of Scripture and Hymns book used by Santals living in the Midnapur and adjoining districts, no Santal text has been printed in the Bengali alphabet. The reason given by those who still adhere to the use of that script is that the Santals for whom these publications are intended are, as a rule, acquainted with it.

Some remarks may be added in this place about the reasons why we have abandoned an Indian system of writing and adopted the Roman alphabet, with the many troublesome diacritical marks.

If we leave out of consideration the question of the shape and the forms of the letters, it may be said that the Indian alphabets are far superior to the Roman Script in so far as the consonants, with the exception of the checked stops, are concerned. Each letter represents practically only one sound; there are separate characters for the dental, palatal and cacuminal stops, unaspirated and aspirated, where we use a combination of characters (as especially in the case of aspirated consonants), or diacritical signs. The difficulty arises when we come to the vowels, because Bengali and Hindi, the only two Indian systems that might be used, have less vowel characters than is needed for writing Santali, and these systems do not easily lend themselves to the use of diacritical marks. The Hindi short *a* and the corresponding short *o̧* in Bengali, have no separate characters at all when preceded by a consonant, with the result that when it is not to be pronounced, special signs or devices have to be applied, while post-consonantic *i* and *u* must be indicated by means of additions to the consonants.

Diacritical signs are a nuisance; but until we get separate and easily written characters for all the different sounds, they cannot be avoided. The Roman alphabet, with all its imperfections, can easily be modified by the use of such signs. In writing Santali, a number has been introduced. A little more will be said on this subject further on. Here, I shall only add one additional reason for using the Roman alphabet. An Indian script would present difficulty to all those who have not been specially taught to use it. One of the chief initial obstacles, when we try to learn a foreign language, and one which also makes it more difficult for different peoples to understand each other, is the bewildering amount of systems of writing. Until we get a practical, workable system, it seems advisable to use an alphabet that is known to and used by the majority of mankind.

Mr. PUXLEY - to use his own words - "adopted a system of letters employed by Forbes, Shakespeare and others for Roman Hindustani," with a few omissions and additions. It was a first attempt; one might have wished that he had made use of LIPSIUS'S Standard Alphabet, which had, in 1868, been available for five years, and in which Mr. PUXLEY'S own Society was especially interested.

So far as the present writer knows, no vocabulary or dictionary of the Santal language was now edited until Mr. ANDREW CAMPBELL'S dictionary appeared in 1899. Before dealing with this book, however, mention has to be made of a work that has had an important on all later treatises of the Santal language, viz., the late Rev. L. O. SKREFSRUD'S "A Grammar of the Santal Language," Benares 1873. It is in certain respects very cumbersome, and unnecessarily so; there are a few mistakes in details, and SKREFSRUD tried to arrange the grammar of an agglutinating language on the pattern of inflexional tongues (Dr. WENGER'S Bengali Grammar seems to have been a kind of model). But with these reservations, it must be said that this grammar is an astonishing work for a man who, when he wrote it, had been among the people for less than four years. SKREFSRUD himself told the present writer, that the grammar was ready from his hand in 1871. SKREFSRUD was an excellent linguist and a practical phonetician. To begin with, he used the Bengali characters for Santali, but gave them up for the system he introduced, which we have since always used with three simplifications, *c* for *ch, ch* for *chh* and *c* for *ċ*. It is not an invention of SKREFSRUD'S, but an application of what he had seen in the above-mentioned work of LIPSIUS. The same system has now been gradually adopted by most people using Santali, except that sometimes no attempt has been made to distinguish the open and closed *e* and *o* sounds, the result having been much mispronunciation and some avoidable misunderstanding.

For all practical purposes, the system has proved to be excellently serviceable. Naturally, it is not expected to be up to the demands of present-day phonetic science, more particularly where the many vowel sounds are concerned.

I have been asked why I have not introduced the system recommended by the International Phonetic Association. My answer is that it is known to phonetic experts only. For practical purposes something much simpler is needed. But I freely acknowledge that it might have been advisable to have given, within parentheses, the Santal words written in this script.

Another complaint has been that no distinction has been made between long and short vowels. The reason is very much the same as that stated above - it would present practical difficulties. Besides, the vowels of Santal words vary very much in practical speech. In certain cases, where a vowel has a special length or shortness affecting the meaning, this has been mentioned.

I may add that length and stress is by no means always the same in Santali loan-words as in the language from which they are borrowed. Take e.g., Santali *mahajo̱n,* pronounced with stress on the first *o* and a short stress less *a,* practically like two words. In Bengali and Hindi the *a* is long and stressed.

Some remarks have also been made about the position in the dictionary of vowels with diacritical signs. The reason why these vowels, *ạ, e̱, ọ, o̱,* have been separated from *a, e, o,* is that they are distinctly separate sounds, and that it has sometimes led to confusion when no distinction has been made. Moreover, we sometimes find exactly the same principle followed in European languages; take e.g., the German *u* and *ũ,* Swedish *a* and *ã, o* or the way in which vowels are separated in Magyar. The diacritical signs in such languages are placed above the vowels, while we have them below. In Santali and other languages many of these modified vowels are "resultant". I am sorry that it is too late now to separate the nasalized vowels in the same way. In their case, however, the vowel sound is the same, with or without nasalization.

As already mentioned, CAMPBELL'S dictionary came in 1899. It is a very creditable work; but phonetically and grammatically it is not wholly satisfactory. When I once asked my old friend why he had not used diacritical marks in order to distinguish the open vowel sounds, his answer was that his ear was not sharp enough to hear the difference between the open and the closed sounds. A similar remark applies to his notation of the checked consonants. In a number of words he has two or even three forms, where only one is correct. When a *k̇, ċ,* or *t'* follows an *i,* it may sometimes be difficult to hear which individual checked consonant is spoken; but is always possible to apply a test. The work is not CAMPBELL'S alone; several of the Scotch missionaries gave what they had collected to CAMPBELL. I have sometimes the impression that a good many of the misspelt words are due to their having been literally copied from what Indians, Santals included, have written. It is not very encouraging to see even school-inspectors and educated Santals write e.g., *Marandi* for *Mạrṇḍi, Hansdah* or *Hansdak* for *Hãsdak̇, ghọ̱ṭọ̱na* (the Bgl. form, never used by Santals) for *ghoṭna,* etc., etc.

The discarding of diacritical marks has led to some curious mistakes. When CAMPBELL quotes the clause *dal olkedeako,* they struck and walled him, he enters it under *ol,* i.e., *o̱l,* to write, draw, etc. The Santal pronunciation is not, however, *o̱l,* but *ọl,* which means fermented, mouldy. *Dal ọl* corresponds exactly to the Norwegian *mørọ̱anke,* to beat soft, to beat to a jelly.

CAMPBELL never writes *ṇ,* This is probably due to the fact that the cacuminal *ṇ* is always found preceding a cacuminal *ḍ* or *ṭ.* But in a few cases the *n* before these cacuminal sounds is dental. CAMPBELL further believed that only *w* and no *v* is found in Santali - a belief which it is difficult to understand.

Something now remains to be said regarding the present work, it is origin, its aims, and the method followed.

When SKREFSRUD sojourned among the Santals, he naturally at once took up the study of their language. The only work he published on Santali, however, was the grammar mentioned above; but from the very first he took care to collect Santali words with the object of ultimately publishing a dictionary. Occupanied as he was with his manifold duties, he could never spare time enough for completing this work. When the present writer came to India in January 1890, SKREFSRUD after a few months asked him to reverse his Santali-English vocabulary into English-Santali, a work that was completed during the rainy season, of that year. This gave an insight into the language that might otherwise have taken a long time to acquire.

As the same time I made a copy of SKREFSRUD'S material for my personal use, and this consequently became the base of my own work. I suppose my mode of working is but little different from that of others who have been similarly occupied. Whenever I heard a word that I did not know, it was noted down, and if not found in the dictionary, entered there. I always carried a notebook where the phrases and expressions I heard were jotted down. Some of the laws regulating the formation of words in the Santal language gradually became apparent, and this also led to the discovery of a large number of words.

SKREFSRUD'S work was a vocabulary, and he had never found the necessary time for any deeper treatment of individual words; in the whole of his work there was scarcely any illustration of the varying use of vocables and terms. After 1890, he did very little in connexion with his dictionary.

When, in 1903, I had provisionally finished the translation of the Bible into Santali, SKREFSRUD asked me to take up the dictionary. He handed his whole material to me, and gave me a free hand to use it, as I might find necessary. SKREFSRUD was, as previously mentioned, an excellent linguist; he had an extraordinary ability to pick up a foreign language and to use it; he had few equals in this respect. He had, moreover, a penetrating intellect, that enabled him to go straight to the centre of anything that occupied him. If he had only had time and leisure to go on with the dictionary. I am confident that the result would have been excellent.

The vocabulary that SKREFSRUD handed over to me contained a little more than 13,000 words. My copy had by then twice that number. While SKREFSRUD'S vocabulary naturally has been my foundation, I wish here to express my indebtedness to CAMPBELL'S dictionary as well. I have had it at hand during the whole of my work, and, as will be seen, I have, for the sake of completeness, entered a number of words found there, but not used or not acknowledged as Santal words by Santals with whom I have had two reasons for incorporating the majority of such words in my dictionary, the one being that they may be found in non-standard writings and need an explanation; the other, that, although a large percentage of these words is unknown to, and not understood by, Santals to the East of Manbhum, where Mr. CAMPBELL lived, many of them may be Kol words used by Santal living more or less in contact with the Muṇḍãs and especially the Ko̱lhe̱s, and consequently of Kherwari interest. The majority are, however, loan-words of Aryan, i.e., Hindi or Bihari, origin. They are of some interest as showing how easily Santals may adopt words from their neighbours, either permanently or only temporarily, and they may be of some little help in showing how the language may develop or be spoilt by borrowing, also how dialects of the language may be formed. All words or forms taken from CAMPBELL and not known by Eastern Santals have been marked by adding “C”; when “not known here” or some similar expression is added, the reference is to the Southern parts of the Santal Parganas district and districts to the East, with the Santal inhabitants of which the writer has been in contact.

To show the difference between the language spoken by Santal Parganas-Santals and Manbhum-Santals the following personal experience may serve : Once when returning from a visit to Mr. CAMPBELL, I was wondering what two Santals who had accompanied me had found to laugh at - they were laughing all the way. When I asked them what the cause of their amusement was, they told me that they were enjoying the funny way in which the Santals of those parts spoke. They spoke like Ko̱lhe̱s, they said, and commenced to repeat what they had heard.

When I started my work on the dictionary in 1903, I was able to devote most of my time to it for about two years. SKREFSRUD had arranged his vocabulary somewhat in accordance with the Devanagari alphabet, commencing with the vowels, and then proceeding to the velars, palatals, etc., an arrangement which has much to recommend it - also from a phonetic point of view. During the two first years I followed the same plan; later, I was prevailed upon to adopt the order of the Roman alphabet. During the two first years I managed to work out all words beginning with a vowel and with *h.* Then regular work on the dictionary to be laid aside for about twenty years, up to 1924 or thereabouts, when I was again able to start in earnest. At present the dictionary is my principal occupation.

In addition to what has already been said about collecting words and phrases, it should be mentioned that my friend the late H. J. MUSTON, a gentleman of considerable linguistic gifts, helped me in such a way that he read through all available Santali prints, and wrote down all words not already entered in the dictionary.

When working on the dictionary, I have always had Santal sitting with me, never less than three at a time. These have been intelligent men with experience and knowledge of the people and their customs, and of their own language - as good men as are to be had - and, especially, also persons who are acknowledged as leaders in their village or other councils. Further, in all my work with the language, I have always made it a point to have about me villagers without any special knowledge of other languages than their own. It is, of course, also necessary to have well educated Santals as assistants; but my experience is, that their language is always more or less liable to be influenced by the foreign language in which they have had their training, and their knowledge of what should be their own is often limited and often peculiar. They have, however, to be used.

I have further copied out lists of all the words of my collection, and given them to Santals, asking them to write down what they understood by each word, and to give examples of how they use it. The written replies that I have obtained in this way in the course of many years have filled shelves.

Besides those already mentioned, I have had other co-workers, men who have collected plants, animals, insects, etc., for which the Santals have special names. In connexion with this I wish to express my indebtedness to the gentlemen in charge of the zoological section of the Indian Museum in Calcutta and of the Botanical Garden at Sibpur, who have always been ready to help me.

It should also be mentioned that I have tried to obtain words adopted by Santals who have emigrated to East Bengal and Assam, or such old words as have come to have a special meaning in those parts. I have also persuaded some Santal women of age and experience to write down special women's words and phrases. Santal women have a rich vocabulary and many curious expressions, especially, perhaps, terms of abuse. It is significant that the language has different words for scolding by a woman and scolding by a man. The women have also conserved quite a number of expressions which men may know, but do not generally use.

It is superfluous to say that every word has been tested and retested as to its meaning and use. I have never rested satisfied with what my predecessors have stated; it now and then happens that my assistants flatly deny the possibility of meanings and uses given even by SKREFSRUD. When "uncertain" is added to a word, it means that I have found the word in SKREFSRUD'S vocabulary, but have been unable to trace it anywhere else. In some cases, however, the addition refers to words copied from Mr. PUXLEY.

I need not add that all my illustrating examples have been taken down from the mouth of Santals; I have bit personally "prepared" any, nor have I entered any sentence which, in reality, is a translation from another language. All the examples are intended to show how a word is used; an English translation is always appended. As a rule it is literal, so far as this possible, even with some disregard of the exigencies of good English. In many cases a literal translation has not been possible. I trust the reader will be able to see the Santal's way of thinking and of giving expressions to his thoughts.

In giving illustrations so numerously, it has been my wish not only to show the language as it is spoken at the present time, but also to try to help those who have to use the language to avoid common mistakes. I have not had in view those who believe in their own ability to develop the language by introducing personal idioms.

The language shows the mental working of a people; many expressions will, better than lengthy explanations, give a glimpse into their mode of thinking and their association of ideas.

A number of ethnological and descriptive statements will be found in the dictionary. My principal reason for introducing them has been my wish to help all those who use the book to a clearer understanding of what each word stands for or refers to, without having to do independent research work; with the little literature that at present exists on these matters such research work could only be undertaken among the Santals. The ethnological remarks are not exhaustive; but they are, I hope, generally sufficient to give a correct idea of what a custom, etc., is. It is my intension, when the whole is ready, to publish an index of such matters, so that everybody will be able to turn up what is written on the subjects referred to without having to make a long search.

Within parentheses at the end of each article I have, so far as possible, added some etymological matter.

The Santals, as also the other Kol peoples and tribes, show a peculiar aptitude and propensity for adopting foreign words. This may be abundantly observed even at the present time. In very many cases these borrowed words represent what has been new or unknown to the people - what they have seen and heard of others. Words of this kind are of interest as giving information about the sate of Santal civilization and about the history and development of the people or their ancestors. It should be borne in mind that, so it is possible to judge, the Santals have been a wandering and migratory people.

In some cases these borrowed words represent what the Santals have seen with others, but have not had themselves.

Take e.g.; words like *naṅgraha, bajar,* and recently, *sǫhǫr,* words in common use for city, town, etc. The Santals have no towns of their own, but will often see such places abroad, and then adopt the foreign designation together with the notion. On the other hand, they possess villages, and will use their own word for "village", *ato,* for the villages of Hindus and Mohammedans. I certain expressions the Hindi words may be heard, e.g., *ga* or *gao, ga gǫṇḍa, bạsti,* but not attached to the name of a village. On the other hand, with reference to the present administration of the villages, and to the divisions of a village, we have borrowed words such as *mạṅjhi, paranik, jǫg mạṅjhi, goḍet, ṭola,* etc.

It is a well-known fact that the Santals preferably use separate words for the manifold objects observed by the senses, and that they have an immense number of words for things heard or seen, etc., whereas we are satisfied with fewer, and more general terms, to which we may, if needed, add some specializing word. Consequently, it is not possible for us to give a literal single-worded translation of all Santal expressions in English or any European tongue, and, when a Santal hears an alien world which seems to convey a notion even slightly different from what his own vocabulary will cover, it is natural for him to adopt the foreign word.

It will be understood from what has just been stated, that when a word in the dictionary has been characterized as "the same as" or "equal to" some other word, - provided the difference is not due to phonetic reasons -, there may, to the Santal mind, be an infinitesimal difference in connotation, perhaps only half conscious. The terms "same" or "equal" must in many touching on a subject which must be treated in connexion with word-information and cannot be properly dealt with in this place.

The words referred to above are such as the Santals

have borrowed from Aryan or, through them, from Semitic languages. In many, or perhaps in most cases, the words may not be absolutely identical in form, the difference often being due to the phonetically tendencies of the languages concerned. I have, in many such cases, quoted only the infinitive of the corresponding base in Hindi, etc.

Strangely enough, the Santals use some pure Sanskrit words, which, so far as I know, are not heard in present-day Hindi.

With regard to a considerable number of such apparent loan-words, the question has been raised whether they are really of Aryan origin, or whether, in their turn, they have been borrowed by the Aryans from another, non-Aryan language. This is a matter which must, and certainly will, be properly investigated. Though they have reached such a high state of formal development and possess such a richly varied vocabulary, Sanskrit and the Sanskritic languages are subject to the same laws as all other human tongues.

In addition to the words already referred to, which Santali has in common with Aryan languages, and which form the majority of the vocabulary of present Santali, there is a large number of words which, found in some Aryan language, cannot well be of Aryan stock, but must have often been explained as originally derived from the language of the Santals or their ancestors. Here we are met with some curious facts that have been much discussed of more recent years. We find that the same, or practically the same, words are widely spread over Asia and parts of Europe, and possibly also over some of the Pacific Islands. One of the very first to draw attention to possible connexion between Santali and languages spoken in the East, even so far as the Pacific islands and Australia, was the late Professor VILHELM THOMSEN of Copenhagen, one of the most eminent philologists of modern times. More recently, Pater W. SCHMIDT has discussed a number of languages which he brought together as a definite linguistic family and called Austric. He wanted also to include the Kol or Muṇḍã languages in this group. There is undoubtedly a number of common words. The same is, however, the case with other languages that have not been included in the Austric family. We find in Japanese a number of words for "eye" and "hand". It has happened that, when I have been looking for parallels, I have found nothing until I reached Japanese; e.g., *ko̱e,* to beg, to pray, in Japanese *koi.* Or to mention another word, the Santal name for village *ato.* In a Phillippine dialect we have the same word with the same meaning; in Muṇḍãri it is *hatu;* and in Japanese we find *satu.*

On the other hand, I have met with several Magyar words which sound like the corresponding Santal ones, but which I have not found elsewhere, e.g., Santali *bạ̈i,* convulsions, or an involuntary or unconscious state or movement of the body, and Magyar *baj,* with a similar meaning; or Santali *co̱k̇,* to kiss, Magyar *csȯk,* Finnish *suokko,* Lappish *čukle* - this may, however, be onomatopoeic; or Santali *kol,* Kurku *kul,* to send, and Lappish *kule,* the same, and so on. I shall not enter into further particulars. The parallels are so many that it is tempting to draw certain conclusions. Though I am not at present prepared to go so far as to say that Magyar and connected languages are of the same stock as Santali, it seems possible that the two groups have, in a remote past, been in close contact with each other or with another language from which they have both borrowed. To prove real relationship, more is required than a certain number of words in common - the grammatical system and structure will have to be carefully and historically examined.

Quite recently the question whether the Muṇḍã languages originally belonged to the Finno-Ugrian family, has been made the subject of a comprehensive study by the Hungarian scholar WILHELM VON HEVESY, and something has also been written about apparent traces of a certain influence exercised by some as yet not clearly defined old language or languages on Sanskrit and other oriental tongues. In this place, however, I shall not enter into a discussion of such far-reaching problems. In the etymological remarks in the Dictionary I have, in several places, taken notice of such correspondences in vocabulary as I have found especially noteworthy, without, however, wanting to claim a common origin in all such cases.

In closing these introductory remarks, I wish to express my deep gratitude to the Norwegian Academy of Science and Letters at Oslo for undertaking the publication of this work; to Professor Dr. STEN KONOW for his very careful reading of the proofs, and to the Printers for their excellent work in seeing the Dictionary through the press.

Mohulpahari, July 5th, 1932. P. O. Bodding

II

The above is not an excerpt but the contents are still very much relevant with regard to the Santals and their language Santali besides their present census.

P. O. Bodding a Norwegian Missionary came to India in January, 1890 and stayed at Mohulpahari, Santal Parganas, Jharkhand. He lived among the Santals and worked for them for 40 years. P. O. Bodding was an eminent anthropologist and the greatest Santali linguist. Bodding published more than twenty-five works on the Santals, including books, monographs, articles, three grammars and a dictionary, covering every aspect of Santal life. His greatest work is without doubt the Santal dictionary, published in five volumes over 1932-36, which is a comprehensive encyclopaedia of everything that concerns the Santals. In fact, the author's intention in bringing out this work was, as he himself remarked, to show the Santal - how he thinks, speaks and understands life, Bodding's last literary work, which he completed before he died in 1938, was the translation into English of Skrefsrud's book *Hoṛkoren Mare Hapṛamko reak̓ Katha.* He also wrote *Materials for a Santali Grammar* in two parts, published over 1923-29, which is still considered to be the best source for an advanced study of the Santali language. For the use of beginners he published *A Santali Grammar for Beginners* in 1929. In Santal Folktales published in Oslo in three volumes, he made available a rich treasure of genuine Santal folktales. He also furnished the Ethnographical Museum at Oslo with probably the richest collection of Santal implements that can be found anywhere. The Asiatic Society of Bengal published a number of his articles and also a series of two monographs on *Studies in Santal Medicine and Connected Folklore* and a monograph entitled *How the Santals Live.* These are invaluable contribution the scientific study of the literature of the Santals. A number of unpublished manuscripts are still held with Oslo University and preserved through micro-film. However, the copy of micro-films are available in India too.

Rev P. O. Bodding published two books - *Materials for a Santali Grammar, Part-I (Phonetics) & Part-II (Morphology).* This work is so called because the writer wanted to have a wider latitude than would have been possible with another title. The second part deals principally with the morphology of the language, while the first part is mostly phonetic. The two parts are still considered to be the best sources for an advanced learning of the Santali language. Bodding also published a book titled - *A Santali Grammar for Beginners.* Feeling the need for a short grammar for the use of beginners to the study of

Santali, the writer was prevailied upon to give a sketch of the language. This grammar was first published in 1929 and again re-published in 1944 and 1952.

In view of the above, it is amply clear that Bodding's contributions with regard to the Santals and their language Santali cannot be ignored as far as Santali is concerned. Rev P. O. Bodding did not publish any such Santali Grammar book but he contributed to us *A Materials for a Santali Grammar.* Considering these valuable materials, present writers dare to publish modern Santali Grammar book titled - ***Santali Beakoron*** *(Santali Grammar) Part-I, Based on P. O. Bodding's Materials for a Santali Grammar.* The book will certainly be helpful to those, who are interested to learn the Santali by adopting modern techniques.

Last but not least, *Kiạ Jharna So̱no̱do̱r Kạmiṭi* as well as the authors of this book wish to express their deep gratitude to the Gyan Publisher, New Delhi for undertaking the publication of this work.

Johar !

Kiạ Jharna So̱no̱do̱r Kạmiṭi
Sahibgõ̱ńj (Santal Pargana)
Jharkhand, India.

20th May, 2019

SARHAO SAKAM!

Johar!

Jạruṛ dọ bań tahẽkana, mẹnkhan ọktẹ reak̓ khọj lekate noa puthi disạm họṛko samańre sọdọrọk̓kanre nokokoak̓ dọ ạḍi marań ẹnẹm menak̓a, ar onko dọko hoyok̓kana :-

Charushila Kisku - Lạikak̓ dọ niạge je Rạghunath Hãsdak̓ mahasọe dọ noa puthi reak̓ bisijań sajao-sapṛaore gẹl serma gan lagaoade tahẽkana. Rạghunath mahasọe dọ noa puthi sapṛaore muć lekaye laṭkaoakanre uniren oṛak̓ bońga Man Charushila Kisku dọ sat kam bạgikate uniye gọṛọade tahẽkana. Oṛak̓ bońgataeak̓ rạskạ hõ inạrege ṭehạḍ tahẽkana jẹmọn noa puthi dọ jãhã lekatege disạm họṛko samańre sọdọrọk̓. Ar ńẹlme nit sạrige noa puthi dọ amak̓ tire menak̓a. Ona iạte Man Charushila Kisku dọ Kiạ Jharna Sọnọdọr Kạmiṭi sẹć khọn ạḍi-ạḍi gun manao ar johar sandese ẹm ocok̓kana.

Sushila Soren - Alakjạ̃ṛĩ Murmuren oṛak̓ bońga Man Sushila Soren sarhaoe lạgit̓ dọ sabadge bań ńamok̓kana. Man Sushila Soren ghọrer ghirni reak̓ jọtọ lekan kạmimae purạuet̓kange, tọbẹ lạikak̓ dọ niạge je nui hõ Man P. O. Boḍińren dọ mit̓ marań cela hõ kanae. Cedak̓je nui dọ Boḍiń sahebe lạiakat̓ *ẹ* ar *ọ* reak̓ arań dọ jivẹt̓ ḍiksinạri lekaye bạḍaea. Noa puthi disạm họṛko hạbić sẹṭẹr ocoere Man Sushila Sorenak̓ hõ ạḍi marań hãt menak̓a. Ona lạgit̓te Man Sushila Soren hõ Kiạ Jharna Sọnọdọr Kạmiṭi sẹć khọn ạḍi-ạḍi gun man Johar!

Bańgaladẹsren bạbu gidrạko - Man P. O. Boḍiń sahebe lạiakat̓ leka kạmpuṭar lạgit̓ Santali phoṇṭ reak̓ dọ ạḍi marań anaṭ tahẽkana. Cedak̓je Santali Beakọrọn (Grammar) reak̓ katha kana, onate judi noa Beakọrọn puthi Santali lipite bań chapa daṛeak̓kan khan dọ Santali pạrsi lạgit̓ ạḍi marań bẹbhạg reak̓ kathage. Khan Kiạ Jharna Sọnọdọr Kạmiṭi sẹć khọn Bańgladẹsren bạbu gidrạ **Man Samar M. Soren** ar **Piṭạr S. Ṭuḍu** Santali phoṇṭ benao lạgit̓kin nẽhõr ocoena. Ar nukin dọ sạrige sin̓ ar ńindạ khaṭaokate Santali phoṇṭkin benao sạtkeda. Nukin bạbu gidrạ sarhaokin lạgit̓ sabadge bạnuk̓a. Ẹntere hõ nukin dọ ạḍi-ạḍi gun manao ar sarhao ẹmakinkana, ẹnte nukinak̓ binạ gọṛọte noa puthi dọ ọhọge sọdọr daṛelena.

Gyan Books Publisher - Noa Santali Grammar puthi dọ Man P. O. Boḍińak̓ umul pańjakatege ọlakana bạḍaekate Gyan Books dọ mẽt̓ jạpit̓kate puthi chapaye rẹbẹnena. Noa lạgit̓ Gyan Books hõ ạḍi-ạḍi gun man ar sarhao ẹmaekana.

KIẠ JHARNA SỌNỌDỌR KẠMIṬI

Unuduk̓

Bisạị **Sakam**

Bisại **Sakam**

Bisại		**Sakam**

1

SANTALI PẠRSI REAK̓ HARO̱PMALA

Santali pạrsi o̱lo̱k̓ lạgit̓ do̱ jo̱to̱re 59 haro̱p reak̓ jạruṛ menak̓a. Onako saṇam do̱ latarre e̱mo̱go̱k̓kana. Noa Haro̱pmalare pạhilre Be̱hạṭiṅõ̱k̓ Haro̱p inạ tayo̱m Hạṭiṅõ̱k̓ Haro̱p ar inạkate do̱ Ke̱ce̱t̓ Haro̱p reak̓ bibro̱nko e̱mo̱go̱k̓kana :–

Be̱hạṭiṅõ̱k̓ Haro̱p *(Vowels)*

a, e, e̱, i, o, o̱, u

ạ, ẹ, ọ

ã, ạ̃, ẽ̱, ẽ, ĩ, õ̱, õ, ũ = 18 go̱ṭe̱c̓

Sadharo̱n Be̱hạṭiṅõ̱k̓ Haro̱p *(Vowels)*

a, e, e̱, i, o, o̱, u = 7 go̱ṭe̱c̓

Gạhlạ Be̱hạ̃ṭiṅõ̱k̓ Haro̱p *(Resultant)*

ạ, ẹ, ọ = 3 go̱ṭe̱c̓

Mũ-aṛaṅ Be̱hạṭiṅõ̱k̓ Haro̱p *(Nasalized Vowels)*

ã, ạ̃, ẽ̱, ẽ, ĩ, õ̱, õ, ũ = 8 go̱ṭe̱c̓

Hạṭiṅõ̱k̓ Haro̱p *(Consonants)*

k, kh, g, gh, ṅ

c, ch, j, jh, ń

ṭ, ṭh, ḍ, ḍh, ṇ

t, th, d, dh, n, nh

p, ph, b, bh, m

y, yh, r, l

v, w, s, h, ṛ, ṛh = 36 goṭeċ

Keceṭ' Harop ***(Checked Consonants)***

k̇, ċ, t', ṗ, ḣ = 5 goṭeċ

Beḥaṭińõk̇, Haṭińõk̇ ar Keceṭ' Harop jotore = 59 goṭeċ

Beste bujhau lagit' mimit' aṛaṅ dol reak̇ haropko emogok̇kana :–

1. **Naṇḍri Aṛaṅ** ***(Velar/Guttural)***

   k, kh, g, gh, ṅ, k̇ - *k* dol

2. **Taru Aṛaṅ** ***(Palatal)***

   c, ch, j, jh, ń, y, yh, ċ - *c* dol

3. **Bhitri Taru Aṛaṅ** ***(Cacuminal/Cerebral)***

   ṭ, ṭh, ḍ, ḍh, ṇ, ṛ, ṛh - *ṭ* dol

4. **Ḍaṭa Aṛaṅ** ***(Dental)***

   t, th, d, dh, n, nh, r, l, t' - *t* dol

5. **Luṭi Aṛaṅ** ***(Labial)***

   p, ph, b, bh, m, v, w, ṗ - *p* dol

6. **Jambe Aṛaṅ** ***(Glottal)***

   h, ḣ - *h* dol

7. **Cetan Alaṅ Aṛaṅ** ***(Sibilant)*** **-** ***s***

k̇, ċ, t', ṗ, ḣ noako harop do aċ motore sadhin rupre do oho ucraṇ daṛelena, bickom sabad sãote ucraṇ daṛeak̇a.

AṚAṄ
(PHONEME)

Aṛaṅ do sabad reak̇ reheṭteṭ kana, ona begorte sabad do ohoge ohma daṛekok̇a. *a, ạ, e, e̱, ẹ, i, o, o̱, ọ, u* aṛaṅ emanko dọ manwawaḱ aṛaṅ thạilạḱ họtẹte sọdọrọḱkana, tọbẹanẹćge noa dọ aṛaṅbo metaḱkana. Noage ọlkate sọdọr rupge harọp dọbo metaḱkana. Harọp dọ Aṛaṅ Cinhạ họ̃ko metaḱa. Iṅgrạji reaḱ *Bag* ar Santali reaḱ *Bẹg*re nasenaḱge begar menaḱa; maraṅ begar dọ bạnuḱa, cedaḱje banar pạrsirege miṫ lekanaḱge aṛaṅ menaḱa. Mẹnkhan ọlọḱre banar reaḱ aṛaṅ cinhạ miṫ eṭaḱaḱ khọn thoṛa judạgea. Onka lekabo ńẹleda je noare aṛaṅ reaḱ benegar dọ bạnuḱa; mẹnkhan harọp reaḱ benegar dọ jạruṛge menaḱa. Aṛaṅ dọbo ucrạn arbon aṅjọm daṛeaḱa; mẹnkhan harọp dọbo ọl, paṛhao arbo ńẹl ńam daṛeaḱa. Ona iạte jọtọ khọn kạṭić ucrạn-aṛaṅ dọ Harọpbo metaḱkana.

HARỌP REAḰ AĆAḰ RUP

Harọp dọ ona mul aṛaṅko metaḱkana, okaṭaḱ dọ ọhọ hạṭiń daṛelen, jeleka – *a, ạ, ẹ, ọ, ḱ, ć, ṫ* emanko. Daka sabad reaḱ barea aṛaṅ menaḱa – *da* ar *ka*. Noa reaḱ họ̃ ponea kuṭrạ menaḱa – *d+a* ar *k+a*. Inạ tayọm noa ponea aṛaṅko dọ ar ọhọge kuṭrạ daṛelena, ona iạte noako dọ harọp kana. Khaṭọte dọ niạge je noa dọ kạṭić khọn kạṭić aṛaṅ kana, ọnẹ oka dọ lutur reaḱ bisọe kan ar ona dọ ọhọge kuṭrạ daṛelena. Harọp dọ aboaḱ ucrạnọḱ pạrsi sẹ aṛaṅ reaḱ jọtọ khọn kạṭić utạraḱ hạṭiń kana. Noa kạṭić hạṭiń milạukatege sabad ar ayat dọ benaoḱkana. Saphate bạdaena je Harọp ar Ucrạnre ạdige ạdi bhitri reaḱ sọmbọnd menaḱa. Noa dọ miṫ eṭaḱaḱ khọn ọhọge begar daṛelena. Santali lipire (Lạṭin) 59 gọṭẹć harọp reaḱ miṫṭẹn malage Harọpmala dọko metaḱkana.

Nọṇḍẹ beste bujhạu lạgiṫ mimiṫ aṛaṅ dọl reaḱ harọpko ẹmọgọḱkana :-

1. **Sadharọn Bẹhạṭińọ̃ḱ Harọp** ***(Vowels)***: *a, ẹ, e, i, ọ, o, u*

   Bẹhạṭińọ̃ḱ Gạhlạ aṛaṅ *(resultant)* : *ạ, ẹ, ọ*

   Bẹhạṭińọ̃ḱ Mũ aṛaṅ *(nasalized)* : *ã, ạ̃, ẹ̃, ẽ, ĩ, ọ̃, õ, ũ*

2. **Hạṭińọ̃ḱ Harọp** ***(consonants)***

   Nạṇḍri aṛaṅ *(velar/guttural)* : *k, kh, g, gh, ṅ, ḱ*

Samaṅ tạru aṛaṅ *(palatal)* : *c, ch, j, jh, ń, y, yh, ċ*

Tạru aṛaṅ *(cacuminal/cerebral)* : *ṭ, ṭh, ḍ, ḍh, ṇ, ṛ, ṛh*

Ḍaṭa aṛaṅ *(dental)* : *t, th, d, dh, n, nh, r, l, t'*

Luṭi aṛaṅ *(labial)* : *p, ph, b, bh, m, v, w, ṗ*

Cetan jambe aṛaṅ *(glottal)* : *h, ḣ*

Cetan alaṅ dọl reak̇ aṛaṅ *(sibilant)* : *s*

3. **Kẹcẹt' Harọp Aṛaṅ** *(Checked Consonants)*: *k̇, ċ, t', ṗ, ḣ*

SANTALI REAK̇ HARỌPMALA

Ucrạn reak̇ dọ pea asọl hạṭińko menak̇a; ar onako dọ hoyok̇kana – Bẹhạṭińȭk̇ Harọp, Hạṭińȭk̇ Harọp ar Kẹcẹt' Harọp :-

i) **Bẹhạṭińȭk̇ Harọp:** Bẹhạṭińȭk̇ Harọp dọ onako metak̇kana; ọnẹ okaṭak̇ reak̇ ucrạn dọ bẹgọr akọṭte sẹ moca khọn ucrạnok̇ họe bahrete ọḍokok̇kan. Noa reak̇ucrạn dọ eṭak̇ak̇ harọp reak̇ bẹgọr gọṛọte hoyok̇kana. Noa dọ sạdhingea. Noa ucrạn jọkhẹċ bhitri khọċ ọḍokok̇ họe moca khọn bẹgọr akọṭte ọḍokok̇kana. Noa ucrạnok̇re nạṇḍri ar tạruge laṛcaṛok̇kana, alaṅ ar luṭi dọ baṅ. Mẹnkhan *o* ar *u* ucrạn jọkhẹċ luṭi dọ laṛcaṛok̇kangea, mẹnkhan thoṛa cokṛo ńȭk̇kate.

ii) **Hạṭińȭk̇ Harọp :** Hạṭińȭk̇ Harọp dọ onako metak̇kana, ọnẹ oka dọ ucrạn jọkhẹċ Bẹhạṭińȭk̇ Harọp ucrạnok̇re miṭ'ṭẹn baṅ ńẹl ńamok̇ Bẹhạṭińȭk̇ Harọp reak̇ aṛaṅ oko menak̇, oka dọ Santali harọpre baṅko bọndọbọsakada; ọnẹ oka dọ bẹgọr ńẹl ńamok̇ak̇ Bẹhạṭińȭk̇ Harọp bẹgọrte baṅ ucrạn daṛekok̇. Nạmuna – *k* dọ sạdhin rupre dọ ọhọ ucrạn daṛelena. Ona sãote miṭ'ṭẹn bin ńẹl ńamok̇ Bẹhạṭińȭk̇ aṛaṅ *(sound)* menak̇a. Jãhãn katha sẹ jãhãnak̇ harọp ucrạnok̇ jọkhẹn jọtọ khọn lahare Bẹhạṭińȭk̇ aṛaṅge ucrạn lahak̇a, adọ inạ tayọmge Hạṭińȭk̇ aṛaṅ dọ ucrạnok̇kana. Ona iạte Hạṭińȭk̇ Harọp dọ ona aṛaṅ kana, ọnẹ oka dọ ucrạnok̇ jọkhẹċ moca bhitri khọn hijuk̇ak̇ họe mocare jãhã baṅ jãhã ṭhen jãhã ruprege akọṭọk̇kana. Ona iạte Bẹhạṭińȭk̇ Harọp reak̓ aṛaṅ dọ sạdhingea ar Hạṭiń̄ọk̓ Harọp reak̓ aṛaṅ dọ ṭehaḍgea.

iii) Kẹcẹt' Harọp : *k̓, c̓, t̓, p̓, h̓.* Noako sanam harọp dọ Kẹcẹt̓ Harọpko *(Checked Consonants)* metak̓kana. Noako sanam harọp dọ adọm-adọm sabadko chaḍakate jaoge sabad reak̓ mucạt̓re lagaok̓kana. Noako harọp dọ tinre sabad reak̓ mucạt̓re hijuk̓kana, un jọkhẹc̓ ona harọp reak̓ ucrạn aṛaṅ dọ ackage hoyok̓kana ar bại-bạite ackage mucạdok̓kana. Noako Kẹcẹt̓ Harọp dọ ac̓ mọtọre sạdhin rupre dọ ọhọge aṛaṅ daṛelena bickọm sabad sāo milạukate ucrạnok̓a. Ẹnte noa reak̓ gunge noṅkana je jāhā lekatege ucrạn reak̓bon kurumuṭui baṅbon ucrạn jut daṛeak̓a. Noa dọ adha ulạ ruạṛket̓ leka ar adha dọ jọm ruạṛket̓ leka ucrạnok̓a. Noako dọ Santali pạrsi baṅ baḍae họṛ dọ ekalte baṅgey ucrạn jut daṛeak̓a. Ona iạte ẹkẹn puthi paṛhao mọtọte dọ baṅ hoyok̓a.

ÃṬ-AṚAṄ AR NASE-AṚAṄ *(ASPIRATE SOUND & NON-ASPIRATE SOUND)*

Santali lipire mõ̱ṛẽ̱ dọl Hạṭiń̄ọk̓ Harọpkore pạhilak̓ dọ Hạṭiń̄ọk̓ Harọp Nase-Aṛaṅ *(Non-Aspirate Sound)* ar dosarak̓ ar ponak̓ dọ Ãṭ-Aṛaṅ *(Aspirate Sound)* Hạṭiń̄ọk̓ Harọp kana. Ucrạnok̓re moca khọn họe ọḍokok̓ dharate Hạṭiń̄ọk̓ Harọp reak̓ dọ bar hạṭiṅre hạṭiń daṛeak̓a : i) Nase-Aṛaṅ; ar ii) Ãṭ-Aṛaṅ.

Tin jọkhẹc̓ moca bahrete họe ọḍoṅok̓kana, tọbẹ ona dọ sanam aṛaṅre mit̓ leka moca khọn họe baṅ ọḍokok̓kana. Adọmak̓ Hạṭiń̄ọk̓ Harọpko ucrạn jọkhẹc̓ kọm ń̄ọk̓ họe moca khọn bahre ọḍoṅok̓kana ar adọmak̓ dọ ḍher ń̄ọk̓. Pạrtul - Moca samaṅre sor ń̄ọk̓re diuhạ dọhọkate *k* ar *kh* harọp reak̓bon ucrạnlege. Abo dọ noabo ńẹla je *kh* harọpbon ucrạnlere *k* khọn ḍher họe moca khọn bahrete ọḍoṅok̓kana. Arbon ńẹla je judi *k* aṛaṅte diuhạ baṅ ĩṛĩjọk̓re hõ̱ *kh* aṛaṅ onḍoṅlenre dhọrage diuhạ dọ ĩṛĩc̓ bọtẹjọk̓gea. Ona iạte okaṭak̓ harọpko ucrạn jọkhẹc̓ nasenak̓ họe ọḍokok̓kana, ona Hạṭiń̄ọk̓ Harọp dọ Nase Aṛaṅko *(non-aspiration)* metak̓kana ar okaṭak̓re jạsti họe moca bahrete oḍoṅokkana, ona do Ãṭ-Aṛaṅko *(aspiration)* metakkana.

Santali lipire mõṛẽ dol Haṭiṅõk Harop do Nase-Aṛaṅ Haṭiṅõk Harop kana ar dosarak ar ponak Haṭiṅõk Harop do Ãṭ Aṛaṅ Haṭiṅõk Haropko metakkana. Santali lipire Haṭiṅõk Harop reak do noako kana :-

Nase-Aṛaṅ *(Non-Aspirate)*	**Ãṭ-Aṛaṅ** *(Aspirate)*
k, g	*kh, gh*
c, j	*ch, jh*
ṭ, ḍ	*ṭh, ḍh*
t, d	*th, dh*
p, b	*ph, bh*

TARKO-AṚAṄ AR BE-TARKO AṚAṄ *(VOICED SOUND AND VOICELESS SOUND OR ROARING AND NON-ROARING SOUND)*

Inboro khon moca haḅic hijukak hoe sojhe mocare do baṅ hijukkana. Abo sanam horak naṇḍrire mit lekanak aṛaṅ jontro menaka. Aṛaṅ jontrore *(sound gland)* jeleṅte benaoakan barea birni menaka. Ona do behla banam retae jokhec tarkok leka onakin birni hõ tarkokkana, okaṭak do aṛaṅok-thaiḷakbon *(sound gland/sound box)* menkea. Noa aṛaṅok thaiḷak do adom-adom oktere mit eṭakak sãote aḍi sor hijukkana. Tin jokhec ona aṛaṅ thaiḷak mit eṭakak sorre hijukkana, un jokhec judi inboro khon hijukak hoe onare ṭakijokkana, tobe ona do tarko rãwãokkana. Tobeanecge aṛaṅok thaiḷak reak tarko rãwão moca haḅic seṭerokak hoere mesalokkana. Menkhan tinre noakin aṛaṅok birni mit eṭakak khon saṅgiṅ-saṅgiṅre tahenkana, unre hoe do sojhe aṛaṅok thaiḷak begor tarkoe tuluc moca haḅic hijukkana. Tarko *(Voiced)* sabad reak manege rãwão se reta kana. Nonde do tarko reak mane jãhãn jinis tarkok reak sompok são do baṅ dohoakana, bickom hoe reak tarko naṇḍrire menak barea birni sãote tarko são sọmpọk dọhọakana. Ona iạte jãhãṭaḱ Hạṭińõḱ Harọpge ucrạn jọkhẹć ucrạnoḱ birni oḍokoḱ rãwão reta são milạu tahẹnkana, ona Hạṭińõḱ Harọpge tarko aṛańoḱ Hạṭińõḱ Harọp *(Voiced consonants)* dọko metaḱkana. Mẹnkhan okaṭaḱ Hạṭińõḱ Harọp ucrạn jọkhẹć aṛańoḱ birni mit́ eṭaḱaḱ khọn sạńgiń-sạńgińre tahẹnkan karọnte noa họe dọ rãwão sãote bań mesaloḱkana, ona Hạṭińõḱ Harọp dọ Bẹtarko *(Voiceless)* Hạṭińõḱ Harọpko metaḱkana.

Santali lipite ọlọgọḱ Santalire mõṛẽ dọl Hạṭińõḱ harọpkorebon ńẹla je mimit́ dọl reaḱ pạhilaḱ barea Hạṭińõḱ Harọp dọ nońka leka kana:-

k	*kh*
c	*ch*
ṭ	*ṭh*
t	*th*
p	*ph*

Noako sanam harọp dọ Bẹtarko Aṛań Hạṭińõḱ *(Voiceless sound)* kana. Mẹnkhan tesaraḱ ar ponaḱ harọp, jeleka :- *g, gh, j, jh, ḍ, ḍh, d, dh, b, bh;* noako sanam harọp dọ Tarko Aṛań Hạṭińõḱ Harọp kana. Ona iạte Tarko Aṛań Hạṭińõḱ Harọp *(Voiced sound consonants)* reaḱ mane dọ ona Hạṭińõḱ Harọp kana, ọnẹ okaṭaḱ dọbon ucrạnlere aṛańoḱ birni tarko rãwão họe são mesal tahẹnkan ar Bẹtarko Aṛań dọ ona Bẹhạṭińõḱ Harọp kana, okaṭaḱ dọbon ucrạnlere, ona họe dọ tarko rãwãoḱ họe são mesal bań tahẹnkan.

ẠKIL BHAŃJAO - 1

A. Ṭọyọt'kate jobab ẹmọḱme :-

1. Santali Harọpmalare tinạḱ harọp menaḱa?

   (a) 89 (b) 34 (c) 59 (d) 30

2. Beḥaṭińõk̓kak̓ tinạk̓ harop menak̓a?

   (a) 12 (b) 53 (c) 18 (d) 45

3. Gạhlạ Beḥaṭińõk̓ Harop do okaṭak̓ kana?

   (a) a (b) h (c) ṭ (d) ạ

4. Mũ-Aṛaṅ Beḥaṭińõk̓ Harop do okaṭak̓ kana?

   (a) ń (b) ṇ (c) k̓ (d) ĩ

5. Hạṭińõk̓ Harop do tinạk̓a?

   (a) 30 (b) 45 (c) 24 (d) 36

6. Santali pạrsi reak̓ Haropmalare Kecet̓ Harop do tinạk̓a?

   (a) 5 (b) 3 (c) 6 (d) 8

7. Santali haropmalare Kecet̓ Harop do okaṭak̓ kana?

   (a) ń (b) c (c) h̓ (d) ạ

8. Noa Beakoron puthi lekate okako kana nãwã harop do?

   (a) g (b) ń (c) h̓ (d) ṭ

9. Noako mod khon okaṭak̓ kana Kecet̓ Aṛaṅ do?

   (a) ạ (b) ń (c) c̓ (d) ṭ

10. Okaṭak̓ kana Mũ Aṛaṅ do?

    (a) ĩ (b) ṛ (c) l (d) k

11. Okaṭak̓ Luṭi Aṛaṅ kana?

    (a) k (b) p (c) ạ (d) t̓

12. Santalire haropko do tinạk̓ aṛaṅ dolre hạṭińakana?

    (a) 6 (b) 7 (c) 3 (d) 9

13. Gạhlạ Beḥaṭińõk̓ Harop do tinạk̓a?

    (a) 7 (b) 2 (c) 3 (d) 6

14. Latarre emakan Nase Aṛaṅ harop do okaṭak̓ kana ?

(a) ṅ (b) k (c) ạ (d) k̓

15. Latarre e̱makan Ãṭ Aṛaṅ haro̱p do̱ okaṭak̓ kana?

(a) gh (b) l (c) ḍ (d) ũ

B. O̱lkate jobab e̱mo̱k̓me :-

1. *ẹ* ar *ọ* do̱ Beako̱ro̱n reak̓ niạm lekate ce̱t̓ aṛaṅ kana?
2. *ṅ* do̱ Beako̱ro̱n reak̓ niạm lekate ce̱t̓ aṛaṅ kana?
3. *s* do̱ Beako̱ro̱n reak̓ niạm lekate ce̱t̓ aṛaṅ kana?
4. *e̱* do̱ Beako̱ro̱n reak̓ niạm lekate ce̱t̓ haro̱p kana,?
5. *ạ, ẹ, ọ* do̱ Beako̱ro̱n reak̓ niạm lekate ce̱t̓ haro̱p kana?
6. Jo̱to̱ Be̱hạṭinõ̱k̓ Haro̱p o̱lme.
7. Jo̱to̱ Hạṭiṅõ̱k̓ Haro̱p o̱lme.
8. Be̱hạṭiṅõ̱k̓ Haro̱p do̱ ce̱t̓ kana?
9. Hạṭiṅõ̱k̓ Haro̱p do̱ ce̱t̓ kana?
10. Jo̱to̱ Ke̱ce̱t̓ Haro̱p o̱lme.
11. E̱ke̱n bhitri Tạru Aṛaṅ o̱lme.
12. Luṭi ar Jambe Aṛaṅ o̱lme.
13. Aṛaṅ do̱ Beako̱ro̱n reak̓ niạm lekate ce̱t̓ kana?
14. Aṛaṅge o̱lkate so̱do̱r do̱ ce̱t̓ko metak̓a?
15. Aṛaṅ do̱bo ceka daṛeak̓a?
16. Haro̱p do̱bo ceka daṛeak̓a?
17. Haro̱p do̱ Beako̱ro̱n reak̓ niạm lekate ce̱t̓ kana ?
18. Ce̱t̓ *a, ạ, e̱, o̱* ar *k̓* do̱ kuṭrạ daṛeak̓a ?
19. Haro̱p do̱ aboak̓ pạrsi reak̓ ce̱t̓ kana ?
20. Haro̱p ar Ucrạnre ce̱t̓ so̱mbo̱nd menak̓a?
21. Ucrạn ar Haro̱p reak̓ so̱mbo̱nd do̱ begar daṛeak̓a se̱ baṅ ?

22. *daka* do̱ pon kuṭṛạre hạṭiń daṛeak̕a, ona kho̱n jạsti do̱ bań. Cedak̕?
23. Ucrạn ar Haro̱pre ạḍi khạndri so̱mbo̱nd menak̕a me̱nte cekatem bujhạu ńama?
24. Santalire 59 go̱te̱c̕ haro̱p reak̕ jạruṛ paṛaok̕kana me̱nte cekatem baḍaekeda? Lại bho̱ńme?
25. Be̱hạṭińo̱k̕ Haro̱p do̱ ce̱t̕ kana? Bean se̱le̱t̕ pạrtul e̱mme .
26. Hạṭińo̱k̕ Haro̱p reak̕ bean o̱l tuluc̕ pạrtul e̱mme.
27. Ke̱ce̱t̕ Haro̱p reak̕ bean o̱l tuluc̕ pạrtul e̱mme.
28. Ãṭ Aṛań ar Nase Aṛań reak̕ bean lại me.

2

SANTALI UCRẠN BESTE HOE OCOERE BE̱HẠṬIṄŌK̇ HARO̱P AR HẠṬIṄŌK̇ HARO̱P

CETAN-LATARRE LAGAOK̇ CINHẠKO *(DIACRITICAL MARKS)*

- Be̱hạṭiṅõk̇ Haro̱pko *(Vowels)* cetanre lagaok̇ cinhạ *(tilde above)* (˜) do̱ mũ ar moca *(nasalization)* aṛaṅ udug lạgiṫ kana; jeleka – *ã, ạ̃, ẽ̱, ẽ̱, ĩ, õ, õ̱, ũ.*

- Be̱hạṭiṅõk̇ Haro̱pko *(Vowels)* latarre lagaok̇ cinhạ *(dash below)* (_) do̱ khulạ aṛaṅ udug lạgiṫ kana ar noa cinhạ do̱ *e* ar *o* latarre lagaok̇kana, jeleka – *e̱, o̱.*

- Be̱hạṭiṅõk̇ Haro̱pko *(Vowels)* latarre lagaok̇ cinhạ *(dot below)* (.) do̱ gạhlạ metak̇me jo̱r e̱mak̇ lạgiṫ aṛaṅ kana ar noa cinhạ do̱ *a, e* ar *o* latarre lagaok̇kana, jeleka – *ạ, ẹ, ọ.*

- Hạṭiṅõk̇ Haro̱p cetanre lagaok̇ cinhạ *(acute accent above)* (ˊ) do̱ tạrute aṛaṅok̇ Hạṭiṅõk̇ *(nasal) n* cetanre lagaok̇a, jeleka – *ń*. Noa reak̇ aṛaṅ do̱ mũ ho̱rte oḍokok̇kana.

- Hạṭiṅõk̇ Haro̱p cetanre lagaok̇ cinhạ *(apostrophe above or on the right hand top side)* (ʾ) do̱ *k, c, t, p* ar *h* cetan se̱ jo̱jo̱m nakhare ke̱ce̱ṫ aṛaṅ udug lạgiṫ kana, jeleka :- *k̇, ċ, ṫ, ṗ* ar *ḣ*.

- Hạṭiṅõk̇ haro̱p cetanre lagaok̇ cinhạ *(dot above)* (˙) do̱ mũ aṛaṅ udug lạgiṫ *n* cetanre lagaok̇kana, o̱ne̱ oka do̱ *ṅ* mũ aṛaṅ *(nasal)* hoyok̇kana.

□ Họṭịńõk̓ Harọp latarre lagaok̓ cinhạ *(dot below)* (.) dọ bhitri ṭạru reak̓ aṛaṅ udug lạgiṭ kana. Noa cinhạ dọ *t, th, d, dh, n* ar *r* harọpre lagaok̓a, jeleka :- *ṭ, ṭh, ḍ, ḍh, ṇ* ar *ṛ*

UCRẠN GUN
(ORTHOGRAPHY)

ạ, e, ẹ, ẹ, o, ọ, ọ, k̓, c̓, t̓, p̓, ṅ ar *ṇ* harọpko reak̓ ucrạn gun :

ạ - *ạ* harọp reak̓ ucrạn dọ *a* harọp reak̓ ucrạnok̓ họe nạṇḍrire khulạ (dabao) ńõk̓kate oḍoṅok̓kan aṛaṅge gạhlạ aṛaṅko metak̓kana ar ona aṛaṅge gạhlạ rupre hoyok̓kana. Noa dọ *a* latarre gạhlạ ṭuḍạk̓ (.) hõko metak̓a. Noa aṛaṅge eṭak̓ pạrsi aṛaṅ khọn Santali dọe begaret̓kana. Noa harọp tayọmre dọ bar harọp *(dipthong)* reak̓ mit̓ ucrạn rupre noa sãote *i* ar *u* hẹc̓ daṛeak̓a, *e* ar *o* dọ baṅ, jeleka :- *ạ+i = ại (ạ+e dọ baṅ) = ạimại; ạ+u = ạu (ạ+o = ạo dọ baṅ)= pạtiạu.* Noa harọp dọ sabad reak̓ ẹtọhọp̓re, talare ar mucạt̓re ar sạdhin rupre; metak̓me sabad reak̓ sanam ṭhãirege laṛcaṛok̓kana; jeleka :-

Sabad ẹtọhọp̓re	Sabad talare	Sabad mucạt're
ạgu, ạlu, ạbuk, ạliń, ạn, ạri, ạmsi, ạrji,	*sạgại, kạmi, jạli, mạli, khạlại, bhạlại, dạl, kại*	*mạilạ, kubạ, kumbạ, bitạ, mạndạṛiạ,cạndlạ*

e - *e* aṛaṅ dọ alaṅ mucạt̓ bhitri nakhare alaṅ gọṇḍa khọn nọtẹ ńõk̓ reak̓ alaṅ reak̓ mit̓ hĩs cọṭ ńõk̓ alaṅ kọṭ kọṭọ ńõk̓kate moca khọn oḍokok̓ họe sakṛae tuluc̓ aṛaṅok̓kana.

Noa *e* reak̓ aṛaṅ beste babon ańjọm lekhac̓ *i* leka hõ aṛaṅok̓bon ańjọma, jeleka: -

cele (who, which), -ge (mit̓ lekan tayọm joṛao), *se (louse), edre (anger).* Noa harọp dọ Iṅgrạji reak̓ *men* leka aṭaṅok̓a, jẹmọn – *en-len* (Kạjnum reak̓ mucạt̓ joṛao) ar sẹ *eṅgot̓ (stoop), elem celem (watch for an opportunity), -kede-* (kạjnum reak̓ tala joṛao), *eto (break in)*. Thoṛabon digdha ńõ̱gọk̓a je *e* ar *i* re aṛań reak̓ benegar udugrebon e̱ṭke̱ṭõ̱ṛẽ̱k̓a, esto̱-be̱sto̱ ńõ̱go̱k̓abo. Bań baḍae ho̱ṛ do̱ *ge* do̱ *gi* leka hõ̱bon o̱la se̱bon ro̱ṛa. Nạmuna lekate - *sereń, dereń, terel, bele* eman do̱ *siriń, diriń, tiril, bili* lekabon o̱l/ro̱ṛ bhule̱t̓kana.

e̱ - e̱ haro̱p reak̓ aṛań do̱ Hindi ए harop aṛań leka aṛańok̓a ar Ińgrạji reak̓ do̱ *air* leka. Noa haro̱p reak̓ aṛań do̱ bhitri alań mucạt̓ nạṇḍri se̱ bhitri moca alań latar se̱c̓ pheḍ ńõ̱k̓kate se̱ khulạ ńõ̱k̓kate ucrạnlenkhan hoyok̓kana. Noa aṛań reak̓ aṛań gun aṛańkatege beste do̱ bujhạu daṛeak̓a. Noa haro̱pre *e* latarre khaṭo̱ dag lagaokate e̱ benaok̓kana. Aboren o̱no̱liạko *e* ar e̱re jãhãn begar bako bujhạu daṛeak̓kana. Noakin banar haro̱p beoharre begar menak̓a, je̱mo̱n - *jive̱t̓ (life), ile̱t̓ (plaster over)*. Noa haro̱p reak̓ begar do̱ noa ayatre beste bujhạuk̓a – *Chitạ do̱ o̱ko̱eren era (wife)* kanae? *Jonḍra do̱ ạurile e̱ra (to sow)*. Noa haro̱p do̱ sabad reak̓ e̱to̱ho̱p̓, tala ar mucạt̓re lagaok̓kana, jeleka:-

Sabad e̱to̱ho̱p̓re	Sabad talare	Sabad mucạt̓re
e̱r, e̱m, e̱ge̱r, e̱n, e̱ne̱m, e̱ṇḍe̱, e̱nte̱, e̱se̱l, e̱se̱r	*be̱re̱l, he̱re̱l, he̱ṛe̱m, le̱he̱r, je̱re̱ṛ, sare̱ṛ, je̱r*	*bo̱le̱, ge̱ḍe̱, ge̱le̱, e̱pṛe̱,*

ẹ - ẹ haro̱p reak̓ ucrạn do̱ *e* haro̱p ucrạnok̓ jo̱khe̱c̓ oḍokok̓ ho̱e thoṛa tala alań cetan se̱c̓ rakap̓ ńõ̱k̓kate ar dabao ńõ̱k̓kate oḍokok̓ aṛań kana, *e* aṛań leka bań ucrạnkate ẹ leka ucrạnok̓kana. Noa do̱ sạri Santali ro̱ro̱ṛ ho̱ṛge beste do̱e bujhạu daṛeak̓a. Santali aṛań baḍae ho̱ṛge noa reak̓ sebelte̱t̓ do̱e bujhạua. Pusṭạute bujhạu lạgit̓ latarre e̱makan ayatrebon mo̱ne̱ak̓ma :-

(a) Bạjun do̱ patare pajhẹṛ *kẹṛ-kẹṛ*e ho̱ho̱leda.

(b) Noa hasa do̱ setońte ro̱ho̱ṛ *ke̱ṛ-ke̱ṛ*ena.

Cetanre e̱makan ayatbon mo̱ne̱akawat̓khan pata-chata reak̓ so̱go̱e ho̱ho̱ *kẹṛ-kẹṛ* sabad jaegare setońte ro̱ho̱ṛakan *ke̱ṛ-ke̱ṛ* sabad do̱ ayatre o̱ho̱bon laṛcaṛ daṛekea. No̱mbo̱r (a) reak̓ ayatre laṛcaṛakan *kẹṛ-kẹṛ* aṛaṅ ṭhã̤ire nọmbọr (b) reaḱ *kẹṛ-kẹṛ* laṛcaṛlen khan sajao dọ baṅ aṅjọmọḱa. Rọṛ reaḱ mọtlọb dọ noage je Santali pạrsire noṅkan gun menaḱa je okaṭaḱ dọ aboaḱ sọmajrebo beoharetḱana. *ẹ* harọp dọ sabad reaḱ tala ar mucạt́re asọkaete beoharoḱkana. Sabad ẹtọhọp̍re *ẹ* harọp dọ ạḍi kọmge lagaoḱkana, jeleka :-

Sabad ẹtọhọp̍re	Sabad talare	Sabad mucạt́re
ẹi (jãhãe họhọae)	*pajhẹṛ kẹṛ-kẹṛ, lẹṅ-lẹṅ (seta họhọae jọkhẹċ)*	*rẹ- rẹ, rẹ- rẹ (Sọhrae jọkhẹċ gạí jagao sereṅ)*

o - o harọp reaḱ ucrạn dọ moca khọn oḍokoḱ họe banar luṭi cokṛo ṅõḱkate moca bahrete họe oḍokoḱkana, jeleka:-

Sor (near), koṛa (boy), hoṛo (paddy), oṛaḱ (house, home, family, abiding place), ot́ (mushroom, toadstool), osar (broad), wide, to make broad) eman. Abo Santal ọnọliạko adọm jọkhẹċ dọbo digdhạḱkan iạte *o* jaegare ghane dọ *u* hõbo ọlẹt́kana. *o* dọ *u* sor reaḱ aṛaṅ kangea. Mẹnkhan *u* utạr hõ baṅ kana. Abo ọnọliạko dọ ọlọḱre noṅkanaḱ bhul hõbo hoe ocoeda :-

po jaegare *pu* (joṇḍra po)

lo jaegare *lu* (daḱ lo)

poho jaegare *puhu*

jol jaegare *jul* (sẹṅgẹl jol)

goḍo jaegare *guḍu*

hako jaegare haku

joroḱ ar jọrọḱ reaḱ begar baṅbon bujhạu daṛeaḱkana.

(Sẹṅgẹl phẹḍre gidrạko joroḱkana; Sạṛim khọn daḱ jọrọḱkana.)

hoe (be, become) ar *họe (air)* reaḱ begar baṅbon bujhạu daṛeaḱkana.

(Ne̱s cas do̱ ạḍi mõ̱ńj hoyakana; tạpis ho̱e karo̱nte, sạṛim do̱ oṭańena.)

hoyok̓ (become) ar *ho̱yo̱k̓ (shave)* reak̓ begar bańbon bujhạu daṛeak̓kana.

(Kạṭic̓re paṛhaok̓me, lạṭukate am lạgit̓ge po̱rho̱ hoyok̓a; Rimil do̱ setak̓re gocoe ho̱yo̱k̓a.)

hoṛo jaegare *huṛu* (hoṛo cas)

kol jaegare *kul* (ciṭhi kol)

lolo (to fetch water) (Kuṛikin do̱ kuńre dak̓kin lolokana)

lo̱lo̱ (hot) (Teheń do̱e setońakada, onate ạḍi ãṭ lo̱lo̱kana.)

Ro̱ṛ reak̓ mo̱tlo̱b do̱ noage je mimit̓ sabad reak̓ banan *(spelling)* ar mane do̱ judạ-judạgea. Mane judạk̓kan khan banan hõ̱ judạk̓ jạruṛkana. Mit̓ bar sabad chaḍakate.

o̱ - *o̱* haro̱p reak̓ aṛań do̱ bhitri alań reak̓ mucạt̓re nạṇḍri kho̱n oḍokok̓ ho̱e latar ńõ̱k̓kate khulạ ńõ̱k̓ aṛań tuluc̓ oḍok bahrek̓kana. *o̱* do̱ Iṅgrạji reak̓ *law* leka aṛańok̓a. Noa haro̱p do̱ sabad reak̓ e̱to̱ho̱p̓, tala ar mucạt̓re lagaok̓kana; jeleka:-

Sabad e̱to̱ho̱p̓re	Sabad talare	Sabad mucạt̓re
o̱l, o̱r, o̱po̱l, o̱mo̱n, o̱t, o̱kte̱, o̱bra, o̱po̱man	*ko̱lo̱m, ho̱po̱n, ho̱ṛ, so̱l, do̱l, ko̱l, sado̱m*	*lo̱lo̱, ro̱ṅgo̱, jo̱to̱, mo̱to̱, khaṭo̱, dho̱dro̱*

ọ - ọ haro̱p reak̓ aṛań do̱ *o̱* ar *o* tala reak̓ aṛań kana. Noa do̱ nońka benaoakana :-

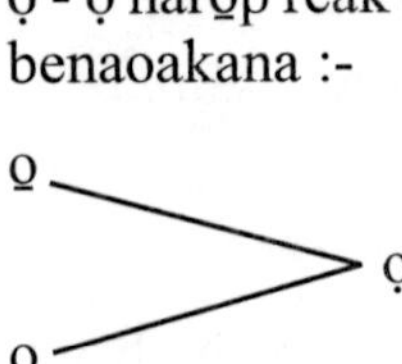

o̱ ar *o* tala reak̓ aṛań kan iạte bań do̱ *o̱* leka aṛańok̓ ar bań do̱ *o* lekage, metak̓me *kọl (cuckoo)* cẽṛẽ do baṅ do *kol (machinery)* ar baṅ do *kol (to send)* lekage aṛaṅok̓. Noa do *o* ar *o* aṛaṅ khon begar leka aṛaṅok̓a. Noa do sabad reak̓ etohop̓, tala ar mucạt̓re lagaok̓a; jeleka :-

Sabad etohop̓re	Sabad talare	Sabad mucạt̓re
ọl (lolote sakam ọlena) *ọṅ- ọṅ (bhabna aṛaṅ)*	*kọl (cẽṛẽ)* *sọl (hako)*	*sọlọ (gel turui)*

Kecet̓ Harop Aṛaṅ *(Checked Consonants)* : *k̓, c̓, t̓, p̓, ṅ*

k̓, c̓, t̓, p̓, ṅ - Noako sanam harop do kecet̓ harop kana *(checked consonants).* Noako sanam haropko do adom-adom sabadko chaḍakate jaoge sabad reak̓ mucạt̓re lagaok̓kana. Noa harop do tinre sabad reak̓ mucạt̓re hijuk̓kana, unjokhec̓ noa harop reak̓ ucrạn aṛaṅ do ackage hoyok̓kana ar bại-bạite ackage mucạdok̓kana. Noako kecet̓ harop ac̓ motore sạdhin rupre do ohoge aṛaṅ se ucrạn daṛelena, bickom sabad são milạukatege ucrạnok̓a. Ente noa reak̓ gun noṅkana je jãhã lekatege ucrạn reak̓bon kurumuṭui baṅgebon ucrạn jut daṛeak̓a. Noa do adha ut̓ket̓ leka ar adha do ulạ ruạṛket̓ leka ucrạnok̓a. Noako do Santali pạrsi baṅ baḍae hoṛ do ekalte baṅgey ucrạn jut daṛeak̓a. Ona iạte eken puthi paṛhao moto/hotete do baṅ hoyok̓a. Santali reak̓ ucrạn se galmarao lạgit̓ do Santali bhasa-bhạsi hoṛ tuluc̓ galmarao se roroṛ hoyok̓a.

Santali pạrsi reak̓ ucrạn ced lạgit̓ do aṛaṅkatege bujhạuk̓a. Ona iạte pạhil do noako mõṛẽ goṭec̓ kecet̓ harop reak̓ ucrạn okare hoyok̓kana, onabon cet̓lege. Noako harop do mit̓ bar sabad talare laṛcaṛok̓ chaḍakate jaoge sabad reak̓ mucạt̓re hijuk̓kana, jeleka :-

Harop	Sabad etohop̓re	Sabad talare	Sabad mucạt̓re
k̓	-	*dak̓edae, rak̓edae*	*ak̓, jak̓, marak̓*

ċ	-	*go̱ċiċ, re̱pe̱ċiċ*	*aċ, laċ, ce̱pe̱ċ*
ť	-	*mẽ̱ťạniċ, mẽ̱ťdak̇*	*uť, ge̱ť, jạpuť*
ṗ	-	*sasaṗiċ, uṗạniċ*	*aṗ, saṗ, rakaṗ*
ḣ	-	*ọḣ-ọḣkedae*	*lẹḣ-lẹḣwaeme*

k̇ - *k̇* Noa aṛaṅ do̱ nạṇḍri kho̱n oḍokok̇ ho̱e nạṇḍri bhitrirege adha do̱ jo̱m ruạṛkeť leka bhitrirege tahẽ̱ ruạṛok̇ ar adha do̱ nạṇḍri bahrete oḍoṅok̇kante ackage mucạdok̇ leka aṭkarok̇a. Noa do̱ ackage aṛaṅkate nạṇḍri bhitrirege pho̱so̱ṅ mucạdok̇a. *k̇* do̱ aċ mo̱to̱ sạdhin rupre do̱ o̱ho̱ge ucrạn daṛelena.

ċ - *ċ* Noa aṛaṅ hõ̱ onkage nạṇḍri bhitri kho̱n oḍokkate ackage mucạdok̇ leka ar cetan ḍaṭa tạru phẹḍre alaṅ nase macha jak̇ ṅõ̱k̇kate ackage moca bhitrire pho̱so̱ṅ mucạdok̇a.

ť - *ť* Noa hõ̱ onkage aṛaṅ mucạdok̇ leka aṭkarok̇a ar cetan ḍaṭa phẹḍre alaṅ rakaṗkate nasenak̇ jag tuluċ ackage moca bhitrirege ho̱e do̱ pho̱so̱ṅ mucạdok̇a. Noa hõ̱ sabad são milạukatege ucrạnok̇a.

ṗ - *ṗ* Noa hõ̱ onka kangea. Latar luṭi, cetan luṭire jo̱po̱go̱k̇ tuluċ ạḍi nase nõ̱k̇ jag tuluċ ackage aṛaṅkate moca bhitrirege ho̱e do̱ pho̱so̱ṅ mucạdok̇a. *ṗ* haro̱p aċ mo̱to̱ sạdhin rupre o̱ho̱ ucrạn daṛelena. Noa haro̱p do̱ sabad são milạukatege ucrạnok̇a.

ḣ - *ḣ* Noa aṛaṅ do̱ ackage *h*re nạṇḍri kho̱n ho̱e oḍoṅkate mucạdok̇a. Me̱nkhan *k̇, ċ, ť, ṗ* ar *ḣ* kho̱n thoṛa judạ ṅõ̱k̇gea. Moṭa-muṭi *ḣ* aṛaṅkate nạṇḍri bhitrirege ackage pho̱so̱ṅ mucạdok̇a.

Disạ do̱ho̱ : Metak̇me *k̇, ċ, ť, ṗ* ar *ḣ* haro̱p do̱ aċ mo̱to̱ do̱ sạdhin rupre o̱ho̱ ucrạn daṛelena, bicko̱m sabad são milạukatege ucrạnok̇a.

ṇ - *ṇ* reak̇ ucrạn do̱ co̱ṭ alaṅ ulṭạute lạṭiċ rakaṗkate bhitri no̱ro̱m tạru co̱ṭ alaṅte jak̇kate hoyok̇kana. Noa mũ aṛaṅ Hạṭiṅõ̱k̇ Haro̱p do̱ *ṭ, ṭh, ḍ, ḍh* sãoge hẹċ daṛeaǩa ar ona hõ noa harop reaǩ ṭhik ẹṇḍẹge lahare hijuǩkana, jẹmọn – *ọṇḍẹ (there), kaṇṭa (throat), biṇṭhi (kind of knife), ạṇḍiċ (seduce), gaṇḍke (a log), oṇḍga (ogre), guṇḍri (a quail), kuṇḍlạṅ (lie down), muṇḍhạt' (stump of a tree, log), kaṇḍwer (a certain tree), kohṇḍa (pumpkin), khokṇḍo (ill conditioned), bharṇḍo (whirlwind), phupṇḍa (mouldy), bhosṇḍo (slovenly), ghạṇṭi (bell), Jharkhaṇḍ (name of a state in India).*

ẠKIL BHAŃJAO - 2

A. Ṭọyọt'kate jobab ẹmọǩme :-

Sạhi sabad bachaome :-

1. … dọ bhugạǩreko tahẽna.

 (a) guḍu (b) gọḍu (c) goḍo (d) gọḍọ

2. Nẹtar ciṭhi … reaǩ jug dọ cabaena.

 (a) kọl (b) kul (c) kọl (d) kol

3. Bhugạǩ sạṛim khọn dọ daǩ …

 (a) joroǩa (b) jọrọǩa (c) juruǩa (d) juroǩa

4. … ca ẹm họṭ'ạṅpe.

 (a) lulu (b) lolo (c) lọlọ (d) lọlọ

5. Chitạ dọe ọkọeren … kana?

 (a) ira (b) era (c) ẹra (d) ẹra

6. … cẽṛẽ dọ ạḍi mõńjko kuhuia.

 (a) kọl (b) kọl (c) kol (d) kul

7. Sạhi banan dọ okaṭaǩ kana?

 (a) binṭhi (b) benṭhe (c) biṇṭhi (d) binṭhu

8. Latarre ẹmakan khọn bachaome okaṭaǩ dọ Ãṭ Aṛaṅ baṅ kana.

(a) kh (b) ch (c) c (d) ph

9. *ṇ* dọ okaṭak̓ harọp lahare hijuk̓a?

(a) p (b) ṭh (c) ạ (d) ṛ

10. Noako mod khọn okaṭak̓ dọ Kẹcẹt̓ Aṛaṅ kana?

(a) ũ (b) k̓ (c) ọ (d) ẹ

11. Sạhi banan lạime.

(a) siriń (b) sẹrẹń (c) sereń (d) seriń

12. Okaṭak̓ banan sạhia?

(a) mẹt̓ (b) mẽd (c) mẽt̓ (d) met̓

B. Ọlkate jobab ẹmọk̓me :-

1. *ạ* dọ cẹt̓ lekan Bẹhạṭińõk̓ aṛaṅ kana?
2. *e, ẹ, ẹ, ṇ, o, ọ* ar *ọ* reak̓ ucrạn gun lạime.
3. *ạ* reak̓ ucrạn gun lạime ar ona *ạ*te sabad benaome.
4. *kọl* ar *kọl* sabad reak̓ begar lạime.
5. *ẹ* ar *ẹ* reak̓ begar lạime.
6. *kẹṛ-kẹṛ* ar *kẹṛ-kẹṛ* ayat beoha reak̓ begar lạime.
7. *k̓, ċ, t̓, ṗ* dọ oka ṭhẹċ beoharok̓a?
8. Tarko aṛaṅ reak̓ 6 gọṭẹċ pạrtul ẹmme.
9. Ãṭ Aṛaṅ reak̓ 6 gọṭẹċ pạrtul ẹmme.
10. Nase Aṛaṅ reak̓ 6 gọṭẹċ pạrtul ẹmme.
11. Mũ Aṛaṅ reak̓ 6 gọṭẹċ pạrtul ẹmme.
12. Kẹcẹt̓ Aṛaṅ reak̓ 6 gọṭẹċ pạrtul ẹmme.
13. *ṭ* dọ oka dọl reak̓ aṛaṅ kana?
14. *t̓* dọ oka dọl reak̓ aṛaṅ kana?
15. *ṇ* dọ oka aṛaṅ dọl reak̓ harọp kana?
16. *ṭ* ar *ṭh* aṛaṅre cẹt̓ begar menak̓a?

3

SANTALI HARO̱PMALARE BEOHARAKAN HARO̱PKO REAK̇ UCRẠN GUN

a, ạ, e, e̱, ẹ, i, o, o̱, , u ar mũ-moca aṛaṅ so̱do̱r lạgit̓ Be̱hạṭiṉ́ok̓ Haro̱p cetanre ' ˜ ' cinhạko lagaok̓kana; metak̓me – *ã, ạ̃, ẽ, ẽ̱, ĩ, õ, õ̱, ũ* emanko.

Santali pạrsire Hạṭiṉ́ok̓ Haro̱pko do̱ turui dhara reak̓ menak̓a :-

1.Tarko Aṛaṅ *(Voiced)*; 2. Be̱tarko Aṛaṅ *(Voiceless);* 3. Ãṭ Aṛaṅ *(Aspirate);* 4. Nase Aṛaṅ *(Non-Aspirate)*; 5. Mũ Aṛaṅ *(Nasal);* ar 6. Ke̱ce̱t̓ Aṛaṅ *(Checked consonants)* :-

1. Tarko Aṛaṅ : *g, gh, ṅ, ḍ, ḍh, ṇ, d, dh, n, b, bh, m, y, r, ṛ, ṛh, l, v, w, h, nh, yh*
2. Be̱tarko Aṛaṅ : *k, kh, c, ch, ṭ, ṭh, t, th, p, ph, s*
3. Ãṭ Aṛaṅ : *kh, gh, ch, jh, ṭh, ḍh, th, dh, ph, bh*
4. Nase Aṛaṅ : *k, ṅ, c, j, ń, ṇ, ṭ, ḍ, t, n, p, b, m, y, r, ṛ, l,v, w*
5. Mũ Aṛaṅ : *ṅ, ń, ṇ, m, n*
6. Ke̱ce̱t̓ Aṛaṅ : *k̓, ċ, t̓, ṗ, h̓*

Cetan reak̓ haro̱pko do̱ eae (7) do̱lre hạṭińakana :-

(i) Cetan jambe aṛaṅ *(Glottal)* : *h, h̓*

(ii) Nạṇḍri aṛaṅ *(Velar guttural)* : *k, kh, g, gh, ṅ, k̓*

(iii) Samaṅ tạru aṛaṅ *(Palatal)* : *c, ch, j, jh, ń, y, ċ, yh*

(iv) Tạru aṛaṅ *(Cacuminal cerebral)* : *ṭ, ṭh, ḍ, ḍh, ṛ, ṛh, ṇ*

(v) Ḍaṭa aṛaṅ *(Dental)* : *t, th, dh, n, nh, r, l, t́*

(vi) Luṭi aṛaṅ *(Labial)* : *p, ph, b, bh, m, v, w, ṗ*

(vii) Gasaok̇ aṛaṅ *(Sibilant)* : *s*

NAṆḌRI AṚAṄ DO̲L
(VELAR)

k - *k* do̲ nase aṛaṅ ar Be̲tarko Aṛaṅ kana. Santalire *k* aṛaṅ reak̇ ucrạn do̲ noṅka hoyok̇kana – alaṅ reak̇ tayo̲m hĩste cetan reak̇ no̲ro̲m (lạbit́) tạrui dabaoet́kana ar moca reak̇ oḍokok̇ ho̲ye ako̲ṭe̲t́kana.

Noa *k* do̲ sabad reak̇ e̲to̲ho̲ṗ, tala ar mucạt́re hijuk̇kana. Ar noa sãote *ṭ, ṭh, ṇḍ, ṛ, t, n, r, l, y, w* ar *s* do̲ lahare tahe̲nkangea, mit́ bar sabad chaḍakate. Nạmuna – *kan, kul, koṛa, kurud, hako, hũk, lakṭha, hakrao, khaṇḍo̲, sĩkṛĩć, cakta, jạknuć, se̲kre̲ć, ke̲kle̲se̲t́, kho̲kyo̲, sakwa, lo̲ksan, thokṛe, kohṇḍa, kombṛo, kaṭko̲m, kabra, kaera* eman.

kh - *kh* do̲ *k* reak̇ Ãṭ Aṛaṅ ar Be̲tarko Aṛaṅ kana. Santalire *kh* aṛaṅ reak̇ ucrạn do̲ noṅka hoyok̇kana – noa do̲ *k* reak̇ aṛaṅ lekage alaṅ reak̇ tayo̲m hĩste cetan reak̇ no̲ro̲m (lạbit́) tạrui dabaoet́kana. Me̲nkhan moca reak̇ oḍokok̇ ho̲e ãṭ ńõ̲k̇ ako̲ṭkate ucrạn aṛaṅok̇kana. *kh* do̲ sabad reak̇ e̲to̲ho̲ṗ ar talarre hijuk̇kana, mucạt́re do̲ baṅ ar noa sãote lahare *ṛ, n, r, l* ar *m* hijuk̇kana. Pạrtul – *khan, khe̲t, jo̲khe̲ć, akhṛa, cikhnạ, bakhra* eman.

g - *g* do̲ nase Aṛaṅ ar Tarko Aṛaṅ hõ̲ kana. Noa reak̇ ucrạn do̲ noṅka hoyok̇kana – alaṅ reak̇ tayo̲m hĩs reak̇ alaṅ, tạru reak̇ no̲ro̲m hisạ jak̇ ńõ̲k̇kate moca reak̇ ho̲ye ako̲ṭe̲t́kana. Me̲nkhan oḍokok̇ ho̲e do̲ tarkok̇kana se̲ gondrao ńõ̲go̲k̇kana. Ona iạtege noa do̲ tarko aṛaṅ manaoakana. *g* do̲ sabad reak̇ e̲to̲ho̲ṗ, tala ar mucạt́re hijuk̇kana ar noa *g* do̲ *j, ḍ, dh, n, r, l, m* ar *w* sãote lahare hijuk̇kana. Pạrtul – *ge̲l, go̲l, guhum, laga, rag, mag, kạgji, ro̲gdo̲, digdhạ, bhạgnạ, lạgti, pagra* eman.

gh - Noa dọ Ãṭ Aṛaṅ ar Tarko Aṛaṅ hõ kana. Noa reaḱ ucrạn dọ alaṅ reaḱ tayọm hĩs reaḱ alaṅ, cetan tạru reaḱ nọrọm hisạ jaḱ ńõḱkate ãṭ macha moca reaḱ họye akọṭeťkana. Ar oḍokoḱ họe dọ tarkoḱkana sẹ gondrao ńõgọḱkana. *gh* dọ sabad reaḱ ẹtọhọṗ ar talare hijuḱkana, mucạťre dọ baṅ. Noa *gh* dọ *r* sãote lahare hijuḱkana. Pạrtul – *ghạl, ghao, ṭaghẹn, righi, aghrao* eman.

ṅ - *ṅ* dọ nạṇḍri aṛaṅ dọl reaḱ mũ aṛaṅ kana. Santalire noa aṛaṅ dọ ẹtọhọṗre dọ baṅ hijuḱa. Noa dọ ẹkẹn sabad reaḱ tala ar mucạťre hijuḱa. Tinre noa *ṅ* talare hijuḱkana, tọbẹ noa reaḱ ucrạn dọ adọm jọkhẹċ dọ *n* leka hoyoḱkana. Mẹnkhan sanam họṛ miť leka bako ucrạneťkana. Adọmko dọ *n* ko ucrạna ar adọmko dọ *ṅ*. Disạ dọhọe jạruṛkana je *ṅ* re dọ *g* reaḱ ucrạn dọ mesalakae tahẹnkana. Disạ dọhọkaḱ jạruṛkana je *onka, enko, onko* emanre dọ *n* ge lagaoḱa *ṅ* dọ baṅ. Adọm jaegare *ṅ* bọdọlte *n* hõ aṅjọmọḱkangea. *ṅ* dọ asọkaete *k, kh, g, gh* lahare hijuḱaḱ harọp kana. Adọmaḱ miť bar sabadge noṅkanaḱ ńamoḱkana, oka dọ *ṭ, ṛ, t, d, n, m* ar *s* sãote tahẹnkana. Pạrtul – *baṅ, baṅa, enaṅ, laṅṭa, koṅka, ṭiṛiṅ, eṅga, ḍaṅgra, ọṅsọ, kaṅkha, kaṅdọṛ, gọṅgha, guṅgṛạ, baṅ* eman.

ḱ - *ḱ* dọ nạṇḍri aṛaṅ dọl reaḱ Kẹcẹť Hạṭiṅõḱ aṛaṅ kana. Noa aṛaṅ dọ moca khọn oḍokoḱ họe nạṇḍri bhitrirege adha dọ jọm ruạṛkeť leka bhitrirege tahẽ ruạṛoḱa ar adha dọ nạṇḍri bhitrirege phọsọṅ mucạdoḱa. *ḱ* dọ aċ mọtọ sạdhin rupre ọhọge ucrạn daṛelena. Noa reaḱ aṛaṅ dọ aċ phẹḍ reaḱ Bẹhạṭiṅõḱ aṛaṅre ṭehaḍ menaḱa sẹ ạyuroḱa. Noa dọ bẹjivianaḱ Niṭ Lạlạiaḱ Tayọm Joṛao *(aḱ)* dọ oko kuṛại reaḱ ọktẹ *(tense)* tayọm bẹjivianaḱ lạgiť hõ beoharoḱkana ar kạmie kạjnumre *(active verb)* hõ hoyoḱkana *(aḱ)*. Ar hukum ayatre bẹjivianaḱ oko kuṛại sãoteaḱre hõ *(aḱ)* lagaoḱkana. Noa *ḱ* dọ Mẹnjọṅ ayat reaḱ Kạjnum, Bẹniṭ sẹ Bhạbisọt ayat reaḱ Kạjnum sabad aḱarjao rup *(-ḱ)*re ar adọm jọkhẹċ dọ Hạhạṭiṅ Lekha *(-ḱ)* tala joṛao *(iṅfix)* rupre hijuḱkana. Pạrtul – *aḱ* – bogeaḱ (bẹjivianaḱ niniṭ lạlạiaḱ tayọm joṛao), *ạguaḱa, ọlakaťaḱ* (bẹniniṭ lạlạiaḱ tayọm joṛao), *dulak̇me* (hukum ayatre tala joṛao), *juṭuċak̇ae* (bhạbisǫt ayat) *bęṅgęťak̇kan tahẽkanako* (bęjivianak̇ lạgiť oko kuṛại – *inam, ind, ob.)*

ǫk̇ – (bękạmi kạjnum tayǫm joṛao –*passive verbal suffix*), jeleka: - *sǫrǫmǫk̇kanae, idik̇, ikạk̇, sorok̇.*

kak̇ – giḍikak̇me, lạikak̇kạnạń (hukum kạjnum)

kok̇ – thirkok̇ae (bęniṭ bhạbisǫt rup))

lak̇ – rǫṛlak̇ae (pạhil hoyakanak̇ ǫktę reak̇- *anterior past*)

kǫk̇ – ęmkǫk̇am (bęniṭ bhạbisǫt rup- *indirect object*)

k̇ – ǫk̇ǫl, uk̇ur, ęk̇ęr (sabad bek̇nao rup)

ik̇irae - (hạhạṭiń lekha *(distributive number)*

ạk̇ạkriń – (sabad benao rup)

bik̇cạr, bak̇ńcao, kok̇ṅga, tik̇irpit, gǫk̇ṛǫ, bạk̇ndi (sabad benao rup)

ǫk̇, rǫk̇, uduk̇ – (Kạmie Kạjnum Rup)

TẠRU AṚAṄ DǪL
(PALATAL)

c - *c* dǫ tala tạrute aṛaṅok̇ harǫp kana. Noa dǫ nase aṛaṅ harǫp hǫ̃ kana. *c* dǫ alaṅ reak̇ tala hĩste kęṭęċ tạru ṭhęċ hǫye akǫṭęťkana. Ar noa aṛaṅ dǫ bętarko aṛaṅ hǫ̃ko metak̇kana. Santalire *c* dǫ sabad reak̇ ętǫhǫṗ, tala ar mucạťre hijuk̇kana. Pạrtul – *cal, lac-laca, lęcṛę, acel*. Noa harǫp dǫ *k, ṭ, ṛ, n, r, l, m* lahare hijuk̇kana. Pạrtul – *backǫm, bạckạr, pạcla, pocra, picnuċ, mocṛa-mucṛi* eman.

ch - Noa dǫ *c* reak̇ Ãṭ Aṛaṅ ar Bętarko Aṛaṅ hǫ̃ kana. Noa reak̇ ucrạn dǫ *c* khǫn ãṭ machatege aṛaṅok̇a, męnkhan aṛaṅ reak̇ ṭhại dǫ miťgea. Metak̇me *c* ar *ch* reak̇ aṛaṅ ṭhại dǫ miťṭęngea. Noa dǫ sabad reak̇ ętǫhǫṗ ar talare *ṛ, n* ar *l* lahare hijuk̇kana. Pạrtul – *bạchṛi, chal, lacha, bachnao, bichnạu, pichlạu* eman.

j - *j* do̠ nase ar tarko ạṛaṅ kana. Noa haro̠p do̠ tala alaṅ, co̠ṭ ke̠ṭe̠c̓ tạru ṭhe̠c̓ ho̠e ako̠ṭkate thoṛa tarko ńõ̠k̓kate ho̠e do̠ moca bahrete oḍokok̓kana. *j* do̠ tala alaṅ ar co̠ṭ tạru reak̓ ke̠ṭe̠c̓ hisạ talare ạṛaṅ thoṛa gondrao *(vibrate)* oḍokok̓kana. Noa ạṛaṅ do̠ nase ạṛaṅ hõ̠ kana. *j* do̠ sabad e̠to̠ho̠p̓, tala ar mucạt̓re hijuk̓kana. Pạrtul – *jel, ajare, raj* eman. *j* do̠ *g* (j) *ṛ, n, r, l, b, m* ar *w* lahare hijuk̓kana. Pạrtul – *ạjgut, gijṛi, bajṛa, jojnao, bujri, he̠jle̠c̓, khijlạu, ajbajao, ajmao, gajwak̓* eman.

jh - *jh* do̠ Tarko Ãṭ Ạṛaṅ kana. *jh* do̠ *j* reak̓ Ãṭ Ạṛaṅ kana. Noa do̠ *j* kho̠n do̠ thoṛa ãṭge ạṛaṅok̓a. Ar banar reak̓ge ucrạnok̓ ṭhãi do̠ mit̓ṭe̠c̓gea. E̠ke̠n ạṛaṅ reak̓ ãṭ ar naserege benegar menak̓a. Noa do̠ tarko ạṛaṅ hõ̠ kana. Noa haro̠p do̠ sabad reak̓ e̠to̠ho̠p̓ ar talare hijuk̓kana. Pạrtul – *jhĩk, jhạl, jho̠l, bojha* eman. Noa haro̠p do̠ *ṛ, n, l* ar *m* lahare hijuk̓kana, jeleka – *ojhṛao, lijhṛạk̓, ajhnar, ujhlạu* eman.

ń - *ń* do̠ tạru ạṛaṅ do̠l reak̓ mũ ạṛaṅ kana. Ar Nase Ạṛaṅ ar Be̠tarko Ạṛaṅ hõ̠ kangea. Noa reak̓ ucrạn do̠ tạru ṭhen tala alaṅte ako̠ṭkate ado̠mak̓ moca reak̓ oḍokok̓ ho̠e mũ ho̠rte ho̠ye pãeṛẽ̠ye̠t̓kana ar ona reak̓ ạṛaṅ do̠ thoṛa mũte hõ̠ hoyok̓kana. Ar ona iạte noa do̠ Mũ Ạṛaṅ Hạṭińõ̠k̓ Haro̠p hõ̠ko metak̓kana. Noa haro̠p do̠ sabad reak̓ e̠to̠ho̠p̓, tala ar mucạt̓re hijuk̓kana, jeleka – *ńe̠l, le̠ń, teńań, ạńu* eman. *ń* do̠ sabad reak̓ *c, j* ar *jh* lahare hijuk̓kana. Pạrtul – *ańcar, ańjle, mạńjhi, mạńjhlạ, mõ̠ńj, ańjo̠m, khańca, pańja* eman.

y - *y* do̠ khulạ tala tạru gasaok̓ ạṛaṅ ar tarko ạṛaṅ hõ̠ kana. Co̠ṭ alaṅ thoṛa laha se̠c̓ ḍhil ńõ̠k̓kate latar reak̓ samaṅ ḍaṭa se̠c̓te ho̠ye oḍoket̓kana. Tala alaṅ cokṛo ńõ̠k̓kate ar tạru ho̠rte sakṛa-sakṛate ho̠ye bahreyet̓kana.

Noa *y* do̠ hahaṛa (hirkhạ/rạskạ/bhabna/ạṛis katha so̠do̠ret̓re hõ̠ beoharok̓kana), jeleka – *hijuk̓me yại! e̠ yại! me̠n yại! dạṛme, ḍạr ńũruk̓kana.* Noa do̠ sabad reak̓ e̠to̠ho̠p̓, tala ar mucạt̓re ńamok̓kana, jeleka – *yại, ya; uniye, ạyur, yona* eman. Ado̠m jọkhẹċ barea Bẹhạṭińŏk̕ Harọp mit̕ ucrạn lekae *(dipthong)* kạmi khan tọbẹ *y* leka hõ ucrạnok̕kana, jeleka – *gại (gạy) – gại gupiyiċ (gupieiċ); lạiet̕ae (lạyet̕ae).*

yh - *yh* dọ *y* reak̕ Ãṭ Aṛaṅ kana. Ar Tarko Aṛaṅ hõ kana. *yh* ar *y* reak̕ aṛaṅ ṭhãi dọ mit̕gea. *yh* dọ *y* khọn thoṛa ãṭ ńŏk̕ tarko aṛaṅok̕a ar gondraoate họye oḍok bahreyet̕kana. *yh* dọ ẹkẹn sabad reak̕ talarege ńamok̕a eṭak̕ ṭhẹċ dọ baṅ, jeleka – *kuṛhiyhạ (kuṛiyhạ).*

ċ - *ċ* dọ tạru aṛaṅ dọl reak̕ Kẹcẹt̕ Hạṭińŏk̕ aṛaṅ kana. *ċ* dọ aċ mọtọre sạdhin rupre baṅ ucrạnok̕a. Noa *ċ* reak̕ ucrạnre họe dọ ạḍi nase bại ńŏk̕te ackage ucrạn mucạdok̕kana, adha dọ oḍoken leka ar adha dọ bọlọ ruạṛen leka ucrạnok̕a. Ar *ċ* dọ tạru ṭhen calaokate họe ạḍi nase parọmọk̕ leka ạikạuk̕a.

BHITRI TẠRU AṚAṄ DỌL
(CACUMINAL CEREBRAL)

Tạru Aṛaṅ dọl reak̕ noa sanam harọp reak̕ ucrạn dọ cọṭ alaṅ tayọm sẹċ lạṭiċ ruạṛkate cetan tạrui jọṭẹt̕ ńam tuluċ moca reak̕ họye akọṭẹt̕kana. Santali reak̕ noa aṛaṅ dọ alaṅ cetan tạrure ulṭạu ńŏk̕kate kiṛbit̕ rakab tuluċ cọṭ alaṅ tạrui jak̕ ńamet̕kana.

ṭ - *ṭ* dọ bhitri tạru aṛaṅ dọl reak̕ Bẹtarko Aṛaṅ kana ar Nase Aṛaṅ hõ kana. *ṭ* reak̕ ucrạn dọ cọṭ alaṅ ulṭạute lạṭiċ rakap̕kate latar nakha reak̕ alaṅ hạṭiń samaṅ tạru ṭhẹċ rakap̕kate họe akọṭ tuluċe oḍok ocoak̕kana. Noa harọp dọ sabad reak̕ ẹtọhọp̕, tala ar mucạt̕re hijuk̕kana. Pạrtul - *ṭuạr, ṭọṭọk̕, rọṭẹ, laṭ, haṭ, chaṭka, cạṭki, muṭi, chuṭki, chiṭkiṛiċ* eman.

ṭ dọ *k, ṛ, n, r, l, b, v, w* ar *m* lahare hijuk̕a, jeleka - *ṭọṭkọ, koṭko, kọṭrẽ, kaṭra-kuṭrạ, bạṭvi, jhaṭwa-jhạṭwi.*

ṭh - *ṭh* dọ ãṭ aṛaṅ ar Bẹtarko Aṛaṅ harọp hõ kana. Noa reak̕ ucrạn dọ *ṭ* lekage hoyok̕a, mẹnkhan ãṭge aṛaṅok̕a. Ucrạn ṭhãi dọ mit̕gea. Noa harọp dọ sabad reak̕ ẹtọhọp̕ ar talare hijuk̕a, mucạt̕re dọ baṅ hijuk̕a. Ar *ṭh* dọ sabadre *ṛ, n, r, l, w, ṅg* lahare hijuǩa. Pạrtul – *ṭheṅga, ṭhaǩ-ṭhoͅǩ, reͅṭheͅ, kạṭhnạu, aṭhr̃eͅ, kạthli, kuṭhri, Aṭhwar, kaṇṭhaṛ* eman.

ḍ - *ḍ* doͅ bhitri tạru aṛaṅ doͅl reaǩ tarko aṛaṅ ar nase aṛaṅ kana. *ḍ* reaǩ ucrạn doͅ *ṭ* lekage hoyoǩkana, meͅnkhan tarkoate hoͅe doͅ moca bahretey oḍok ocoaǩkana. Noa reaǩ ucrạn ṭhã̤i doͅ *ṭ* ar *ṭh* leka miṭ ṭhenge hoyoǩkana. Noa haroͅp doͅ sabad reaǩ eͅtoͅhoͅp̌, tala ar mucạṭre hijuǩkana. *ḍ* doͅ sabadre *g, n, r, l, b, v, w* ar *m* lahare hijuǩkana. Pạrtul - *ḍạn, geͅḍeͅ, haḍgar, gaḍ-guḍ, guḍnạ, buḍruč, uḍli, guḍmạ, kuḍbur, ṭiḍvi* eman.

ḍh - Noa doͅ *ḍ* khoͅn begargea. *ḍh* doͅ *ḍ* reaǩ Ãṭ Aṛaṅ kana. Noa doͅ Ãṭ Aṛaṅ ar Tarko Aṛaṅ kana. Noa reaǩ ucrạn ṭhã̤i doͅ *ṭ, ṭh, ḍ* leka miṭ ṭheͅčgea. Noa haroͅp doͅ sabad reaǩ eͅtoͅhoͅp̌ ar talare hijuǩkana, mucạṭre doͅ baṅ hijuǩkana. Pạrtul - *ḍhạrwạǩ, ḍạḍhiṭ* eman.

ṇ - *ṇ* doͅ Bhitri Tạru Aṛaṅ doͅl reaǩ mũ aṛaṅ haroͅp kana. Noa doͅ tarko ar nase aṛaṅ hõ kana. Noa reaǩ ucrạn doͅ coͅṭ alaṅ lạṭič rakap̌kate bhitri tạru ṭhen tạru ṭuṇḍu tiạǩkate hoͅye akoͅṭeͅṭkana. Bhitri reaǩ coͅṭ noͅroͅm tạru ṭhen hoͅe akoͅṭkate adoͅmaǩ hoͅe doͅ mũ hoͅrtey pãeṛẽͅ goͅṭkaǩkana ar thoṛa mũte hõ aṛaṅoǩkana. Ona iạtege noa haroͅp doͅ Mũ Aṛaṅ Haroͅp doͅko metaǩkana Noa doͅ *ṭ, ṭh, ḍ* ar *ḍh* lahare hijuǩkana. *ṇ* doͅ eṭaǩ doͅl reaǩ haroͅp sãote baṅ heͅč daṛeaǩa seͅ noa doͅl reaǩge *ṛ* lahare baṅ hijuǩa.

ṇ doͅ sabad reaǩ eͅtoͅhoͅp̌re doͅ ekalte baṅ hijuǩa *ṭ, ṭh, ḍ, ḍh* lahare heͅčkate benaoǩ sabad – *jhạṇṭi, rạṇḍi, mạṇḍi, hạṇḍi, jạrṇḍi, kohṇḍa, mohṇḍa, biṇṭhi, ạṇḍič, gaṇḍke, oṇḍga, guṇḍri, kuṇḍlạṅ, muṇḍhạṭ, bhãrṇḍo* eman.

ṛ - *ṛ* doͅ Nase Aṛaṅ ar Tarko Aṛaṅ kana. Noa reaǩ ucrạn doͅ coͅṭ alaṅ cetan reaǩ keͅṭeͅč tạru seͅč ulṭạu rakap̌kate hoͅye akoͅṭeͅṭkana, meͅnkhan tạru doͅ nasenaǩ baṅ jaǩ ńamoǩkana. Coͅṭ alaṅ cetan tạru ṭhen laṛaoǩa, tạru doͅ bae tiạga ar moca reaǩ hoͅe doͅ coͅṭ alaṅ cetan-cetante paroͅm calaǩa. Santalire *ṛ* sabad reaǩ eͅtoͅhoͅp̌re doͅ ekalte baṅ hijuǩa. *ṛ* doͅ sabad tala ar mucạṭre hijuǩkana. Noa doͅ *h, k, g, ṅg, c, ch, j, jh, y, v, t, d, dh, n, r, p, b, m, v, w* ar *s* lahare hijuk̓kana. Pạrtul – *lạṛhại, ãṛgo, e̱ṛe̱c̓-e̱ṛe̱c̓, pạṛchạu, hãṛjaṅ-huṛjuṅ, ko̱ṛńje, e̱ṛjhe̱-be̱ṛjhe̱, ge̱ryo̱m, kẽ̱ryo̱t̓, bạ̃ṛti, kạṛdhup̓-kạṛdhup̓, khạ̃ṛduk̓, koṛra, laṛpe, hạṛbuṅ, ho̱ṛmo̱, bẽ̱ṛbak̓, ghaṛvi, kãṛwãt̓, ghaṛwa, oṛsa, aṛak̓* eman.

ṛh - *ṛh* do̱ *ṛ* reak̓ Ãṭ Aṛaṅ ar Tarko Aṛaṅ kana. Noa reak̓ ucrạn do̱ *ṛ* leka hoyok̓kana ar ucrạn ṭhại hõ mit̓ṭe̱ngea. Me̱nkhan *ṛh* do̱ *ṛ* kho̱n ãṭge ucrạnok̓a. *ṛh* do̱ sabad reak̓ talarege hijuk̓a e̱to̱ho̱p̓ ar mucạt̓re do̱ baṅ hijuk̓a. Pạrtul – *kuṛhiạ, buṛhi* eman.

ḌAṬA AṚAṄ DO̱L
(DENTAL)

Noa do̱ Ḍaṭa Aṛaṅ Do̱l reak̓ haro̱p kana. Noa reak̓ ucrạn do̱ co̱ṭ alaṅ reak̓ latar nakha hisạte cetan ḍaṭa goṇḍa ṭhen se̱nkate ho̱ye ako̱ṭe̱t̓kana, to̱be̱ge noa do̱l reak̓ haro̱p do̱ ṭhik-ṭhik ucrạn daṛeak̓kana.

t - *t* do̱ Nase Aṛaṅ *(unaspirated)* ar Be̱tarko Aṛaṅ kana. Noa do̱ cetan ḍaṭa reak̓ bhitri nakhare alaṅ jagok̓a ar ho̱e ako̱ṭkate *t* reak̓ ucrạnok̓kana. Co̱ṭ alaṅ cetan ḍaṭa ṭhen se̱nkate ho̱ye ako̱ṭ ruạṛet̓kana.

t do̱ sabad reak̓ e̱to̱ho̱p̓, tala ar mucạt̓re hijuk̓kana ar noa haro̱p do̱ *k, ṛ, n, r, l, b, m, v* ar *w* lahare hijuk̓kana. Pạrtul – *ạtkir, bo̱tke̱, bhotṛo, atnak̓, citri, ạtruń, hatlak̓, gutlu, matbo̱r, etbar, thutmạ, hatwa-hạtvi, tetaṅ, ti, itil, bat, bhit, bitkil, matko̱m, catra, patṛa, ghatra, jatra, khunta* eman..

th - *th* do̱ sabad laha ar talare hijuk̓ak̓ Ãṭ Aṛaṅ ar Be̱tarko Aṛaṅ kana. Noa do̱ *t* reak̓ Ãṭ Aṛaṅ kana. *t* lekage noa reak̓ ucrạn ṭhại do̱ mit̓ṭe̱ngea. Me̱nkhan *th* reak̓ ucrạn do̱ *t* kho̱n do̱ jạstigea ar ãṭ ńõk̓ge aṛaṅok̓a. Santalire noa haro̱p do̱ e̱to̱ho̱p̓ ar talare he̱c̓kate *ṛ, n* ar *r* lahare hijuk̓a. Pạrtul – *tho, lathak̓, le̱thṛe̱c̓, ko̱thne̱, muthni, ge̱ndṛe̱c̓-ce̱thṛe̱c̓, tho̱kṛe̱, tho̱tho̱t̓, thapram* eman.

d - *d* do̱ Nase Aṛaṅ ar Tarko Aṛaṅ kana. Noa do̱ Santalire bhitri nakha cetan ḍaṭa ṭhen cọṭ alaṅ sẹnkate alaṅ jalaṫ ńõk̇kate hoye akoṭeṫkana, mẹnkhan noa reak̇ aṛaṅ dọ gondrao ńõgọk̇kana. Noa harọp dọ sabad reak̇ ẹtọhọṗ, tala ar mucạṫre hijuk̇kana ar *g, ṛ, n, l, m* ar *w* lahare hijuk̇kana. Pạrtul – *dạd, dada, dhadra, hodgo, ludguṗ, gudṛi, lẹdṛẹṫ, khudni, udgạr, ada, edre, udri, khadle, dhodlo, adwa* eman.

dh - *dh* dọ sabad ẹtọhọṗ ar talare hijuk̇ak̇ ãṭ aṛaṅ ar tarko aṛaṅ kana. Noa dọ *d* reak̇ Ãṭ Aṛaṅ kana. *dh* reak̇ ucrạnre dọ *d* khọn dọ ãṭ ńõk̇ge hoyok̇a ar *d* ar *dh* reak̇ ucrạn ṭhại dọ miṫgea. Noa harọp dọ sabad reak̇ ẹtọhọṗ ar mucạṫre hẹc̓kate *ṛ, n, r, m* lahare hijuk̇a. Pạrtul – *dhar, dhẹdrẹ, badha, odhrao, lẹdhra, godhnao* eman.

n - *n* dọ ḍaṭa aṛaṅ dọl reak̇ Mũ Aṛaṅ harọp kana. Santalire noa reak̇ ucrạn dọ cọṭ alaṅ cetan ḍaṭa ṭhen rakaṗkate moca reak̇ hoye akoṭeṫkana. Noa dọ Nase Aṛaṅ ar Tarko Aṛaṅ hõ kana. Noa reak̇ ucrạn dọ ekal cetanre ḍaṭa ṭhen rakaṗkate ucrạnok̇ noṅkan katha hõ baṅ kana, bickọm cetan ḍaṭa ṭhen khọn thoṛa pạclạ ńõk̇ cọṭ alaṅte jagok̇kana.

n dọ sabad reak̇ ẹtọhọṗ, tala ar mucạṫre hijuk̇a ar *h, k, kh, g, t, th, d, dh, w* ar *s* lahare hijuk̇a. Pạrtul – *nanha, bana, cun, janhẹ, nonkan, chingạu, jante, kantha, cũnd, dundu, ńindir, gẹndrẹc̓, endrae, khandlak̇, khạndri, sendra, kandha, andhra, gạndhuạ, pondhaṛ, janwar, banwãṛ, ansa, gunsi* eman.

Santalire Iṅgrạji pạrsi khọn miṫ bar noṅkan sabad hẹc̓ bọlọakana ar Santali reak̇ sọbhab lekate Santalire ạḍi jạsti beohar hẹc̓akana. Adọ noare miṫ lekanak̇ sabad reak̇ harọpre hẹc̓akana. Adọ noare miṫ lekanak̇ sabad reak̇ harọpre bọnọdọl ńẹlọgọk̇kana. Iṅgrạji reak̇ *n* dọ Santalire *l* bọdọlọk̇kana ẹnte noa dọ Santali reak̇ sọbhab ar gun kana ar noa dọ Iṅgrạji khọn Baṅglate bọlọena ar inạkate bại-bạite Santalire hõ beoharok̇ ẹhọṗena sẹ Iṅgrạji khọn Hindire bọlọena ar inạkate Santalire bọlọ taṗena. Ar noa bọnọdọl dọ sabad reak̇ ẹtọhọṗ ar talare hoyok̇kana. Pạrtul – *lil* dọ *nil* lạgiṫ bọdọlena; *lọṭ* dọ *note*; *pilsiṅ* dọ *pension*; *lalṭọn* dọ *lantern*. Mẹnkhan adọm jọkhẹċ dọ *l* khọn *n* re bọdọlọk̉kana. Pạrtul - *list* dọ *nisṭi* lạgit̉ bọdọlọk̉kana.

nh - *nh* dọ Ãṭ Aṛaṅ ar Tarko Aṛaṅ kana. Noa reak̉ ucrạn dọ *n* lekage hoyok̉kana ar ucrạn ṭhã̱i hõ̱ mit̉gea. Mẹnkhan *nh* dọ thoṛa *n* khọn dọ ãṭ ńõ̱k̉katege ucrạnok̉kana. *n* lekage moca reak̉ họe akọṭkate thoṛa dọ mũ họrtey pãẹṛẽ̱yet̉kana. Noa harọpte sabad benaok̉kan khan Isạra Ujnum ar Isạra Kạjnum Gunum reak̉e kạmiet̉kana, jeleka – *nhui, nhại, nhaṇḍẹ, nhako, nhạk̉ại* eman. Judi noa talare hijuk̉khan *n* leka Nase Aṛaṅ ańjọmọk̉a, jeleka – *nonka*.

r - *r* dọ Nase Aṛaṅ ar Tarko Aṛaṅ kana. Noa harọp reak̉ ucrạn dọ cọṭ alaṅ pạclạ sẹċ họye parọm ocoe tuluċ sọsrọċko rag leka alaṅ thar tharaok̉a ar *r* reak̉ ucrạn hoyok̉kana. Cọṭ alaṅ cetan ḍaṭa ṭhenak̉ mạskuṛa ṭhen calaokate ucrạnok̉kana. Cọṭ alaṅ cetan cokṛo ńõ̱k̉kate metak̉me kạṭiċ camọc leka khã̱iduk̉kate moca họye akọṭẹt̉kana.

Santali pạrsire *r* dọ sabad ẹtọhọp̉, tala ar mucạt̉re hijuk̉kana. Pạrtul – *rici, rõ̱, ọr, dereń* eman.

r dọ *h, k, kh, g, ṅg, c, ch, j, ṭ, ṭh, ṇḍ, ṛ, t, th, d, dh, n, l, p, ph, b, bh, m, v, w* ar *s* lahare hijuk̉kana; *ḍ, r* ar *v* chaḍakate. Pạrtul – *darha, ńũrhạ, murhuċ (murhut̉), jọm, parkọm, cạrkhi, urgum, jarge, kharṅgao, sarṅga, bạrchi, ạrji, sarjọm, cọrṭha, purṭhạ, bharṇḍo, kurṇḍạ, ghirni, gharṛa, harta, dhạrti, bertha, ardas, tẹrdẹċ, kirdhum, jharna, birni, orlo, bọrlọm, khọrlọṅ, arpa, kurphạ, bạrphại, narba-kharba, gạrbhạ, urmạl, jarmak̉-tormak̉, sormbot̉, ervel, orwal, parwa, ạrsi, marsal, bursi* eman.

l - *l* dọ Nase ar Tarko aṛaṅ kana. Noa reak̉ ucrạn dọ cọṭ alaṅ samaṅ reak̉ cetan ḍaṭa ṭhen calaokate họye akọṭẹt̉kana ar alaṅ ẹtọm-kõ̱yẽ̱ sẹċte moca reak̉ họe dọ oḍoṅok̉kana. Noa aṛaṅ dọ Bẹtarko Aṛaṅ leka hõ̱ aṭkarok̉a.

Santali pạrsire noa dọ sabad ẹtọhọp̉, tala ar mucạt̉re

hijuk̓kana, jeleka – *lil, lin, soͅl, bale* eman.

l doͅ *h, k, kh, g, ṅg, c, ch, ńj, ṭ, ḍ, ḍh, t, d, dh, n, p, ph, b, m, v, w* ar *s* lahare hijuk̓kana. Pạrtul – *lelha, lulhạ, teͅlheͅċ, lilkạr, pạlkui, alga, kulkhi, ulku phulku, ulkhạ ulkhi, lạlci, pilcu, telńjo, ulṭạ-palṭa, khilḍu, ulḍhạ, belteń, caldha, silpiń* eman.

t̓ - *t̓* doͅ Ḍaṭa aṛaṅ doͅl reak̓ Keͅceͅt̓ Beͅhạṭińoͅk̓ Haroͅp kana. *t̓* reak̓ ucrạn doͅ coͅṭ alaṅ seͅċte paroͅmoͅk̓ hoͅe ạḍi nasenak̓ ạikạuk̓a. Alaṅ mucạt̓ hoͅe heͅċ heͅċte ackage phoͅsoͅṅ mucạt̓enge. Noa aṛaṅ doͅ adha ulạket̓ leka ar adha doͅ joͅm ruạṛket̓ leka ucrạnok̓a. *t̓* doͅ kạjnumre lagaok̓ tayoͅm joṛao kana. Noa doͅ Beͅhạṭińoͅk̓ Haroͅp tayoͅmre asoͅkaete taheͅnkana. Pạrtul – *at̓, goͅt̓, mat̓, ot̓, ut̓, mẽt̓, mucạt̓, lat̓, sit̓, mit̓ eman. -eͅt̓, -et̓, -keͅt̓, -ket̓, -leͅt̓, -let̓, -akat̓, -at̓, -kat̓* ko doͅ Kạjnum tayoͅmre lagaok̓ Tayoͅm Joṛao kana.

LUṬI AṚAṄ DOͅL
(LABIAL)

p - *p* doͅ Luṭi Aṛaṅ Doͅl reak̓ Nase Aṛaṅ ar Beͅtarko Aṛaṅ kana. Noa haroͅp doͅ moca reak̓ adoͅmak̓ hoͅe cetan ar latar luṭitey akoͅṭeͅt̓kana ar ackage luṭire posak̓en leka hoͅe oḍokok̓kana.

Noa haroͅp doͅ sabad reak̓ eͅtoͅhoͅp̓, tala ar mucạt̓re hijuk̓kana. Ar *k, c, t, ṭ, ṭh, ṇḍ, ṛ, t, n, r, l, s* doͅ *p* lahare hijuk̓kana.

Pạrtul - *panahi, parkoͅm, apnar, apat, lapṛe, lap-lapa, upkạr, ḍoͅpkoͅċ, gapca, hiptiċ, ceͅpṭeͅ, apṭhao, phupṇḍo, hapta, suptiċ, apṛẽ, eͅpṛeͅ, hapṛak̓, jhạpni, pipni, apṛãṛ, eͅpeͅr, upriạ, thara-thoͅpre, thapṛa, aple, ṭuplạk̓, bapla, oͅpsoͅr, lipsạ, jhopsa* eman.

ph - *ph* doͅ Luṭi Aṛaṅ Doͅl reak̓ Ãṭ Aṛaṅ ar Beͅtarko Aṛaṅ kana. Noa reak̓ ucrạn doͅ *p* lekage hoyok̓kana, meͅnkhan *p* khoͅn doͅ ãṭge aṛaṅok̓kana ar ucrạnok̓ ṭhại doͅ mit̓gea. *ph* doͅ sabad reak̓ eͅtoͅhoͅp̓ ar talare hijuk̓kana, meͅnkhan ạḍi koͅmge sabad mucạt̓re doͅ hijuk̓kana. Pạrtul – *pheͅpṛa, phãkṛãk̓, uphnạu, haphsao, phuṭ, phuṛuk̓, phurkạu, phala, phạ̃uti, pharak, phạudạri, dhapadar* emanko.

b - *b* dǫ Tarko ar Nase aṛaṅ kana. *ǫ* reaḱ ucrạn dǫ *p* khǫn dǫ thoṛa luṭi ṭhen tarko ńõ̱gǫḱkana ar aṛaṅ dǫ moṭa ńõ̱gǫḱkana. Noa harǫp reaḱ ucrạn dǫ banar luṭi saṛpa miṫkate tarko machawate moca khǫn hǫe dǫe oḍok ocoaḱkana.

Noa harǫp do sabadre ẹtǫhǫp̉, tala ar mucạṫre hijuḱkana, jeleka – *bar, babẹr, baba, lebṛa, lǫb, ub, ḍhǫb* eman. Noa harǫp dǫ *k, g, j, ḍ, ḍh, ṛ, d, dh, n, r* ar *l* lahare hijuḱkana. Pạrtul – *dabka, abge, ǫbjǫs, kạbjui, kabjho (jh* lahare hõ̱ hijuḱkana*), jǫbdhao, khabṛaha, jambṛe, babṛẽ̱, thubṛạ, labda, kuḍhạ, labdhao, obra, kabra, gubri, khablǫḱ* eman.

bh - *bh* dǫ luṭi aṛaṅ dǫl reaḱ ãṭ aṛaṅ ar tarko aṛaṅ kana. Noa reaḱ ucrạn dǫ *b* lekage hoyoḱkana, mẹnkhan banar luṭi ṭhen hǫe dǫ raṅgao ńõ̱ḱ ṭhuen leka aṛaṅoḱa. Noa reaḱ ucrạn dǫ *b* khǫn dǫ ãṭge aṛaṅoḱa. Noa reaḱ ucrạn ṭhãi dǫ *b* ar *bh* dǫ miṫgea ẹkẹn ãṭ aṛaṅ ar nase aṛaṅrege begar dǫ menaḱa.

Noa sabad reaḱ ẹtǫhǫp̉ ar talare hijuḱkana, jeleka – *bhạlại, bhagao, lubhi, bhugạḱ, abhran, libhạr, libhrạ* eman. Noa harǫp dǫ *r* lahare hijuḱkana. Pạrtul – *abhra, abhran, libhrạ* eman.

m - *m* dǫ luṭi aṛaṅ dǫl reaḱ Tarko Aṛaṅ, Mũ Aṛaṅ ar Nase Aṛaṅ kana. Noa reaḱ ucrạn dǫ banar luṭi bǫndkate moca reaḱ hǫe akǫṭkate nǫrǫm tạru sẹc̓te thoṛa hǫe dǫ mũ hǫrtey pãeṛẽ̱yeṫkana ar thoṛa kǫm ńõ̱ḱge moca khǫn dǫ hǫe oḍokoḱkana.

Santalire noa *m* dǫ banar aṛaṅge ńamoḱkana, metaḱme tarko aṛaṅ ar bẹtarko aṛaṅ. Judi noa harǫp sabad ẹtǫhǫp̉ ar talare hẹc̓len khan Bẹtarko hoyoḱkana ar mucạṫre hẹc̓len khanre hõ̱ Bẹtarko hoyoḱkana. Ar adǫm jǫkhẹc̓ dǫ Hạṭińõ̱ḱ Harǫp lahare ar mucạṫre hẹc̓len khan Bẹtarko Aṛaṅ leka aṛaṅoḱa, jeleka – *ma, mama, am, ram* eman.

m harǫp dǫ *h, k, g, c, ch, j, jh, ṭ, ṭh, ḍ, ḍh, ṛ, t, d, th, n, r (ǫr), l (ǫl), p, ph, b, bh* ar *s* lahare hijuḱkana. Pạrtul – *kạmhại, gamhãṇḍ, dumhẹ, gomke, cẹmkẹċ, jạmki, dạmgi, dẹmcǫk̓ (ḍhẹńcǫk̓), humcạk̓, gamcha, lamjak̓, rạmjạu, umjhạu, sạmjhạu, humṭạk̓, amṭha, cẹmḍẹń, kumḍhuċ, kạmṛĩ (kạṛmi), umtạ-umti, amdaj, umdhi, ǫmnẹ, ṭạmni, ạmrit (ambrit-papaya), amla, mamla (mambla), campa, ampa ompo, lampha, campel, ombak̓, kumbẹt̓, jhumbri, hẹmbrǫm, kombṛo, jambṛo, kumlạu, bambkao, sambhe, kambhao, kumbhir, gạmbhrạ, amsam, rimsiċ, dhumsạ* eman.

v - *v* dǫ Khulạ Ḍaṭa Luṭi Aṛaṅ kana. Noa dǫ Tarko Aṛaṅ ar Nase Aṛaṅ hõ kana. Noa harǫp reak̓ ucrạn dǫ latar luṭi reak̓ bhitri hisạte cetan reak̓ samaṅ ḍaṭa jak̓ ńamkate moca reak̓ hǫe dǫe akǫṭẹt̓kana.

w - *w* dǫ Tarko Aṛaṅ ar Nase Aṛaṅ kana. Noa harǫp reak̓ ucrạn dǫ latar luṭi cetan reak̓ samaṅ ḍaṭa bae jak̓ ńamet̓kana. Cetan ḍaṭa ạurie jak̓ ńamrege pharak lahak̓kana. Noa dǫ Khulạ Luṭi Aṛaṅ kana. Noa aṛaṅ jǫkhẹċ luṭi dǫ ekal baṅ cokṛok̓kana. Adǫm hǫṛ dǫ *v* ar *w* reak̓ begar baḍae baṅ iạte *v* jaegare *w* hõko beohareda ar adǫm jǫkhẹċ dǫ *w* jaegare *v* hõko laṛcaṛet̓kangea. Noa dǫ bhulogok̓kana ẹnte banar reak̓ ucrạn gun begargea. Mẹnkhan noa hõ mit̓ṭẹn katha *v* dǫ adǫm jǫkhẹċ *bh* leka hõ aṛaṅok̓gea, metak̓me Ãṭ Aṛaṅ leka.

v ar *w* dǫ sabad reak̓ talarege, ar baṅ khan barea Bẹhạṭiṅõk̓ Harǫp talare hijuk̓a sẹ talare Hạṭiṅõk̓ Harǫp lahare hõ ar inạ aċ tayǫmre Bẹhạṭiṅõk̓ Harǫp hijuk̓a.

Santalire *v* ar *w*te dǫ sabad baṅ ẹhǫbǫk̓a. Barea Bẹhạṭiṅõk̓ talare, jẹmǫn - *jivi, jivẹt̓, livẹt̓, ever, nãwã, rãwão* eman.

v ar *w* dǫ *k, g, c, j, ṭ, ṭh, ḍ, ṇḍ, ṛ, t, d, n, r, l* ar *s* tayǫmre hijuk̓a. Pạrtul - *sakwa, sagwan, kacwan, gajwak̓, lẹṭwẹt̓, paṭwa, aṭhwar, ṭiḍvi, maṇḍwa, liwạ-lawe, latwak̓, adwa, manwa, parwa, palwa, aswar* eman.

w ar *v* dǫ Santali sabad reak̓ ẹtǫhǫp̓ ar mucạt̓re baṅ hijuk̓a.

ṗ - *ṗ* dọ Kẹcẹt́ Luṭi Aṛaṅ kana. *ṗ* dọ *p* reaḱ lekage ackage aṛaṅ mucạdoḱ harọp kana. Noa harọp dọ *ḱ, ċ, t́* ar *ń* lekage aċ mọtọre sạdhin rupre dọ baṅ ucrạnoḱa. Sanam kẹcẹt́ harọpge aċ mọtọre dọ baṅ ucrạnoḱa, bickọm sabad sāo hẹċkatege ucrạnoḱa, mẹnkhan noa reaḱ aṛaṅ dọ baṅ lekage aṅjọmọḱ leka ại kạuḱa, metaḱme adha dọ ucrạnket́ leka ar adha dọ jọm ruạṛket́ leka aṭkaroḱa.

ṗ dọ sanam Bẹhạṭiṅõḱ Harọp tayọmre hẹċ daṛeaḱa sẹ hijuḱkana. Pạrtul – *lạṗ, aṗ, saṗ, leṗ, seleṗ, ruṗ, ṭhẹṗ, ḍẹṗ-ḍẹṗ, ṭhọṗ-ṭhọṗ, ḍhọṗ-ḍhọṗ, ciṗ-ciṛiṗ, kaṗ-koṗ* eman.

ḱ, ċ, t' ar *ṗ* reaḱ *g, j, d, b*re BỌDỌLỌḰ REAṄ

Tinre sabad mucạt́re kạjnum *(verb)* rupre kẹcẹt́ harọpko beoharoḱa ar ona dọ jọs kạjnum *(transitive)* reaḱ manere laṛcaṛoḱa ar onare kạjnumanaḱ Ọktẹ Tayọm Joṛao *(verbal tense suffix)* joṛaolenre ar onare kuṛại Tayọm Joṛao *(object suffix)* tahẹnkhan, metaḱme *iń* ar *e* beoharlen khan tọbẹ *t'* dọ hijuḱkana. Pạrtul – *t'* – *iń* ar *e* sāo, *let́-iń* (kuṛại tayọm joṛao *(object suffix)*

let́(a) (kạjnum ọktẹ tayọm joṛao kuṛại tayọm joṛao, (*verbal tense suffix obj. Inp*)

sit' (a)-e (verbal tense suffix obj. Inp)

sit' iń (verbal tense suffix obj. Inp)

t' dọ *d*re unre bọdọlọḱkana tinre Bhạbisọt Ọktẹ *(future tense)* ar Hukumanaḱ ayat reaḱ Kạjnum *(Imperative sentence with verb)* sāote sọdọr Bẹjivianaḱ Kuṛại *(direct inanimate object)* sāo hẹċlen khan ar Sọdọr Jivianaḱ Kuṛại Tayọm Joṛao *(direct animate object infix)* hẹċlenre hõ *t'* khọn *d*re bọdọlọḱkana. Ar noa dọ Kạmiạ Pạhil Họṛ *(first person)* ar Eṭaḱ Họṛ *(third person)* mit́ lekha tahẹn khan hoyoḱkana. Pạrtul:–

sit' + ạ + ń = sidạń (bhạbisọt ọktẹ-*(FT – First person singular number) sit' + a+e = sidae (-do-Third person singular number)*

sit' (me) = sidme (hukum) – sǫdǫr bẹjivianak̓ kuṛại

(i) Adǫm jǫkhẹc̓ judi Kạjnum *(passive voice)* tayǫm joṛao *(suffix)ok̓/ǫk̓* hẹc̓lenre kẹcẹt̓ harǫp dǫ purạu tarko harǫpre bǫdǫlǫk̓a. Pạrtul :- *gẹt'* (ok̓) = *gẹdǫk̓*; *mak̓* (ok̓) = *magok̓*; *mẽt̯'* (ok̓) = *mẽdok̓*; *up̓* (ok̓) = *ubok̓*.

(ii) Tinre tayǫmre joṛaoak̓ tayǫm joṛao *(suffix)* judi mucạt̓re kẹcẹt̓ harǫp tahẹn khan ar ona ǫcǫk̓lenkhan purạu tarko aṛaṅ benaok̓kan khan, tǫbẹ ona dǫ mul sabad *(root word)* leka kạmikana ar ona são *ok̓/ǫk̓* joṛaolen khan hõ purạu tarko aṛaṅ harǫpre bǫdǫlǫk̓kana. Pạrtul :–

iṅak̓ = iṅagae; lạgit' = lạgidok̓; lagat' = lagadok̓;

rinic̓ = rinijok̓ae

(iii) Kạjnumre hijuk̓ak̓ tayǫm joṛaore :-

(a) Santali sabadre judi *k̓*te mucạdok̓ khan ar ona tayǫm *ok̓/ǫk̓* menak̓ khan tǫbẹ ona dǫ *g*re bǫdǫlǫk̓a. Ar noa dǫ ac̓ dǫl reak̓ harǫpge hẹc̓len khan noa niạm dǫ cạluk̓a; mẹnkhan kạjnumre hoyok̓ jạruṛkana. Pạrtul :–

ṅẹlǫk̓ = ṅẹlǫgǫk̓; gẹt' = gẹdǫgǫk̓

Ayatre judi katha mẹnjǫṅ leka beoharlenkhan, metak̓me jãhãnak̓ reak̓ katha bạḍaeok̓khan tǫbẹ kẹcẹt̓ harǫp dǫ baṅ bǫdǫlǫk̓a ar *ok̓/ǫk̓* dǫ baṅ joṛaok̓a. Pạrtul –

calak̓iṅ mẹnlak̓a; onaṅ kạmikak̓a.

(b) Judi sabadre bẹjivianak̓ tayǫm joṛao *(suffix)* lagaolen khan *k̓* dǫ baṅ bǫdǫlǫk̓a. Pạrtul :–

haṛamak̓, rạput'ak̓, jeleṅak̓, mat'kak̓ae, mak̓let'ae eman.

(c) *t'* reak̓ kạjnum sãote tayǫm joṛao *(suffix)* – *-et', -ket', -let', -kat'* ar *-akat'* tahẹnkhan ar ona tayǫm *c* ar *iṅ* hẹc̓lenkhan *t'* dǫ *d* tarko aṛaṅ harǫpre bǫdǫlǫk̓a, judi *c* ar *iṅ, -ko, -ben,*

-*kin* eman sọdọr kuṛạị talajoṛao tahẹnkhan. Pạrtul :-

rạput'-et' = rạput'idạń, rạput'edae, rạput'edakin/ rạput'edaben, rạput'edako,

rạput'-kẹt' = rạput'kẹt'ạń, rạput'kedae, rạput'kedakin, rạput'kedaben, rạput'kedako,

rạput'-lẹt' = rạput'lidạń, rạput'ledae, rạput'ledakin/ rạput'ledaben, rạput'ledako,

rạput'-akat' = rạput'akadạń,rạput'akadae, rạput'akadakin/ rạput'akadaben, rạput'akadako.

(d) *t'* reak' kạjum sãote tayọm joṛao *(verbal suffix)* – - *at'* ar *akawat'* tahẹnkhan ar ona sãote họraranak' kuṛạị tala joṛao *(prominal object infix)* tahẹnkhan metak'me *e, iń.*

Pạrtul -:

lạị-at' = lạị-adeae, lạị-ạdińae

lạị-akawat' = lạị-akawadeạń, lạị-akawadeae

ẹm-at' = ẹma-deae, ẹmadiạń

ẹm-akawat' = ẹm-akawạdińae, ẹm-akawadeae

(e) Adọm jọkhẹc̓ mucạtre *t'* tahẹnkhan inạ tayọm *a* hẹc̓lenkhan baṅ hõ bọdọlọk'a, kạjnum tayọm joṛao tahẹnre hõ. Pạrtul :– *gẹt'-a = gẹt'-akat'ae, gẹt'-at'ae*

Adọm sabad judi *k'* te mucạdok'kan khan ar mucạt' utạrak' akhọr *(last syllable)* buṭạ sabad lekae kạmikhan *k'* dọ gre ar *c̓* dọ *j*re bọdọlọk'kana.Pạrtul :- *ac̓ – ajak', lac̓ – lajok', dẹc̓ – dẹjọk', sẹc̓ – sẹjọk', mak' – magok', eṭak'–eṭagak'/eṭagok'.*

CETAN JAMBE AṚAṄ
(GLOTTAL)

h - *h* dọ cetan jambe aṛaṅ dọl reak' ragṛao-gasaok' Tarko Aṛaṅ ar Nase Aṛaṅ kana. Noa reak' ucrạn dọ cetan jambe sẹc̓te họe ragṛao-gasaoate moca kho̱n ho̱e oḍokok̕kana. Noa haro̱p do̱ Santali sabadre e̱to̱ho̱p̕, talare hijuk̕a; mucạt̕re do̱ baṅ hijuk̕kana, jeleka – *hạr, hạni, hul, tahe̱n, o̱ho̱c̕, mahle.*

h do̱ *k, g, c, j, ń, ṭ, ṇ, ṛ, t, d, n, r, l, p, b* ar *m* lahare hijuk̕kana.

Pạrtul :- *ahkao, sohga, bạhcạ, ohjao, mohńjam, ohṭao, kohṇḍa, kuhṛạ, kạhtuk, rahdạni, gahna, lahra, ạhluṅ, jạhpuṅ, so̱hbo̱d, ohma* eman.

ḣ - *ḣ* do̱ cetan jambe aṛaṅ do̱l reak̕ ke̱ce̱t̕ haro̱p kana. Noa do̱ ac̕ mo̱to̱re do̱ baṅ ucrạnok̕a, e̱ke̱n sabad são he̱c̕katege ucrạnok̕a. Noa reak̕ ucrạn do̱ *h* lekage hoyok̕kana, me̱nkhan moca reak̕ ho̱e adha do̱ ackage ucrạn ruạṛket̕ leka ạikạuk̕a ar adha do̱ ackage ut̕ ruạṛket̕ lekage ucrạnok̕a. Noa do̱ sạdhin rupre baṅ ucrạnok̕a.

Noa *ḣ* do̱ e̱ke̱n mit̕ bar sabadrege ńamok̕kana, ona hõ̱ sabad reak̕ mucạt̕re. Pạrtul :- *aḣ, uḣ, ạḣ, e̱ḣ, le̱ḣ-le̱ḣ, iḣ*

GASAOK̕ AṚAṄ
(SIBILANT)

s - *s* do̱ Be̱tarko Aṛaṅ kana. Noa aṛaṅ oḍok lạgit̕ do̱ co̱ṭ alaṅ cetan se̱c̕ rakap̕ ńõ̱k̕kate gasaok̕kana ar ho̱e do̱ khulạ o̱ṇḍokok̕kana. Noa do̱ Iṅgrạji reak̕ *sink, cease* são ạḍige jurik̕kana. Noa *s* aṛaṅok̕ do̱ Ḍaṭa Aṛaṅ *t, d* ar *n* lekage hoyok̕kana. *s* do̱ sabad reak̕ e̱to̱ho̱p̕, tala ar mucạt̕re lagaok̕kana, je̱mo̱n – *si, so̱, as, se̱s, lase̱r eman.*

Noa *s* tayo̱mre do̱ noako haro̱p hijuk̕kana – *k, ṭ, ṇḍ, ṛ, t, n, r, l, (p), b, m, (mb)* ar *w*. Nạmuna – *iskir, uskur, kasko̱m, rạskạ; asṭaṅ, ṭesṭa; bạsṇḍi, bhosṇḍoṅ; gusṛi, le̱sṛo̱k̕; e̱sto̱ be̱sto̱; posta; kisni, dhasna, ạsrạ̃ṭ, so̱sro̱c̕, ho̱sro̱t̕, lasro̱; hạ̃sli, bạslạ, muslạ; ispat; ko̱sbat̕; o̱smao; kasmar, kismo̱t; ke̱smbe̱t̕, kusmbi; aswar* eman.

BẸHẠṬIŃÕ̱Ḱ HARỌP
(VOWELS)

Santalire menaḱ sanam Bẹhạṭińõ̱ḱ Harọp dọ tarko aṛaṅ kana, metaḱme :

a, ẹ, e, i, ọ, o, u

ạ, ẹ̣, ọ̣

ã, ạ̃, ẹ̃, ẽ, ĩ, ọ̃, ũ, õ, ũ

Noako mod khọn adọmaḱ dọ moca mọtọte aṛaṅokaḱkana ar adọmaḱ dọ mũ ar moca banartege. Ẹkẹn moca mọtọte aṛaṅokaḱ Bẹhạṭińõ̱ḱ Harọp : *a, ẹ, e, i, ọ, o, u, ạ, ẹ̣, ọ̣*

Mũ ar mocate : *ã, ạ̃, ẹ̃, ẽ, ĩ, ọ̃, õ, ũ*

Noa reaḱ ucrạnre thoṛa mọnẹaḱ jạruṛkana – *ã, ạ̃, ẹ̃, ẽ, ĩ, ọ̃, õ* ar *ũ* reaḱ ucrạnre mũte dọ ạḍi kọm sahẹt́ oḍokoḱkana ar mocate dọ jạstige họe oḍokoḱkana.

MOCA-MŨ AṚAṄ HARỌP
(NASAL CONSONANTS)

Adọmaḱ Hạṭińõ̱ḱ Mũ Aṛaṅ Harọp, metaḱme *n, ṅ, ṇ, v, m* reaḱ ucrạnre moca reaḱ họe (sahẹt́) mũte dọ jạsti oḍokoḱa ar mocate dọ kọmge.

oḱ, ọḱ, uḱ Tayọm Joṛao ar *ḱ* Tayọm Joṛaoḱ

Noa dọ Bẹkạmi Kạjnum *(passive verb)* sãote lagaoḱa. *oḱ/ọḱ* dọ sabad mucạt́re Hạṭińõ̱ḱ Harọp sãote mucạdoḱkhan lagaoḱa, jeleka - *ńam + (oḱ/ọḱ) = ńamoḱ, dul= (oḱ/ọḱ) = duloḱ.*

Buṭạ sabadre judi Khulạ Bẹhạṭińõ̱ḱ Harọp tahẹnkhan, metaḱme *ọ* sẹ *ẹ* tahẹnkhan ona tayọm -*oḱ* hijuḱkhan ona dọ – *ọḱ* benaoḱkana. Pạrtul :-

ẹm = (oḱ) = ẹmọḱ, ẹhọb + (oḱ) = ẹhọbọḱ,

lẹbẹd + (oḱ) = lẹbẹdọḱ

u harọpante judi miṫ akhọranaḱ *(monosyllabic)* buṭạ sabad tahẹnkhan – *oḱ* tayọm joṛao dọ *uḱ*re bọdọlọḱa ar baṅkhan *ạ, ẹ, ọ* aṛaṅ leka hõe ucrạn ocoea. Pạrtul :–

ńũr + (oḱ) = ńũruḱ, bul + (oḱ) = buluḱ,

chur + (oḱ) =churuḱ, gur + (oḱ) = guruḱ

Buṭạ sabad sãote mucạṫre judi miṫṭẹn Bẹhạṭińõḱ Harọp tahẹnkhan ar noa buṭạ sabad bẹkạmie kạjnumrey *(passive verb)* kạmiekhan tọbẹ onare ẹkẹn *ḱ*ge lagaoḱa. Pạrtul :–

laṅga + (-ḱ)=laṅgaḱ; teṅgo + (-ḱ) = teṅgoḱ;
ạgu = (-ḱ) = ạguḱ; idi = (-ḱ) =idiḱ; ẹṛẹ + (-ḱ) = ẹṛẹḱ;
dọhọ + (-ḱ) = dọhọḱ; bạhu + (-ḱ) = bạhuḱ.

Miṫ akhọran kạjnum *(monosyllabic)si* são dọ *oḱ* hijuḱkana ar ona dọ *sioḱ* sẹ *siḱ* hõ hoyoḱkana.

Jãhãn sabad barea Bẹhạṭińõḱ harọp *ae* sẹ *ạu* sãote mucạṫlenkhan ona sãote Bẹkạmi Kạjnum Joṛao *(passive suffix)* *ḱ*ge lagaoḱa. Pạrtul :–

baḍae + (-ḱ) = baḍaeoḱ; ạikạu + (-ḱ) = ạikạuḱ;

sambṛao + (-ḱ) = sambṛaoḱ; bhiṛạu + (-ḱ) = bhiṛạuḱ;

aḍrao + (-ḱ) = aḍraoḱ; bhokrao + (-ḱ) = bhokraoḱ;
ạulạu + (-ḱ) = ạulạuḱ; laṛao + (-ḱ) = laṛaoḱ;

bujhạu + (-ḱ) = bujhạuḱ eman.

Buṭạ sabad reaḱ dosar Bẹhạṭińõḱ Harọp *e* sẹ *i* tahẹnkhan Bẹkạmi Kạjnum Joṛao *(passive suffix) -oḱ* hijuḱkana. Pạrtul :–

baḍa(e) + (-oḱ) = baḍaeoḱ; lạ(i) + -ọḱ) = lạiọḱ;

bạḍạ(i) + (-ọḱ) = bạḍạiọḱ; lạṛhại + (-ọḱ) = lạṛhạiọḱ eman.

Jãhãn sabad tinre kẹcẹṫ harọpante mucạṫlenre ar ona Bẹkạmi Kạjnum Joṛao *(Passive Suffix) – oḱ* hẹc̓lenkhan ona kẹcẹṫ harọp dọ purạu tarko aṛaṅre bọdọlọḱa, metaḱme :

ḱ te mucạṫlen khan – *g* benaoḱkana

ċ te mucaṭ́len khan – *j* benaok̇kana

ṗ te mucaṭ́len khan – *b* benaok̇kana

ť te mucaṭ́len khan – *d* benaok̇kana.

Noa disại jạrurkana je ona kẹcẹt́ harop tayom-*ok̇* hijuk̇ jạrurkana ar tobẹaneċ Bẹkạmi Kạjnume benaoeťkana. Pạrtul :–

mẽť + (ok̇) = mẽdok̇, mẽť + (ok̇) = mẽdok̇;

lẹbẹť + (ok̇) = lẹbẹdok̇; laċ + (oċ) = lajok̇,

bak̇ + (ok̇) = bagok̇; saṗ + (ok̇) = sabok̇

Kạjunum sabadre judi -*ok̇* mucaṭ́re hẹċlenkhan ona tayom arhõ -*ok̇* sẹ -*uk̇* hẹċkate Bẹkạmi Kạjnum *(Passive Verb)* benaok̇khan -*ok̇* do -*ogok̇* sẹ *ogok̇*, sẹ *gok̇* sẹ *gok̇* noa do *ok̇ok̇* sẹ *ok̇ok̇* hẹċlenkhan hoyok̇kana. Pạrtul :–

ńam(ok̇) = (ok̇) = ńamogok̇

ńẹlo (ok̇) = (ok̇) = ńẹlogok̇

umuk̇ = (ok̇) = umugok̇

Kạmi Kạjnum *(Active Verb)* Bhạbisot Oktẹ *(Future Tense)* lạgiť -*ok̇* = -*ok̇* sẹ -*ok̇* = -*ok̇* sẹ -*k̇* = -*ok̇* lagaokate Bẹkạmi Kạjnum benaok̇khan ona do -*ogok̇*, -*ogok̇* sẹ -*gok̇*re bodolok̇a ar mucaṭ́re miťẹnge Bẹhạṭińõk̇ Harop hẹċlenre sẹ barea Bẹhạṭińõk̇ Harop hẹċlenre ar ona são -*k̇* tahẹnkhan, tobẹ *k̇* + *ok̇* do *gok̇*re bodolok̇a. Pạrtul :–

ẹmok̇ + (ok̇) = ẹmogok̇, rorok̇ + (ok̇) = rorogok̇

Ayat :-

onka do bań rorogok̇a.

bań lạiok̇a = bań lạiogok̇a.

ńẹlok̇ak̇ = ńẹlogok̇ak̇, siok̇ak̇ = siogok̇ak̇, hoyok̇ak̇ = hoyogok̇a, ucrạnok̇a = ucrạnogok̇a

Sọdọr Kuṛại Ujnum tayọm Tala Joṛao *(Direct Object infix Pronoun)* Pạhil Họṛ Miť Lekha *(Ist Person Singular = iń)* sãote -*keť* tahẹnkhan ar -*ť* dọ *d*re bọdọlkate ẹ dọ *i*re bọdọlọǩa.

Pạrtul :– *dalkidińae* ar judi eṭaǩ họṛ miť lekha tahẹnkhan ẹ dọ *e*re bọdọlọǩa jẹmọn -*kẹť* = *dalkedeae*

-*oǩ*=-*ọǩ* dọ tinre -*ọǩ* = -*ọǩ*re bọdọlọǩa ar -*ǩ* = -*oǩ* dọ tinre

-*ǩ* = - *ọǩ*re sẹ *ogoǩ* dọ *ọgọǩ*re sẹ *goǩ* dọ *gọǩ*re bọdọlọǩa.

Niạm : Judi buṭạ sabadre Khulạ Bẹhạṭińọǩ Harọp metaǩme *ẹ*, *ọ* tahẹnkhan ar ona tayọm bẹkạmi kạjnum reaǩ tayọm joṛao -*oǩ* hẹc̓lenre tọbẹ -*ǩ* dọ *g*re bọdọlọǩa ar ona laha-tayọm *o* latarre *dash* (-) lagaoǩa. Pạrtul :–

ńẹlọǩa = ńẹlọgọǩa (ńẹl = ọǩ + ọǩa) = ńẹlọǩ + oǩa = ńẹlọgọǩa

rọṛọǩa = rọṛọgọǩa (rọṛ = ọǩ + ọǩ) = rọṛọgọǩa

jọmọǩa = jọmọgọǩa (jọm = ọǩ+ọǩa) = jọmọgọǩa

ẠKIL BHAŃJAO - 3

A. Ṭọyọť kate jobab ẹmọǩme :-

1. Santali aṛańoǩ dharate tinạǩ dọlre hạṭiń daṛeaǩa? Ar okako?

   (a) 5 (b) 4 (c) 6 (d) 7

2. Cetan jambe aṛań reaǩ harọp dọ okaṭaǩ kana?

   (a) kh (b) h (c) ṭ (d) w

3. Gasaoǩ aṛań dọ okaṭaǩ kana?

   (a) s (b) k (c) c (d) t

4. Okaṭak̓ banan reak̓ sabad ṭhika?

   (a) so̱ro̱k̓ (b) sorok̓ (c) suruk̓ (d) surok̓

5. Okaṭak̓ banan ṭhika?

   (a) daea (b) daya (c) daia (d) daiea

6. *ṇ* do̱ okaṭak̓ haro̱p lahare lagaok̓a?

   (a) ṭ (b) th (c) ph (d) ṛh

7. Okaṭak̓ banan ṭhika?

   (a) mẽ̱d (b) me̱d (c) mẽ̱t̓ (d) met̓

8. Okaṭak̓ banan ṭhika?

   (a) eh (b) ẹh̓ (c) e̱h (d) e̱h̓

9. Be̱kạmi Kạjnum Joṛao *k̓* do̱ ce̱t̓ haro̱pre bo̱do̱lo̱k̓a?

   (a) g (b) kh (c) gh (d) c

10. Be̱kạmi Kạjnum Joṛao *p̓* do̱ ce̱t̓ haro̱pre bo̱do̱lo̱k̓a?

    (a) ph (b) b (c) dh (d) p

B. O̱lkate jobab e̱mo̱k̓me :-

1. *k̓, c̓, t̓, p̓* do̱ cekate *g, j, d, b*re bo̱do̱lo̱k̓a?
2. *e̱* do̱ tinre *i* re bo̱do̱lo̱k̓a?
3. *ok̓* do̱ tinre *uk̓* re bo̱do̱lo̱k̓a?
4. o̱k̓ + o̱k̓ do̱ tinre o̱go̱k̓ *re* bo̱do̱lo̱k̓a?

4

LAṬIN SANTALI REAK̓ ASO̠L-ASO̠L NIẠMKO

O̠lo̠k̓ reak̓ ạn se̠ ạri do̠ko metak̓kana Banan *(Spelling)*. Jãhãṭak̓ pạrsi reak̓ge sanam aṛaṅko jothat ṭarikate ucrạn lạgit̓ge banan reak̓ sanam ho̠ṛ mit̓ leka o̠l lạgit̓ ạnko *(rules)* ṭarhaoet̓kana. Okaṭak̓ pạrsi reak̓ bananre ac̓ak̓ pạrsi são eṭak̓ pạrsi reak̓ aṛaṅko apnar reak̓ tinạk̓ daṛe menak̓, ona pạrsi reak̓ banan unạk̓ge daṛeanak̓ pạrsi bujhạuk̓a. Ona banan reak̓ sidhạ so̠mbo̠nd pạrsi reak̓ aṛaṅko reak̓ ucrạn são menak̓a.

Mit̓ bar niạmko :-

Judi kạjnum tayo̠mre e̠ke̠n Be̠hạṭiṅõ̠k̓ tahe̠nkhan, to̠be̠ ona Kạjnum do̠ Jo̠s Kạjnum *(transitive verb)* lekae kạmiet̓kana ar ona sãote Ujnumanak̓ Kuṛại Tala Joṛao *(pronominal object infix)* baṅ tahe̠nkana. Buṭạ Sabad *(base word)* mucạt̓re *a, o, o̠* tahe̠nkhan - *e* lagaok̓a; je̠mo̠n – *baḍa-e-ae, ho̠ho̠-e-ae, teṅgo-e-ae*

Buṭạ sabad mucạt̓re *ạ* se̠ *u* tahe̠nkhan *i* lagaok̓a, jeleka - *ạgu-i-ae, bạgi-ae, kạmi-ae, idi-ae, ạ-i-kạ-u = ạikạu, uihạṛ, nạihạṛ, bạihạṛ* eman. Noa do̠ e̠ke̠n Kạmi Kạjnum *(active verb)* sãoge hoyok̓a.

Judi *kana* do̠ ṅunum *(noun)* lại lạgit̓ beoharok̓kana, to̠be̠ *kana* do̠ judạre o̠lo̠go̠k̓a, jeleka :- Noa do̠ ul bele *kana*; uni ac̓ babawak̓ ṅutum do̠ Marsal *kana*; eman.

Judi *kana* do̠ kạjnum *(verb)* sãote ro̠ṛo̠go̠k̓kana, to̠be̠ noa do̠ Kạjnum são milạukate o̠lo̠go̠k̓a, jeleka – *jo̠met̓kan tahẽ̠kanae*; uni do̠e *calak̓kana;* eman.

ạ sãote *i* lagaok̓a *e* do̱ baṅ, jeleka :- *ạ+i=* ạikạu (ạekạu do̱ baṅ)

ạ sãote *u* lagaok̓a *o* do̱ baṅ, jeleka:- *ạ+u=* ạulạu (ạolạo, ạwlạwdo̱ baṅ)

a sãote *e* lagaok̓a *y* do̱ baṅ, jeleka:- *a+e=* baḍae (baḍay do̱ baṅ)

a sãote *o* lagaok̓a *u, w* do̱ baṅ, jeleka:- *a+o=* benao (benau, benaw do̱ baṅ)

e sãote *o* lagaok̓a *u*, *w* do̱baṅ, jeleka:- *e+o = ḍheo (ḍheu se̱ ḍhew* do baṅ*)*

e̱ sãote *o* lagaok̓a *u, v. w* do̱ baṅ, jeleka:- *e̱+o=* he̱o (heu, hev, hew do̱ baṅ)

uni ujnum sãote *e* lagaok̓a *y* do̱ baṅ, jeleka:- *uni+e=* unie (uniy do̱ baṅ)

u sãote *i* lagaok̓a *e, y* do̱ baṅ, jeleka:- *u+i=* uihạr (uehạr, uyhạr do̱ baṅ)

e tayo̱mte *a* hijuk̓a *y* do̱ baṅ, jeleka:- *se+a=* sea (seya do̱ baṅ)

i sãote *ạ* lagaok̓a *y* do̱ baṅ, jeleka:- *i+ạ=* kuṛhiạ (kuṛhiyạ do̱ baṅ)

o sãote *a* lagaok̓a *w* do̱ baṅ, jeleka:- *o+a=* oar, koa (owar, kowa do̱ baṅ)

u sãote *ạ* lagaok̓a *w* do̱ baṅ, jeleka:- *u+ạ=* ruạ, cuạ (ruwạ, cuwạ do̱ baṅ)

i sãote*, ạ* lagaok̓a *y* do̱ baṅ, jeleka:- *i+=* piọ (piyo do̱ baṅ) *i+ạ=* piạ (piyạ do̱ baṅ)

Metak̓me mit̓ ucrạno̱k̓ barea Be̱hạṭiṅõk̓ haro̱p *(dipthong)* do̱ noṅka o̱lo̱go̱k̓a :-

a tayo̱mre do̱ *e* = *ae*

a tayo̱mre do̱ *o* = *ao*

ạ tayo̱mre do̱ *i* = *ại*

ạ tayo̱mre do̱ *u* = *ạu*

e tayo̱mre do̱ *a* = *ea*

e tayo̱mre do̱ *o* = *eo*

e̱ tayo̱mre do̱ *o̱* = *e̱o̱*

e̱ tayo̱mre do̱ *o* = *e̱o*

ẹ tayo̱mre do̱ *i* = *ẹi*

ẹ tayo̱mre do̱ *o* = *ẹo*

i tayo̱mre do̱ *ạ* = *iạ*

i tayo̱mre do̱ *o* = *io*

i tayo̱mre do̱ *u* = *iu*

o tayo̱mre do̱ *a* = *oa*

o tayo̱mre do̱ *e* = *oe*

o tayo̱mre do̱ *e* = *oe*

o̱ tayo̱mre do̱ *e* = *o̱e*

ọ tayo̱mre do̱ *i* = *ọi*

u tayo̱mre do̱ *ạ* = *uạ*

u tayo̱mre do̱ *i* = *ui*

Santalire mit̓ ucrạno̱k̓ pea Be̱hạṭińõ̱k̓ Haro̱pante *(tripthong)* hõ̱ sabad benaok̓kana, je̱leka :-

ea+e = eae *(seven)*

oa+o = *oao - joao (mature)*

iạ+u = *iạu* - riạu *(invite to come along)*

ae+o = *aeo* – baḍaeok̓ *(be known)*

o̱e+ea+e = *o̱eeae – ko̱eeae (he will ask)*

o̱e+ae+ae = *o̱eaeae – ko̱eaeae (he will ask for him)*

BANANRE BHUL SUDHAṚ

do ar *do̱* talare begar

do do̱ hukum katha beoharre laṛcaṛok̇a ar *do̱* do̱ ayat reak̇ Juṭiċak̇ *(Particle)* kana. Nạmuna:-

do ya, amge calak̇me; iń *do̱* bạń calao daṛeak̇kana.

oko ar *o̱ko̱* talare begar

oko do̱ Gunum *(Adjective)* kana ar *o̱ko̱* do̱ Kukli Ujnum *(Interrogative Pronoun)* kana. Nạmuna:-

o̱ko̱ baṛae, okare co̱e *oko*akan tahẽ̱kan.

jorok̇ ar *jo̱ro̱k̇* do̱ judạ-judạ sabad kana.

Nạmuna:-

jorok̇ - Culhạ ṭhenle *jorok̇*akana.

jo̱ro̱k̇ - Sạṛim kho̱n dak̇ *jo̱ro̱k̇*kana.

lo ar *lo̱* reak̇ begar

lo̱ ar *lo* do̱ banarge Kạjnum *(Verb)* kana. Me̱nkhan onakin sabad do̱ dohṛakate beoharlen khan mane do̱ judạk̇ kangea.

Nạmuna:-

lo̱ - Chạmi do̱ kicriċe *lo̱*keda.

lo̱lo̱ - De̱n se̱ *lo̱lo̱* ca imạńpe.

lo - Do, dak̇ *lo* ạguime.

lolo - Ạḍi khạndri kho̱n dak̇ *lolo* hoyok̇kana.

kol, ko̱l ar *kọl* sabadre begar

kol do̱ Kạjnum ar *ko̱l* ar *kọl* do̱ Ńunum *(Noun)* kana.

Nạmuna:-

kol - Ciṭhi do̱ń *kol*keda.

ko̱l - Dak̇ *ko̱l*te guhumko paṭaokeda.

kọl - *Kọl* cẽṛẽ do ạḍi mõńje ńeloḱkana.

hoe ar _hoe_ sabadre begar

hoe do Kạjnum *(Verb)* ar *hoe* do Ńunum *(Noun)* kana.

Nạmuna:-

hoe - Nes horo do *hoe* lạṭiċakana.

hoe - Khiṛki sińkam, reaṛge *hoe* hijuḱkana.

hoyoḱ - Bạń paṛhaolen khan ceṭ *hoyoḱa*?

hoyoḱ - Rạskạ do setaḱre gocoe *hoyoḱa.*

ocoḱ - Noa ciṭhitepe baḍae *ocoḱkana.*

ocoḱ - Noṇḍe khon usạra *ocoḱme.*

ceṭ' ar _ceṭ'_ sabadre begar

ceṭ' do Kạjnum ar *ceṭ'* do Gunum kana. Nạmuna:-

ceṭ' - Iskulre do paṛhaoḱle *ceṭ'*eda.

ceṭ' - One coń emaṭme, *ceṭ'* adom khojoḱkana?

ceṭ', ceṭ' - Iskulre do *ceṭ'em ceṭ'eda?*

hoṛo, hoṛo, hoṛo sabadre begar

hoṛo, hoṛo do Ńunum *(Noun)* kana ar *hoṛo* do Puḱrạu *(Particle)* sabad kana. Nạmuna:-

hoṛo - *Hoṛo* do ạurile rohoea.

hoṛo - *Hoṛo-hoṛo* lạḍu emakope.

hoṛo - Dhạrti do *hoṛo* deare menaḱa.

goḍo ar _godo_ sabadre begar

goḍo do Ńunum ar *godo* do Puḱrạu sabad kana. Nạmuna:-

goḍo - *Goḍo* do bhugạḱreko tahena.

godo - *Godo-godo* daḱ ạtuḱkana.

kẹṛ-kẹṛ ar kẹṛ-kẹṛ sabadre begar

kẹṛ-kẹṛ dọ Gunum *(Adj.)* ar *kẹṛ-kẹṛ* dọ Puk̇rạu *(Particle)* sabad kana. Nạmuna:-

kẹṛ-kẹṛ - Setoṅte hasa dọ rọhọṛ *kẹṛ-kẹṛena.*

kẹṛ-kẹṛ - Sọgọe koṛa dọ pajhẹṛ *kẹṛ-kẹṛ*ko họhọkeda.

sọl ar sọl sabadre begar

Noakin dọ banarge Ńunum *(Noun)* kana. Nạmuna:-

sọl - *Sọl* dọ rawalgea, noa dọ pukhrire janamok̇a.

sọl - *Sọl* hako dọ gaḍareko ńamok̇a.

era ar era sabadre begar

era dọ Ńunum *(Noun)* ar *era* dọ Kạjnum *(Verb)* kana. Nạmuna:-

era - Uni dọe ọkọeren *era* kana?

era - Jonḍra dọ ạurile *era.*

ọl ar ọl sabadre begar

ọl dọ Kạjnum ar *ọl* dọ Gunum *(Adj.)* kana. Nạmuna:-

ọl - Ciṭhi dọń *ọlkeda.*

ọl - Noa dọ dare bele dọ baṅ, noa dọ *ọl* beleak̇kana.

jolok̇ ar juluṫ sabadre begar

Nạmuna:-

jolok̇ - Amak̇ marsal dọ *jolok̇*tege tahẹnma.

juluṫ - Bakjunu dọko *juluṫ-juluṫ* baṛaea.

Santalire ạḍi ḍher onkan sabadko menak̇a, oka dọ miṫ sabad reak̇ge aema mane ar baṅkhan inạ sabadge ucrạn gunre thoṛa-thoṛa begar menak̇a. (Noa babọt jạsti baḍae lạgiṫ dọ *Homographs* ar *Homonyms* paṭbon ńẹlma.)

DABAṚ AṚAṄ
(WORD STRESS)

Sabad rọṛ jọkhẹć mane sẹ saphate ucrạn lạgiť tinre abo dọ ucrạn jọkhẹć jãhã akhọr ṭhẹć jạsti jọrbon ẹmaḱkana, tọbẹ ona kạmi dọ Dabaṛ-Aṛaṅ mẹntebon metaḱkana. Santalire akhọrtẹťre dabaṛ-aṛaṅte dọ sabad reaḱ mane bae bọdọl daṛeaḱa, mẹnkhan noa reaḱ mane dọ ekalte noa dọ baṅ kana je Santali sabad reaḱ mimiť akhọr reaḱ dabaṛ-aṛaṅ dọ miť sọmangea mẹnte. Santalire hõ eṭaḱ pạrsi lekage judạ-judạ akhọrko reaḱ ucrạn dọ dabaṛ-aṛaṅ sãote bọdọl dọ bọdọlọḱkangea; mẹnkhan akhọrre dabaṛ-aṛaṅ karọnte mane dọ baṅ bọdọlọḱa, ẹkẹn ucrạnge ucrạnoḱkana dabaṛ aṛaṅte. Mẹnkhan noṅkan dabaṛ-aṛaṅ dọ eṭaḱ pạrsirenko tinre Santali rọṛ reaḱko kurumuṭuieda, onkan họṛ họtẹtege jãhãman tãhãko rọṛa sẹko dabaṛ-aṛaṅa. Santalire okaṭaḱ sabadre okaṭaḱ akhọrre cẹť ar cẹť leka ar tinạḱ ãṭ dabaṛ-aṛaṅ rọṛ jạruṛa, okaṭaḱte dọ Santali rọrọṛ họṛ lekan ucrạn sẹy rọṛ daṛeaḱ, ona dọ Santali gọ-pạrsi rọrọṛićge beste dọe bạḍaea. Mẹnkhan ọkọe họṛ noa bae bạḍaea, uniaḱ ucrạnre bạḍae họṛ dọ bhule ńam gọda. Nõḱõe noa iạtege Santali baṅ baḱḍaić dọ *duṛup̀* dọ *duṛup*, *calaḱ* dọ *cala*, *daḱ* dọ *da, bạnuḱa* dọ *banua* eman lekako ucrạn ocoeťkana.

Santali sabadre sabad reaḱ okaṭaḱ akhọrre dabaṛ hoyoḱ, noa dọ laha khọnge niṭgea. Ar baṅkhan dọ jãhãman tãhã dabaṛ-aṛaṅlen khan noṅka hõ hoe daṛeaḱa, oka dọ jãhãn manege baṅ hoyoḱkan, jeleka :- *khạclạḱ-khạclạ, baḱḍae-bạḍaḱae, mamaḱić-maťmaić,* eman.

Santali sabadre sabad reaḱ okaṭaḱ akhọrre dabaṛ-aṛaṅ hoyoḱ, noa dọ laha khọnge bạḍaema menaḱge, ona iạte Santali ceceťić họṛ dọ noa hõ lạiae jạruṛkana je uni dọ ona sabadko reaḱ ucrạn dọ ganoḱaḱ akhọrrege jẹmọn dabaṛ-aṛaṅ dọe hoe ocoe.

RAṚ BOḌOLOḰ AṚAṄ
(INTONATION)

Tinre sabadbon ucrạneṫkana, tobe sabadko do ucrạn jokhec̓ miṫ lekan rạṛ do babo roṛeṫkana. Ucrạn jokhec̓ rạṛ do cetan ar lataroḱtege tahenkana. Roṛ jokhec̓ noa cetanoḱ ar lataroḱ reaḱ begarteṫge rạṛ-bodol rạṛ doko metaḱkana. Roṛ jokhec̓ *(pitch)* bodoloḱ do manwawaḱ sobhab kana. Rạṛ bodoloḱ do aema karonte hoyoḱkana. Adom jokhec̓ aṛaṅ thạilạḱ jạsti ńõḱ orkate tarkolen khan hoyoḱkana ar adom jokhec̓ do inboro khon hoe bahre oḍoṅlenkhan hõ ar adom jokhec̓ do ucrạn okte do alaṅ reaḱ jelre ḍher laṛaole khanre hõ rạṛ bodoloḱkana. Ona iạte rạṛ hõ miṫṭen ṭehaḍ aṛaṅ kana, okaṭaḱ do bodoloḱkan duniạ reaḱ aema pạrsikore Santali ayatko reaḱ maney bodol daṛeaḱkana.

Roṛ bodoloḱ karonte ucrạnoḱkan roṛ cetanoḱ ar latar rạṛko do latar-cetanoḱ rạṛko metaḱkana *(intonation)*. Tinre miṫ lekan roṛtebon roṛle khan ora-sora se barabạri roṛbon metaḱkana. Menkhan tinre ucrạn reaḱ roṛ cetanoḱkana tobe ona do cetanoḱ rạṛ *(ascending)* ar lataroḱkan rạṛ *(decending)* do lataroḱ rạṛbo metaḱa. Pạrtul lạgiṫ miṫ bar ayatbon ńellege :-

(i) Somae Pạuṛia doe ḍakṭor kana. *(General statement)*

(ii) Somae Pạuṛia doe ḍakṭor kana? *(Interrogative sentence)*

(iii) Somae Pạuṛia doe ḍakṭor kana! *(Exclamatory sentence)*

DOBẠṬIẠ AṚAṄ
(JUNCTION SOUND)

Ńel baṛaedabon je pạrsikore sabadko ucrạn jokhec̓ miṫṭen aṛaṅ tayom ar eṭaḱ aṛaṅbon ucrạneṫkana, adom jokhec̓ do begor thiroḱtebon aṛaṅeṫkana ar adom jokhec̓ do miṫṭen aṛaṅ ucrạn tayom eṭaḱaḱ aṛaṅ reaḱ ucrạnre thoṛagan thir ńõḱkate hoyoḱkana. Aema pạrsikore miṫṭen sabad reaḱ aṛaṅ ucrạn jokhec̓ talare hijuḱkan thiroḱ hǫtẹte sabad reaḱ maney bǫdǫlẹt́kana. Mit́ṭẹn sabad reaḱge barea aṛaṅ talare hijuḱkan thoṛa thir ńõḱkate ṛạṛge Dǫbạṭiạ Aṛaṅ dǫko metaḱkana. Pạrtulbon ńẹla :-

ạimại reaḱ mane dǫ *woman, ại* dǫ hǫhǫjǫṅ sạgại chǫnd cinhạ *(case)* kana ar *mại* reaḱ mane dǫ – hara gǫdǫḱ kuṛi *(teenage girl)*. Noa reaḱ benegar bạḍae lạgit́ge latarre pạrtul ẹmǫgǫḱkana :-

(A) (i) Uni dǫe *ạimại* kana sẹy hẹrẹl kana?

(ii) *Ại mại*, okaren kanam?

(B) (i) Guhum *arjao* dǫ ạḍi jạruṛgea.

(ii) Guhum *ar jao* dǫ ạḍi mõńj hoyakana.

Ona iạte okako pạrsikore dǫbạṭiạ-aṛaṅ karǫnte sabad reaḱ mane bǫdǫlǫḱkana, ona dǫ ona pạrsi reaḱ Dǫbạṭiạ-Aṛaṅtạri reaḱge manaoḱkana.

Dǫbạṭiạ-Aṛaṅ dǫ bujhạu lạgit́ (+) cinhạ hǫtẹte udugǫḱa. Metaḱme judi barea sabad talare (+) cinhạ lagaoakan khan noa reaḱ mane dǫ noage je sabad ucrạnre thoṛa jirạu sẹ thir menaḱa. Dǫbạṭiạ-Aṛaṅ dǫ jaoge barea aṛaṅ talarege asǫkaetey kạmia. Santalire hõ adǫm-adǫm sabadko dǫ Dǫbạṭiạ-Aṛaṅ karǫnte sabad reaḱ maney bǫdǫlẹt́kana, jeleka :-

ạimại - ại + mại

kạṭkǫm - kaṭ + kǫm

sarjǫm - sar + jǫm

dǫkhǫl - dǫ + khǫl

mit́sae - mit́ + sae

dǫpe - dǫ + pe

Noage ayatre laṛcaṛkatebon ńẹllege, tǫbẹanẹćge saphatebo bujhạu utạra :-

1. (a) Uni dǫe *ạimại* kana sẹy hẹrẹl kana?

(b) *Ại mại,* am dọm okaren kana?

2. (a) *Kaṭkọm* dọ bhugạk̓reko tahẹna.

(b) Noa oṛak̓ reak̓ dọ saṅga *kaṭ kọm*gea.

3. (a) Sukri dọ *sar jọm*katey dạṛkeda.

(b) Jahẹrre ạḍi saṅge *sarjọm* dare menak̓a.

4. (a) Bạjun dọ khas jumie *dọkhọl*keda.

(b) Noa matkọm dare *dọ khọl*gea.

5. (a) Noa sagaṛ dọ kulhi khọn *mit̓sae*pe.

(b) Noa puthi reak̓ dam dọ *mit̓ sae* ṭaka kana.

6. (a) Bọhọk̓ suṛẹ *dọpe* jọmkeda?

(b) Bọhọk̓ suṛẹ *dọ pẹ* hĩsre hạṭiṅpe.

Cetanre ẹmakan sanam sabadko dọ ayatre laṛcaṛkate pạrtulbon ńẹlkeda. Onkage ayat tala reak̓ mane bọdọl daṛeak̓ aṛaṅ laṛcaṛkate, sabad thir ńõk̓kate rọṛ sẹ aṛaṅlen khan mane bọdọlọk̓ reak̓ eṭak̓ak̓ ayat arhõ ẹmọgọk̓ pạrtulre sabad dọ baṅ hạṭiṅõk̓a, bickọm ayat reak̓ mit̓ hĩsre thir ńõk̓kate aṛaṅok̓a, oka dọ ayat reak̓ maney bọdọlẹt̓kana ar ona dọ *comma* (,) họtẹte begarok̓a, jeleka :-

1. (a) *marak̓, tukạre.*

(b) *marak̓ tukạre, ayaṅ biń.*

2. (a) *daka ṭukuc̓, cọṭre.*

(b) *daka, ṭukuc̓ cọṭre.*

3. (a) *gạḍi cọṭre.*

(b) *gạḍi, cọṭre.*

AṚAṄ AR LIPI
(PHONEME AND SCRIPT)

Aṛaṅ dọ manwa ar janwar banarak̓ge menak̓a. Ar bẹjivianak̓

jivire hõ aṛaṅ menaḱa. Jivianaḱ ar bẹjivianaḱ jinisre niạge begar menaḱa je bẹjivianaḱ jinis dọ manwae beohar khange saḍea ar baṅkhan dọ baṅ. Setawaḱ *bhoḱ* ar pusiaḱ *miyuṅ-miyuṅoḱ* dọ janwaraḱ moca khọn oḍokoḱ aṛaṅ kana. Bẹjivianaḱ jinis aṛaṅbon ńẹl lekhan noako hõ hoe daṛeaḱa :- ṭamak sẹ tumdaḱ ru aṛaṅ sẹ daḱ ạtuḱ sọkọjọḱ aṛaṅ, banam saḍe reaḱ aṛaṅ, thạri-bạṭi ńũruḱ aṛaṅ eman emanko. Beakọrọnre ẹkẹn manwawaḱ moca khọn oḍokoḱ sẹ ucrạnoḱ aṛaṅ babọt reaḱge bọrnọn ẹmọgọḱkana.

Manwa họtẹte ucrạnoḱ aṛaṅ dọ aema lekana. Adọmaḱ aṛaṅ noṅkanaḱ hõ menaḱa, ọnẹ oka dọ manwawaḱ moca khọn gọlẹť aṛaṅ, raḱeť aṛaṅ, landae aṛaṅ, sereń aṛaṅ, thayoḱ, cirhạť-cọrhọť taṛameť aṛaṅ, udureť aṛaṅ, gẹraṅ aṛaṅ, sahan paṛať jọkhẹć *hũḣ-hũḣ* ar manwa aćaḱ mẹnjọṅte aćaḱ moca khọn ucrạn aṛaṅ. Noa dọ abo manwawaḱ aṛaṅbon mẹn daṛekea. Aṛaṅ maneanaḱ ar bẹmaneanaḱ banarge hoe daṛeaḱa. Bẹmaneanaḱ aṛaṅ dọ pạrsi sẹ bhasabo metaḱkana. Noa aṛaṅ họtẹte abo dọ aboaḱ mẹnjọṅ, hudis-bicạr sẹ aṭkarkobo lại sọdọrẹťkana. Rọṛ dọ sabad họtẹte benaoḱkana ar sabad dọ aema lekanaḱ maneanaḱ aṛaṅ milạu-kate hoyoḱkana.

Pạhilre manwa akoaḱ hudis-bicạr sẹ pạtiạu emanko rạkhi-jogao lạgiť ạḍi jạruṛko aṭkarleda. Pạhil dọ manwa katha sọdọr lạgiť ayat sọdọr lekanaḱ cinhạ họtẹte kạmiko calao-banao hataṛeť tahẽkana, inạkate ọtọṅ-taenọm sabad cinhạ *(words symbol)* ar aṛaṅ cinhạ *(sound symbol)* benao tayọm pasẹć lipi cinhạko benaoana. Cinhạko dọ ọktẹ nạpitre bọdọl idiena. Nitaḱ lipi cinhạ dọ mucạť rup kana. Mẹnkhan nitaḱ noa kạmi dọ baṅ mucạťakana.

Nit hạbić Santali lạgiť ạḍi ḍher lipiko sirjạuakana, mẹnkhan onako modre bigyanik dharate *(scientifically)* jọtọ bọḍọ jọtọ khọn sọrọs utạraḱ dọ Man P. O. Boḍiṅ họtẹte sajao-sapṛaoakať Santali lipi kana.

ẠKIL BHAŃJAO - 4

A. Ṭoyoṭ'kate jobab ẹmok̇me :-

1. Latarre ẹmakan harọp bachaome, okaṭak̇ dọ *ạ* sãote hijuk̇a (*dipthong* benaok̇re)?

   (a) e (b) i (c) y (d) o

2. Latarre ẹmakan harọp bachaome, okaṭak̇ dọ *u* sãote hijuk̇gea (*dipthong* benaok̇re)?

   (a) i (b) e (c) y (d) ẹ

3. *Dipthong* benaok̇re *i* sãote cẹṭ hijuk̇a?

   (a) y (b) ạ (c) d (d) k̇

4. Ẹmakan sabadte khạli jaga pẹrẹjme.
   Sạṛim khọn dak̇ … kana.

   (a) jorok̇ (b) jọrọk̇ (c) juruk̇ (d) jọrok̇

5. Ciṭhi … hoyok̇a.

   (a) kọl (b) kul (c) kol (d) kọl

6. Gocoń … kana.

   (a) hoyok̇ (b) họyọk̇ (c) huyuk̇ (d) họyọk̇

7. Joṇḍra dọ ạurile …

   (a) era (b) ẹra (c) ira (d) ẹra

8. Ghãs … saphaepe.

   (a) ocok̇ (b) ọcọk̇ (c) ucuk̇ (d) ọcọk̇

9. Nẹs … dọ ạḍi mõ̃ńj hoyakana.

   (a) huṛu (b) họṛọ (c) hoṛo (d) họṛọ

10. Jalna bhugạk̇ khọn … hijuk̇kana.

(a) hg̱e (b) hoe (c) hui (d) hg̱y

B. O̱lkate jobab e̱mo̱ḱme :-

1. *Sidạń* reaḱ mul rupre o̱l begarme.
2. *Ge̱do̱ḱ* reaḱ mul rupre o̱l begarme.
3. go̱ć ar go̱j ayatre laṛcaṛme.
4. *go̱ć* kho̱n *go̱j* ce̱ṫ lekate benaoena?
5. *lại* sabad *first person singular number*re ce̱ṫ lekam beohara?
6. *jo̱m* sabad *first person singular, second person, third person*re ce̱ṫ lekam beohara?
7. *re̱pe̱ć* sabad *intransitive* ar *passive verb*re beoharme.
8. -*aeo*te ce̱ṫ sabad benaoḱa?
9. -*o̱ee*te ce̱ṫ sabad benaoḱa?
10. -*e̱a*te ce̱ṫ sabad benaoḱa?
11. Bar akho̱ranaḱ miṫ ucrạn *(dipthong)* sabad do̱ okaṭaḱ kana?
12. Pe̱ akho̱raḱ miṫ ucrạn *(tripthong)* sabad do̱ okaṭaḱ kana?
13. *Dipthong* do̱ ce̱ṫko metaḱa?
14. *Tripthong* do̱ ce̱ṫko metaḱa?
15. Dabaṛ aṛań do̱ ce̱ṫ kana? Pạrtul se̱le̱ṫ lạime.
16. Rạṛ Bo̱do̱lo̱ḱ Aṛań do̱ ce̱ṫ kana? Pạrtul se̱le̱ṫ lạime.
17. Aṛań do̱ ce̱ṫ kana? Pạrtul se̱le̱ṫ lạime.
18. Lipi do̱ ce̱ṫ kana?
19. Aṛań ar Lipire ce̱ṫ so̱mbo̱nd menaḱa?

5

BEAKO̱RO̱N REAḰ MAJTE̱Ṫ
(DEFINATION OF GRAMMAR)

Beako̱ro̱n do̱ ce̱ť kana? Beako̱ro̱n do̱ pạrsi reaḱ onkan ạn-ạri kana, okare pạrsi do̱ sạhi-sạhi ro̱ṛ ar sạhi-sạhi o̱l daṛeaḱ reaḱ niạme lạieťkan. No̱ṇḍe̱ baḍaejo̱ṅ katha do̱ niạge je jãhãe o̱no̱liạko ho̱te̱te Beako̱ro̱n do̱ baṅ benaoakana. Bicko̱m tis sedae kho̱n co̱ṅ Beako̱ro̱n do̱ pạrsirege menaḱ ạgua. Pạrsi do̱ ce̱ť leka sạhi ro̱ṛ ar se̱ o̱l daṛekoḱ; ona ạn-ạriko ruti-ruti lại so̱do̱rge Beako̱ro̱n do̱ko metaḱkana. Noa katha pusṭạuḱ lạgiť miťṭe̱n pạrtul e̱mo̱go̱ḱkana :–

Lukhi kana jo̱jo̱m do̱ dakae.

Noa ayatte ce̱ťbo bujhạueda? Dho̱rage noa ayat reaḱ do̱ jãhãn manege baṅ oḍokoḱkana. Noa ayat do̱ pạrsi reaḱ oka niạmtege baṅ o̱lakana. Jãhãtinạḱ noa ayatre beoharakan sabadko reaḱ mane hõ sạhige, me̱nkhan Beako̱ro̱n lekate baṅ o̱lakan karo̱nte, noa ayat do̱ bhulgea. Ona iạte pạrsi reaḱ niạmko paṅjakate, oka ạn-ạriko o̱l so̱do̱ro̱ḱkan, onage Beako̱ro̱n do̱. Cetanre lạien ayat do̱ Beako̱ro̱n lekate noṅka o̱lo̱go̱ḱa :–

Kạmiạ	+	**Kuṛại**	+	**Kạjnum**
(Subject)	+	*(Object)*	+	*(Verb)*
Lukhi do̱	+	*dakae*	+	*jo̱jo̱mkana*

E̱ṇḍe̱khan ạḍi mõṅjte pusṭạuena je Beako̱ro̱n reaḱ niạm lekate miťṭe̱n sạhi ayat ro̱ṛ se̱ o̱l lạgiť do̱ maṛaṅre Kạmiạ, inạkate do̱ Kạjnum beoharoḱ reaḱ niạm menaḱa. Ayatre ar ce̱ťko babo̱t baḍae daṛekoḱ, ona do̱ nahaḱ ar eṭaḱ paṭkore lạiạgo̱ḱa.

No̱ṇḍe̱ miť katha pusṭạu ocoḱkana je ạkhir ayat do̱ ce̱ť kana?

Noa do̱ sạrigea je bin sabadte ayat do̱ o̱ho̱ge benao daṛelena. Onate, ayatre beoharakan aṛaṅ se̱ ro̱ṛ do̱ sabadko metak̓a. Judi sabad se̱ rạṛ se̱ ro̱ṛ reak̓ jãhãn manege bạnuk̓khan, ona do̱ sabad o̱ho̱ge lekhalena. Sabad do̱ e̱ṇḍe̱khan onako metak̓a; oka do̱ so̱maj reak̓ anaṅgo̱c menak̓tae. Metak̓me sabad do̱ onage, oka do̱ ro̱ro̱ṛic̓ ar ak̓ńjo̱mic̓ bana ho̱ṛkin bujhạu daṛeak̓kan.

Sabad do̱ aema lekanak̓ hoe daṛeak̓a. Me̱nkhan Beako̱ro̱nre noa sabad do̱ irạl (8) go̱ṭe̱c̓ hạṭiṅre hạṭiṅakana. Noa hạṭiṅ do̱ Iṅgrạjite do̱ *Part of Speech*-ko metak̓kana. Noage Santalite do̱ *Sabad hạṭiṅ* se̱ *Beako̱ro̱n hạṭiṅko* metak̓kana. Beako̱ro̱n reak̓ ona hạṭiṅ do̱ noako kana :-

1. Ńunum *(Noun)*
2. Ujnum *(Pronoun)*
3. Kạjnum *(Verb)*
4. Gunum *(Adjective)*
5. Kạjnum-Gunum *(Adverb)*
6. Puk̓rạu Sabad *(Particle)*
7. Jok̓ṛao Sabad *(Conjunction)*
8. Hahaṛa/Bhabna/Rạskạ Lạlạiak̓ Sabad *(Interjection)*

Cetanre e̱makan Beako̱ro̱n hạṭiṅ reak̓ sabadko do̱ ayatre jạruṛok̓ lekate laṛcaṛo̱go̱k̓kana. Sabad do̱ ayat reak̓ jo̱to̱ kho̱n kạṭic̓ utạr hĩs kana ar maneanak̓ hạṭiṅ kana. Pạrtul leka mit̓ṭe̱n sabadbon hataoa – *ho̱ṛ*. *Ho̱ṛ* sabad do̱ ulṭạ-palṭakate do̱ho̱lekhan noṅka hoyok̓a – *ṛho̱, ṛo̱h, o̱ṛh, hṛo̱.* Me̱nkhan noako Haro̱p Joṛo *(Alphabet Group)* do̱ sabad o̱ho̱ me̱n daṛelena. Cedak̓je noa reak̓ mane baṅ oḍokok̓kana. Onate ayatre sabad beohar lạgit̓ maneanak̓ sabad hoyok̓ jạruṛkana. Beako̱ro̱n noae lạiabonkana je ayatre laṛcaṛakan mimit̓ sabad do̱ oka Beako̱ro̱n hạṭiṅ kana se̱ Beako̱ro̱n dharate mimit̓ ayat reak̓ mimit̓ sabad do̱ ce̱t̓ kana se̱ ayatre ce̱t̓e kạmiet̓kana? Pạrtulbo ńe̱la – *Sunạ do̱ ṭheṅgate setae dalkedea.* Noa ayatrebo gaṇḍo̱n baṛalege :-

- *Suną* do Ńunum *(Noun)* kana,
- *do* do Puk̓rąu Sabad *(Particle)* kana,
- *ṭheṅga* do Ńunum *(Noun)* kana,
- *dal* do Kąjnum *(Verb)* kana, ar ona sãote joṛaoakan
- *kedea* do Jivianak̓ okte Tayom Joṛao *(Animate Tense Suffix)* kana; Metak̓me –

- *Suną, ṭheṅga, seta* do – Ńunum kana.
- *do* do – Puk̓rąu sabad kana.
- *te* do – Tayom japak̓ kana. *(Instrumental Postposition)*
- *-e* do – Hoṛ Ujnum reak̓ kąṭić rup kana ar Kąmią *(Subject)* reak̓e kąmieda.
- *dal* do – Kąjnum kana.
- *-kedea* do – Jivianak̓ okte Tayom Joṛao kana. Noare *-e* tala joṛao menak̓a ar kuṛąi reak̓e kąmikana.

Santalite ayat benao reak̓ nią̣m do noṅka kana:-

Kąmią + Kuṛąi + Kąjnum

Cetanre emakan ayat goṛhon ńellekhan noṅka hoyok̓a :–

Kąmią+Puk̓rąuak̓ Sabad+Sapap̓ Ńunum+Sapap̓ Tayom Japak̓+ Sodor Kuṛąi+Kuṛąi Ujnum+Kąjnum+Okte Tayom Joṛao

Metak̓me – *Suną do ṭheṅga (-te) seta (-e) dal (-kedea).*

Iṅgrąjite do noṅka :-

Subject+Particle+Instrumental Noun+Instrumental Postposition+Direct Object+Subject Pronoun+Verb+Tense Suffix

ẠKIL BHAŃJAO - 5

A. Ṭọyọṭ'kate jobab ẹmọk̓me :-

1. *Part of Speech* dọ tinạk̓ hạṭińre hoe daṛeak̓a?
   (a) 6 (b) 7 (c) 8 (d) 9

2. Beakọrọn lekate Kạmiạ tayọm dọ cẹt̓ hijuk̓kana?
   (a) Kạjnum (b) Kuṛại (c) Ujnum (d) Gunum

3. *Sunạ* dọ Beakọrọn lekate cẹt̓ kana?
   (a) Ńunum (b) Ujnum (c) Kạjnum (d) Gunum

4. Beakọrọn lekate *dọ* dọ cẹt̓ kana?
   (a) Puk̓rạu Sabad (b) Ńunum (c) Kạjnum (d) Ujnum

5. Beakọrọn lekate *dal* dọ cẹt̓ kana?
   (a) Ńunum (b) Kạjnum (c) Ujnum (d) Gunum

B. Ọlkate jobab ẹmọk̓me :-

1. Beakọrọn dọ cẹt̓ kana? Pusṭạu lạgit̓ pạrtul ẹmme.
2. Sabad dọ tinạk̓ hạṭińa? Ona reak̓ hạṭińko lạime.
3. *Sunạ dọ ṭheṅgate setae dalkedea.* Noa ayat reak̓ sabad hạṭiń lạime·
4. Ayat dọ cẹt̓te benaok̓kana?
5. *ṛhọ*te mit̓ṭẹn maneanak̓ sabad benaome.

6

ŃUNUM
(NOUN)

Ńunum do̱ ona sabadko metak̓kana, o̱ne̱ oka do̱ ac̓ak̓ rupe bo̱do̱l daṛeak̓. Noa sabadte jãhãn jinis *(object),* ḍhạu (भाव) ar jivianko babo̱t baḍaeok̓kan; cahe ńe̱l ńamok̓ak̓, cahe tunum ńamok̓ak̓, cahe jivianko se̱ bạjivianak̓ sanamge Ńunum kana. Ro̱ṛ reak̓ mo̱tlo̱b do̱ noage je noa so̱ṅsar *(universe)* reak̓ se̱ serma co̱ṭren bin ńe̱l ńamok̓ jinis se̱ ńe̱l ńamok̓ jinis sanamge Ńunum kana. Metak̓me jãhãn ho̱e se̱ jinis se̱ ḍhạu reak̓ ńutum babo̱t baḍaege Ńunum do̱ko metak̓a.

Cetanre Ńunum reak̓ rup bo̱do̱lo̱k̓ babo̱t bibro̱n emakante no̱ṇḍe̱ ona rup bo̱do̱lo̱k̓ babo̱tre lại saphae reak̓ jạruṛ paṛaok̓kana. Santali reak̓ sanam sabad reak̓ rup bo̱do̱lo̱k̓kana. Sabadre laṭhe̱kate hõ sabad o̱lo̱go̱k̓kana; jeleka :–

co̱ṭ - *co̱ṭre, co̱ṭte, co̱ṭo̱k̓, co̱ṭṭe̱t̓*

ıń - *ıńre, ıńren, ıńko, ıńben, ıńte*

do̱ - *do̱e, do̱kin, do̱ko, do̱le, do̱lıń, do̱ben*

sakam - *sakamre, sakamte, sakamak̓* eman.

Latarre ńe̱l ńamok̓ak̓, tunum ńamok̓ak̓ ar bin ńe̱l ńamok̓ak̓ ńunum babo̱tre mõńjte lạiạgo̱k̓a ar Ńunum reak̓ sanam bhe̱d babo̱t reak̓ hõ e̱mo̱go̱k̓a, to̱be̱ane̱c̓ge Ńunum ce̱t̓ kana me̱ntebo bujhạu daṛeak̓a.

Ńunum babo̱t bibro̱n e̱m lahare arhõ Ńunum ce̱t̓ leka benaok̓kana, ona babo̱tre thoṛa lạiạgo̱k̓a.

Santalire Ńunum sabad benao lạgit̓ sabad reak̓ pạhil Be̱hạṭıńõk̓ Haro̱p tayo̱mre *-n* se̱ *-t* sabad reak̓ talare lagaokate hoyok̓kana se̱ noa Hạṭıńõk̓ Haro̱p *(Consonant)* tayo̱m Hạṭıńõk̓

Harop dohraḱkana. Metaḱme, sabadre pahil Behatińok̇ Harop do *-e* kana ar dosaraḱ do *-o* se *-o* kana. Tobe dosaraḱ Behatińok̇ Harop *(Vowel)* do *-t* lahare joraokate rorogoḱa. Noa *-n* se *-t* lagaokate benaoḱ Ńunum sabad reaḱ jãhãn nit niam do banuḱa. Noakin haropte benaoḱ miť bar benaoakan sabadbon ńela, partul :–

t te - (i) *ehop̍* khon *etohop̍* (ii) *seleť* khon *seteleť*

(iii) *saheť* khon *sataheť* (iv) *jeleń* khon *jeteleń*

(iv) *sareċ* khon *satareċ* (v) *rok̇* khon *rotok̇*

n te - (i) *mucať* khon *munucať* (ii) *ãrgo* khon *anãrgo*

(iii) *rakap̍* khon *ranakap̍* (iv) *lebeť* khon *lenebeť*

(v) *bodol* khon *bonodol* (vi) *ńel* khon *ńenel*

(vii) *acur* khon *anacur* (viii) *beť* khon *beneť*

(ix) *haso* khon *hanaso* (x) *bak̇* khon *banak̇*

(xi) *bar* khon *banar* (xii) *pe* khon *pene*

(xiii) *pon* khon *ponon* (xiv) *sudur* khon *sunudur*

(xv) *eteť* khon *eneteť* (xvi) *atań* khon *anatań*

(xvii) *osar* khon *onosar* (xviii) *disa* khon *dinisa*

(xix) *bida* khon *binida* (xx) goṅ khon gonoṅ

Adom sabad do noṅka ho menaḱa, one oka do *-t* se *-n* talare lagaokate Ńunum do baṅ benaoḱkana, bickom adom do Kajnumge tahenkana ar adom do Gunum *(Adjective)* benaoḱkana, jeleka – *or* khon *otor*, *um* khon *unum, em* khon *enem*.

Adomaḱ buta *(root)* sabadre *ok̇/ok̇* lagaokate Tala Kurai Tayom Jorao *(Medium Suffix)* Kajnum sabad benaoḱkana, jeleka *–jom* khon *jomok̇*. Adom sabad do *goċ* khon *gojok̇/gujuk̇*.

Adomaḱ sabad tayomre *-teť* lagaokate Dhau Ńunum , *(Abstract Noun)* benaoḱkana, jeleka :–

(i) *jeleń* kho̱n *jeteleńte̱t'* (ii) *lo̱lo̱* kho̱n *lo̱lo̱te̱t'*

(iii) *jo̱jo̱* kho̱n *jo̱jo̱te̱t'* (iv) *juạn* kho̱n *juạnte̱t'*

(v) *koṛa* kho̱n *koṛate̱t'* (vi) *haṛam* kho̱n *haṛamte̱t'*

(vii) *gạndhuạ* kho̱n *gạndhuạte̱t'* (viii) *rạskạ* kho̱n *rạskạte̱t'*

ŃUNUM REAK̇ HẠṬIŃ
(KIND OF NOUN)

Ńunum do̱ pạhilre bar hạṭińre hạṭiń daṛeak̇a :-

1. Ńe̱l Ńamok̇ak̇ Ńunum ***(Visible Noun)***

2. Bin Ńe̱l Ńamok̇ak̇ Ńunum ***(Invisible Noun)***

1. Ńe̱l Ńamok̇ak̇ Ńunum (*Visible Noun*) – Ńe̱l ńamok̇ jinis do̱ onako metak̇a, o̱ne̱ oka do̱ ńe̱l se̱ jo̱ṭe̱t' daṛeak̇, jeleka – *sado̱m, ho̱ṛ, buru, dare-ñạṛĩ, sim, sukri, dhiri, gaḍa, gitil, daka, taben, lạṭu, khạjạṛi, ṭukuċ, jo̱no̱k̇, haṭak̇, nahel, ãṛgo̱m, kuḍi, datro̱m, jhuṛi, ṭạmni, pạńci, paṛhạṇḍ, me̱ro̱m, bhiḍi, kaḍa, ḍaṅgra, saera, ṭo̱ro̱ḍaṅ* eman.

2. Bin Ńe̱l Ńamok̇ak̇ Ńunum ***(Invisible Noun)*** - Bin Ńe̱l Ńamok̇ jinis do̱ onako metak̇kana, o̱ne̱ oka do̱ baṅ ńe̱l ńam daṛeak̇, e̱ke̱n ạikạu se̱ bujhạu ńam daṛeak̇, jeleka – *ho̱e, haso, bhut, boṅga, cando, sebelte̱t', jo̱jo̱te̱t', haṛamte̱t', reaṛte̱t', rabaṅte̱t', ạkil, lelhate̱t', gạndhuạte̱t', khacaṛte̱t', rạskạte̱t',* eman.

Ńe̱l ńamo̱k̇ jinisko mod kho̱n Ńunum do̱ arhõ bar hạṭińre hạṭiń daṛeak̇a, jeleka :-

Ńe̱l Ńamok̇ak̇ Ńunum *(Visible Noun)*

Jivianak̇ Ńunum *(Animate Noun)*

Be̱jivianak̇ Ńunum *(Inanimate Noun)*

Jivianak̇ Ńunum - Jivianak̇ Ńunum do̱ onako metak̇a, o̱ne̱ okaṭak̇re do̱ jivi menak̇ se̱ jio̱n menak̇ se̱ ona do̱ mit̀ ṭhāi kho̱n eṭak̇ ṭhāite he̱c̀ daṛeak̇, jeleka – *sado̱m, sukri, sim, kaḍa, cē̱ṛē̱, ḍaṅgra, tayan, parwa, kạhũ, nāṛī* eman.

Be̱jivianak̇ Ńunum - Be̱jivianak̇ Ńunum do̱ onako metak̇kana, o̱ne̱ oka do̱ baṅ he̱c̀-se̱n daṛeak̇ se̱ hara hō̱ baṅ hara daṛeak̇ ar go̱c̀ge, metak̇me be̱jivianak̇ jinisge Be̱jivianak̇ Ńunum do̱ko metak̇a.

Disạ do̱ho̱ katha: Santali pạrsire dare-nāṛīko do̱ be̱jivianak̇ lekage ayatre beoharok̇kana Noa do̱ Santali pạrsire be̱jivianak̇ me̱ntege aṅgo̱co̱k̇kana, jeleka – (i) *Noa do̱ ul dare kana.* (sạhi); (ii) *Nui do̱e ul dare kana* se̱ *Nui do̱e ul kana.* (bhulgea)

O̱po̱wad ***(exception)*** – Ạikhạ *kạuḍi, guṭi, kạti, lạṭhu* eman do̱ jivianak̇ ńunum kana, je̱mo̱n – (i) *Kạuḍi e̱mkaetiṅme.* (sạhi);(ii) *kạuḍi e̱mkạtiṅme.* (bhulgea)

Ńe̱l Ńamok̇ Ńunum ***(Visible Noun)*** do̱ arhō̱ bar lekate hạṭiń daṛeak̇a, jeleka – Lekha Ńamok̇ Ńunum *(Visible Noun)/ (Countable Noun)* ar Be̱lekha Ńamok̇ Ńunum *(Uncountable Noun).*

Lekha Ńamok̇ Ńunum - Lekha Ńamok̇ Ńunum do̱ onageko metak̇a, o̱ne̱ oka do̱ uduk̇kate se̱ jo̱ṭe̱t̀kate se̱ halaṅkate lekha daṛeak̇, jeleka – *puthi, kaḍa, me̱ro̱m, dare, gaṇḍo, mạci, parko̱m, oṛak̇, ho̱ṛ, baksa* eman.

Be̱lekha Ńamok̇ Ńunum - Be̱lekha Ńamok̇ Ńunum do̱ onageko metak̇a, o̱ne̱ oka do̱ baṅ lekha daṛeak̇ se̱ lekha hō̱ muskilge, jeleka – *sunum, buluṅ, dạl, caole, dak̇, setoṅ, umul, māyām, aṭa, daka, rase, hạṇḍi, pạuṛạ, sindur, arta, gitil, ipil, uṗ, ghās, tuṛi, hoṛo, joṇḍra, bajṛa, guhum* emanteak̇.

Ayatre Ńunum kana me̱nte cekate baḍaeok̇a se̱ cekate bujhạuk̇a je noa se̱ hana do̱ Ńunum kana me̱nte? Ayatre Ńunum do̱ ado̱m jo̱khe̱c̀ do̱ Kạmiạ *(Subject)* reak̇, ado̱m jo̱khe̱c̀ do̱ Kuṛai

(Object) reaḱ, adom jokheć do Oko Kuṛạị *(Indirect Object)* reaḱ, adom jokheć do Sodor Kuṛạị *(Direct Object)* reaḱe kạmieda. Noako bujhạu lạgiṫ metaḱme Ńunum do Oko Kuṛạị, Sodor Kuṛạị, Kạmiạ, Kuṛạị ńam oḍok lạgiṫ *ceṫ kana, okoe kanae, okoe lạgiṫ;* kukli hotete kukli rakaṗlenkhan, oka jobab ńamoḱ, onage Ńunum kana.

Disạ dohoe katha: Noa kuklire Ujnum *(Pronoun)* hõ kukli reaḱ jobab rupre ńam daṛeaḱa, menkhan ona do Ńunum do baṅ lekhaḱa.

(a) **Jivianaḱ Ńunum *(Animate Noun)*** sendra ńam lạgiṫ - Jivianaḱ Ńunum sendra ńam lạgiṫ *okoe, okoye, okoe lạgiṫ, ceṫ, cele, celeye*; noako kuklite kuklilenkhan ar ona reaḱ oka jobab ńamoḱkana, ona do ńunumge ńam oḍokoḱa, pạrtul :–

(i) *Lubin do haḍgare tuńkedea.*

Kukli – Okoe tuńkedea?

Jobab – Lubin (Kạmiạ-*Subject*)

Kukli - Celeye tuńkedea?

Jobab – Haḍgar (Sodor Kuṛạị-*Direct Object*)

(ii) *Dhumạ do Coron lạgiṫ lạḍui ạgukeda.*

Kukli - Okoe ạgukeda?

Jobab - Dhumạ (Kạmiạ – *Subject*)

Kukli - Ceṫe ạgukeda?

Jobab - Lạḍu (Sodor Kuṛạị–*Direct Object*)

Kukli – Okoe lạgiṫe ạgukeda?

Jobab – Coron (Oko Kuṛạị – *Indirect Object*)

(b) **Bejivianaḱ Ńunum *(Inanimate Noun)*** sendra ńam lạgiṫ – Bejivianaḱ Ńunum sendra ńam lạgiṫ *ceṫ, ceṫe* kuklite kukli dohol enkhan ar ona reaḱ oka jobab ńamoḱkana,ona do Bejivianaḱ Ńunumge oḍokoḱkana, pạrtul –

(i) *Lukhi do̱ hasae ạgukeda.*

Kukli – Ce̱t̓e ạgukeda?

Jobab – Hasa (So̱do̱r Kuṛạỉ –*Direct Object*)

(ii) *Lukhi do̱ oṛak̓ je̱re̱ṛ lạgit̓ hasae ạgukeda.*

Kukli – Ce̱t̓e je̱re̱ṛ lạgit̓?

Jobab – Oṛak̓ (Oko Kuṛạỉ – *Indirect Object*)

ŃUTUM LẠLẠIAK̓ ŃUNUM *(PROPER NOUN)*

Okaṭak̓ sabad ho̱te̱te jãhãe ho̱ṛ se̱ jinis reak̓ ńutum babo̱t se̱ jãhãe ho̱ṛak̓ ńutum babo̱t baḍaeok̓, onage Ńutum Ńunumko *(Proper Noun)* metak̓a. Duniạre aema ho̱ṛ menak̓koa se̱ aema jinisko menak̓a. Sanam ho̱ṛak̓ se̱ jinis reak̓ ńutum menak̓a. Be̱go̱r ńutumte ho̱ṛ se̱ jinis o̱ho̱ baḍae daṛelena. Ona baḍae lạgit̓ge ńutum do̱ do̱ho̱ hoyok̓kana. Ar ńutum ńumlen khange, ona do̱ Ńutum Ńunum hoyok̓kana, jeleka – *Sidạ, Kạnhu, Tilkạ, Lo̱kho̱n, Sunạ, Co̱ro̱n, Budhrạỉ, Bãsnạ̃i Gaḍa, Pańcet Buru, Ḍumkạ, Hirạn, Sahebgõ̱ńj, Gańga* eman. *Sidạ* ńumlen khan ho̱ṛak̓ ńutum babo̱t baḍaeok̓kana. *Bãsnạ̃i Gaḍa* me̱nlen khan mit̓ṭe̱n gaḍa reak̓ ńutum baḍaeok̓kana. *Nagraha, puthi, mãhã, cando, po̱ro̱b* reak̓ ńutum hõ̱ noarege hijuk̓kana.

Nagamiạ lạṛhạỉ reak̓ ńutum hõ̱ noarege hijuk̓a, jeleka – *Sagrampur Lạṛhạỉ, Pealapur Lạṛhạỉ, Santal Hul, Kirtạ Kãṇḍ, Bạńjhi Kãṇḍ,* eman.

Po̱ro̱b reak̓ ńutum – *So̱hrae, Mak̓ Mõ̱ṛẽ̱, E̱ro̱k̓, Baha, Janthaṛ* eman.

Puthi ńutum - *Haṛmawak̓ Ato, O̱jo̱e Gaḍa Ḍhipre, Ho̱ṛ So̱mbad, Jug Sirijo̱l* eman.

Nagraha reak̓ ńutum – *Dilli, Kolkata, Pako̱ṛ, Maldo̱, Mumbạỉ* eman.

JẠT LẠLẠIAK̉ ŃUNUM
(COMMON NOUN)

Okaṭak̉ sabad hotete mit̉ jạt reak̉ jinis se hoṛko babotre baḍaeok̉ se mit̉ jạt reak̉ jinis babotre baḍaeok̉ se mit̉ jạt janwar lekan babotre baḍaeok̉kana, onage Jạt Lạlạiak̉ Ńunum doko metak̉kana, jeleka - *manwa, hoṛo, jonḍra, oṛak̉, buru, cẽṛẽ, gại, ḍańgra, merom, seta, pusi, puthi, dare, gaḍa* eman.

Manwa menlekhan duniạren sanam manwa jạt babot reak̉ baḍaeok̉kana. *Oṛak̉* menlekhan duniạ reak̉ sanam lekan oṛak̉ babotre baḍaeok̉kana, onkage ar emanteak̉.

ḌHẠU LẠLẠIAK̉ ŃUNUM
(ABSTRACT NOUN)

Okaṭak̉ Ńunum sabadte jãhãe hoṛak̉ se jãhãn jinis reak̉ gun se obostha babotre baḍaeok̉kan, onage Ḍhạu Lạlạiak̉ Ńunum doko metak̉kana, jeleka – *nindhạntet̉, haṛamtet̉, rabańtet̉, lolotet̉, bujhạutet̉, jeleńtet̉, koṛatet̉, hasotet̉, lelhatet̉, końkatet̉* eman.

Sońsar reak̉ mimit̉ jinis reak̉ ac̉ak̉ gun *(nature)* menak̉a. Ac̉ak̉ gun lekae beohara se ac̉ak̉ obostha lekae beohara. Bińak̉ bis do eken dak̉ do oho men daṛelena. Onare mit̉ lekan gun se daṛe menak̉a, One oka do ac̉ak̉ sobhab se beohartege baḍaeok̉a. Bis reak̉ sobhab kana je jãhãeak̉ hoṛmo reak̉ bhitri hĩsre mit̉ ṭhop paṛaolenkhan, uni hoṛak̉ nạṭkạ (sir) laṛaok̉ bondok̉taea ar onare mãyãm hõ bań calak̉a. ente bis reak̉ sobhab kana; hoṛmore mãyãme gaṛdhaea ar nạṭkạre mãyãm bań calak̉ iạte hoṛe gujuk̉a. ente bis reak̉ sobhabge noa kana. Onkage hạnḍi se pạurạ hõ hoyok̉kana. Hoṛmore bololenkhange hoṛmo doe lebṛeja ar buluk̉a, ente pạurạ reak̉ gunge onkana.

Manware *manwatet̉ (humanity)* reak̉ gun menak̉a. Janwarre *janwartet̉* reak̉ gun menak̉a. Janwar do manwa leka do̱ o̱ho̱e beohar daṛelea. Jãhãtinạk̉ge oṛak̉reye ạsule. Jãhãn jinis reak̉ gunte̱ť do̱ begarkate eṭak̉re o̱ho̱ do̱ho̱ daṛelena. Ar miťṭe̱n pạrtulbo ńe̱la – *Rạghu do̱ ạḍie onḍyoťgea.* Noa *onḍyoťte̱ť* do̱ Rạghu ṭhen kho̱n do̱ o̱ho̱ begar daṛelena, ona do̱ Rạghu sãotege tahe̱na. Rạghu do̱ aċak̉ *onḍyoťte̱ť* do̱ho̱ oṭokate jãhã se̱ċ o̱ho̱e calao daṛelena. Ona iạte *onḍyoťte̱ť* do̱ Rạghuak̉ gun kana.

Ḍhạu Lạlạiak̉ Ńunum do̱ Jạt Lạlạiak̉ Ńunum *(Common Noun),* Gunum *(Adjective)* ar Kạjnumre *(Verb)* Tala Joṛao *(Infix)* ar Tayo̱m Joṛao *(Suffix)* lagaokate benao daṛeak̉a, pạrtul :–

(a) Jạt Lạlạiak̉ Ńunum kho̱n Ḍhạu Lạlạiak̉ Ńunum benaore - *-te̱ť* tayo̱m joṛaokate hoyok̉kana, jeleka :-

kuṛi + te̱ť	*= kuṛite̱ť*
koṛa + te̱ť	*= koṛate̱ť*
gate + te̱ť	*= gatete̱ť*
manwa + te̱ť	*= manwate̱ť*
janwar + te̱ť	*= janwarte̱ť*

(b) Ḍhạu Lạlạiak̉ Ńunum benao lạgiť do̱ Gunum *(Adjective)* sabadre --*te̱ť* tayo̱m joṛao lagaokate hoyok̉kana, jeleka :-

lo̱lo̱ + te̱ť	*= lo̱ló̱te̱ť*
lelha + te̱ť	*= lelhate̱ť*
onḍyoť + te̱ť	*= onḍyoťte̱ť*
khacaṛ + te̱ť	*= khacaṛte̱ť*
bo̱be̱ + te̱ť	*= bo̱be̱te̱ť*
co̱ṭkar + te̱ť	*= co̱ṭkarte̱ť*

(c) Kạjnum kho̱n Ḍhạu Lạlạiak̉ Ńunum benaore Kạjnum sabadre *n* Tala Joṛao *(Infix)* lagaokate hoyok̉kana, jeleka :-

rakaṗ	*= ra + (na) + kaṗ*	*= ranakaṗ*
bo̱do̱l	*= bo̱ + (no̱) + do̱l*	*= bo̱no̱do̱l*
ạcur	*= ạ+ (nạ) +cur*	*= ạnạcur*

um	= *u* + *(nu)* +*m*	= *unum*
ãṛgo	= *ã* + *(na)* +*ṛgo*	= *ãnaṛgo*
e̠se̠t'	= *e̠* + *(ne̠)* +*se̠t'*	= *e̠ne̠se̠t'*

Ḍhạu Lạlạiaǩ Ńunum benao lạgiť ńunum ar gunum sabadre - *-te̠t'* joṛaolenkhan hoyoǩkana.

DO̠L LẠLẠIAǨ ŃUNUM *(COLLECTIVE NOUN)*

Okaṭaǩ kathate jãhãn jinis miť ṭhen jarwa se̠ ṭhạrwạ reaǩ katha baḍaeoǩkana, onage Do̠l Ńunum do̠ko metaǩkana. Miť ṭhen jarwa reaǩ ńutum tahe̠nkana, jeleka – *mela, bạisi, sabha, bhiṛ, do̠l, akhṛa* eman.

DURIB LẠLẠIAǨ ŃUNUM *(MATERIAL NOUN)*

Okaṭaǩ kathate jãhãn jinisko tulạ se̠ so̠ṅ daṛeaǩ kathako baḍaeoǩkan, onage Durib Ńunumko metaǩkana, jeleka – *sona, cạndi, hirạ, rupạ, sunum, caole, joṇḍra, toa, tuṛi* eman.

Jạt Lạlạiaǩ Ńunum kho̠n Ńutum Ńunum orom lạgiť latarre miť bar nạmuna e̠mo̠go̠ǩkana :–

Jạt Lạlạiaǩ Ńunum *(Common Noun)*	Ńutum Lạlạiaǩ Ńunum *(Proper Noun)*
hoṛo	*bhạdạị, he̠nde̠ bhạdạị, poṇḍ bhạdạị, bis-phuṭiạ, ciṅgul hoṛo, sạṭi bhạdạị, e̠r hoṛo, bismuniạ, iṛi bhạdạị, sorna hoṛo, so̠ hoṛo, rạghusạl eman.*

puthi	*Haṛmawak̓ Ato, Hoṛkoren Mare Hapṛamko Reak̓ Katha, Hoṛ Hoponkoak̓ Sedae Katha, Pạrsi do Somaj Reak̓ Ạrsi, Pạrsi do Ame Sãohãmea eman.*
cẽṛẽ	*kạ̃hũ, kisni, kõk̓, kikir, gunḍri, potam, miru, ṭoya, kokor eman.*
gaḍa	*Bãsnạ̃i Gaḍa, Nạ̃i Gaḍa, Ojoe Gaḍa, Gumạni Gaḍa eman.*
hoṛ	*Coron, Som, Pagan, Somae, Budhrại, Lukhi, Bahamuni, Surujmuni eman.*

ẠKIL BHAŃJAO - 6

A. Ṭoyot'kate jobab emok̓me :-

1. *ehop̓* Kạjnum khon Ńunum okaṭak̓ hoyok̓a?

   (a) epohop̓ (b) etohop̓ (c) enohop̓ (d) esohop̓

2. *sareć* Kạjnum khon Ńunum okaṭak̓ hoyok̓a?

   (a) satareć (b) sapareć (c) sakareć (d) sanareć

3. *rakap̓* Kạjnum khon Ńunum okaṭak̓ hoyok̓a?

   (a) rapakap̓ (b) ranakap̓ (c) rapapak̓ (d) ranatap̓

4. *osar* Kạjnum khon Ńunum okaṭak̓ hoyok̓a?

   (a) oposar (b) onosar (c)opsor (d) onsor

5. *suḍur* Kạjnum khon Ńunum okaṭak̓ hoyok̓a?

   (a) suḍuḍur (b) subuḍur (c) sunuḍur (d) soboḍor

B. Olkate jobab emok̓me :-

1. Ńunum do cet̓ kana? Noa reak̓ pạrtul lạime.

2. Ńunum reaḱ do̱ tinạḱ hạṭiń menaḱa? Hạṭińko reaḱ ńutum lạime.
3. *sahe̱ť* reaḱ Ńunum lạime.
4. *sare̱ċ* reaḱ Ńunum lạime.
5. *haso* reaḱ Ńunum lạime.
6. *ataṅ* reaḱ Ńunum lạime.
7. *gạndhuạ* reaḱ Ńunum lạime.
8. *rạskạ* reaḱ Ńunum lạime.
9. Ńutum Lạlạiaḱ Ńunum do̱ ce̱ť kana? Pạrtul se̱le̱ť lạime.
10. Jạt Lạlạiaḱ Ńunum do̱ ce̱ť kana? Pạrtul se̱le̱ť lạime.
11. Ḍhạu Lạlạiaḱ Ńunum do̱ ce̱ť kana? Pạrtul se̱le̱ť lạime.
12. Do̱l Lạlạiaḱ Ńunum do̱ ce̱ť kana? Pạrtul se̱le̱ť lạime.

7

UJNUM
(PRONOUN)

Ujnum do̱ ona sabadko metak̇kana, o̱ne̱ oka do̱ Ńunum bo̱do̱lte hijuk̇kan se̱ beoharok̇kan, jeleka – *iń, am, uni* eman. Ayatre ho̱ṛak̇ Ńunum se̱ jinis reak̇ Ńutum mit̕ ro̱go̱ṛ laṛcaṛ do̱ sajao baṅ aṅjo̱mo̱k̇a. Ona iạtege Ujnum do̱ko beoharet̕kana. Pạrtulbon ńe̱lma :–

Bạjun do̱ ạdi bhage ho̱ṛ kanae. Bạjunren do̱ pea koṛa menak̇kotaea. Bạjun do̱ sanam koṛa moṭa ḍạrrey aṗakat̕koa. Bạjun do̱ nitok̇ ạdi sukre menaea.

Noa pạrtul reak̇ sanam ayatre *Bạjun* beoharakana, oka do̱ sajao baṅ aṅjo̱mo̱k̇kana. Ona do̱ Ńunum bo̱do̱lte, ona jaegare Ujnum noṅka beoharo̱k̇a –

Bạjun do̱ ạdi bhage ho̱ṛ kanae. Uniren (Bạjunren) do̱ pea koṛa menak̇kotaea. Uni (Bạjun) do̱ sanam koṛa moṭa ḍạrrey aṗakat̕koa. Uni (Bạjun) do̱ nitok̇ ạdi sukre menaea.

Ujnum do̱ noa leka hạṭiń daṛeak̇a :-

1. Ho̱ṛ Ujnum *(Personal Pronoun)*
2. Nij Ujnum *(Reflexive Pronoun)*
3. Isạra Lạlạiak̇ Ujnum *(Demonstrative Pronoun)*
4. Be̱niṭ Ujnum *(Indefinite Pronoun)*
5. E̱ktiạri Ujnum *(Possesive Pronoun)*
6. Kukli Ujnum *(Interrogative Pronoun)*
7. Hạhạṭiń Ujnum *(Distributive Pronoun)*
8. So̱mpo̱k Ujnum *(Relative Pronoun)*

HOṚ UJNUM
(PERSONAL PRONOUN)

Hoṛ Ujnum do arhõ pe haṭińre haṭiń daṛeak̓a, jeleka :–

1. Paḥil Hoṛ ***(First Person)***

2. Dosar Hoṛ ***(Second Person)***

3. Tesar Hoṛ ***(Third Person)***

Mit̓ bar ayat goṛhon chaḍakate Bharot reak̓ mimit̓ paṛsi reak̓ Beakoron reak̓ sobhab do moṭa-muṭi mit̓gea. Ona iạte Santali reak̓ Beakoron babot sobhab do oho begar daṛelena. Onate Santali reak̓ Beakoron haṭiń hõ milạuk̓kangea. Onage cetanre emakan Ujnum haṭiń reak̓ biboron sapha-sạphi latarre emogok̓kana :-

1. Paḥil Hoṛ ***(First Person)*** – Paḥil Hoṛ do onageko metak̓a, one oka do roroiće aćtet̓ kange, jeleka – *iń.*

2. Dosar Hoṛ ***(Second Person)*** – Dosar Hoṛ do onaṭak̓ko metak̓a, one oka do roroṛićak̓e ak̓ńjomkan, jeleka – *am.*

3. Tesar Hoṛ ***(Third Person)*** – Okaṭak̓ sabad hotete roroṛić ar ak̓ńjomić chaḍakate eṭak̓ hoṛ babotre baḍaeok̓kan, onage Tesar Hoṛ se Eṭak̓ Hoṛ doko metak̓kana, jeleka – *uni.*

Arhõ baḍae lek katha do noage je Ektiạri Ujnum ar Sompok Ujnum lạgit̓ judạte sabad bạnuk̓a, noare do Tayom Joṛao lagaokate sabad benaok̓kana, ar adom jokheć do Hoṛ Ujnum, Isạra Ujnum ar Kukli Ujnumre Tayom Joṛao, Laha Joṛao se Tayom Japak̓ *(Postposition)* hõ lagaok̓kangea ar bań hõ. Adomak̓ sabad chaḍakate Ujnum do mul rupre tahẽkate Ńunum, Gunum ar Kạjnum leka hõe kạmiet̓kana. Noa do jạruṛok̓ak̓ tayom joṛao lagaokatey kạmiet̓kana.

Isạra Ujnum, Kukli Ujnum, Beniṭ Ujnjum do jivianak̓ ar bejivianak̓ lạgit̓ judạ-judạ Tayom Joṛao lagaok̓kana.

Jivianaǩ Ho̱ṛ Ujnum *(Animate Personal Pronoun)* do̱ Lekha *(Number)* dharate noṅka haṭiń daṛeaǩa :-

Ho̱ṛ Ujnum *(Personal Pronoun)*	**Mit' Lekha** *(Singular Number)*	**Bar Lekha** *(Dual Number)*	**Saṅge Lekha** *(Plural Number)*
Pạhil Ho̱ṛ *(First Person)*	*iń, tiń*	*ạliń, talaṅ, tạliń*	*ale, abo, abon, tabon, tale*
Dosar Ho̱ṛ *(Second Person)*	*am, tam, me*	*aben, taben*	*ape, tape*
Eṭaǩ Ho̱ṛ *(Third Person)*	*uni*	*ạkin, unkin*	*ako, onko*

Jivianaǩ Ho̱ṛ Ujnum reaǩ kạṭiċ rup do̱ lekha dharate noṅka haṭiń daṛeaǩa, noa do̱ Oko Kuṛại *(Indirect Object)* ar So̱do̱r Kuṛại *(Direct Object)* lạgiť laṛcaṛoǩa :–

Ho̱ṛ Ujnum *(Personal Noun)*	**Mit' Lekha** *(Singular Number)*	**Bar Lekha** *(Dual Number)*	**Saṅge Lekha** *(Plural Number)*
Pạhil Ho̱ṛ *(First Person)*	*ń*	*laṅ, liń*	*bo, bon, le*
Dosar Ho̱ṛ *(Second Person)*	*me, m*	*ben*	*pe*
Eṭaǩ Ho̱ṛ *(Third Person)*	*e*	*kin*	*ko*

E̱ktiạri Ujnum *(Possessive Pronoun)* lạgiť aso̱kaete noako kạṭiċ rup laṛcaṛoǩkana :-

(i) Miť Lekha Pạhil Ho̱ṛre do̱ - *tiń*
Miť Lekha Dosar Ho̱ṛre do̱ - *tam*
Miť Lekha Eṭaǩ Ho̱ṛre do̱ - *tae*

(ii) Bar Lekha Pạhil Hore dọ - *talaṅ, tạliń*
Bar Lekha Dosar Hoṛre dọ - *taben*
Bar Lekha Eṭak̓ Hoṛre dọ - *tạkin*

(iii) Saṅge Lekha Pạhil Hoṛre dọ - *tabo, tabon, tale*
Saṅge Lekha Dosar Hoṛre dọ - *tape*
Saṅge Lekha Eṭak̓ Hoṛre dọ - *tako*

Santalire dọ Bẹjivianak̓ Ujnum *(Inanimate Pronoun)* hõ menak̓a ar Santal lẹgcarre laṛcaṛok̓kana. Noa reak̓ pạrtul dọ latarre ẹmọgọk̓kana ar ona dọ ẹkẹn Eṭak̓ Hoṛ reak̓ mit̓ lekha, Eṭak̓ Hoṛ reak̓ bar lekha ar Eṭak̓ Hoṛ reak̓ saṅge lekharege ńamok̓kana, jeleka :-

(i) Eṭak̓ Hoṛ reak̓ Mit̓ Lekha - *ona*

(ii) Eṭak̓ Hoṛ reak̓ Bar Lekha - *onakin*

(iii) Eṭak̓ Hoṛ reak̓ Saṅge Lekha - *onako*

NIJ UJNUM
(REFLEXIVE PRONOUN)

Nij Ujnum ho̱te̱te do̱ nij se̱ aċte̱t́ babo̱tre baḍaeoḱkana. Noa Ujnum do̱ Ho̱ṛ Ujnum *(Personal Pronoun)* reaḱ sanam ho̱ṛre *(person)* ńamoḱkana, jeleka – *aċ, unite̱t́, ińte̱t́, ạlińte̱t́, alete̱t́, abente̱t́, onkote̱t́, amte̱t́, abote̱t́, abonte̱t́.*

Noako sanam do̱ pe̱ne̱ lekhare sanam ho̱ṛre noṅka do̱ho̱ḱa. Noa do̱ jivianaḱ rupre *(animate form)* noṅka hoyoḱa –

Ho̱ṛ *(Person)*	**Mit' Lekha** *(Singular Number)*	**Bar Lekha** *(Dual Number)*	**Saṅge Lekha** *(Plural)*
Pạhil Ho̱ṛ *(First Person)*	*ińte̱t́*	*ạlińte̱t́*	*alete̱t́*
Dosar Ho̱ṛ *(Second Person)*	*amte̱t́*	*abente̱t́*	*apete̱t́*
Eṭaḱ Ho̱ṛ *(Third Person)*	*unite̱t́, aċte̱t́*	*unkinte̱t́*	*onkote̱t́*

Noa Ujnumge Be̱jivianaḱ rupre do̱ e̱ke̱n Eṭaḱ Ho̱ṛ *(Third Person)* reaḱ pe̱ne̱ lekharege ńamoḱkana, jeleka :–

(i) Eṭaḱ Ho̱ṛ Mit́ Lekhare - *onate̱t́, onaṭaḱte̱t́*

(ii) Eṭaḱ Ho̱ṛ Bar Lekhare - *onakinte̱t́, onaṭaḱkinte*

(iii) Eṭaḱ Ho̱ṛ Saṅge Lekhare - *onaṭaḱte̱t́, onaṭaḱkote*

Ayatre laṛcaṛkate noṅka hoyoḱa :–

(i) *onate̱t́* - O̱ne̱m me̱nle̱t́, *onate̱t́ge* ạguime.

(ii) *onaṭaḱte̱t́* - O̱ne̱m me̱nle̱t́, *onaṭaḱte̱t́ge* ạguime.

(iii) *onakinte̱t́* - O̱ne̱m me̱nle̱t́, *onakinte̱t́ge* ạguime.

(iv) *Onaṭaḱkinte̱t́* - *Onaṭaḱkinte̱t́ge* ạguime, o̱ne̱ okam me̱nle̱t́.

(v) *onakotẹt'* - Okakom halaṅakat', *onakotẹt'ge* ạguime.

Nij Ujnum benao lạgit' Pạhil Họṛ, Dosar Họṛ ar Eṭak' Họṛ reak' sanam lekhare *-tẹt'* Tayọm Joṛao *(Suffix)* lagaokate benaok'kana. Mẹnkhan Bẹjivianak' Ujnumre dọ ẹkẹn Eṭak' Họṛ *(Third Person)* reak' pẹnẹ lekhare *-tẹt'* Tayọm Joṛao lagaok'kana. Pạhil Họṛ ar Dosar Họṛre dọ baṅ lagaok'kana.

ISẠRA LẠLẠIAK' NIṬ UJNUM *(DEMONSTRATIVE PRONOUN)*

Oka Ujnum họtẹte rọrọṛić ṭhen sẹ sạṅgiń reak' jãhãn niṭ utạrak' jinis babọte uduk'et'kan sẹ sor ar sạṅgiń reak' niṭ jinis babọtrey isạraet'kan bạḍaeok'kan sẹ sor ar sạṅgiń reak' jinis sẹ jivianak' jinis udug reak' katha bạḍaeok'kan, onage Niṭ Ujnum dọko metak'kana ar ona dọ Ńunum babọte uduk'et'kana. Ńunum jẹmọn mit' rọgọṛ baṅ beoharok', ńutum aema dhao beohar dọ sajao baṅ aṅjọmọk' iạte Unjum dọko beohara.

Isạra Ujnum beste bujhạu lạgit' Unjum ayatre laṛcaṛogok'a ar noa dọ Jivianak' ar Bẹjivianak' Isạra Ujnumre begar-begar hõ; pạrtul ẹmọgọk'kana :–

no - nu - Noa Ujnum họtẹte dọ sor reak' jinis sẹ jivianak' jinis babọte uduk'et'kana. Mit'ṭẹn dọ jivianak' sẹć ar mit'ṭẹn dọ bẹjivianak' sẹće isạraet'kana, jeleka :–

nu - (i) *nu + (i)* = *Nui* họṛ dọ nọtẹgey hijuk'kana.

(ii) *no + (a)* = *Noa* dare dọ ọkọeak' kana?
Noa nakha hijuk'me.

(iii) *no + (ko)* = *Noko* mẹrọm gupi hataṛkom.

ni - ni - nẹ ar *ni* dọ banarge ora-soragea. *ni* dọ jivianko lạgit' laṛcaṛok'a ar *nẹ* dọ bẹjivianak' lạgit' beoharok'kana. *nẹ* dọ adọm jọkhẹć sọmọe reak' babọt hõe lạiet'kana, jeleka :– *Ni; gidrạ hẹo hataṛem, caoleń gumlege.* (jivian); *Nẹ; ataṅme, gochareń emama.* (bẹjivian). *Nẹ uḍiće emamkana, ẹnte bạnuk'takoa.*

ni ar *nẹ* – *ni* ar *nẹ* dọ banarge ora-soragey kạmietkana. Noa dọ aṛaṅ reaḱ ulạṭ-palạṭoḱ iạte adọm jọkhẹc̓ dọ *ni* leka ar adọm jọkhẹc̓ dọ *nẹ* leka aṅjọmọḱa, pạrtul :–

ni – (i) *Niko* gidrạ gate hataṛkom.

(ii) *Nikin* gidrạ gate hataṛkinme; sẹ *nẹko* gidrạ gate hataṛkom.

un – on/nẹ – nẹ - Noako dọ beoharoḱ lekate banarge ora-soragea. Mit̓ṭẹn dọ jivianaḱ ar mit̓ṭẹn dọ bẹjivianaḱ sẹc̓e uduḱet̓kana. Mẹnkhan ac̓ sorre dọ bạnuḱa. Beste bujhạu lạgit̓ latarre ayat ẹmọgọḱkana :-

(i) *na* - *Naḱae* ṅẹlme. (bẹjivianaḱ)

(ii) *nạ* - *Nạḱại* ṅẹlẹme. (jivianaḱ)

(iii) *un* - *un (i)* = *Uni* ṅẹlẹme. (jivianaḱ)

(iv) *ọn* + *(ẹ)*= *Ọnẹ* ṅẹlme. (bẹjivianaḱ)

uni/un – *on* : *un* ar *on* hõ banarge ora-soragea. Noa hõ sor-sạṅgiṅ reaḱe uduḱet̓kana, mit̓ṭẹn dọ jivianaḱ ar mit̓ṭẹn dọ bẹjivianaḱ sẹc̓e uduḱet̓kana. Nọṇḍẹ *uni* ar *un* dọ mit̓ṭẹnge mane dọe ẹmẹt̓kana. Beste bujhạu lạgit̓ latarre pạrtul ẹmọgọḱkana :–

(i) *un* – *un* + *(i)*= *Uni* ṅẹlẹme. (jivianaḱ)

(ii) *ọn* – *ọn* + *(ẹ)*= *Ọnẹ* ṅẹlme. (bẹjivianaḱ)

ini/in – Noa banarge mit̓ṭẹn reaḱe kạmiet̓kana, banarge mit̓ jinis kana. Noate hõ sor-sạṅgiṅ reaḱge baḍaeoḱkana sẹy uduḱet̓kana. Noate jivianaḱ ar bẹjivianaḱ banar leka hõe uduḱ daṛeaḱa. *Morphology* aṛaṅ karọnte adọm jọkhẹc̓ *in* dọ *n* leka aṅjọmọḱa, jeleka :–

(i) *in* – *in* + *(i)* = *Ini* am phẹḍre menae, inigey daṛeaḱa.

(ii) *in (ạ)* *Inạṭaḱ* nọtẹ gọt̓kaḱme. (bẹjivianaḱ)

(iii) *en (ko)* *Enkoge* ạgukom.

ẹn - noa họ Santali pạrsire Ujnum ruprey kạmiet̓kana. Noa

Ujnumte do somoe reak̇e lạieťkana, jeleka :–

(a) *Enbetar* coḍgoc̆ hako ạdi ãṭko saeraeťko tahẽkana.

(b) *Enhilok̇* ceťem roṛleda?

Noṇḍe latarre emakan Ujnum ayatre laṛcaṛkate beste bujhạu lạgiť kurumuṭuakana :–

(i) *hone* - Datrom *hone* hoṇḍe menak̇a.

(ii) *hoṇḍe* - *Hoṇḍe* calak̇me.

(iii) *huni* - *Huni* tora bhurni bhugạk̇ khone dạṛkeda.

(iv) *hini* - *Hini* sec̆gey dạṛ idia.

(v) *hinạ* - *Hinạṭak̇* noteyme.

(vi) *hana* - *Hanaṭak̇* ạguime.

(vii) *nhawa* - *Nhawaṭak̇* ńelme.

(viii) *nhại* - *Nhạiṭak̇* hohowaeme.

(ix) *ene* - *Ene* oṇḍe dohoeme.

(x) *eṇḍe* - *Eṇḍe* dohoeme.

(xi) *hane* - *Hane* ńelme.

(xii) *nhowa* - *Nhowa* katwar iń ṭhec̆ge ạtu hijuk̇kana.

(xiii) *noa* - *Noa* dhiri do ocogme.

(xiv) *hene* - *Hene* haṇḍe menak̇a.

(xv) *ote* - *Ote* tạrup̆ak̇ hạṇḍrạu ańjomok̇kana.

Noṇḍe miťbar jivianak̇ ar bejivianak̇ Isạra Ujnum babot latarrebon ńela. *ote, hote, ete, ate* eman do aṛań *(sound)* sec̆e uduk̇ sey isạraeťkana :-

Jivianak̇ ***(Animate)***	**Bejivianak̇** ***(Inanimate)***
nui – Nui sec̆ hijuk̇me.	*noa – Noa ńelme.*
uni – Uni sec̆ beńgedme.	*ona – Ona ńelme.*

huni – Huni ho̱ṇḍe̱ menaea.	*hana – Hana ńe̱lme.*
ni – Ni gidrạ he̱olem.	*nią – Nią̣tegebo aṇṭaoka̓.*
ini – Ini hõ̱ bam ḍaṇṭaoe-dekana.	*iną – Iną no̱te̱ go̱ťkaǩme.*
hini – Hini se̱ċ lebda go̱ťkam.	*hiną – Hinạṭaǩ no̱te̱yme.*
ạni – Hạnikin sap̓ ạgukedea.	*hana – Hanakin no̱te̱yme.*
hạni – Hạni ńe̱le̱me.	*nõ̱ǩõ̱e –Nõ̱ǩõ̱e nią̣tege hoyoǩa.*
nũǩui – Nũǩui he̱oeme.	*nẽ̱ǩẽ̱ – Nẽ̱ǩẽ̱ nią̣ge menaǩa.*
niǩi – Niǩi he̱oeme.	*nhãwã - Nhãwãṭaǩ ạguime.*
nhą̃i – Nhãiṭaǩ ho̱ho̱waeme.	*nhoa – Nhoako ạguime.*
nhui – Nhuiṭaǩ ho̱ho̱waeme.	*nhią – Nhią̣ko ro̱ho̱eme.*
nhi – Nhuṭaǩ sao̱eme.	*nhõ̱ǩõ̱e– Nhõ̱ǩõ̱e noako ńe̱lme.*
nhũǩũi – Nhũǩũi nho̱te̱y he̱ċena.	*nhẽ̱ǩẽ̱ – Nhẽ̱ǩẽ̱ ninạǩgea.*
nhĩǩĩ – Nhĩǩĩ niṭaǩ sao̱eme.	*nhako – Nhakoṭaǩ ạgukom. (jivianaǩ)*
nhą̃ǩą̃i – Nhą̃ǩą̃i nhatey dạṛkeda.	*nhãǩãe – Nhãǩãe nhaṇḍe̱ menaǩa.*
nhạ̣i – Nhạigey baḍaekana.	

1. Miť bar Isạra Ujnum menaǩa, o̱ne̱ oka do̱ joṛare bar dhao leka ạikạuǩa. Me̱nkhan *n* haro̱p do̱ banar sabadre tahe̱ngea. Pạrtul :–

uni – nui, onko – nhoko, hanko – neko, hana -nhawa

2. Ado̱maǩ noa Ujnum noṅkanaǩ tahe̱nkana; miťṭe̱n do̱ khaṭo̱ rup ar dosaraǩ do̱ purạ rup miť dhaote beoharoǩkana Moṭa-muṭi barea sabad joṛare hijuǩkana, pạrtul :–

un – uni, un – unkin, on – ona, on – onko, ọn – ọnẹ, ọn – ọntẹ, ọn – ọṇḍẹ, in – ini, in – inkin, on – onko, ọn – ọnẹ, ẹn – ẹnẹ, hen – hẹnẹ, in – inạ, hạn – hạni, hạn – hạnkin, han – hanko, han – hanẹ, ẹn – ẹnko, ẹn – ẹṇḍẹ.

ọnẹ – onko, ọnẹ – inạ, ọnọ – ọṇḍẹ, ona – ọnẹ, ọnẹ – uni, ọnẹ – unkin, ọnẹ – ona, ọnọ – onka, ọnọ – ọntẹ, ọnọ – ọṇḍẹ, ọnọ – uni, ọnẹ – inạ, ọnẹ – hinạ.

ọnẹ – ini, ọnẹ – inạ, ọnẹ – ẹnka, ẹnẹ – ẹṇḍẹ, ẹnẹ – ẹntẹ, hẹnẹ – hinạ, hanẹ – hana, hanẹ – hạni, hanẹ – haṇḍẹ – hantẹ.

noko – nui, nũk̓ĩ – ni, nọ̃k̓ọ̃e – noa, nhũk̓ũi – nhũi, nhũk̓ũi – nui.

Isạra Ujnum *(Demonstrative Pronoun)* dọ Kạjnum-Gunum *(Adverb)* reak̓ Isạra Kạjnum-Gunum reak̓ họ̃e kạmieda. Kạjnum-Gunum dọ noṅka lekana :–

(i) Sọmọe Kạjnum-Gunum *(Time Adverb)*

(ii) Ṭhại Kạjnum-Gunum *(Place Adverb)*

(iii) Dik Kạjnum-Gunum *(Directive Adverb)*

(iv) Ṭewan Kạjum-Gunum *(Position Adverb)*

Noa chaḍa arhọ̃ aema menak̓a. Noa dọ laha sẹc̓re ẹmakan Kạjnum-Gunum Paṭre menak̓a. Mẹnkhan nọṇḍẹ mit̓ bar disại lạgit̓ ẹmọgọk̓kana :–

nọṇḍẹ, ọṇḍẹ, haṇḍẹ, họṇḍẹ, ẹṇḍẹ, ọntẹ, hantẹ, nhọtẹ, nạtẹ, nhatẹ, nun, un, nhun ar emanteak̓.

ISẠRA UJNUM
(DEMONSTRATIVE PRONOUN)

Jivianak̓ Ujnum

Isạra Ujnum *(Demonstrative Pronoun)* reak̓ sanam họṛ *(person)* ar sanam lekhare *(number)* dọhọkate beste bujhạu lạgit̓ kurumuṭuakana. Noa bujhạu lạgiť latarre pạrtul e̱mo̱go̱k̓kana :-

Isạra Ujnum (Jivianak̓ Ujnum)	**Ho̱ṛ** *(Person)*	**Miť Lekha** *(Singular)*	**Bar Lekha** *(Dual)*	**Saṅge Lekha** *(Plural)*
ini	Pạhil Ho̱ṛ	*iniń*	*iniliń*	*inile*
ini	Dosar Ho̱ṛ	*inim*	*iniben*	*inipe*
ini	Tesar Ho̱ṛ	*inie*	*inkin, inikin*	*iniko, enko*
uni	Pạhil Ho̱ṛ	*uniń*	*uniliń*	*unile*
uni	Dosar Ho̱ṛ	*unim*	*uniben*	*unipe*
uni	Tesar Ho̱ṛ	*unie*	*unkin, unikin*	*onko, uniko*
huni	Pạhil Ho̱ṛ	*huniń*	*huniliń*	*hunile*
huni	Dosar Ho̱ṛ	*hunim*	*huniben*	*hunipe*
huni	Tesar Ho̱ṛ	*hunie*	*hunkin, hunikin*	*honko, huniko*
hini	Pạhil Ho̱ṛ	*hiniń*	*hiniliń*	*hinile*
hini	Dosar Ho̱ṛ	*hinim*	*hiniben*	*hinipe*
hini	Tesar Ho̱ṛ	*hinie*	*hinikin, hinkin*	*hinko, hen-ko*
nhại	Pạhil Ho̱ṛHo̱ṛ	*nhạń*	*nhạiliń*	*nhạile*
nhại	Dosar Ho̱ṛ	*nhạiem*	*nhạiben*	*nhạipe*
nhại	Tesar Ho̱ṛ	*nhạie*	*nhạikin*	*nhạiko*

ạni	Pạhil Ho̱ṛ	*ạniń*	*ạniliń*	*ạnile*
	Dosar Ho̱ṛ	*ạnim*	*ạniben*	*ạnipe*
	Tesar Ho̱ṛ	*ạnie*	*ạnikin*	*ạniko*
hạni	Pạhil Ho̱ṛ	*hạniń*	*hạniliń*	*hạnile*
	Dosar Ho̱ṛ	*hạnim*	*hạniben*	*hạnipe*
	Tesar Ho̱ṛ	*hạnie*	*hạnikin, hạnkin*	*hanko, hạniko*

Onkage noa pạrtul pańjakate :– *nuk̓ui, nik̓i, nhui, nhi, nhin.* Onkage noa pạrtul pańjakate - *nuk̓ui, nik̓i, nhui, nhi, nhuk̓ui, nhạk̓ại, un-uni, in-ini, nui, o̱ne̱-uni, e̱ne̱-ini, hane̱-hạni, ni* eman do̱ho̱ daṛeak̓a.

Nitok̓ do̱ be̱jivianak̓ Isạra Ujnum sanam lekhare do̱ho̱kate pạrtul e̱mo̱go̱k̓kana :-

Isạra Ujnum *(Demonstrative Pronoun)*	**Mit' Lekha** *(Singular)*	**Bar Lekha** *(Dual)*	**Saṅge Lekha** *(Plural)*
noa	*noa*	*noakin*	*noako*
ona	*ona*	*onakin*	*onako*
hana	*hana*	*hanakin*	*hanako*
niạ	*niạ*	*niạkin*	*niạko*
inạ	*inạ*	*inạkin*	*inạko*
hinạ	*hinạ*	*hinạkin*	*hinạko*
hona	*hona*	*honakin*	*honako*
nõ̱k̓õ̱e	*nõ̱k̓õ̱e*	*nõ̱k̓õ̱ekin*	*nõ̱k̓õ̱eko*
nẽ̱k̓ẽ̱	*nẽ̱k̓ẽ̱*	*nẽ̱k̓ẽ̱kin*	*nẽ̱k̓ẽ̱ko*

nhawa	*nhawa*	*nhawakin*	*nhawako*
nhoa	*nhoa*	*nhoakin*	*nhoako*
nhiạ	*nhiạ*	*nhiạkin*	*nhiạko*
nhõ̱k̇õ̱e	*Nhõ̱k̇õ̱e*	*nhõ̱k̇õ̱ekin*	*nhõ̱k̇õ̱eko*
nhe̱k̇e̱	*nhe̱k̇e̱*	*nhe̱k̇e̱kin*	*nhe̱k̇e̱ko*
nhãk̇ãe	*nhãk̇ãe*	*nhãk̇ãekin*	*nhãk̇ãeko*
on-ona	*on-ona*	*on-onakin*	*on-onako*
o̱ne̱-ona	*o̱ne̱-ona*	*o̱ne̱-onakin*	*o̱ne̱-onako*
o̱ne̱-inạ	*e̱ne̱-inạ*	*e̱ne̱-inạkin*	*e̱ne̱-inạko*
hane̱-hana	*hane̱-hana*	*hane̱-hanakin*	*hane̱-hanako*
he̱ne̱-hinạ	*he̱ne̱-hinạ*	*he̱ne̱-hinạkin*	*he̱ne̱-hinạko*
in-inạ	*in-inạ*	*in-inạkin*	*in-inạko*

Santalire mit̓ lekan gun menak̓a ar ona do̱ Ujnum reak̓ kạṭić rup Kạjnum são joṛaokate So̱do̱r Kuṛai *(Direct Object)* ar Oko Kuṛại *(Indirect Object)* lạgit̓e kạmiet̓kana. Noa Ujnum reak̓ kạṭić rup sanam ho̱ṛ *(person)* ar sanam lekhare *(number)* noṅka beoharok̓a :-

Isạra Ujnum (Kạṭić rup)	**Ho̱ṛ** *(Person)*	**Mit̓ Lekha** *(Singular)*	**Bar Lekha** *(Dual)*	**Saṅge Lekha** *(Plural)*
	Pạhil Ho̱ṛ	*iń*	*laṅ* (se̱le̱t̓), *liń*	*bo, bon* (se̱le̱t̓)
ń	Dosar Ho̱ṛ	*me*	*ben*	*pe*
	Tesar Ho̱ṛ	*e* (jivianak̓re)	*kin* (jivianak̓re)	*ko* (jivianak̓re)

Santalire noṅkanak̓ Ujnum hõ̱ menak̓a, o̱ne̱ oka do̱ sabad

reak̓ talare *(infix)* ar mucạt̓re *(suffix)* lagaokate Ektiạri Ujnum reak̓ kạṭic̓ rupre laṛcaṛok̓kana. Noa kạṭic̓ rup Ujnum do jãhãn jinis reak̓ ektiạri se ạdhikar reak̓e bạḍae ocoet̓kana ar noa do sanam hoṛ *(person)* reak̓ sanam lekhare dohokate beste bujhạuk̓a :-

Isạra Ujnum (Kạṭic̓ rup)	Hoṛ *(Person)*	Mit' Lekha *(Singular)*	Bar Lekha *(Dual)*	Saṅge Lekha *(Plural)*
tiń	Pạhil Hoṛ	*tiń*	*talaṅ, tạliń*	*tabo, tabon* (selet̓)
	Dosar Hoṛ	*tam*	*taben*	*tape*
	Tesar Hoṛ	*tae*	*tạkin*	*tako*

BENIṬ UJNUM
(INDEFINITE PRONOUN)

Okaṭak̓ sabad hotete jãhãn niṭ jinis babot baṅ bạḍaeok̓kan, ona do Beniṭ Ujnumko *(Indefinite Pronoun)* metak̓kana. Jãhãn jinis babotte jãhãn niṭ katha baṅ bạḍaeok̓ do beniṭgebon mena. Eken bejivian babot moto do baṅ bickom sanam jivian babot hõ onkagey kạmia. Ona beniṭ lạlại lạgit̓ hõ sabad menak̓a, jeleka – *jãhãe, jãhãn, thoṛa* eman. Ayatre laṛcaṛkate beste do bujhạuk̓a :–

(i) *jãhãe* - *Jãhãe* hoṛko hec̓lenkhan note kolkom.

(ii) *thoṛa* - *Thoṛa* caole imạńme.

Nonḍe jãhãe niṭ hoṛ babttre baṅ niṭ utạrakana ar *caole* hõ tinạk̓e emaea, ona hõ baṅ niṭa. Menkhan noa *thoṛa* do Kạjnum-Gunum *(Adverb)* leka hõe kạmikana.

Santalire Beniṭ Ujnum chạḍa arhõ mit̓ten Ujnum menak̓a, ona do Kukli Ujnumko metak̓a. Noaṭak̓ dol reak̓ Ujnum do bar lekan Ujnum sãote biboron emkatege beste dǫ bujhạuk̇a. Santalire Kukli Ujnum sãote *cǫṅ, hǫ̃* sẹ *-ge* lagaolenkhan, tǫbẹ ona dǫ Bẹniṭ Ujnum reak̇e kạmieda. Adǫmak̇ Bẹniṭ Ujnum dǫ Bẹjivianak̇ Unjum *(Inanimate Pronoun)* rupre hǫ̃ beoharok̇kangea ar adǫmak̇ dǫ jivianak̇ rupre hǫ̃ laṛcaṛok̇kangea. Adǫmak̇ noṅkanak̇ Bẹniṭ Ujnum menak̇a, ǫnẹ oka dǫ lekha reak̇ Tayǫm Joṛao *(Suffix)* lekae kạmiet̕kana. Ona Ujnum sãote *-ṭak̇* joṛaoakan tahẹnkana. Adǫm jǫkhẹc̕ noṅkan Ujnum Bẹniṭ Ujnum sẹ Kukli Ujnum reak̇ hǫ̃e kạmieda ar ona dǫ Tayǫm Joṛao *(Suffix)* lekae kạmiet̕kana. Ona Ujnum sãote *-ṭak̇* joṛaoakan tahẹnkana. Adǫm jǫkhẹc̕ noṅkan Ujnum Bẹniṭ Ujnum sẹ Kukli Ujnum reak̇ hǫ̃e kạmieda ar ona dǫ Tayǫm Joṛao *(Suffix)* reak̇ rup hǫ̃e hataoet̕kana. Bẹniṭ Ujnum jãhãre *-n* joṛaolenkhan; metak̇me *jãhãn* hoelenkhan tǫbẹ noa ayatre Gunum *(Adverb)* lekae kạmiet̕kana ar Bẹjivianak̇ Bẹniṭ Ujnum *(Inanimate Indefinite Pronoun)* rupre beoharok̇kana.

Noa Ujnum babǫt beste bujhạu lạgit̕ jivianak̇ Bẹniṭ Ujnum ar bẹjivianak̇ Bẹniṭ Ujnum latarre pạrtul ẹmǫgǫk̇kana:-

Lekha	**Jivianak̇**	**Bẹjivianak̇**
(i)	*Jãhãe hǫhǫakome.*	*Jãhãnak̇ ạguime.*
(ii)	*Jãhãe ǫkǫekin hǫhǫakoa?*	*Jãhãnak̇ cẹt̕iṅ ạguia?*
(iii)	*Jãhã-jãhã okateṅ calak̇a?*	*Jãhãṭak̇ ạguime.*
(iv)	*Jãhãman tãhãe calak̇kana.*	*Jãhãn kaṭ ạguime.*
(v)	*Jãhãeṭak̇ hǫhǫaeme.*	*Jãhãnak̇ ạgu daraeme.*

cǫṅ - Noa judi Kukli Ujnum são joṛaolen khan sẹ Tayǫm Joṛao *(Suffix)* leka lagaolenkhan, Bẹniṭ Kukli Ujnum lekae kạmia, jeleka :–

(i) *ǫkǫe cǫṅ* - *Ǫkǫe cǫṅe* hǫhǫet̕kana?

(ii) *cele coṅ* - Birre *cele coṅe* rak̇et̓kan botorge?

(iii) *cet̓ coṅ* - *Cet̓ coṅe* roṛet̓kan?

(iv) *okaṭak̇* - *Okaṭak̇* coṅe lạiạdiń tahẽkan?

coṅ do ekal lagaote hõ lagaok̇gea, onkan katha do baṅ kana. Noa *coṅ* do *coṅ* rupre baṅ hõ lagaok̇kana. *co* sãote Tayom Joṛao *(Suffix) -ko* lagaokate Kukli Beniṭ Ujnume *(Interrogative Indefinite Pronoun)* benaoet̓kana, jeleka –

(i) Okoe *coṅko* (coko) hec̓akana.

(ii) Okarenkan *coṅko* (coko)?

(iii) Cet̓ko *coṅe* (coe) roṛet̓kan.

hõ - Noakin sãote *baṅ, alo, oho* Kukli Ujnum tahẽlenkhan Beniṭ Ujnum reak̇e kạmieda, jeleka :–

(i) Okoe *hõ* bako calaolena.

(ii) Cele *hõ* babo calaolena.

(iii) Oka *hõ* baṅ cekalena.

(iv) Cet̓ *hõ* baṅ hoelena.

Noa chaḍakate *bạnuk̇* beoharlenkhan Beniṭ Ujnum do noṅka benaok̇kana. Noate cet̓ niṭ jinis babot khạṭite bae lại daṛeak̇kana. Onate *cet̓* sãote *hõ* ar *bạnuk̇* lagaok̇kana, jeleka :–

hõ

Cet̓ *hõ* bạnuk̇takoa.

oho laṛcaṛkate hõ Beniṭ Ujnume kạmiet̓kana, jeleka :–

Cet̓ hõ *oho* emlena.

alo sãote do noṅka benaok̇kana :–

Cele hõ *alom* lạiakoa.

ge sãote do noṅka Beniṭ Ujnum benaok̇kana :–

Okoege bako hec̓lena; *Cet̓ge* alom mena.

cetat sãote *hõ̱* se̱ *ge* ar ona sãote *baṅ* ar *ba(e)* tahe̱nkhan Be̱niṭ Ujnum do̱ noṅka benaok̓kana :–

Cetat *hõ̱* baṅ dhe̱jaea; *Cetatge* bae dhe̱jana; *Cetatak̓ hõ̱* baṅ jạruṛa.

Kukli Ujnum *(Interrogative Pronoun)* *o̱ko̱e* ar *oka* bar dhao dohṛalenkhan, to̱be̱ ona do̱ Be̱niṭ Ujnum reak̓e kạmiet̓kana. Noakin banar bar lekanak̓ jivianak̓ ar be̱jivianak̓ reak̓e kạmiet̓kana, jeleka – *o̱ko̱e* do̱ jivianak̓ sabad reak̓e kạmieda ar *oka* do̱ be̱jivianak̓ reak̓e kạmieda.

Judi *o̱ko̱e* do̱ bar dhao dohṛalenkhan, to̱be̱ ona do̱ jivianak̓ ar saṅge lekhare hõ beoharok̓gea ar *oka* dohṛalenkhan do̱ be̱jivianak̓ ar sanam lekhare beoharkate Be̱niṭ Ujnum reak̓ hõe̱ kạmieda, jeleka :–

(i) *O̱ko̱e-o̱ko̱e* do̱ko me̱na; baṅma ayo ho̱ṛ do̱ sạṛimre de̱jo̱k̓ baṅ ganok̓a. (Saṅge Lekha)

(ii) *Oka-oka* jaega do̱ butạhagea. (Mit̓ Lekha)

(iii) *Oka-oka* jaegareko ńamok̓a. (Saṅge Lekha)

o̱ko̱e & oka – Noakin sabad Be̱niṭ Ujnum leka do̱ ạikạuk̓kangea, me̱nkhan Go̱ṛo̱ Ayat *(Clause)* leka arhõ̱ he̱c̓kate Be̱niṭ Saṅge Lekha reak̓ hõe̱ kạmieda, jeleka :–

(i) *O̱ko̱e*ko do̱ko baḍae, *o̱ko̱e*ko do̱ baṅ?

(ii) *Oka* ho̱r do̱ ṭhika, *oka* ho̱r do̱ baṅ?

ja & je – Noakin sãote *-ge* ar eṭak̓ sabad tahe̱nkhan, Be̱niṭ Ujnum reak̓e kạmiet̓kana, jeleka :–

(i) *Ja* uḍic̓ hoṛo hoeakantalea.

(ii) *Jage* utu leka hakole go̱c̓akat̓koa.

(iii) *Je* kichu ńamen napaege hoena.

Ado̱mak̓ noṅkan sabad menak̓a, o̱ne̱ oka do̱ Gunum se̱ Ńunum Huḍạ *(Noun Phrase)* rupre hijuk̓kana. Ar noa do̱ jivianak̓ ar bejivianak̓ rupre saṅge lekha leka hijuk̓kana. Ar Beniṭ Ujnum reak̓e kạmiet̓kana. Pạrtul :–

(i) *adom-adom* - *Adom-adom* hoṛ doko calaoena.

(ii) *adomko* - *Adomko* doko calaoena.

(iii) *adomak̓* - *Adomak̓* do bạṛic̓gea.

(iv) *adomak̓* - *Adomak̓ko* do seaena.

(v) *adom-adomak̓ko* - *Adom-adomak̓ko* do mõńjgea.

(vi) *adom hoṛ* - *Adom hoṛ* doko lahaena.

(vii) *adom sakam* - *Adom sakam* do paloena.

(viii) *adom do ... adom do* – *Adom do* seaena ar *adom do* mõńjgea.

(ix) *adha* - *Adha* doko calaoena, *adha* doko taenomena.

(x) *kichu-kichu* - *Kichu-kichue* disạet̓kangea.

(xi) *eṭak̓-egak̓* - *Eṭak̓-eṭak̓e* roret̓kana.

ar - Noa *ar* do adom jokhec̓ do Jok̓ṛao *(Conjunction)* reak̓ ar adom jokhec̓ do Ujnum *(Pronoun)* lekae kạmiet̓kana. Noa banarge jivianak̓ ar bejivianak̓ leka laṛcaṛok̓kana, jeleka :–

(i) Jel *ar* hakoko utuat̓lea. *(Conjunction)*

(ii) Ape dope seṭerena *ar*ko do okare menak̓koa? *(Pronoun)*

(iii) Bạń bilena *ar*hõ den imạńme. *(Pronoun)*

ar-ar – Noa sabad bar dhao dohṛakate Beniṭ Ujnum reak̓e kạmiet̓kana, jeleka :–

(i) *ar-ar* - Ape dope hec̓ena *ar-ar*ko doko okaena?

(ii) *ar-ar* - Am moto lạgit̓ do alom hudisa, *ar-ar*ko lạgit̓ hõ dandok̓ jạruṛkana.

ạḍi ar *uḍic̓* – *ạḍi* ar *uḍic̓* hõ Beniṭ Ujnum reak̓e kạmieda, judi uḍiċ lahare *ja* sẹ *tin* lagaolenkhan ar judi Ńunum lahare *ạḍi* lagaolenkhan Ńunum hudạ *(Noun Phrase)* reaǩe kạmieťkana sẹ Bẹniṭ Ujnum reaǩ hõe kạmieda, jeleka :–

(i) Ja *uḍiċ* hoṛole ńamkeda.

(ii) Tin *uḍiċko* ẹmena?

(iii) *Ạḍi* hoṛko chuṭạuena.

iạ – iạ dọ Ńunum, Gunum, Kạjnum sẹ Kạjnum-Gunum reaǩ kạmi são-sãote Bẹniṭ Kạjnum reaǩ hõe kạmieťkana. Adọm jọkhẹċ dọ noa *iạ, -re, -te* Tayọm Japaǩ *(Postposition)* lagaokate *iạ*te benaoente karọne *(cause)* baḍae ocoeťkana. Noa sabadte jãhãnaǩe hiṛińkaǩkhan ar bae disạeťkhan, tọbẹ disại lạgiť *iạ-iạ* ko rọṛa. Ar adọm jọkhẹċ dọ dukrey paṛaolenkhan hõ *iạ* dọko laṛcaṛeťkana. Adọm jọkhẹċ dọ họhọae reaǩ katha lạgiť hõ laṛcaṛoǩkana. Ar adọm jọkhẹċ dọ katha ẹhọb jọkhẹċ hõ *iạ*ko rọṛeťkana ar adọm jọkhẹċ dọ katha aċaǩ ańjọm ocoe lạgiť hõ *iạ – iạ*ko rọṛa, jeleka :–

(i) Ẹ *iạ*, hijuǩme! (Họhọ, *Vocative case*)

(ii) *Iạ,* ańjọmlem sẹ! *(Interjection)*

(iii) *Iạ* gọ, gapa nãhãǩ paesa imạńme! *(Interjection)*

(iv) *Iạ* do sẹ calaolenme, ḍakṭọr họhọ ạguem! *(Interjection)*

(v) *Iạń* ńẹlledea. *(Pronoun)*

(vi) *Iạkedeako,* ḍaṇḍọmkedeako. *(Verb)*

(vii) *Iạǩkanae,* ńũruǩkanae. *(Verb)*

eman – Noa dọ Ńunum leka hõe kạmia ar Bẹniṭ Ujnum leka hõ, ọnẹ oka dọ jãhãe hoṛ sẹ jãhãnaǩ jinis babọte lạieťkana. Noa Ńunum ruprey kạmikhan dọ jaoge saṅge lekha ruprey kạmia. *eman* dọ Gunum leka hõe kạmia. Noa dọ Iṅgrạjite dọ *such like, and so on, etcetra*ko metaǩa. Pạrtul :–

(i) Ńindạ dọ alom daṛana, *emankoko* ńamoǩa. *(Indefinite Pronoun)*

(ii) *Emantenkoko* bolo̱k̔a, duạr siṅkak̔me.
(Indefinite Pronoun)

(iii) *Emanteak̔ko* e̱m emankema. *(Pronoun)*

(iv) *Emanteak̔bo* jo̱ma. *(Pronoun)*

eman do̱ ado̱m jo̱khe̱c̔ *dara* lagaokate noṅka beoharok̔a :–

(i) Katha *eman darate* do̱ o̱ho̱ń pạtiạulena.

(ii) Uni *darate* calak̔me.

tan – Noa do̱ Be̱niṭ Tayo̱m Japak̔ juk̔ṭuc̔ak̔ kana se̱ Ujnumanak̔ *(Pronominal)* kana. Noa do̱ Iṅgrạjite do̱ *Indefinite Postposition Particle*ko metak̔a. Noa do̱ Niniṭ Tayo̱m Joṛao *(Determinative Suffix) -ko* lagaokate laṛcaṛok̔kana, jeleka – *tan + ko, tạn + ic̔* eman hoyok̔kana. Noako do̱ e̱ke̱n jivianak̔ jinis lạgit̔ge laṛcaṛok̔a. Me̱nkhan *tan + ak̔, tan + ak̔ + kin, tan + ak̔ + ko* do̱ e̱ke̱n be̱jivianak̔ jinis lạgit̔ge laṛcaṛok̔kana. Noa be̱jivianak̔ak̔ do̱ *O̱te̱* isạra aṛaṅate hõ laṛcaṛok̔gea. *-tanak̔* do̱ Kạjnum sãote hõ joṛaok̔gea ar sãote *pase̱c̔* lagaokate ayatre laṛcaṛok̔kana. Noako beste bujhạu lạgit̔ pạrtulbo ńe̱la :–

(i) O̱te̱ toyo *tanak̔* kanae pase̱c̔.

(ii) Pase̱c̔ unie dal *tanak̔lem* khan!

(iii) Pase̱c̔em bajao *tanak̔akade!*

(iv) O̱te̱ *tanko* pase̱c̔ko onko kangeako.

(v) Uni *tạnic̔* kangeae.

mit̔ – Noa hõ Be̱niṭ Ujnum reak̔e kạmieda. Noa sãote *ṭe̱c̔, ṭaṅ, ṭe̱n* joṛaolen khan be̱jivianak̔ ar Jivianak̔ Ujnum hoyok̔kana, jeleka – *mit̔ ho̱ṛ, mit̔ṭe̱c̔ dare, mit̔ṭaṅ raja, mit̔ṭe̱c̔ raja, mit̔ṭaṅ dhiri, mit̔ṭe̱n dhiri* eman.

E̱KTIẠRI UJNUM
(POSSESSIVE PRONOUN)

Okaṭak̓ Ujnum ho̱te̱te ayatre jãhãṭak̓ eṭak̓ Ujnum se̱ Ńunum ona são so̱mpo̱k do̱ho̱kate e̱ktiạri reak̓ so̱mpo̱k babo̱t baḍaeok̓kan, onage E̱ktiạri Ujnum *(Possesive Pronoun)* do̱ko metak̓kana, jeleka – *ok̓/o̱k̓, ona ... oka do̱; oka ... ona; o̱ne̱ ... ona; ce̱t̓ ... ona; , uniak̓, aboak̓, onkoak̓, aleak̓, -ren, reak̓* emanko. Noa Ujnum beste bujhạu lạgit̓ mit̓ bar ayat latarre e̱mo̱go̱k̓kana :–

(i) ona … oka do̱ - *Onageń* emat̓mea; *oka* do̱m me̱nle̱t̓.

(ii) oka … ona - *Okam* me̱nle̱t̓; *ona* do̱ bạń ńamleda.

(iii) o̱ne̱ … oka - *O̱ne̱m* me̱nle̱t̓; ona do̱ bạnuk̓a.

Santalire mit̓ lekanak̓ E̱ktiạri Ujnum do̱ bạnuk̓a. Ado̱m jo̱khe̱c̓ noare Laha Joṛao *(Prefix)* se̱ Tayo̱m Joṛao *(Suffix)* se̱ Tayo̱m Joṛao *(Postposition)* hõ lagaok̓kana ar ado̱m jo̱khe̱c̓ do̱ be̱go̱r tayo̱m joṛaoante hõ hijuk̓kangea. Noa Ujnum do̱ Kukli Ujnum ar Isạra Ujnum hõ noa do̱l reak̓e kạmiet̓kana. Ho̱ṛ Ujnum *(Personal Pronoun)* reak̓ sạdhin rup do̱ Ńunum lahare he̱c̓kate E̱ktiạri Ujnum reak̓e kạmiet̓kana. Ado̱m jo̱khe̱c̓ noa Ujnum do̱ Gunum reak̓e kạmiet̓kana. Ho̱ṛ Ujnum do̱ Be̱jivianak̓ Ńunumre laṛcaṛlenkhan, ona do̱ E̱ktiạri Ujnum reak̓e kạmiet̓kana. Ado̱m jo̱khe̱c̓ noa do̱ Ńunum tayo̱mre he̱c̓ milạukate beoharok̓a. Noa babo̱t latarre pạrtul e̱mo̱go̱k̓kana :–

(i) iń - *Kiminiń* (ińren kimin); *ho̱po̱niń* (ińren ho̱po̱n); *ạpuń* (ińren ạpu).

(ii) ale - *Ale* koṛa (aleren koṛa)

(iii) ape - *Ape* haṛam (aperen haṛam)

(iv) ale - *Ale* mại (aleren mại)

(v) reak̓ - *Kod* reak̓ kaṭ kana.

(vi) renak̓ - Ato *renak̓* jahe̱r kana.

Adom jokheċ judi Ektiạri Ujnum rupre lạrcạrlenkhan tobe onare – *ak̓, -ak̓kin, -ak̓ko* jorạolenre bejivianak̓ rup hoyok̓kana. *-ren* do jivianak̓ lạgit̓ beoharok̓kana.

re (re) – Noa sãote – *-ak̓/-ak̓kin/-ak̓ko* do bejivianak̓ tayom jorạo kana. *-re* sãote *-n* ar *–ak̓, -n* sãote *–aṅ* jorạolenre hõ bejiianak̓ hoyok̓kana. Nonḍe noa hõ disại lek kana je aċ sãote *-riniċ* jorạolenkhan *-aċriniċ,* Ektiạri Ujnum hoyok̓kana.

Cetan reak̓ ạn lekate noa do noṅka hoyok̓kana –

re	- (i) renak̓	- Cet̓ *renak̓* kana?
	(ii) reaṅ	- Cet̓ *reaṅ* kana?
	(iii) reak̓	- Cet̓ *reak̓* kana?

Cetan reak̓ ponon Ektiạri Ujnum *renak̓, reak̓* ar *reaṅ* jotoge ora-sorae kạmiet̓kana ar bejivianak̓ lekage kạmik̓kana.

Mit̓ bar Santal somajre sombond se sạgại menak̓a. Ona sombond katha sãote Hoṛ Ujnum reak̓ kạṭiċ rup *-ń, -m* ar ona sãote *-t* ar *-tet̓* jorạokate hõ Ektiạri Ujnum benaok̓kana se *-iń, -m, me* jorạokate hõ Ujnume benaoet̓kana, pạrtul :-

ń - *ạpuń, kiminiń, iṅgạń, miserań, bokoń, goṅgoń, hoponerań, dadań, ạjiń, jae dadań, mamoń, kạkiń, bạhuń, balań* eman.

hopon + iń	*= hoponiń*
gorom + iń	*= goromiń*
hatom + iń	*= hatomiń*
hanhar + iń	*= hanhariń*
hõehar + iń	*= hõehariń*

m - *eṅgam, ạpum, miseram, bokom, goṅgom, eram, hoponeram, dadam, ạjim, jaedadam, mamom, kạkim, balam* eman.

m - *hoponme, gorome, hatomme,koraṛme, jãwãeme, hõeharme, ạpumme, ạjimme, dadamme, balamme, miseramme, hoponme, kiminme, jaekoraṛme* eman.

t - Noa hō̱ sạgại reak̇ kathare lagaolen khan Ẹktiạri Ujnume hoe ocoet̕kana, jeleka :–

eṅgat, apat, miserat, mamot, bạhut, dadat, bo̱ko̱t, goṅgot, kạkit, jaedadat, balat eman.

te̱t̕ - Noa hō̱ sạgại kathare lagaolen khan Ẹktiạri Ujnume benaoet̕kana, jeleka :–

apatte̱t̕, eṅgate̱t̕, miseratte̱t̕, mamotte̱t̕, bạhutte̱t̕, dadatte̱t̕, bo̱ko̱tte̱t̕, goṅgotte̱t̕, kạkitte̱t̕, jaedadatte̱t̕, hanharte̱t̕, hō̱eharte̱t̕, he̱re̱lte̱t̕, ạimạite̱t̕, bo̱ko̱tte̱t̕ eman.

Ẹktiạri Ujnum reak̇ arhō̱ mit̕ lekan rup menak̇a ar ona do̱ be̱jivianak̇ leka beoharok̇a, me̱nkhan noa do̱ Dosar Ho̱ṛ *(Second Person)* lạgit̕ laṛcaṛok̇kana. Noa do̱ dosar ho̱ṛ *-me* joṛaokate hoyok̇kana, jeleka :–

(i) *Mē̱t̕melaṅ* suṭujtama.

(ii) *Mocamelaṅ* ko̱ṭe̱jtama.

(iii) *Ramamelaṅ* o̱r todtama.

(iv) *Ḍaṭamelaṅ* ko̱ṭe̱ċ ńũrtama.

(v) *Jaṅgamelaṅ* ṭaṭhe̱mea.

(vi) *Baṛgemelaṅ* sietama.

iṅ, am, aben, ape, ạliń, ale, alaṅ, onko sãote *-ak̇* Tayo̱m Joṛao joṛaolenkhan Be̱jivian Ujnum reak̇ so̱mbo̱nd benaok̇kana, jeleka –

ak̇ - *(i) iṅak̇ khe̱t, (ii) amak̇ khe̱t, (iii) abenak̇ khe̱t, (iv) apeak̇ khe̱t, (v) alaṅak̇ khe̱t, (vi) onkoak̇ khe̱t*

ren - *(i)iṅren kaḍa, (ii) amren kaḍa, (iii) abenren kaḍa, (iv) aperen kaḍa, (v) alaṅren kaḍa, (vi) onkoren kaḍa.*

Noa do̱ Ho̱ṛ Ujnum *(Personal Pronoun)* sāo *-ak̇, -ren* lagaokatege Ẹktiạri Ujnume benaoet̕kana.

KUKLI UJNUM
(INTERROGATIVE PRONOUN)

Jãhãe ho̱ṛ se̱ jinis babo̱t baḍae lạgit́ okaṭak̇ Ujnum beoharok̇kana, ona do̱ Kukli Ujnumko metak̇kana, jeleka – *o̱ko̱e, ce̱t́, cele* eman.

Santalire bar lekanak̇ Kukli Ujnum menak̇a, mit́ do̱ Jivianak̇ ar dosarak̇ do̱ Be̱jivianak̇. Nạmuna :–

(i) **Jivianak̇ Kukli Ujnum** – *o̱ko̱e, o̱ko̱ekin, o̱ko̱eko, cele, celekin, celeko* eman.

(ii) **Be̱jivianak̇ Kukli Ujnum** – *oka, okakin, okako, ce̱t́* eman.

o̱ko̱e ar *oka* do̱ mit́ lekhare beoharok̇kana, ona sãote joṛaokate *-ṭak̇* se̱ *–ṭaṅ* he̱c̀lenkhan ona do̱ jãhãn jinis babo̱te uduk̇ begareda, jeleka – *okaṭak̇.* To̱be̱ noa reak̇ jobab do̱ noṅka ńamok̇kana – *o̱ne̱ onaṭak̇* se̱ *nõk̇õe noaṭak̇, hinạṭak̇* emanko.

o̱ko̱e+ṭak̇=o̱ko̱eṭak̇, o̱ko̱e+ṭaṅ=o̱ko̱eṭaṅ,
oka+ṭak̇=okaṭak̇, oka+ṭaṅ=okaṭaṅ

ṭak̇ do̱ Gunum rupre hõ ayatre laṛcaṛok̇kana, jeleka :–

(i) *Okaṭak̇* khe̱tem sia?

(ii) *O̱ko̱eṭak̇* gạiem kirińea?

Jãhãe ho̱ṛak̇ ńutumem kuliekhan *cele* hõ beoharok̇kana, jeleka :–

(i) *celeama;* (ii) *celewaea;* (iii) *celeaea;* (iv) *celeaeako;*

(v) *celeko ńumkedea* eman.

Kukli Ujnum do̱ Gunum rupre hõ beoharok̇a ar Kạjnum rupre hõ. Noa Ujnum do̱ banar dhao dohṛakate hõ ayatre beoharok̇kana ar saṅge lekha se̱ Hạṭińõk̇ Rupre *(Distributive)* hõ laṛcaṛok̇a, jeleka :–

(i) *O̱ko̱e-o̱ko̱eko* calaoena?

(ii) *Q̱kq̱ekoko* calaoena?

Noakinre babar dhao Kukli Ujnum beoharoḱa. Noa Ujnum hq̱tẹte hq̱ṛe begareťkoa ar saṅge lekhare beoharoǩkana.

(i) *Q̱kq̱e kanae?* – Ujnum *(Pronoun)*

(ii) *Cele hq̱ṛ kanae?* – Gunum *(Adjective)*

(iii) *Oka hq̱rtem hẹċena?* - Gunum *(Adjective)*

Adq̱m jq̱khẹċ Tayq̱m Japaǩre *(Postposition)* lagaoǩkana. Noako Ujnum dq̱ adq̱m jq̱khẹċ dq̱ Sapaṗaǩ ar adq̱m jq̱khẹċ dq̱ Kạjnum rupre beoaroǩkana, jeleka :–

cẹť + (te+m) = cẹťtem hẹċena? Sapaṗaǩ *(Instrumental)*

Sapaṗaǩ *(Instrumental)* : Noa dq̱ adq̱m jq̱khẹċ dq̱ Gunum, Ujnum, Kạjnum reaǩe kạmieťkana, pạrtul :–

(i) *Cẹť* katha kana? Gunum *(Adjective)*

(ii) *Oka* kathako saṗakada? Gunum *(Adjective)*

(iii) *Cẹť-cẹťkom* ceťkeťa? Hạṭiń Ujnum *(Distibutive Pronoun)*

(iv) *Cẹť-cẹťkope* jq̱mkeťa? Hạṭiń Ujnum *(Distibutive Pronoun)*

(v) *Q̱kq̱e-q̱kq̱e* ṭhenem calaolena? Hạṭiń Ujnum *(DistibutivePronoun)*

(vi) Uni dq̱pe *q̱kq̱ekedea? (Celepe ńutumkedea.)* Kạjnum *(Verb)*

(vii) Uni haṛam dq̱e *q̱kq̱yentapea? (Uni haṛam dq̱ cẹť sạgạile sabtaea?)*

(viii) *Q̱kq̱eq̱ǩq̱e* uni dq̱? *(q̱kq̱e bō̃s?* Kạjnum *(Verb)*

(ix) *Q̱kq̱eko* hẹċaťbona, abo sẹ onko? *(Kuṛi sẹ koṛa gidrại janamena. (Pronoun)*

(x) *Q̱kq̱e* ṭhẹčko ńamkeťa? *(Noa dq̱ q̱kq̱e-q̱kq̱e ṭhen leka hō̃ beoharoḱa. ((Dist. Pro.)*

(xi) *Okoeṭaḱem* ạkhriṅkedea? *(Determinative Pronoun)*

Noṇḍe *cele* hotete ńutum, sạgại, kạmi (nukri) babotre hõ baḍaeoḱkana, jeleka :–

(i) *Celeama? (Ńutum)*

(ii) Onko do *celeḱako/celeaḱako? (Sạgại)*

(iii) *Celeaḱkom* kạmi baṛaeṫa? *(nukri)*

Noṇḍe *oka* hotete *ṭhại* ar *jãhãnić* hoyoḱ reaḱe baḍaeoḱkana ar jãhãnić adoḱ reaḱ hõ baḍaeoḱkana, jeleka : –

(i) *Okam* calaḱa? *(ṭhại)*

(ii) *Okayenae? (Ceṫe benaoena?)*

(iii) Gại dom *okakedea? (Aṫ reaḱ)*

(iv) *Okakoanko* aleaḱ do? *(Jinis reaḱ ạidạri se hoḱ)*

(v) *Oka okape* senlen oṇḍe-oṇḍe idibonpe. *(ṭhại)*

(vi) Katha dom *okaṭaḱkeṫa? (Okaṭaḱ amem kusiaṫ)*

(vii) *Okateyić* hoṛ kanae? *(ṭhại)*

(viii) *Ceṫ lạgiṫ? (Menjoṅ/oka amem menjoṅkan)*

(ix) *Ceṫ iạte? (Karon baḍae sana)*

(x) *Ceṫ baṅ se! (Hahaṛa katha baḍaeoḱ)*

Metaḱme Kukli Ujnum reaḱ sabad hotete aema lekan katha baḍaeoḱkana.

ceṫ ... ceṫ – Noa kukli lahare miṫṭen ona são jojaoḱ sabadtege hijuḱa ar joto reaḱ katha metaḱme sanam reaḱ kathae lạieṫkana, jeleka :–

(i) *Haṛamge ceṫ, buḍhige ceṫ sanamko calao cabawakana.*

(ii) *Nahaḱ do joto hoṛaḱ pagra menaḱtakoa, buḍhige ceṫ, kuṛige ceṫ.*

(iii) *Ạimạige ceṫ, herelge ceṫ, koṛage ceṫ, kuṛige ceṫ*

sanamke sanamko calaoena.

cele – Noa hoteꞔe kukli sãote jãhãnaḱ soṅgete baḍae reaḱ moneу tuluċ kukliḱkana ar noa do ayatre Kạjnum-Gunum *(Adverb)* lekae kạmieťkana, jeleka :–

(i) *Cele,* jarwaenabon, se baṅa?

(ii) *Cele,* tearena se baṅ?

Noṇḍe *cele* hotete jạt *(gender)* ar jãhãniċ ceť lekan hoṛ kanako mente baḍaeoḱ lạgiť hõ, jeleka :–

(i)Uni gại do *cele* mĩhũi busạgea?

(ii) *(*onko) Mõṛẽ hoṛ do *celeko* tahẽkana?

celeċ ar *celeť* – Noakin sabad do banarge Kạjnum-Gunum leka ayatrey kạmieťkana. Aḱṅjomiċ do noa sabad hotete jobab hõe emoḱkana, jeleka :–

(i) Henda hoṛ Budhrại doe heċena se? Hẽ, *celeť* onkageṅ aṅjomakaťa.

(ii) Som do haṭtey calaoena se baṅ? Hẽ, *celeť* onkage holae meneť tahẽkana.

(iii) Hijuḱgeae *celeċ,* ente onkako roṛ baṛaeťa.

celeť – Noa *celeť* sabad hõ kukli sabad kangea. Noa do noṅka hõko beohara :–

Celeťteťko coṅ din hilạḱko hijuḱa.

cetat – Noa sabad do Bejivianaḱ Kukli Ujnum reaḱ manere beoharoḱa ar noa do *ceť* sabad barabạrigey kạmia. Noa sabad sãote hõ *se, -ge* joṛaokate hõ laṛcaṛoḱkana, jeleka :–

(i) Ceťpe cekakeda, *cetatge* bako dheja.

(ii) Ceťge bape baḍaea, *cetat* hõ oṛ bạnuḱtapea.

okor - Noa hõ Kukli Ujnum kangea. Noa do jivianaḱ jinis babot baḍae sana menaḱkhan beoharoḱa. *okor* do Kạjnum-Gunum leka hõ beoharoḱa. P. O. Boḍiṅ do noa sabad jivianaḱ ar bejivianaḱ banarrege beoharoḱ lągiť dạlile emoḱkana. Noa sãote Niṭ Tayom Joṛao *(Determinative Suffix) -ic̓, -an, -anań, -anec̓* hõ hijuḱgea, pạrtul :–

(i) *Okoric̓*, nit hõ bae hec̓akana.

(ii) *Ukuric̓tako* apat hoṛ do?

(iii) *Ukuric̓takoan* bạhu hoṛ do?

(iv) *Okorko* okare?

(v) *Okorantakoanań* onkanaḱ khet do?

(vi) *Okoric̓anec̓* oka ṭhec̓ menaea?

(vii) *Okoranań* oka ṭhec̓em ńamkeťa?

(viii) *Okoric̓an* uni do?

Kukli Ujnum do Kukli Kạjnum-Gunum *(Interrogative Adverb)* rupre hõ laṛcaṛoḱkana ar Isạra Kạjnum-Gunum *(Demonstrative Adverb)* rupre hõ. Menkhan jaoge nońka do bań hoyoḱkana. Ńel baṛaḱkana Kukli Ujnum ar Tayom Japaḱ *(Postposition) -wante* hõ beoharoḱgea. Kukli-Ujnum do Kạjnum-Gunum rupre ṭhãi/jaega sec̓ isạrae lạgiť hõ beoharoḱkana.

oka – Noa do adom jokhec̓ Kạjnum-Gunum rupre begor Tayom Japaḱ – *-te, -re, ṭhen, khon, dhạbic̓, onte* hõ beoharoḱgea. Pạrtul :–

(i) begor *-te* wante – Okam calaḱkana?

(ii) *te* - *Okatem* calaḱkana?

(iii) *re* - *Okarem* ńelakada?

(iv) *sec̓* - Oka *sec̓em* calaḱkana? (dik, ṭhãi)

(v) *ṭhen/ṭhec̓* – Oka *ṭhen* menama? Oka *ṭhec̓* menama?

HẠHẠṬIŃ UJNUM
(DISTRIBUTIVE PRONOUN)

Hạhạṭiṅ Ujnum dọ onageko metaḱkana, ọnẹ okaṭaḱte dọ Ńunume begareťkan sẹ begar begare judạeťkan, jeleka :–

mimiť, sanam, miť ke miť, miť miťte ar *baṅ dọ* … ar *baṅ dọ*

(i) *mimiť* - *mimiť* gọṭẹn emakope.

(ii) *sanam* - *sanamkoko* calaoena.

(iii) *miť ke miť* - *miť ke miť* họṛko calaoena.

(iv) *miť miťte* - *miť miťteko* calao cabaena.

baṅ dọ ar *baṅ dọ*

(i) *Baṅ dọ* Rabọne aguleda ar *baṅ dọ*Lọkhọnge.

(ii) *Baṅ dọ* amem hẹc̓len ar *baṅ dọ* unige.

Inạ chaḍakate hõ eṭaḱ lekanaḱ Hạhạṭiṅ Ujnum menaḱa, ona dọ noako kana – *babar, pẹpẹ, popon, mõmõṛ, tuturui, eḱae, iḱrạl, aḱre, gẹgẹl, mimiť gẹl, babar gẹl* emanko.

Noa Lekhawanaḱ *(Numerical)* Ujnum sãote *gọṭẹn* sẹ *gọṭẹc̓* joṛaolenkhan hõ Hạhạṭiṅ Ujnum benaoḱkana, jeleka :–

(i) *mimiť gọṭẹn* - *Mimiť gọṭẹn* kolkope.

(ii) *babar gọṭẹc̓* - *Babar gọṭẹc̓* kolkope.

(iii) *pẹpẹ* - *Pẹpẹ gọṭẹc̓* kolkope.

Onkage eṭaḱ são hõ beoharoḱkana Noa tayọmre *-kate* lagaolenre hõ Hạhạṭiṅ Ujnum benaoḱkana, jeleka :–

(i) *Babar gọṭẹnkate* kolkope.

(ii) *Pẹpẹ gọṭẹnkate* kolkope.

(iii) *Popon gọṭẹnkate* kolkope.

(iv) Mõmõṛ *gọṭẹnkate* kolkope.

SOMPOK UJNUM
(RELATIVE PRONOUN)

Tinre miťṭen Ńunum eṭakak̕ Ńunum são sombonde benaoeťkana, onage Sombond Sompok Ujnum doko metak̕a. Adom jokhec̕ do Sompok Ujnum ayatre baṅ ńel ńamok̕a. Menkhan sompok reak̕e kạmieda, ayatre *one, okoe, ceť, jãhãe, jãhãe okoe, jãhã-jãhã, jãhã oka ar jãhãṭak̕* hotete miťṭen ayat se Ńunum eṭakak̕ ayat se Ńunum são sompoke joṛaoeťkana.

one ... un - onem hec̕len *unhilok̕.* Noṇḍe Sompok Ujnum *(Relative Pronoun)*

(un) – Noṇḍe *un* hotete somoe reak̕ sombonde joṛaoeťkana. Noa do noṅka hõ hoe daṛeak̕a :-

(i) *Onem* hec̕en hilok̕.

(ii) *One ... ona – onem* metadiń, *onageń* ạgukeda.

Noa Ujnum sãote Hoṛ Ujnum *(person pronoun)* reak̕ pene khaṭo rup *-ń, -m, -e* rup hõ laṛcaṛok̕gea, jeleka :-

(iii) *Oneń* metaťme, *onam* ạgukeda?

(iv) *Onem* menleť, *onań* ạgukeda.

(v) *Ona ... one - Onae* ạgukeda, *onem* menleť.

(vi) *Onań* ạgukeda, *onem* menleť.

Noṇḍe *okoe* do jivianak̕ lạgiť, oka do bejivianak̕ lạgiť beoharok̕kana ar eṭak̕ Ujnum se ayat são sombonde joṛaoeťkana, jeleka :-

(i) Uni hoṛ, *okoe* do *onae* kạmi daṛeak̕. (onae kạmi daṛeak̕ hoṛ; onae kạmi daṛeak̕ miť hoṛ)

(ii) Uni hoṛ, *one okoe* kạmi daṛeak̕.

(iii) *One* uni, *okoe* do *onae* kạmi daṛeak̕.

(iv) *Ona* khet, *okam* losoťakať. (losoťakať khet)

(v) *Ona* khẹt, *ọnẹ onam* lọsọťakať.

(vi) *Ọnẹ okam* lọsọťakať khẹt.

(vii) Sebelaǩ *ọnẹ oka* bam jọm legawakať.

cẹť ar *cele* hǒ Sọmbọnd Ujnum reaǩe kạmieťkana, jeleka :-

(i) *Cẹťe* khọjkan, ona ẹmaeme.

(ii) *Cele* cọko metae, miť hoṛe hẹċakan.

(iii) *Cele* cọe uḍạu hẹċen, bọhọǩrey aṗena. (bọhọǩrey aṗeniċ celekan cọe)

Isạra Ujnum jaoge *-ń, -m, -e* são joṛao miťkate miť eṭaǩaǩ Ujnum são sọmbọnde joṛaoeťkana, jeleka :-

(i) Uni seta, ọnẹ *unim* dallede.

(ii) Ona sahan, *ọnẹm* paṛaǩakať.

sẹ

(iii) Ona sahan, ọnẹ *onam* paṛaǩakať.

(iv) Iń, *ọnẹ, noań* gọǩakawaťpe.

Bẹniṭ Ujnum adọm jọkhẹċ sọmbọnd joṛao ayat lekae kạmieťkana. *jãhãe* ar *jãhãe ọkọe* dọ jivianaǩ lạgiť ar *jãhã, jãhã oka* dọ bẹjivianaǩ lạgiť beoharoǩkana. Ar noa dọ bẹgọr *ọnẹ* lagaokate hoyoǩkana, jeleka :-

(i) *Jãhãepe* ńamko, ạgukope. (ńamoǩko hoṛ)

(ii) *Jãhãe* ọkọepe kọekoa.

(iii) *Jãhãṭaǩ* bogepe metaǩ, ona kạmipe.

(iv) *Jãhã* okaṭaǩpe kạmia, oka bes hoekoǩ.

ẠKIL BHAŃJAO - 7

A. Ṭoyoṭ'kate jobab emok̉me :-

1. Hoṛ Ujnum reak̉ kạṭić rup Pạhil Hoṛ *(First Person)* mit̉ lekha *(Singular Number)* do okaṭak̉ kana?

   (a) liń (b) ń (c) pe (d) m

2. Hoṛ Ujnum reak̉ kạṭić rup Pạhil Hoṛ Bar Lekha do okaṭak̉ kana?

   (a) liń (b) bo (c) ń (d) m

3. Hoṛ Ujnum reak̉ kạṭić rup Saṅge Lekha do okaṭak̉ kana?

   (a) laṅ (b) bo (c) am (d) m

4. Hoṛ Ujnum reak̉ kạṭić rup Dosar Hoṛ *(Second Person)* mit̉ lekha do okaṭak̉ kana?

   (a) m (b) ń (c) le (d) pe

5. Hor Ujnum reak̉ kạṭić rup Dosar Hoṛ Bar Lekha do okaṭak̉ kana?

   (a) me (b) laṅ (c) liń (d) ben

6. Hoṛ Ujnum reak̉ kạṭić rup Dosar Hoṛ Saṅge Lekha do okaṭak̉ kana?

   (a) ben (b) pe (c) le (d) bon

7. Hoṛ Ujnum reak̉ kạṭić rup Eṭak̉ Hoṛ *(Third Person)* mit̉ lekha do okaṭak̉ kana?

   (a) am (b) iń (c) pe (d) uni

8. Hoṛ Ujnum reak̉ kạṭić Eṭak̉ Hoṛ Bar Lekha do okaṭak̉ kana ?

   (a) bon (b) liń (c) ben (d) kin

9. Hoṛ Ujnum reak̉ kạṭić rup Eṭak̉ Hoṛ Saṅge Lekha do okaṭak̉ kana?

(a) liń (b) ko (c) pe (d) le

10. E̱ktiạri Ujnum *(Possessive Pronoun)* reak̓ Pạhil Ho̱ṛ *(First Person)* mit̓ lekha *(singular number)* do̱ okaṭak̓ kana?

    (a) tam (b) ṭạkin (c) ṭạliń (d) tiń

11. E̱ktiạri Ujnum reak̓ Dosar Ho̱ṛ Mit̓ Lekha do̱ okaṭak̓ kana?

    (a) ṭạkin (b) tam (c) tiń (d) tae

12. Be̱jivianak̓ Ujnum reak̓ Eṭak̓ Ho̱ṛ Mit̓ Lekha do̱ okaṭak̓ kana?

    (a) uni (b) ona (c) onakin (d) onako

13. Be̱jivianak̓ Ujnum reak̓ Bar Lekha do̱ okaṭak̓ kana?

    (a) onakin (b) ona (c) unkin (d) onko

B. O̱lkate jobab e̱mo̱k̓me :-

1. Ujnum do̱ ce̱t̓ kana?
2. Santalire Ujnum do̱ tinạk̓ lekana. Bean e̱mme.
3. Sanam Ujnum reak̓ pạrtul e̱mme.
4. Ho̱ṛ Ujnum reak̓ bean e̱mme.
5. *Iń* do̱ Ho̱ṛ Ujnum reak̓ okaṭak̓ Ho̱ṛ kana?
6. *Am* do̱ Ho̱ṛ Ujnum reak̓ okaṭak̓ Ujnum kana?
7. *Uni* do̱ Ho̱ṛ Ujnum reak̓ okaṭak̓ Ujnum kana?

8

GUNUM
(ADJECTIVE)

Santal so̱majre jãhãe boge/bhage/bạṛic̓/mõ̱ń̇j ho̱ṛ hõ̱ menak̓koa. Noako ro̱ṛ lạgit̓ sabadko o̱ne̱ ona sabadan ho̱ṛ boge/bạṛic̓bon metakokana. Onkage jãhãn jinis reak̓ boge/bạṛic̓ baḍae lạgit̓ sabad menak̓a. Okaṭak̓ sabad ho̱te̱te boge ar bạṛic̓bon baḍaet̓kan, ona sabadge Gunum do̱ko metak̓kana.

Gunum do̱ latarre emakan hạṭiń̇rebo hạṭiń̇ daṛeak̓a :-

1. Ujnumanak̓ Gunum *(Pronominal Adjective)*
2. Gun Gunum *(Quality Adjective)*
3. Lekha Gunum *(Quantity Adjective)*
4. Ulphạ Gunum *(Extra Adjective)* (Noa do̱ Kạjnum-Gunum *(Adverb)* hõ̱ko metak̓a.)

UJNUMANAK̓ GUNUM
(PRONOMINAL ADJECTIVE)

iń̇, am ar *uni* chaḍakate eṭak̓ak̓ Ujnum tinre Ń̇unum lahare hijuk̓kana, to̱be̱ ona do̱ Ujnumanak̓ Gunumko metak̓kana, jeleka :-

nui seta; hạni kaḍa; noa oṛak̓; jãhãe ho̱ṛ; noṅkan nahel; ce̱t̓ lekan ho̱ṛ; nhowa dare; neko hako; hini me̱ro̱m; nhako sado̱m; hana dare, ona loṭa eman. *nui, hạni, noa, jãhãe, noṅkan, hini, ce̱t̓ lekan, oka, o̱ko̱e, noko, nhako, hana;* onako do̱ *seta, kaḍa, oṛak̓ ho̱ṛ, nahel, ho̱ṛ, dare, hako, me̱ro̱m, ho̱ṛ, sado̱m, o̱ko̱e ho̱ṛ, tinạk̓ dak̓, ninạk̓ dak̓,* dare ar loṭa lahare he̱c̓akante ona do̱ beako̱ro̱n reak̓ ạn lekate do̱ Gunum manaok̓kana.

GUN GUNUM
(QUALITY ADJECTIVE)

Okaṭak̇ sabad hoṭete Ńunum reak̇ gun, hoṛak̇ dosa, sobhab emane lạiet̓kan, onage Gun Lạlạiak̇ Gunum doko metak̇kana. Jivianak̇ jinis moto reak̇ gun moto do baṅ bickom Bejivianak̇ Ńunum reak̇ gun hõe lạiet̓kana. Noa Gunum do aema lekanak̇ menak̇a, jemon :-

(i) **Okte Lạlạiak̇** - *maren, nãwã, laha, tayom, nitok̇, gapa,meaṅ, mahnder, bhạbisot, on mahnder, setak̇, tikin, ạyup̣, dak̇ lo ber, simrak̇, buḍhi parkom, sidup̣, pạhil simrak̇, paha poho, jeḍer keṭeċ, ńuhum, baskeak̇ bela, kedok̇, hola, endrae, kalom, ńindạ, aṅga, sedae* eman.

(ii) **Ṭhãi Lạlạiak̇** -*purub, pạchim, etom, kõyẽ, Baṅgladesren, Jharkhanḍren, Bharotren, Asamren, Rusren, atoren, disạmren, Nepalren, Bhuṭanren* eman.

(iii) **Gun** - *bhage, cerha, laser, cokhal, coṭkar, nindhạn, soṛa, khacaṛ, liṭhur, livet̓, leṛe theṛe, reaṛ* eman.

(iv) **Dos** - *bạṛiċ, hohak̇, lelha, goda, gadha, katjioạ* eman.

(v) **Roṅ** - *arak̇, ponḍ, hạriạṛ, sasaṅ, mĩhĩ musnạ, hende, esel, tel sãwãr, kursạ baha roṅ, lil, beṅgaṛ roṅ* eman.

(vi) **So** - *sea, sĩṛĩċ, mõńj so* eman.

(vii) **Dosa** -*lohot̓, rohoṛ, oda* eman.

(viii) **Jak̇** - *lạbit̓, keṭeċ, rokoṛ, norom, rodha, saegat̓, leńjer, rukhạṛ, cikạ̃ṛ* eman.

(ix) **Sebel** - *sabak̇, khara, jojo, heṛem, kasa, comkoċ, tạpis, lotoe* eman.

LEKHA GUNUM
(QUANTITY ADJECTIVE)

Okaṭak̇ sabad ho̱te̱te Ńunum se̱ Ujnum lekha/मात्रा babo̱te lạiet̓kan, ona do̱ Lekha/मात्रा Gunumko metak̓kana, jeleka :- *barea kalo̱ṭ, ponea sukri, turui sado̱m, irạl ho̱ṛ, thoṛa ho̱ṛ, sanam ho̱ṛ, aema hoṛo, aema dare* eman. No̱ṇḍe̱ *barea, ponea, turui, irạl, thoṛa* sanam do̱ Lekha Gunum kana.

Noako hõ̱ Gunum kangea – *mit̓, bar, pe̱, pon, mõ̱ṛẽ̱, mõ̱ṛẽ̱iċ (ak̇), turuiċ (ak̇), bar do̱bo̱ṛ, pe̱ do̱bo̱ṛ, pon do̱bo̱ṛ, mõ̱ṛẽ̱ do̱bo̱ṛ, sae do̱bo̱ṛ, banar, pe̱ne̱, ponon, mimit̓, babar, pe̱pe̱, mit̓ pạì, mit̓ pạì tala, tala pạì, mit̓ sạr, mit̓ choṭak, mit̓ suli, bar mũṛĩ, mit̓ isi, mit̓ pạilạ, mit̓ poa, mit̓ se̱r, mit̓ kaṭ, mit̓ po̱so̱ri* eman.

ULPHẠ GUNUM
(EXTRA ADJECTIVE)

Okaṭak̇ sabad ho̱te̱te Gunum reak̇ge gune lạiet̓kan, ona sabad do̱ Ulphạ Gunumko metak̓kana, jeleka :- *ạḍi e̱se̱l, ạḍi poṇḍ, kĩṛĩt̓ reaṛ, ritit̓-ritit̓ reaṛ, ạḍi arak̇, je̱ṅge̱t̓-je̱ṅge̱t̓ arak̇, kaṛaṅ-kaṛaṅ ńũt, te̱he̱-te̱he̱ poṇḍ, kạridaṅ ńũt* eman. No̱ṇḍe̱ do̱ *ạḍi, kĩṛĩt̓-kĩṛĩt̓, je̱ṅge̱t̓-je̱ṅge̱t̓, te̱he̱-te̱he̱, kaṛaṅ-kaṛaṅ*ko do̱ Ulphạ Gunum kana cedak̇ e̱nte̱t̓ *e̱se̱l, poṇḍ, reaṛ, arak̇, ńũt* reak̇ gune lạiet̓kana. Noako chaḍakate E̱ktiạri Cho̱nd reak̇ sanam rup do̱ Gunum reak̇gey kạmiet̓kana, jeleka :- *Sunạ eṅgat, aleren koṛa, So̱mae bạhu, Bharo̱tren ho̱ṛ, Lukhi erve̱lte̱t̓, Ramak̇ nahel, kaḍawan ho̱ṛ, dak̇anak̇ kũi* eman. Ona chaḍakate Kạjnumre Tayo̱m Joṛao lagaokate ona tayo̱m Ńunum he̱ċlenkhan Gunum reak̇e kạmia, jeleka :- *se̱nlen ho̱ṛ, calaoen hapta, he̱ċakan koṛako, janamok̇tae gidrạ* eman. No̱ṇḍe̱ *se̱nlen, calaoen, he̱ċakan, janamok̇tae* do̱ Gunum reak̇e kạmiet̓kana.

Inạ chaḍakate Kạjnum kho̱n eṭak̇ak̇ sabadre Tayo̱m Joṛao he̱ċlenkhan hõ̱ Gunum reak̇e kạmiet̓kana, jeleka :-

cando	- *candokią*
tayom	- *tayomak̉*
laha	- *lahawak̉*
etom	- *etomak̉*
sareċ	- *sareċak̉*
baromas	- *baromąsią*

Noṇḍe mit̉ dhao lạiągok̉kana je *-re* ar *–te, -re, -n* joṛaolenkhan hõ Gunum reak̉e kạmiet̉kana, jeleka :-

oṛak̉ren hoṛ, birren janwar, ato renak̉ko, birtenko, horten-ko eman.

Noṇḍe thoṛa Kạjnumanak̉ Gunumbo *(Adjectival/Particle)* ńela, one oka do Ńunum lahare Kạjnum sãote Tayom Joṛao lagaokate Gunum reak̉e bornonet̉ se gune lạiet̉kan. Noṇḍe Kạmi Kạjnum *(Active Voice)* sãote Sodor Kuṛai reak̉ laṛcaṛbo ńellege, pạrtul :-

(i) *Calak̉ hoṛ.*

(ii) *Hijuk̉ lạgidok̉kan tahẽkan hoedak̉.*

(iii) *Bań hiṛińok̉ katha.*

(iv) *Bạlin̉ hiṛin̉ daṛeae gidrạ.*

(v) *Ḍạkuko jeret̉kede hoṛ;*

(vi) *Mucạt̉ cando.*

(vii) *Bir dare.*

(viii) *Mutul ṭhenak̉ dare.*

(ix) *Dulạṛet̉me eṅgam.*

(x) *Horhoet̉kokan gupiyiċ.*

(xi) *Kuliet̉bon tahẽkan doroga;*

(xii) *Dal got̉ket̉me ḍạku.*

(xiii) *Ńel ńõk̉let̉ko koṛa.*

(xiv) *Ataṅakaťko peṛa.*

(xv) *Ạguakadiń tahẽkan hoṛko.*

(xvi) *Ńapamleťlaṅ gateko.*

(xvii) *Noa menkeť hoṛ.*

(xiii) *Gegerkan seta* eman.

Nitoḱ do Kạmi Kạjnum *(Active Voice)* sãote Oko Kuṛại *(Indirect Object)* reaḱ laṛcaṛbon ńela :-

(i) *daḱ dudul (dulaḱ) mạli.*

(ii) *goṛowạńkan bareń.*

(iii) *ceťapekan tahẽkan pạṇḍit.*

(iv) *saṗ soraťbon maejiu.*

(v) *noa lạiakawaťliń gidrạ.*

(vi) *ṭaka emakawaťko tahẽkan mahajon* eman.

Noṇḍe arhõ Bekạmi Kạjnum *(Passive Voice)* são laṛcaṛoḱ Kạjnumanaḱ Gunum *(Adjectival Particle)*bo ńela, pạrtul :-

(i) *hijuḱ Aṭhwar.*

(ii) *calaḱkantiń hopon.*

(iii) *ạtuḱkan tahẽkan daḱ.*

(iv) *benaoen oṛaḱ.*

(v) *rạpuťlen nahel.*

(vi) *ńapamlen tahẽkan kuṛiko.*

(vii) *pereċakan lạukạ.*

(viii) *aťakan tahẽkan merom* eman.

Noṇḍe aċ lạgiť kạmikan reaḱ Kạjnumanaḱ Gunumbo *(Adjectival Particle)* ńela :-

(i) *bạhu ńamjoṅ koṛa.*

(ii) *koejoṅkan ayo.*

(iii) *kulijoṅkan tahẽkan haṛam.*

(iv) *ạidạriwan hoṛ.*

(v) *ńelakawan buḍhi.*

(vi) *ṭheṅgawan hoṛ.*

(vii) *pegele gidrạwan maejiu.*

(viii) *apatan gidrạ.*

(ix) *ak̓saran hoṛko.*

(x) *tarwaṛean hoṛko* eman.

Sabad tayomre tahenkhan ona hõ Gunum reak̓e kạmia, pạrtul :-

(i) Noa do *ona khon keṭeċgea.*

(ii) Uni do *iń khone maraṅgea.*

Arhõ *arteṭ', bãṛti* lagaokate Ńunum se Ujnum reak̓ gune lạiet̓kana, jeleka :-

(i) Noa do *arteṭ' lebṛeċgea.*

(ii) Uni do *am khon arhõe usulgea.*

(iii) Nui do *bãṛtigeye khaṭoa.*

(iv) Ona ato do *arhõ sạṅgińgea.*

joto khon se *sanam khon* lagaokate hõ Ujnum se Ńunum reak̓ gune lạiet̓kana, jeleka :-

(i) Uni do *sanam khone kisãṛgea.*

(ii) Uni do *joto khone usulgea.*

utạr joṛaokate hõ Ujnum se Ńunum reak̓e kạmiet̓kana, jeleka :-

(i) Uni doe marań *utạrgea.*

(ii) Aema *utạrgeako.*

(iii) Sạri *utạrgea.*

Cetanre emakan Gunumge beste bujhạu lạgiť begar-begar ẹmkate, oka ayatre laṛcaṛoḱkana, ona miť-miťte nọṇḍẹ judạ-judạbo ńẹla :-

(i) Bạjun dọ ạḍi *lasẹr hatańan* koṛa kanae.

(ii) Noa dọ *mõ̱ńj sạṛi* kana.

(iii) Lukhi dọe *cẹrha kuṛi* kana.

(iv) Amṛapaṛa dọ *kạṭič bajar* kana.

Noa ayatre *lasẹr hatań, mõ̱ńj, kạṭičko* dọ Gunum reaḱe bọrnọnẹťkana. Gunum dọ noae lạieťkana je *koṛa, sạri, kuṛi* ar *bajar* dọ cẹť lekana mẹnte.

Oka sabad jãhãe hoṛaḱ, jinis reaḱ sẹ ghoṭna reaḱe bọrnọnẹťkana, onage Gunum dọko metaḱa. Nọṇḍẹ miťṭẹnkate sanam Gunum reaḱ bhẹd ẹm tuluč ayatre beoharkate Gunum babọtrebo ạri bạndhia :-

Ujnumanaḱ Gunum *(Pronominal Adjective)*

(i) *Nui* seta dọe ińren kana.

(ii) *Noa* oṛaḱ dọ ińaḱ kana.

(iii) *Nhawa* dare dọ aleaḱ kana.

(iv) *Nhoko* sadọm dọko aleren kana.

(v) *Nhạko* bhiḍi dọko calaḱkana.

Noa ayat reaḱ *nui, noa, nhawa, nhoko, nhạko* dọ Ujnumanaḱ Gunum kana. Noako tayọmre Ńunum metaḱme *seta, dare, sadọm* ar *bhiḍi* hẹčakana. Noako sabad tayọmre Ńunum hẹčakan iạte noa dọ Gunum reaḱe kạmieťkana. Judi noa sabad tayọmre Ńunum bań hẹčlenkhan Gunum reaḱ bae kạmia. Noage ona reaḱ oprom dọ. Nọṇḍẹ beste bujhạu lạgiť ayat ẹmọgọḱkana:-

(i) *Nui* dọe seta kana.

(ii) *Noa* dọ oṛaḱ kana.

(iii) *Nhawa* do̱ dare kana.

(iv) *Nhoko* do̱ko sado̱m kana.

(v) *Nhạko* do̱ko bhiḍi kana.

Noa ayatre e̱makan *nui, noa, nhawa, nhoko, nhạko* sabad tayo̱mre e̱ṇḍe̱ge Ńunum sabad do̱ bạnuǩa, onate noa sabad do̱ noako ayatre do̱ Ujnum *(Pronoun)* reaǩe kạmieťkana.

No̱ṇḍe̱ arhō̱ eṭaǩ-eṭaǩ lekanaǩ Ujnum Gunumbo ńe̱la :-

(i) *Ce̱ť* dare kana?

(ii) *Okaṭaǩ* aṅgro̱pem kirińa?

(iii) *Oka* ho̱rtem calaǩa?

(iv) *Cele* hakom sap̌kedea?

Noa ayatre *ce̱ť, okaṭaǩ, oka, cele* sabad tayo̱m Ńunum sabad *dare, aṅgro̱p, ho̱r* ar *hako* he̱c̆akana, onate noako do̱ Gunum reaǩe kạmieťkana. Ona tayo̱mre Ńunum sabad baṅ tahe̱nkhan to̱be̱ ona do̱ Gunum reaǩ do̱ bae kạmia. Noa katha bujhạu lạgiť latar reaǩ ayat bestebon bujhạuma :-

(i) *Ce̱ťem* cekaeda?

(ii) *Okaṭaǩem* kạmia?

(iii) *Okatem* calaǩkana?

(iv) *Celekom* ńe̱lleťkoa?

Noa ayatre *ce̱ť, okaṭaǩ, oka, cele* tayo̱mre Ńunum sabad bạnuǩa. Ona iạte Gunum reaǩ do̱ bae kạmieťkana.

Inạkate arhō̱ eṭaǩ lekanaǩ Ujnum-Gunumbo ńe̱la :-

(i) *Ińaǩ* parko̱m do̱ okare menaǩa?

(ii) *Amaǩ* nahel do̱ okare menaǩa?

(iii) *Uniaǩ* puthi do̱ okayena?

(iv) *Onkoaǩ* hoṛo do̱ hoeyena.

Noa ayatre menaḱ *iṅaḱ, uniaḱ, amaḱ, onkoaḱ* tayo̱mre Ṅunum sabad he̱ċakana metaḱme *parko̱m, nahel, puthi, hoṛo* he̱ċakana. Ona ia̱te noako sabad do̱ Gunum reaḱe ka̱mieťkana. Noa tayo̱mre Ṅunum sabad baṅ tahe̱nkhan Gunum reaḱ do̱ bae ka̱mia. Noa bujha̱u la̱giť latarre ayat pa̱rtul e̱mo̱go̱ḱkana :-

(i) *Iṅaḱ* do̱m cekaea, am ṅe̱lme.

(ii) *Amaḱ* do̱ baṅ mõ̱ṅja, iṅaḱge mõ̱ṅja.

(iii) *Uniaḱ* do̱ mõ̱ṅjgea, me̱nkhan iṅaḱ do̱ baṅ.

(iv) *Nokoaḱ* do̱ baṅ kana, aleaḱ kana.

Noa ayatre emakan *iṅaḱ, amaḱ, uniaḱ, nokoaḱ* tayo̱mre Ṅunum sabad baṅ he̱ċakana, ona ia̱te onako do̱ Gunum reaḱ do̱ bae ka̱mieťkana. Noa cha̱da e̱taḱ lekanaḱ Ujnum-Gunumbo ṅe̱la :-

(i) *Mimiť* ho̱ṛko calaḱa.

(ii) *Pe̱pe̱* ho̱ṛko calaḱa.

(iii) *Mimiť* ho̱ṛ a̱di ra̱ska̱re menaḱkoa.

(iv) *Popon* ho̱ṛko calaḱma.

Noa ayatre *mimiť, pe̱pe̱, popon* tayo̱mre Ṅunum sabad *ho̱ṛko* he̱ċakana. Ona ia̱te noako sabad do̱ Gunum reaḱe ka̱mieťkana. Ona tayo̱mre Ṅunum sabad baṅ he̱ċlenkhan Gunum reaḱ do̱ bae ka̱mia. Noa katha bujha̱u la̱giť latarre ayat pa̱rtul e̱mo̱go̱ḱkana :-

(i) *Mimiťaḱ* do̱ hoe idiena.

(ii) *Pe̱pe̱* go̱ṭe̱ċko ha̱rana.

(iii) *Popon* dhaoko do̱nkeda.

No̱ṇḍe̱ *mimiť, pe̱pe̱, popon* tayo̱mre jãhãn Ṅunum sabad baṅ he̱ċakan ia̱te Gunum reaḱ do̱ bae ka̱mieťkana. Arhõ̱ e̱taḱ lekanaḱ Ujnumanaḱ Gunumbo ṅe̱la :-

(i) Uni do̱e *Pa̱ria̱rdaharen* kana.

(ii) Unin do̱e *Nepalren* kana.

(iii) Uni doe *Urisaren* kana.

(iv) Uni doe *Bharotren* kana.

Nonde *Pariardaha, Nepal, Urisa, Bharot* do ńutum lalaiak Ńunum *(Proper Noun)* kana. Noa sabadre *-ren* lagaokate *Pariardaharen, Nepalren, Urisaren, Bharotren* benaoakana. *-ren* joraoen iate noa do Gunum reaḱe kamietkana ar ona do Gunum hoyena. Adomak Gunum do adom jokheč Ńunum lahare hijukkana, jeleka :-

latu orak, latu kora, marań kora, losot khet, hariar sakam emanko.

Santalak somajia *(social)* gorhon, one oka do latu-katič boehako talare tahenkana. Ona do Ńunum lahare hečkate Gunum reaḱe kamietkana, jeleka – *marań kora, tala kora, sańjla kora, sańjli kuri, mańjli kuri, hudiń kora, mańjla kora, hudiń tala kora*. Adom jokheč Ńunum hõ Gunum reaḱe kamieda, ona do Gunum reak unregey kamia tinre do Ńunum lahare hijukkan, jeleka :-

ita orak, hasa orak, tin orak, tali orak, busup orak, tale dhoya orak, simĩt orak, khunti orak, sauri orak, lumań sari, sutam sari, harta panahi, tayar catki eman. Noa do jora sabad hõko metaka (*Compound,* समास) Noako Ńunum lahare Gunum sabad joraokate Ńunum reak sorostet arhõe bãrtietkana. Noa do ayat reak beoharkate arhõ beste bujhauka. Partul ńelkate bestebo bujhaua :-

(i) *arak* - *Arak* ita orak ńelokkan, ondebo calaka.

(ii) *usul* - *Usul* hasa orakren kora kanae.

(iii) *jhalkaok* - *Jhalkaok* tin orak sečtebo calaka.

(iv) *osar* - *Osar* tali orakrebo boloka.

(v) *phedle* - *Phedle* busup orakren kuri kanae.

(vi) *nãwã* - *Nãwã* tale dhoya orak phedtebo calaka.

(vii) *mõ̱ńj* - *Mõ̱ńj* jeleń sasaṅ lumạṅ sạribon kiriṅạṅạ.

No̱ṇḍe̱ beste bujhạu lạgiť ado̱m-ado̱mak̕ Gunum ayatre laṛ-caṛkatebo bujhạua :-

aema -Noa sabad do̱ bar lekanak̕ Gunume lạieťkana. Iṅgrạjite do̱ *much* se *many*ko metak̕kana. Latarre emakan ayatbo ńe̱la :-

(i) *Aema* hoṛo menak̕talea.

(ii) *Aema* tuṛi menak̕talea.

(iii) *Aema* sunum menak̕talea.

(iv) Pukhrire *aema* dak̕ menak̕talea.

(v) Gaḍare *aema* gitil menak̕a.

(vi) *Aema* pạṭạulak̕e jo̱k̕ jaorakeda.

(vii) *Aema* sakam ńũrakana.

Noako ayatre bar lekan Ńunum reak̕ bibro̱n e̱mkate, ona reak̕ gun lekae kạmieťkana. Miť lekan Gunum do̱ baṅ lekha *(uncountable noun)* Ńunum lạgiť *aema (much)* reak̕ beoharakana. Miť do̱ lekha daṛeak̕ Ńunum *(countable Noun)* lạgiť *aema (many)* beoharakana, jeleka :-

(i) *Aema* hoṛo (Baṅ lekha daṛeak̕ Ńunum)

(ii) *Aema* tuṛi (Baṅ lekha daṛeak̕ Ńunum)

(iii) *Aema* sunum (Baṅ lekha daṛeak̕ Ńunum)

(iv) *Aema* dak̕ (Baṅ lekha daṛeak̕ Ńunum)

(v) *Aema* gitil (Baṅ lekha daṛeak̕ Ńunum)

(vi) Aema sakam (Baṅ lekha daṛeak̕ Ńunum)

Arhõ̱ no̱ṇḍe̱ noa aemage lekha daṛeak̕ Ńunum lạgiť beoharakana, jeleka :-

(i) *Aema* dare menak̕talea.

(ii) *Aema* ṭaka menak̕talea.

(iii) *Aema* ṭukuć menak̕talea.

(iv) *Aema* datrom menaǩtalea.

Noṇḍe noa *aema*ge lekha daṛeaǩ Ńunum reaǩ bibron emkate ona reaǩ lekhae lạieťkana. Ona iạte *aema* do Ńunum reaǩ gun lekae kạmikana.

mimiť -Noa reaǩ beohar Ńunum lahare hečkate Gunum reaǩe kạmieťkana. ente Ńunum reaǩ babotge lahare hečkate bibrone lạieťkana, jeleka :-

(i) *Mimiť* hoṛko donkeda.

(ii) *Mimiť* darere jo menaǩa.

(iii) *Mimiť* joṛo emakope.

(iv) *Mimiť* gidrạ utu emakope.

(v) *Mimiť* hoṛaǩ jhola ńeltakope.

Noa *mimiť* hõ Ńunum lahare hečakante Gunum reaǩe kạmieťkana.

sanam/joto - Noa reaǩ laṛcaṛ do latar reaǩ ayatrebon ńela. Menkhan noa do lekha daṛeaǩ ar baṅ lekha daṛeaǩ Ńunum banar lạgiťge :-

(i) *Sanam* hoṛko jomkeda.

(ii) Khet reaǩ *Sanam* daǩ ạtu cabaena.

(iii) *Joto* hako pukhri khonko dạṛ cabakeda.

(iv Pusi *sanam* toae ńũ caba goťkada.

(v) Pusi *joto* toae ńũ cabakeda.

sanam do *hoṛ, daǩ* ar *toa* lahare hečkate ona reaǩ babote lạieťkana. Ona iạte *sanam* do Gunum reaǩe kạmieťkana. Onkage *joto* hõ *hako* ar *toa* reaǩ babote lạieťkan iạte ar Ńunum lahare hečakan iạte Gunum reaǩe kạmieťkana.

banar -Noa do Ńunum lahare hečkate Ńunum reaǩ babote lạieťkana ar Gunum reaǩe kạmia. Noa do eken lekha daṛeaǩ

Ńunum lạgiťge laṛcaṛoǩa, jeleka :-

(i) *Banar* dare magme.

(ii) *Banar* khe̱t si go̱ťkaǩme.

(iii) *Banar* oṛaǩbo saphaea.

(iv) *Banar* duạrre silpińbo lagaoa.

***banar* do̱ e̱ke̱n barea Ńunum lạgiť'ge beoharoǩa.**

thoṛa - Noa do̱ baṅ lekha daṛeaǩ Ńunum lạgiť metaǩme banar lạgiťge laṛcaṛoǩa, jeleka :-

(i) *Thoṛa* thamakur imạńme se̱.

(ii) *Thoṛa* daǩ imạńme se̱.

(iii) *Thoṛa* buluṅ imạńme se̱.

(iv) *Thoṛa* cun imạńme se̱.

(v) *Thoṛa* sakam imạńme se̱.

Metaǩme Ńunum lahare he̱čkate jãhã lekanaǩ sabadge he̱členkhan ar Ńunum babo̱t jãhãnaǩe lạieťkhan, ona do̱ Ńunum reaǩ Gunum lekae kạmia.

ẠKIL BHAŃJAO - 8

A. Ṭo̱yo̱t'kate jobab e̱mo̱ǩme :-

1. Gunum do̱ tinạǩ hạṭińre menaǩa?

   (a) 4 (b) 5 (c) 8 (d) 9

2. *nui seta* do̱ okaṭaǩ Gunum kana?

   (a) Ujnumanaǩ Gunum (b) Gun Gunum

   (c) Lekha Gunum (d) Ulphạ Gunum

3. *pe̱ do̱bo̱ṛ* do̱ okaṭaǩ Gunum kana?

(a) Lekha Gunum (b) Ulphạ Gunum (c) Gun Gunum
(d) Ujnumanak̉ Gunum

4. *baromas* sabad reak̉ Gunum do cet̉ hoyok̉a?
(a) baromantar (b) baromạsiạ (c) barokos (d) baromasa

5. *mit̉ pạilạ* do okaṭak̉ Gunum kana?
(a) Lekha Gunum (b) Ulphạ Gunum (c) Gun Gunum
(d) Ujnumanak̉ Gunum

B. Olkate jobab emok̉me :-

1. Gunum do cet̉ kana?
2. Gunum do tinạk̉ goṭeċa?
3. Gunum reak̉ sanam hạṭiń reak̉ pepe goṭeċ pạrtul emme.
4. Ujnumanak̉ Gunum *(Pronominal Adjective)* do cet̉ kana? Pạrtul selet̉ lạime.
5. Gun Ujnum *(Quality Adjective)* do cet̉ kana? Pạrtul selet̉ lạime.
6. Lekha Ujnum *(Quantity Adjective)* do cet̉ kana? Pạrtul selet̉ lạime.
7. Ulphạ Gunum *(Extra Adjective)* do cet̉ kana? Pạrtul selet̉ lạime.
8. *Nui setagey ạ̃iṭhạkeda.* Noa ayat reak̉ *nui* sabad do oka gunum reak̉ kana?
9. *lelha* sabad do oka Gunum reak̉ kana?
10. *pon hoṛ* reak̉ *pon* do okaṭak̉ Gunum reak̉ sabad kana?
11. *Cando, tayom, laha, etom, sareċ* ar *baromas* khon gunum benaome.
12. *Calak̉, hijuk̉ lạgidok̉kan tahẽkan,* ar *bạliń hiṛiń daṛea*eko

do̱ ayatre Gunum leka laṛcaṛme.

13. *daḱ dudul* ar *go̱ṛo̱ạńkan* do̱ ayatre Gunum leka laṛcaṛme.

14. *Pe̱ge̱le̱ gidrạwan* ar *apatan* do̱ ayatre Gunum leka laṛcaṛme.

15. *Noa do̱ arte̱t' le̱bṛe̱ċgea* ayat reaḱ *arte̱t' le̱bṛe̱ċgea* do̱ ce̱t́ reaḱ gune lạiet́kana?

16. *Amṛapaṛa do̱ kạṭiċ bajar kana.* Noa ayat *kạṭiċ* do̱ ce̱t́ reaḱ gune lạiet́kana ?

17. *Ińaḱ parko̱m do̱ okayena?* Noa ayat reaḱ laṛcaṛakan *ińaḱ* sabad Gunum leka laṛcaṛakana me̱nte cekatem bujhạua.

18. *Iṭạ oṛaḱ kana.*, noa ayatre *iṭạ oṛaḱ* barea Ńunum sabad laṛcaṛakana *iṭa* ar *oṛaḱ*, noakin banar sabad milạukate Joṛa Sabad *(Compound)* benaoakana. Noakin mod kho̱n okaṭaḱ sabad Gunum lekae kạmikana?

19. Bharo̱t sabad do̱ ayatre Gunum leka laṛcaṛme.

20. *Araḱ* do̱ Beako̱ro̱n reaḱ niạm lekate ce̱t́ kana?

9

KẠJNUM-GUNUM *(ADVERB)*

Tinre abo dọ jãhãnaḱ ghoṭna sẹ jãhãnaḱ babọtbon gapalmaraoa, tọbẹ abo dọ ona ghoṭna babọt lạlại sanabon tọbẹ ona dọ Kạmiạ, Kạjnum, Kuṛại sẹ Puḱṛạuaḱ họtẹte dọ baṅ sọdọrọḱkana. Noa reaḱ beohar Kạjnum-Gunum họtẹte sọdọrọḱa. Noa dọ Gunum, Kạjnum sẹ eṭaḱ Kạjnum-Gunum reaḱ gune lạieṭ́kana. Kạjnum-Gunum *(Adverb)* cekatebo oroma, ona ńam lạgiṭ́ dọ *tis/tinre/tinạḱ/cẹṭ́ leka/cekate/cedaḱ/okare/ wante* kukli ọmọnkate, ona reaḱ oka jobab ńamoḱkana, ona dọ Kạjnum-Gunum *(Adverb)* kana mẹntebo bujhạua. Noa Kạjnum-Gunum dọ noṅka leka hạṭiń daṛeaḱa :-

1. Sọmọe Lạlạiaḱ Kạjnum-Gunum *(Adverb of Time)*
2. Ṭhãi Lạlạiaḱ Kạjnum-Gunum *(Adverb of Place)*
3. Dhara/Tạrika Lạlạiaḱ Kạjnum-Gunum *(Adverb of Maner)*
4. Bạ̃ṛti Lạlạiaḱ Kạjnum-Gunum *(Adverb of Degree)*
5. Dhao Lạlạiaḱ Kạjnum-Gunum *(Adverb of Frequecy)*
6. Kukli Kạjnum-Gunum *(Interrogative Adverb)*
7. Sọmbọnd Lạlạiaḱ Kạjnum-Gunum *(Relative Adverb)*
8. Isạra Kạjnum-Gunum *(Demonstrative Adverb)*
9. Bẹniṭ Ujnum Kạjnum-Gunum *(Indefinite Pronominal Adverb)*

SOMOE LALAIAK̇ KAJNUM-GUNUM *(ADVERB OF TIME)*

Oka sabad do somoe/okte reak̇e lạiet̕kana, onage Somoe Lạlạiak̇ Kạjnumbo metak̇kana, jeleka :-

(i) *Teheń* calak̇me.

(ii) *Gapa* do, khetiń sia.

(iii) *Hola* do Aṭhwar tahẽkana.

Noṇḍe *teheń, gapa* ar *hola* do somoye lạiet̕kana. Ona iạte noa do Kạjnum-Gunum kana. Ona chaḍa aema Kạjnum-Gunum menak̇a, oka do somoe reak̇e lạiet̕kan, pạrtul :-

teheńok̇, gapanok̇, holanok̇, teheń gapa, meań, mahnder, nit, endrae, on mahnder, nitok̇, kalom, din kalom, nebetar, satom, hol kalom, pher satom, mah satom, pher kalom, mah kalom, dak̇ lo ber (sun day time), ńindạ, sedae, bela (sun time of day-hour), simrak̇, ańga, setak̇, ạyup̀, tikin eman. Noa chaḍakate adomak̇ Somoe Lạlạiak̇ Kạjnum-Gunum benao lạgit̕ onare Tayom Japak̇ *(Post Position)* lagaokate hõ benaok̇kana, jeleka :-

(i) *nit + re* = *nitre*

(ii) *gapa + te* = *gapate*

(iii) *sạt + ok̇* = *sạtok̇a*

(iv) *teheń + khon* = *teheń khon*

(v) *gapa + hạbiċ* = *gapa hạbiċ*

Adomak̇ do noa hõ kana - *jaoge, jao hilok̇, jao hilok̇ setak̇, jao hilok̇ ạyup̀, ạyup̀ piche, setak̇ piche, siń sạṭup̀, jaejug, din hilok̇, mit̕ din, bạrsiń, mit̕ dinok̇, pe mãhã, ursiń bạrsiń, gel din, gel mãhã, mursiń bạrsiń, mit̕ cando, bar cando, mit̕ serma, mit̕ dhao, bochor din, mit̕ dhaote, bar dhaote, bar dhao, pạhilte, pạhil, lahate, pạhilre, lahare, mạrańre, dinạm hilạk̇, ạuri, dinạm(ge), enan(re), enań(re)* eman.

Adọmak̉ Sọmọe Lạlạiak̉ bar dhao dohṛakate hõ sọmọe reak̉ họṛak̉ hewa lekako kạmia, pạrtul :-

(i) *Setak̉-setak̉iń* ṭahlaok̉kana.

(ii) *Setak̉-setak̉iń* kạmikana.

(iii) *Ạyup̉-ạyup̉iń* calak̉a.

(iv) *Serma-serma* khajna ẹmọk̉ hoyok̉kana.

(v) *Cando-cando* ẹmọk̉ hoyok̉kana.

(vi) *Din-din* inạge kạmi hoyok̉kana.

(vii) *Din-kẹ-dinko* calak̉kana.

(viii) *Cando-kẹ-candoko* calak̉kana.

(ix) *Serma-kẹ-sermako* dạṛjọṅkana.

Mare hapṛamko dọ nẹtar leka sọmọe bạḍae lạgit̉ ghạṛi emanko dọ baṅ tahẽkantakoa. Onate siń ar ńindạ lạgit̉ latarre ẹmakanak̉ lekate sọmọeko bạḍaejọṅkan tahẽkana. Ar onako dọ noṅkako ńutumakada :-

(i) Ghaṭao ńindạ (amdaj 1:00 baje ńindạ)

(ii) Maraṅ simrak̉ (amdaj 3:30 baje ńindạ khọn 4:00 baje simrak̉)

(iii) Huḍiń simrak̉ (maraṅ simrak̉ ọktẹ tayọm reak̉ sọmọe)

(iv) Paha poho (setagok̉ sọmọe ọktẹ laha reak̉ sọmọe)

(v) Pirtạṅ-pọrtọṅ (aṅga poho reak̉ ọktẹ reak̉ sọmọe)

(vi) Piạṅ-payaṅ(noa hõ pirtạṅ-pọrtọṅ ọktẹ reak̉ sọmọegey lạiet̉kana)

(vii) Gại aṛak̉ deladili (sẹ ọktẹ)

(viii) Setak̉ simrak̉ (cando rakap̉ laha reak̉ sọmọe)

(ix) Setak̉ ber rakap̉, jẹḍẹr, jẹḍẹr kẹṭẹc̉ (cando rakap̉ ọktẹ)

(x) Baskeak̉ (ber) (amdaj 9:00 baje setak̉ bela)

(xi) Bạsiạm ber (amdaj 9:00 baje setak̉ bela)

(xii) Khara bạsiạm (khara baskeak̕ bela) (amdaj 11:00 baje setak̕ bela)

(xiii) Tikin dela dili, tikin, tikin ńŏṛak̕ (loṛak̕) (amdaj 1:00 baje ạyup̕ bela)

(xiv) Maraṅ tarasiń (amdaj 2:00 baje ạyup̕ bela)

(xv) Huḍiń tarasiń (amdaj 3:00 baje ạyup̕ bela)

(xvi) Maraṅ dak̕ lo ber (amdaj 4:00 baje ạyup̕ bela)

(xvii) Huḍiń dak̕ lo ber (amdaj 5:00 baje ạyup̕ bela)

(xviii) Ber jhik-jhikạuk̕ (ber hạsurok̕ okte)

(xix) Ber hạsur (ạyup̕)

(xx) Gại ader jokhec̕ (ber hạsurok̕-hạsurok̕ tayom okte)

(xxi) Ńũhum (ńindạk̕ laha reak̕ okte)

(xxii) Gại ader harop̕ (gại goṛare ader okte tayom reak̕ somoe)

(xxiii) Mạci andhar (goṛare gại ader okte tayom khon hŏ tayom)

(xxiv) Kedok̕ jom (ńindạ daka jom okte reak̕ somoe)

(xxv) Kedok̕ jom harop̕ (kedok̕ jom tayom reak̕ okte)

(xxvi) Kaḍa ader jokhec̕ (kedok̕ jom laha reak̕ okte)

(xxvii) Kisạ̃ṛ hoṛ kedok̕ jom okte (kaḍa aderko okte reak̕ somoe)

(xxviii) Reṅgec̕ hoṛ kedok̕ jom okte (kaḍa aderko okte reak̕ somoe)

(xxxix) Gitic̕ jokhec̕

(xxx) Gitic̕ herep̕ (gitic̕ tayom reak̕ okte)

(xxxi) Gitic̕ saṛa sạtiń (be disạ jạpit̕ okte)

(xxxii) Tala ńindạ

(xxxiii) Mit̕ gitic̕ ebhen (amdaj tala ńindạ)

Hapṛamko dọ ipilko ńẹlkate hõ sọmọe reaḱ ńutumko ẹmadawada, jeleka :-

Buḍhi parkọm sidup̀ ọktẹ, sorenko koceyen ọktẹ eman.

Noa chaḍakate sọmọe lại lạgit́ *siń* ar *ńindạ* são cando dọhọlenkhanre hõ sọmọe reaḱe lạieťkana, jeleka :-

(i) *Siń cando rakaboḱ ọktẹ.*

(ii) *Ńindạ cando rakaboḱ ọktẹ.*

Inạkate noako hõ sọmọeye lạieťkana :-

ambas, amba bạsiạ, moloḱ cando eman.

Candoe moloḱlenkhan Họṛ họpọnre okaṭaḱ pạtiạu cọ menaḱte, uni dọ noṅkako joharaea - *Nãwã Cando Johar!*

bale moloḱ, moloḱ tikin, kunạmi, buru kunạmi, ọt kunạmi, kunạmi kecaḱ, ńirjạu dela dili (candoaḱ pon hĩsre mit́ hĩs reaḱ tala hisạ.)

ńirjạu (candoe dạṛ lahae reaḱ ọktẹ)

ńũtạt (kunạmi khọn ambas ọktẹ hạbiċ reaḱ ọktẹ)

Cetanre ẹmakan sanam dọ Sọmọe Lạlạiaḱ Kạjnum-Gunum kana. Cedaḱ ẹnte noa dọ Kạjnum họtẹte kạmie reaḱ sọmọeye lạieťkana.

Noa reaḱ bean dọ noṅka ẹm daṛeaḱa – Kạjnum-Gunum dọ onako metaḱa, ọnẹ okaṭaḱ dọ kạmi sẹ ghoṭna reaḱ sọmọe Kạj-num họtẹte lạiạgọḱkan.

ṬHẠ̃I LẠLẠIAḰ KẠJNUM-GUNUM *(ADVERB OF PLACE)*

Noa họtẹte ṭhạ̃i sẹ dike *(place or direction)* lạieťkana. Onate ṭhạ̃i sẹ dike lạieťkan iạte Kạjnum-Gunum reaḱe kạmieťkana, jeleka :-

(i) *Goṭa ṭaṇḍie* laṭiċ baṛakeda.

(ii) *Goṭa ṭaṇḍi* ḍam ḍaheyena.

(iii) Dayage *ṭaṇḍi-ṭikur*ko ńir baṛaekana.

No̱ṇḍe̱ *goṭa ṭaṇḍi, ṭaṇḍi-ṭikur* do̱ Ṭhãi Lạlạiak̓ Kạjnum-Gunum kana. Onka aema lekanak̓ menak̓a – *sanam ṭaṇḍi, noa sa(re)* (dik=*direction*), jeleka :-

(i) *hana sa(re)*	- (ṭhãi)
(ii) *no̱ paro̱m*	- (dik)
(iii) *ne̱ paro̱m*	- (dik)
(iv) *o̱n paro̱m*	- (dik)
(v) *e̱n paro̱m*	- (dik)
(vi) *ho̱n paro̱m*	- (dik)
(vii) *he̱n paro̱m*	- (dik)
(viii) *han paro̱m*	- (dik)
(ix) *laha-lahate*	- (dik)
(x) *lahare*	- (ṭhãi)
(xi) *laha se̱ċ*	- (dik)
(xii) *laha se̱ċre*	- (ṭhãi)
(xiii) *tayo̱m-tayo̱mte*	- (dik)
(xiv) *tayo̱mre*	- (ṭhãi)
(xv) *tayo̱m se̱ċ(te)*	- (dik)
(xvi) *tayo̱m*	- (dik)
(xvii) *tayo̱m se̱ċ(te)*	- (dik)
(xviii) *lahate*	- (dik)
(xix) *lahare*	- (ṭhãi)
(xx) *latar se̱ċ(te)*	- (dik)
(xxi) *latar se̱ċ(re)*	- (ṭhãi)

(xxii) *cetan(te)* - (dik)

(xxiii) *cetan(re)* - (ṭhại)

(xxiv) *cetan sẹċ(te)* - (dik)

(xxv) *cetan sẹċ(re)* - (ṭhại)

(xxvi) *cọṭ* - (dik)

(xxvii) *cọṭ(re)* - (ṭhại)

(xxviii) *cọṭ sẹċ(re)* - (ṭhại)

(xxix) *cọṭ(te)* - (dik)

(xxx) *cọṭ sẹċ(te)* - (dik)

(xxxi) *beṛhae* - (ṭhại)

(xxxii) *beṛhae(re)* - (ṭhại)

(xxxiii) *beṛhae sẹċ(re)* - (ṭhại)

(xxxiv) *beṛhae(te)* - (dik)

(xxxv) *beṛhae sẹċ(te)* - (dik)

(xxxvi) *bahre(te)* - (dik)

(xxxvii) *bahre(re)* - (ṭhại)

(xxxviii) *bahre sẹċ(re)* - (ṭhại)

(xxxix) *bahre sẹċ(te)* - (dik)

(xl) *bhitri* - (ṭhại)

(xli) *bhitri(te)* - (dik)

(xlii) *bhitri(re)* - (ṭhại)

(xliii) *aṛe-aṛe(te)* - (dik)

(xliv) aṛe(re) - (ṭhại)

(xlv) *dak̇ sẹċ(te)* - (dik)

(xlvi) *mucạt'(re)* - (ṭhại)

(xlvii) *raca(te)* - (dik)

oton̐-tayom - Noa do *Oton̐-tayom* Ṭhãi, Somoe, Ṭarika hõe lạigea.

Noa reak̉ bean do non̐ka em daṛeak̉a :- Ṭhãi Lạlạiak̉ Kạjnum-Gunum do onako metak̉a, one oka do kạmie reak̉ ṭhãi se dike lạiet̉kan.

Noako Somoe Lạlạiak̉ Kạjnum-Gunum do mit̉ bar ayatre laṛcaṛkatebo n̐ela :-

(i) Uni do *latar seċe* dạṛkeda.

(ii) Uni do *latar seċtey* dạṛkeda.

(iii) Uni do *laha-lahatey* calak̉kana.

(iv) Uni do jalapuri *on parome* calaoena.

(v) Uni do *ne parome* heċena.

(vi) Uni do *no parome* heċena.

(vii) *Hanasae* calaoena.

(viii) *Hanasare* menaea.

(ix) Uni *beṛhaetey* ạcurok̉kana.

(x) Uni *beṛhaereko* duṛup̉akana.

(xi) Kuḍạm *beṛhae seċreye* duṛup̉akana.

DHARA LẠLẠIAK̉ KẠJNUM-GUNUM *(ADVERB OF MANNER)*

Dhara/Ṭarika Lạlạiak̉ Kạjnum-Gunum do noae lạiet̉kana je Kạjnum *(Verb)* do cet̉ lekae kạmiet̉kana se oka lekae kạmiet̉kana. Kạjnum oka leka kạmik̉kana, ona reak̉ ḍhon̐ se ṭarika cet̉ lekana. Ona reak̉ metak̉me ona reak̉ cõhõk do cet̉ lekana. Kạjnum reak̉ cõhõktet̉ lạige Ṭarika Lạlạiak̉ Kạjnum-Gunumko metak̉a. Ona reak̉ pạrtul latarrebon n̐ela :-

(i) *Hako-pako* calak̉me.

(ii) *Hare-pharey* calaoena.

(iii) *Caṇḍa-cạṇḍe* calaoena.

(iv) *Odoṛ-dhopoṛe* calaoena.

(v) *E̱ke̱n* tie ruạṛena.

(vi) *Eskargeye* he̱ċena.

(vii) Ho̱ṛ *lekae* ńe̱lo̱ḱkana.

(viii) Bes *lekate* kạmime.

(ix) Sanam *lekatey* pạsuṛena.

(x) Ạḍi *lekatey* bujhạuadea.

(xi) *Bareakateko* jo̱mkeda.

(xii) *E̱ṛe̱kateko* ạsuloḱkana.

(xiii) *Duṛuṗkateko* jo̱meťkana.

(xiv) *Rańgaokateko calaoena.*

(xv) *Ạuṛiaḱtey* e̱ge̱rkana.

Noako ayatre beoharakana *hako-pako, hare-phare, e̱ke̱n ti, ho̱ṛ leka, bes lekate, ạḍi lekate, bareakate, e̱ṛe̱kate, odoṛ-dhopoṛ, duṛuṗkate, rańgaokate ar ạuṛiaḱte* do̱ *calaḱ, ruạṛ, he̱ċ, ńe̱l, kạmi, pạsuṛ, bujhạu, jo̱m, ạsul e̱ge̱r* reaḱ gune lạieťkana. Inạ chaḍa noako hõ̱ Kạjnum reaḱ gun se̱ ḍho̱ń se̱ tạrikae lạieťkana :-

jo̱rmo̱ṭte, miťte(ge), sulukte, mạńgnite, bạ̣i-bạ̣ite, jute-jutete, gitiċ-gitiċte, ho̱r-ho̱rte, taṛam-taṛamte, hiri-hirite, bogege, rạpuťge, se̱n go̱ť (doḱ), he̱ċ ńõ̱ḱ, dạṛ taṗ, tań-tań, ṭạń-ṭạń, ṭuń-ṭuń, ṭaṛań-ṭaṛań, ṭiṛiń-ṭiṛiń, ṭuṛuń-ṭuṛuń, ṭe̱ń-ṭe̱ń, ṭe̱ń-ṭe̱ṭe̱ń, ṭo̱ń-ṭo̱ń, ṭuń-ṭuṛuń, ke̱b-ke̱be̱, ke̱be̱-ke̱be̱, kib-kibi, kibạ-kobo, kibo̱-ko̱bo̱, kobo-kobo, kabaḱ-kabaḱ, kabaḱ-ko̱bo̱ḱ, ko̱bo̱ḱ-ko̱bo̱ḱ, kabaḱ-ko̱bo̱ḱ, kabaḱ-koboḱ, kạbui-kạbui, ko̱bo̱e-ko̱bo̱e, kibạ̣i-ko̱bo̱e, kạbuċ-kạbuċ, kubuċ-cubuċ, kabaṛ-koboṛ, kibiṛ-kibiṛ, koboṛ-koboṛ, kubuṛ-kubuṛ, kubuń-kubuń eman.

gas-gas, gas-gus, gis-gis, gus-gus, gasar-gasar, gasar-gusur, geser-geser, gisir-gisir, gisạr-gosor, gusur-gusur, gạsur-gạsur, gasaṛ-gosoṛ, gisạṛ-go̱so̱ṛ, gosoṛ-gosoṛ, gasrať-gosroť, gisrạť-gosroť, gasaṗ-gusuċ, ge̱se̱ċ-ge̱se̱ċ, gisiċ-gisiċ, gisoċ-gosoċ, gusuċ-gusuċ, gisạṅ-go̱so̱ṅ, go̱so̱ṅ-go̱so̱ṅ, gusuṅ-gusuṅ, giso-goso, gisạ-gase, gisạ-goso eman.

he̱j-he̱je̱, hij-hiji, hoj-hojo, huj-huju, hojo-hojo, he̱je̱-he̱je̱, hijạ-haje̱, hijo-ho̱jo̱, hojo-hojo eman.

lac-laca, le̱c-le̱ce̱, lo̱c-lo̱co̱, lạcuk̇-lạcuk̇, lacak̇-lucuk̇, laca-laca, le̱ce̱-le̱ce̱, licạ-lace̱, licạ-lo̱co̱, lo̱co̱k̇-lo̱co̱k̇ eman.

kar-kur, ker-ker, ko̱r-ko̱r, kạruċ-kạruċ, kạruṛ-kạruṛ, kạruṭ-bạruṛ, kạruċ-bạruċ, karaċ-karaċ, karaċ-kuruċ, ke̱re̱ċ-ke̱re̱ċ, ke̱re̱-ke̱re̱, kereċ-kereċ, kiriṛ-kiriṛ, kiro̱-kiro̱, kiro̱ċ-ko̱ro̱ċ, kiro̱ť-ko̱ro̱ť, ko̱ro̱ť-ko̱ro̱ť, kirạť-ko̱ro̱ť, ko̱ro̱-ko̱ro̱, koro-koro, ko̱ro̱ċ-ko̱ro̱ċ eman. Miť bar ayatre beoharkatebo ńe̱la :-

(i) *Ke̱re̱* dipilakada.

(ii) *Ko̱ro̱ť-ko̱ro̱ťe* dalkedea.

(iii) *He̱j-he̱je̱y* duṛuṗakana.

(iv) *Cucuṅguċtey* duṛuṗakana.

(v) *Paṭ gaṇḍokatey* duṛuṗakana.

(vi) *Tabe̱rkatey* gitiċakana.

(vii) *Sạmbirkatey* gitiċakana.

(viii) *Soṛtatey* gitiċakana.

(ix) *Siduṗtey* do̱ho̱akada.

(x) *Gaṇḍe̱tey* do̱ho̱akada.

(xi) *Rap-rapae* teṅgoakana.

(xii) *ṭap-ṭapae* teljoakada.

(xiii) *Piṛyạk̇-piṛyạk̇e* phandaeda.

Noako hǫ̃ Tạrika Lạlạiak̇ Kạjnum-Gunum kana :-

hãṛãk̇-paṭak̇, ota-tabe̱r, bhindae-bhindaete, hande̱t̕-ṭhape̱t̕, dhaoṛã-dhạuṭĩ, kaḍa-koḍo, jhạluṅ-ghạluṅ, jhalo̱ṅ-jhalo̱ṅ, kodoṛ-kodoṛ, diṛim-diṛim, ṭhae-ṭhae, thiạ-thape, do̱n-kocoṛ, harpa-hurpi, dapa-dạpi, andak̇-tawak̇, asok̇-ṭayok̇, kaḍaṅ-kuḍuṅ kodoṅ-kodoṅ, kaṛaṗ-kaṛaṗ, kaṛdhaṗ-kaṛdhaṗ, kaṛdhaṗ-kuṛdhuṗ, kharaṅ-khacaṅ, utut̕-tumbut̕, hạṇḍrạuate, rak̇ate, landawate eman.

Noṅkage aema utạr Kạjnum-Gunum hoe daṛeak̇a. No̱ṇḍe̱ ayatre beoharkate beste bujhạu lạgit̕ e̱mo̱go̱k̇kana :-

Uni gại do̱ *koboṅ-koboṅ* hoṛo jo̱me mohṇḍaena.

Noa ayatre *koboṅ-koboṅ* laṛcaṛakana. Noa *koboṅ-koboṅ* do̱ ce̱t̕ reak̇ gune lạiet̕kana? Abobon baḍaea je Kạjnum-Gunum orom lạgit̕ do̱ :- *(i) ce̱t̕ leka; (ii) ce̱t̕ lekate; (iii) oka lekate; (iv) okate; (v) oka se̱c̕; (vi) okare; (vii) tinre; (viii) tis; (ix) tisre; (x) oka hilạk̇; (xi) tisok̇; (xii) cedak̇; (xiii) tinạk̇ eman* ho̱te̱te Kạjnum sāo kuklilenkhan oka jobab ńamok̇, onage Kạjnum-Gunum do̱ko metak̇a. Cetanre e̱makan ayat reak̇gebon ạri bạndhilege:-

Kukli - *Ce̱t̕ lekae mohṇḍaena?*

Jobab - *Koboṅ-koboṅ*

No̱ṇḍe̱ ce̱t̕ leka reak̇ jobab do̱ *koboṅ-koboṅ* kana. Ona iạte *koboṅ-koboṅ* do̱ Tạrika Lạlạiak̇ Kạjnum-Gunum *(Adverb of Manner)* kana, o̱ne̱ oka do̱ Kạjnum *mohṇḍa* reak̇ gune lạiet̕kana.

BẠ̃ṚTI LẠLẠIAK̇ KẠJNUM-GUNUM *(ADVERB OF DEGREE)*

Noa Kạjnum-Gunum do̱ ona sabadko metak̇kana; o̱ne̱ oka do̱ Kạjnum-Gunum se̱ Gunum reak̇ge gune lạiet̕kan. Noa bujhạu lạgit̕ latar reak̇ ayatbo ńe̱la :-

(i) Ạḍi *jeleń* ho̱r kana.

(ii) Ạḍi *raṅgaokatey* dalkedea.

Noa ayatre *jeleń* do̱ gunum kana ar *raṅgaokate* do̱ Kạjnum-Gunum kana. *Jeleń* lahare *ạḍi* he̱c̓akana, o̱ne̱ oka do̱ bā̃ṛti jeleńe lạiet̓kan. Noakin ho̱te̱te *ho̱ṛ* reak̓ bā̃ṛti jeleńte̱t̓e lạiet̓kana. Onkage dosar ayatre beoharakan *ạḍi* ho̱te̱te *raṅgaote* reak̓ bā̃ṛti raṅgaote̱t̓e lạiet̓kana. Arhõ no̱ṇḍe̱ ayat e̱mo̱go̱k̓kana :-

(i) *Unạk̓ ḍher* do̱ bạń idia.

(ii) *Inạk̓ ko̱m* do̱ bạń hataoa.

(iii) *Tinạk̓ ḍherem* jo̱ma?

(iv) *Tinạk̓ raṅgaoem* dạṛa?

(v) *Ạḍi ce̱hra* kiminte̱t̓tae.

(vi) *Sạmạni mõ̱ńj* ńe̱lok̓kana!

(vii) *Ạḍi ā̃ṭ* hasokidińa.

(viii) *Ạḍi nase-nase* ro̱ṛme.

Noa ayatre:-

unạk̓ do̱ *ḍher* reak̓ gune lạiet̓kana.

inạk̓ do̱ *ko̱m* reak̓ gune lạiet̓kana.

tinạk̓ do̱ *ḍher* reak̓ gune lạiet̓kana.

tinạk̓ do̱ *raṅgao* reak̓ gune lạiet̓kana.

ạḍi do̱ *cehra* reak̓ gune lạiet̓kana.

ạḍi do̱ *ā̃ṭ* reak̓ gune lạiet̓kana.

ạḍi do̱ *nase-nase* reak̓ gune lạiet̓kana.

sạmạni do̱ *mõ̱ńj* reak̓ gune lạiet̓kana.

DHAO LẠLẠIAK̓ KẠJNUM-GUNUM
(ADVERB OF FREQUENCY)

Noa Kạjnum-Gunum ho̱te̱te Kạjnum tinạk̓ do̱m/dhaoe kạmiet̓kana. Noa reak̓ pạrtul latarre e̱mo̱go̱k̓kana :-

(i) Iń dǫ *mit' dǫmgeń* jǫmakada.

(ii) Uni dǫ *aema dhaoe* bhulakada.

(iii) Nitok̇ ar *tis hõ̱* bạń bạṛija.

(iv) Uni dǫ *jaogey* bạṛija.

Nǫṇḍe̱ :-

mit' dhao dǫ *jǫm* reak̇ gune lạiet̉kana.

aema dhao dǫ *bhul* reak̇ gune lạiet̉kana.

tis hõ̱ baṅ dǫ *bạṛij* reak̇ gune lạiet̉kana.

Jaoge dǫ *bạṛij* reak̇ gune lạiet̉kana.

Nǫṇḍe̱ *jǫm, bhul* ar *bạṛij* reak̇ kạmi dǫ tinạk̇ dhao hoyakana, ona reak̇ jobab dǫ *mit' dhao, aema dhao, tis hõ̱ baṅ* ar *jaoge* kana. Ona iạte noako dǫ Dhao Lạlạiak̇ Kạjnum-Gunum kana.

KUKLI KẠJNUM-GUNUM
(INTERROGATIVE ADVERB)

Kukli Kạjnum-Gunum dǫ ona sabadko metak̇kana, okaṭak̇te dǫ kạmi se̱ gun babǫte kuk̇likan. Kukli Ujnum oka dǫ adǫm jǫkhe̱ċ ayatre tayǫm japak̇ – *-te, -re, ṭhen, se̱ċ, khǫn, dhạbiċ, -wante hõ̱* Kạjnum-Gunum rupre laṛcaṛok̇kana, jeleka :-

(i) *Okatem* calak̇kana? *Okam* calak̇a?

(ii) *Okare* menak̇a?

(iii) *Oka se̱ċ* khǫnem hijuk̇kana?

(iv) *Oka ṭhen* menak̇a?

(v) *Oka khǫn* he̱ċena?

(vi) *Oka hạbiċ* calak̇a?

(vii) *Okare* hõ̱ baṅ ńamok̇a.

(viii) *Okate* hõ̱ baṅ calak̇a?

Nọṇḍẹ :-

okate hoṭẹte dọ ṭhā̦i lạgiť lạieťkana.

okare hoṭẹte dọ ṭhā̦i lạgiť lạieťkana.

oka sẹċ hoṭẹte dọ dike lạieťkana.

oka ṭhen hoṭẹte dọ ṭhā̦ie lạieťkana.

oka hạbiċ hoṭẹte dọ ṭhā̦i lạgiť isạraeda.

okate hõ baṅ hoṭẹte dọ ṭhā̦i lạgiť isạraeda.

ọkọr dọ Bẹjivianak̓ Oko Kuṛạiante Kạjnum-Gunum lekae kạmieťkana :-

(i) *Ọkọre* hẹċlena?

(ii) *Ọkọrem* sẹnlen?

(iii) Calak̓ dọ *ọkọrantae* kana?

(iv) *Ọkọrak̓takoa* ẹmọk̓ dọ?

Jivianak̓ Oko Kuṛạiante dọ noṅka :-

(i) *Okoriċe* hẹċlen?

(ii) *Okorko* onko dọ?

Kukli Kạjnum-Gunum dọ sọmọe reak̓ hõe lạieťkana :-

(i) *Tisok̓em* calak̓a?

(ii) *Tin dinem* tahẽna?

(iii) *Tin ọktẹm* calak̓a?

(iv) *Timin dinem* tahẽna?

(v) *Timinak̓rebo* sẹṭẹra?

(vi) *Tisbo* calak̓a?

Tayọm Japak̓ *(Postposition) – -re, khọn, jọkhẹċ, khọċ, hạbiċ, -te, -kore, -wante* hẹċlenkhan hõ sọmọe reak̓e lạieťkana :-

(i) *Tisrem* sạtakada?

(ii) Tis *khọnẹm* kạmikana?

(iii) Tis *dhạbiċem* kạmia?

(iv) *Tisre* hõ̤ baṅ hoyoḱa?

(v) Tis *jọkhẹċ* ńamoḱa?

(vi) *Tinre* ẹhọbọḱa?

(vii) Tin *khọċko* lalakana?

(viii) Tin *dhạbiċko* kạmia?

(ix) *Tinte* benaoḱa?

Adọm kukli Kạjnum-Gunum dọ tinạḱ ḍher/tinạḱ maraṅ reaḱ babọte lạieťkana, jeleka :-

(i) *Tin maraṅ?*

(ii) *Tin tiriťko* hạṭińana?

(iii) *Tin uḍiko* jọmkeda?

(iv) *Tin uḍiċe* halaṅkeda?

(v) *Timin maraṅe* haraena?

(vi) *Ẹhẹtiń* lẹdọr-pẹdọr gochare!

(vii) *Ẹhẹ-ẹhẹtạliń* jọṇḍra ata!

(viii) *Italaṅ* khại ata.

(ix) *I maraṅiń* ńẹlledea tạruṕ.

(x) *Ẹhẹ tiriťe* jọmeda.

Adọmaḱre -*aḱ* joṛaokate noṅka hoyoḱkana :-

(i) *Ninạḱko* ẹmadińạ.

(ii) *Nunạḱko* ẹmadińạ.

(iii) *Inạḱge* imạńme.

(iv) *Hạnạḱe* jọmkeda.

(v) *Unạḱ* phạdko dạṛkeda.

(vi) *Unąk* hoṛko heċlena.

Adomak̇ Kąjnum-Gunum do sor/sąṅgiń reak̇ hõe lạiet̕kana, jeleka :-

(i) *Inąk̇gan* sorok̇me.

(ii) *Unąk̇ jeleń* hor calak̇ hoyok̇a?

Adomak̇re *-te* ar *-re* joṛaokate ḍher ar kom reak̇e lạiet̕kana, jeleka :-

(i) *Inąk̇te* do bale aṇṭaok̇a.

(ii) *Nunąk̇re* hõ bape aṇṭaoak̇a?

Kukli Kąjnum-Gunum hotete Tạrika Lạlạiak̇ leka hõe kạmia. Noa do Kukli Ujnum *(Interrogative Pronoun)* são leka joṛaolenkhan ar ona sãote Tayom Japak̇ *(Postposition)-te,* se *-re* hõ lagaolenkhan hoyok̇kana, jeleka :-

(i) Cet̕ *lekam* taṛameda?

(ii) Cet̕ *lekate* hoyok̇a?

(iii) Cet̕ *lekare* peṛtaena?

(iv) Oka *lekam* kạmieda?

(v) Oka *lekateń* dohoea?

(vi) Oka *lekate* hõ bań jutuk̇a.

(vii) Cet̕ *lekam* dohoeda?

Noṇḍe :-

cet̕ leka do *taṛam* reak̇ tạrikae lạiet̕kana.

cet̕ lekate do *hoyok̇* reak̇ tạrikae lạiet̕kana.

cet̕ lekare do *peṛtaen* reak̇ karone lạiet̕kana.

oka leka do *kạmi* reak̇ tạrikae lạiet̕kana.

oka lekate hõ bań do *jut* reak̇ bań jutuk̇ reak̇ tạrikae lạiet̕kana.

ceka ar *hõ* Kukli Kąjnum-Gunum reak̇e kạmiet̕kana, jeleka

:-

(i) *Cekam* hẹċena?

(ii) *Ceka lekaniċ* kanam?

(iii) *Ceka lekankin* kanakin?

(iv) *Ceka lekanko* kanako?

(v) *Cekan lekaniċ* kanae?

(vi) *Cekan lekankin* kanakin?

(vii) *Cekan lekanko* kanako?

SỌMBỌND LẠLẠIAḰ KẠJNUM-GUNUM *(RELATIVE ADVERB)*

Noa Kạjnum-Gunum họtẹte dọ barea huḍiń ayate joṛaoeťkana, pạrtul :-

(i) Un hilạḱko calaolena *ọnẹ oka* hilạḱ dọ Sọhrae tahẽkan.

(ii) Iń baḍaea *ọkọe* dọko dallede.

(iii) Tinạḱem jọm *unạḱiń* ẹmama.

(iv) Ḍaṇḍọmkedeako *cedaḱ ẹntey* bạṛiċakada.

(v) Ọṇḍẹń calaḱa *okare* dọ suluk ạikạuḱ.

(vi) Onageń jọma *oka* dọ apepe jọm.

Nọṇḍẹ ayat no. (i) reaḱ *ọnẹ oka*; ayat no. (ii) reaḱ *ọkọe*; ayat no. (iii) reaḱ *unạḱ*; ayat no. (iv) *cedaḱ ẹnte*; ayat no. (v) reaḱ *okare dọ*; ayat no. (vi) *oka dọ* dọ eṭaḱ huḍiń ayat *hilạḱ dọ Sọhrae, dọko dalkedea, emama*, *bạṛiċakada, suluk ạikạuḱ* ar *apepe* jọm são sọmbọnde joṛaoeťkana. Onate ona dọ Sọmbọnd Lạlạiaḱ Kạjnum-Gunumko metaḱkana.

Nọṇḍẹ arhõ jạsti ńõḱ bujhạu lạgiť pạrtul ẹmọgọḱkana. Noabo baḍaegea je Kạjnum-Gunum baḍae lạgiť jãhãnaḱ ghoṭna hoyoḱ reaḱ *sọmọe, ṭhại, tạrika, ḍher-thoṛa* sẹ karọn babọt katha baḍae lạgit́ beoharok̀kana, pạrtul :-

(i) Oka serma amko baplalet́me *ona* serma dọ kạṭic̀geń tahẽkana. (sọmọe reak̀e lạiet́kana)

(ii) Okare Sidạko pạsikede *ọnḍẹ* dọ bạṛe dare menak̀a. (ṭhạ̃i reak̀e lạiet́kana)

(iii) Uni oka leka hoṛoe rọhọe daṛeak̀ iń hõ *onkageń* rọhọe daṛeak̀a. (tạrika)

(iv) Oka-oka jọkhẹc̀ Santalko kọclọn ocolena *un-un-ọktẹ* Jahẹr Erae sọdọrlena. (sọmọe)

(v) Jẹmọnge huḍurkeda *tẹmọnge* cẹṭẹr ńũr gọt́ena. (sọmọe)

(vi) Noa nahel dọ ọnḍẹge dọhọ oṭokak̀me *okare dọ* tahẽkan. (ṭhạ̃i)

(vii) Cẹt́ leka ińiń mẹnjọṅkan *onka* bań hoyok̀kana.(tạrika)

(viii) Tinạk̀ amem khọjkan *unạk̀* bạń ẹm daṛeama. (ḍher-thoṛa)

(ix) Noa gharõńjren kimin kạnạń, *ona iạte* ińak̀ hõ họk menak̀tińạ. (karọn)

(x) Judi amem mẹnjọṅkhan *tọbẹ* ińiń gọṛọama. (karọn)

(xi) Judi ińak̀ katham ańjọma *tọbẹ* ḍạnḍọm khọnem bańcaok̀a. (karọn)

(xii) Ḍạr mak̀ giḍikam *jẹmọn* sisir ńũruk̀. (karọn)

(xiii) Paesa imạńe mẹnẹt́re hõ *ẹnhõń* lajaok̀kana. (karọn)

Rọṛ reak̀ mọtlọb dọ noage je okaṭak̀ sabad barea ayate joṛaoet́kan ar *tạrika, sọmọe, ṭhạ̃i, ḍher-kọm, karọn, ekraṛ, pontha* bak̀ḍae sabad bik̀rudak̀ baḍae katha baḍaeok̀kan, ona dọ Sọmbọnd Kạjnum-Gunum sabadko metak̀kana.

ISẠRA KẠJNUM-GUNUM *(DEMONSTRATIVE ADVERB)*

Santali pạrsire Kạjnum-Gunum dọ aemak̕gea. Isạra Kạjnum-Gunum sabad họtẹte jãhãnak̕ jinis reak̕ sor-sạṅgiń babọt kathae lạiet̕kana. Bean *(defination)* lekatebo ńẹllekhać noṅka mẹnọgọk̕a – Isạra Kạjnum-Gunum dọ onako metak̕a, ọnẹ okaṭak̕ sabad họtẹte jãhãnak̕ jinis reak̕ sor sẹ sạṅgińre menak̕ reak̕ kathae lạiet̕kana. Sãote ṭhạ̃i reak̕ katha hõe lạiet̕kana,

jeleka :-

(i) *nọṇḍẹ* - Nahel dọ *nọṇḍẹ* menak̕a.

(ii) *nẹṇḍẹ* - *Nẹṇḍẹgebo* duṛup̕a.

(iii) *ọṇḍẹ* - *ọṇḍẹ* laeme.

(iv) *ẹṇḍẹ* - *ẹṇḍẹge* duṛup̕me.

(vi) *họṇḍẹ* - *họṇḍẹ* menak̕a.

(v) *haṇḍẹ* - *haṇḍẹ menak̕a.*

(vi) *hẹṇḍẹ* - *hẹṇḍẹ menak̕a.*

Okaṭak̕ Kạjnum-Gunum sabad lahare ẹtọhọp̕re *n* menak̕, ona sabad họtẹte dọ sor jaegare jãhãnak̕ menak̕ reak̕e isạraet̕kana, jeleka – *nẹṇḍẹgebo* duṛup̕a.

Okaṭak̕ Kạjnum-Gunum sabad reak̕ ẹtọhọp̕re Bẹhạṭińõk̕ Harọp *(Vowel)* metak̕me -*ẹ* hẹćlenkhan, ona sabad họtẹte dọ *ẹṇḍẹ* sabad thoṛa sạṅgiń ṭhạ̃i reak̕e isạraet̕kana, jeleka – *ẹṇḍẹge* duṛup̕tabonpe.

Okaṭak̕ Kạjnum-Gunum sabad ẹtọhọp̕re -*h* tahẹnkana, ona sabad họtẹte dọ noae isạraet̕kana je okaṭak̕ ṭhạ̃i thoṛa sạṅgińak̕ ṭhạ̃i reak̕ thoṛagan sạṅgiń reak̕e lạiet̕kana, jeleka – *haṇḍẹ* teṅgok̕me.

Adọm jọkhẹć abo Họṛ dọ -*n* sãote -*h* harọp milạukate -*nh* ãṭ aṛań *(aspirate)*bo laṛcaṛet̕kana, jeleka – *nh – nhaṇḍẹ, nhẹṇḍẹ,* *nhoṇḍe.*

Adom jokheċ abo Hoṛ noako sabad joṛare dohokate hõbo beohareťkana. Menkhan thoṛa sabad lahare Beḥaṭińõk Harop *(Vowel)* ar Haṭińõk Harop *(Consonant)* ar Ãṭ Aṛaṅ *(aspirate)* harop beoharkate bodolokkana, jeleka :-

oṇḍe – noṇḍe	*oṇḍe – nhoṇḍe*
eṇḍe – nheṇḍe	*eṇḍe – neṇḍe*
haṇḍe – nhoṇḍe	*haṇḍe – nhaṇḍe*

Adomak noṅkan Isaṛa Kajnum-Gunum sabad hõ ńamokkana, oka do Hoṛ hopon teheń khon 160 serma lahakoreko beohareťkan tahẽkana. Onako sabad do noako kana – *neman, eman,noman* ar *oman* eman. Ayatrebo ńela :-

(i) *neman* - *Nemanre doń calaoakana.*

(ii) *noman* - *Nomanre doń calaoakana.*

(iii) *oman* - *Oman darakate doń dãṛãwakada.*

(iv) *eman* - *Iń khonak eman darateko senena.*

Cetanre emakan Isaṛa Kajnum-Gunum são Tayom Japak *(Postposition)* lagaolenkhan hõ Kajnum-Gunum lekae kamia, jeleka :-

(i) *noṇḍe* - *Noṇḍere ńelogok.*

(ii) *hoṇḍere* - *Hoṇḍerebon ńela.*

(iii) *eṇḍere* - *Eṇḍerebon ńela; eṇḍerema bogege.*

(iv) *noṇḍe khon* - *Noṇḍe khon calakme.*

(v) *noṇḍe habiċ* - *Noṇḍe habiċ laeme.*

(vi) *haṇḍe lagiť* - *Haṇḍe lagiť idieme.*

(vii) *noṇḍeaneċ* - *Noṇḍeaneċ atu ocoakme.*

Adomak Isaṛa Kajnum-Gunum do *dik (direction)* reak hõe isaṛaeťkana. Noa Kajnum-Gunum sãote *-te* Tayom Japak

(Postposition) lagaokate mit̕ṭe̱n nãwã sabade benaoet̕kana, metak̕me banar hạṭiń milạukate mit̕ṭe̱n nãwã sabad benaok̕kana, jeleka :-

(i) *no̱te̱* - *no̱te̱ hijuk̕me.*

(ii) *ne̱te̱* - *ne̱te̱ hijuk̕me.*

(iii) *o̱nte̱* - *o̱nte̱ calak̕me.*

(iv) *e̱nte̱* - *e̱nte̱ ńõ̱go̱k̕me.*

(v) *he̱nte̱* - *he̱nte̱ ńõ̱go̱k̕me.*

(vi) *ho̱nte̱* - *ho̱nte̱ ńõ̱go̱k̕me.*

(vii) *hante̱* - *hante̱ ńõ̱go̱k̕me.*

(viii) *nhe̱te̱* - *nhe̱te̱ ńõ̱go̱k̕me.*

(ix) *nho̱te̱* - *nho̱te̱ ńõ̱go̱k̕me.*

(x) *nhate̱* - *nhate̱ ńõ̱go̱k̕me.*

Ado̱mak̕ Isạra Kạjnum-Gunum sãote *-te* ar *se̱c̕* lagaokate *dik* reak̕e isạraet̕kana. Ar *kho̱n* se̱ *-re̱* lagaokate hõ̱ eṭak̕ *dik* reak̕e isạraet̕kana, pạrtul :-

no̱te̱te̱, ne̱te̱te̱, ho̱nte̱te̱, he̱nte̱te̱, e̱nte̱te̱, o̱nte̱te̱, e̱nte̱te̱, hante̱te̱, nho̱te̱te, nhe̱te̱te̱, nhate̱te̱, no̱te̱ se̱c̕, no̱te̱re̱, hante̱re̱, no̱te̱ se̱c̕re̱, ne̱te̱ kho̱n, no̱te̱ kho̱n eman.

Ado̱mak̕ Isạra Kạjnum-Gunum joṛare he̱c̕kate hõ̱ laṛcaṛok̕kana, jeleka :-

o̱nte̱-no̱te̱, o̱nte̱-nho̱te̱, e̱nte̱-ne̱te̱, e̱nte̱-nhe̱te̱, he̱nte̱-nho̱te̱, hante̱-nhate̱, he̱nte̱-nho̱te̱ eman.

Ado̱mak̕ Isạra Kạjnum-Gunum onkanak̕ hõ̱ menak̕a, oka do̱ Gun ar Tạrika *(Manner)* reak̕e isạraet̕kan. Nońkanak̕ Kạjnum-Gunum benao lạgit̕ *non, on, nen, en, hon, hen, han* sãote *-ko* joṛaokate hoyok̕kana, jeleka :-

(i) *non + ka* = *nonka*

(ii) *on+ ka* = *onka*

(iii) *nen+ka* = *nenka*

(iv) *en+ka* = *enka*

(v) *hon ka* = *honka*

(vi) *han+ka* = *hanka*

(vii) *hen+ka* = *henka*

(viii) *nhon+ka* = *nhonka*

(ix) *nhen+ka* = *nhenka*

(x) *nhan+ka* = *nhanka*

Cetanre ẹmakan sanam Kạjnum-Gunumre leka toṅgelen khan noa lekan Kạjnum-Gunum benaok̇kana, ọnẹ oka dọ cetanre ẹmakan. Ẹkẹn ńẹlọk̇ lekate begar ńẹlọk̇kana, mane dọ mit̓gea sẹ manere *(meaning)* jãhãn begar dọ bạnuk̇a. Noa reak̇ pạrtul dọ latarre ẹmọgọk̇kana :-

noṅka leka, nenka leka, onka leka, enka leka, honka leka, henka leka, honka leka, nhonka leka, nhenka leka, nhanka leka eman.

Adọmak̇ Ujnumre *(Pronoun)* Ńunumre leka toṅgelenkhan hõ Kạjnum-Gunum lekae kạmiet̓kana sẹ eṭak̇ sabadre toṅgelenre hõ hoyok̇kana, jeleka :- *noa leka, am leka, dak̇ leka, toa leka* eman.

Adọmak̇ Isạra Kạjnum-Gunum gun ar tạrika lại lạgit̓ Tayọm Japak̇ *(Postposition)* *-te* ar *-re* lagaokate hõ benaok̇kana, jeleka - *onkate, enkate, enkare, enka lekate* eman.

Adọmak̇ Kạjnum-Gunum *n* toṅgekate dohṛalenkhan hõ hoyok̇kangea, jeleka :-

(i) *onka* - *noṅka*

(ii) *onka* - *nhonka/nonka*

(iii) *enka* - *nenka*

(iv) *enka* - *nhenka/henka*

(v) *honka* - *nonka/nhonka*

(vi) *honka* - *nhonka*

(vii) *enka* - *nenka; eman.*

Adọmaḱ Isạra Lạlạiaḱ Ujnum *(Demonstrative Pronoun)* reaḱ ẹtọhọṗ reaḱ harọp bọdọl ńõḱkate ọllenkhan Isạra Kạjnum-Gunum reaḱe kạmieťkana, jeleka :-

(i) *nun* - *Nun marań* bin dọ bạń ńẹlakaťkoa.

(ii) *nin* - *Nin marań* hakoń saṗledea.

(iii) *un* - *Un marańak* dọń cekaea.

(iv) *in* - *In marańaḱ* dọń cekaea.

(v) *nhun* - *Nhun marań* họṛ dọ bạń ńẹlakaťkoa.

(vi) *nhin* - *Nhin marań* hakoń saṗledea.

(vii) *nhạn* - *Nhạn marańaḱ* ạguime.

Cetanre ẹmakan Kạjnum-Gunumko dọ ḍher/thoṛa reaḱ hõẹ lạieťkana. Mẹnkhan *-ạḱ* joṛaoanẹċgey kạmia, jeleka :-

(i) *nunạḱ* - *Nunạḱ ḍher* daka dọ bạń cabaea.

(ii) *unạḱ* - *Unạḱ thoṛa* dọ bạń hataoa.

(iii) *ninạḱ* - *Ninạḱ kọm* hoṛo dọ bạń idia.

(iv) *inạḱ* - *Inạḱ kọm* paesa dọ bạń hataoa.

(v) *nhunạḱ* - *Nhunạḱ* poṇḍ kicriċ dọ bạń kirińa.

(vi) *nhinạḱ* - *Nhinạḱ kọm* sunum dọń cekaea.

(vii) *nhạnạḱ* - *Nhạnạḱ* jeleń bińiń ńẹlledea.

nun, un, nin, in emanko dọ sọmọe reaḱ hõẹ lạieťkana, jeleka :

(i) *nun* - *Nun serma* dọ cẹťem cekaeťkan tahẽkana?

(ii) *un* - *Un din* dọ cẹt́em cekaet́kan tahẽkana?

(iii) *nin* - *Nin din* dọ cẹt́pe ńamkana?

(iv) *in* - *In din* dọ cedak̓pe thirakan tahẽkana?

(v) *in* - *Inanẹċpe* sạtkeda?

(vi) *in* - *In dhao* dọ cedak̓pe ạcurkeda?

Santalire dọ noako Isạra Kạjnum-Gunumko hõ beoharok̓kana, jeleka :

(i) *numin* - *Numin din* dọ okarem tahẽkana?

(ii) *numin* - *Numin marań* dhạrti dọ bhala tọkọe haleye benaolet́a?

(iii) *nimin* - *Nimin din* dọ mại tokarem tahẽkana?

Noako hahaṛa lạlạiak̓ sabadko ḍher/thoṛa/marań/uḍiċ/uḍi reak̓ lạlại tuluċ Isạra Kạjnum-Gunum reak̓e kạmiet́kana, jeleka :-

(i) *nẹ* - *Nẹ ninạk̓le* halańkeda.

(ii) *ẹhẹ* - *Ẹhẹ tirit́tako* rọkọċ jel!

(iii) *ẹhẹ* - *Ẹhẹ marań* hakoko sap̓akadea.

(iv) *i* - *I marań* bińiń ńẹlakadea.

(v) *nẹ* - *Nẹ uḍi* jọmme.

(vi) *ẹhẹ* - *Ẹhẹ tirit́e* jọmet́a.

un, in, nin, *-re* ar *-te* lagaolenkhan sọmọe reak̓e lạiet́kana ar sọmọe reak̓e lạiet́khan Kạjnum-Gunumge lekhak̓kana, jeleka :-

(i) *unre* - *Unre* cẹt́em cekakeda?

(ii) *inre* - *Inre* họtẹċem sẹnlen khanem paṛaokok̓a.

(iii) *inte* - *Inte* amak̓ kạmi hoekok̓a.

(iv) *ninte* - *Cẹt́* adọm teṅgoakana, ninte amak̓ kạmi benaokok̓a.

(v) *inkote* - *Inkote* kạmi hoekok̓tama.

(vi) *onkate* - *Onkatege* ona ghoṭna do̠ hoyena.

Ado̠mak̓ Isạra Ujnum-Gunum lekae kạmiet̓kana, jeleka :-

inạk̓gan sorok̓me; unạk̓ phẹḍ; unạk̓ marañ dare; unạk̓ ho̠ṛ; inạk̓ usul dare; ninạk̓e emadińạ; unạk̓ena eman.

Noako sabadre *-te* ar *–re* lagaokate hõ̠ Kạjnum-Gunum reak̓e kạmiet̓kana, jeleka :-

(i) *inạk̓te* - *Inạk̓te* do̠ ce̠t̓ hoyok̓a?

(ii) *nunạk̓re* - *Nunạk̓re* hõ̠ bape aṇṭaok̓a.

Santali reak̓ ado̠mak̓ Isạra Kạjnum-Gunum bar do̠m dohṛalenkhan Ńunum, Gunum ar Kạjnum reak̓e kạmiet̓kana, jeleka :-

(i) *unạk̓-unạk̓* - *Unạk̓-unạk̓* ho̠ṛ. (Gunum rupre)

(ii) *inạk̓-ninạk̓* - *Inạk̓-ninạk̓et̓kanae.* (Kạjnum)

Santali reak̓ sanam Isạra Kạjnum-Gunum do̠ Isạra Ujnum lekae kạmia. Judi ona lahare Isạra Ujnum reak̓ kạṭić rup metak̓me *un, on, o̠n, in, en, e̠n, hun, ho̠n, he̠n, han, hạn* joṛaokate ona tayo̠m -e̠ lagaolenre noṅka beoharok̓kana – *o̠ne̠, e̠ne̠, ane̠, ho̠ne̠, he̠ne̠, hane̠, hune̠* emanko.

Ado̠mak̓ do̠ ṭhã̠i udug lạgit̓ noṅkanak̓ hõ̠ beoharok̓kana ar Kạjnum-Gunumgey kạmieda – *o̠n-o̠ṇḍe̠; o̠ne̠-o̠ṇḍe̠; e̠ṇḍe̠; e̠ne̠-e̠ṇḍe̠; he̠n-he̠ṇḍe̠; he̠ne̠-he̠ṇḍe̠; han-haṇḍe̠; hane̠-haṇḍe̠; ho̠n-ho̠ṇḍe̠; he̠ne̠-he̠ṇḍe̠; o̠n-e̠nte̠; han-hante̠; o̠ne̠-onka; han-hanka; un-unạk̓; in-inạk̓; o̠ne̠-unạk̓; e̠ne̠-inạk̓; hạn-hạnạk̓; hạn-hạnạñ* emanko.

Ado̠mak̓ Kạjnum-Gunum lahare *n* he̠ćkate jivianak̓ ar be̠jivianak̓ babo̠te uduk̓et̓kana, jeleka – *nuk̓ui no̠ṇḍe̠; nik̓i ne̠te̠; nõ̠k̓õ̠e no̠ṇḍe̠; ne̠k̓e̠ ne̠ṇḍe̠* eman.

Ado̠m-ado̠m jaegaren Santal metak̓me Baṅgal reak̓ uttạr

nakharen Santal, Asamren Họṛ họpọnko dọ sanam Isạra Ujnum, Kạjnum-Gunum rupre beoharok̇ Isạra Kạjnum-Gunum reak̇ mucạt̔ Bẹhạṭiṅọ̃k̇ Harọpre *-n* joṛaokate noṅkanak̇ sabadko beohareťkana. Inạkate dạkhin-pạchim Baṅgal ar Uṛisaren Họṛ họ̃ *-n* ante beoharok̇ sabadko beohareťkana. *-n* joṛaokate jaoge beoharok̇a mẹnte P. O. Boḍiṅ dọ dạlile ẹmọk̇kana, jeleka :-

(i) *Onako* kangea aleak̇ dọ.

(ii) *Onan* dharae ạikạuk̇kana.

(iii) *Unin* kanae.

(iv) Noko họ̃ko *onkangea.*

(v) *Inạn* họṛako.

(vi) Onko tinạk̇ menak̇ko, noko họ̃ko *inạnena.*

(vii) *Ọnẹn ọnẹn* dọ cẹt̔ kana?

(viii) *Ọnẹnić* dọe aleić kana.

(ix) *Ọtẹnak̇* dọ cẹt̔ aṅjọmọk̇kana.

(x) *Ọtẹnko.*

ọṇḍẹn; ọṇḍẹnak̇; ọṇḍẹnić; ọntẹnić; ọntẹnkin; ọntẹko; ọntẹnak̇; ọntẹnak̇kin; ọntẹnak̇ko; onkan; onkanić; onkankin; onkanko; onkanak̇; onkanak̇kin; onkanak̇ko.

uni lekan; uni lekanić; uni lekankin; uni lekanko; onka lekan; onka lekanić; onka lekankin; onka lekanko; onka lekanak̇; onka lekanak̇kin; onka lekanak̇ko; onkan lekan, onkan lekanić; onkan lekankin; onkan lekanko; onkan lekanak̇; onkan lekanak̇kin; onkan lekanak̇ko; nẹṇḍẹren; nẹṇḍẹrenić; nẹṇḍẹrenkin; nẹṇḍẹrenko. nọtẹren; nọtẹrenić; nọtẹrenkin; hantẹrenko; hantẹten; hantẹtenić; hantẹtenkin; hantẹtenko eman.

BẸNIṬ UJNUM KẠJNUM-GUNUM
(INDEFINITE PRONOMINAL ADVERB)

Bẹniṭ Ujnum-Kạjnum-Gunum dọ onageko metaḱa, okaṭaḱ dọ Ujnum dọ bẹniṭ reaḱe lạieťkan. Mẹnkhan Kạjnum-Gunum lekae kạmieťkana. Noa reaḱ dọ *jãhã* kana. Noare Tayọm Japaḱ *(Postposition) -re, sẹċ, tinre/tisre* leka aema lagaoḱkana. Noa sabad tayọmre *-n* joṛaolenkhan Gunumre *(Adjective)* bọdọlọḱkana. Nitoḱ bẹgọr *-n* te benaoakan Kạjnum-Gunumbo ńẹla, jeleka :-

(i) *Jãhãgem* calaḱ idi torayińme.

(ii) *Jãhãre* baṅ ńamoḱa.

(iii) *Jãhãte* alom calaḱa.

(iv) *Jãhã sẹċ* alom calaḱa.

(v) *Jãhã khọn* ạguime.

(vi) *Jãhã* tinạḱem rọṛ bako bataotama.

(vii) *Jãhãtinre* hijuḱme.

(viii) *Jãhãtisre* hoelena.

(ix) *Jãhãtis jãhãtis* hẹċ baṛaḱme.

(x) *Jãhãtin jãhãtinrey* hẹċ baṛaḱgea.

(xi) *Jãhã lekate* hijuḱme.

(xii) *Jãhã tãhã (kãhã)* alom calaḱa.

(xiii) *Jãhã tãhã/jãhãn tãhãn* alom calaḱa.

(xiv) *Jãhãman tãhã* alom daṛana.

(xvi) *Jãhãnman tãhãn* alom calaḱa.

(xvii) *Jande mande* alom tahẹna.

(xviii) *Jande tande* alom daṛana.

(xix) *Jandeman tande* alom calaḱa.

(xx) *Jande mande* alom calaḱa.

(xxi) *Jane tane* alom calaḱ.

(xxii) *Jane man tande* alom dạṛa.

jãhã tayom jạruṛaḱ lekanaḱ Tayom Japaḱ lagaokate Kạjnum-Gunum reaḱe kạmietḱana.

ẠKIL BHAŃJAO - 9

A. Ṭoyot'kate jobab emoḱme :-

1. Kạjnum-Gunum do tinạḱ lekana?
   (a) 8 (b) 9 (c) 5 (d) 7

2. *serma ke serma* do okaṭaḱ Kạjnum-Gunum kana?
   (a) Somoe Lạlạiaḱ Kạjnum-Gunum (b) Sombond Lạlạiaḱ Kạjnum- Gunum (c) Isạra Kạjnum-Gunum
   (d) Kukli Kạjnum-Gunum

3. *on parom* do okaṭaḱ Kạjnum-Gunum kana?
   (a) Ṭhại Lạlạiaḱ Kạjnum-Gunum
   (b) Sombond Lạlạiaḱ Kạjnum-Gunum
   (c) Isạra Kạjnum-Gunum (d) Kukli Kạjnum-Gunum

4. *sạmạni mõń* do okaṭaḱ Kạjnum-Gunum kana?
   (a) Ṭhại Lạlạiaḱ Kạjnum-Gunum
   (b) Bạ̃ṛti Lạlạiaḱ Kạjnum-Gunum
   (c) Isạra Kạjnum-Gunum (d) Kukli Kạjnum-Gunum

5. *jãhãtis jãhãtis* do okaṭaḱ Kạjnum-Gunum kana?
   (a) Beniṭ Ujnum Kạjnum-Gunum
   (b) Bạ̃ṛti Lạlạiaḱ Kạjnum-Gunum
   (c) Isạra Kạjnum-Gunum (d) Kukli Kạjnum-Gunum

B. O̱lkate jobab e̱mo̱k̓me :-

1. Kạjnum-Gunum do̱ ce̱t̓ko metak̓a?
2. Kajnum-Gunum do̱ tinạk̓ lekana? Ona reak̓ ńutum o̱lme.
3. Ṭhą̃i lạlạiak̓ Ujnum-Gunum *(Adverb of place)* do̱ ce̱t̓ko metak̓a? Pạrtul hõ̱ lạime.
4. So̱mo̱e Lạlạiak̓ Kạjnum-Gunum *(Adverb of Time)* do̱ ce̱t̓ko metak̓kana? Pạrtul hõ̱ lạime.
5. Dhara Lạlạiak̓ Kạjnum-Gunum *(Adverb of Manner)* do̱ ce̱t̓ko metak̓a? Pạrtul hõ̱ lạime.
6. Bą̃ṛti Lạlạiak̓ Kạjnum-Gunum *(Adverb of Degree)* do̱ ce̱t̓ko metak̓kana? Pạrtul hõ̱ lạime.
7. Dhao Lạlạiak̓ Kạjnum-Gunum *(Adverb of Frequency)* do̱ ce̱t̓ko metak̓kana? Pạrtul hõ̱ lạime.
8. Kukli Kạjnum-Gunum *(Interrogative Adverb)* do̱ ce̱t̓ko metak̓kana? Pạrtul hõ̱ lạime.
9. So̱mbo̱nd Lạlạiak̓ Kạjnum-Gunum *(Relative Adverb)* do̱ ce̱t̓ko metak̓kana? Pạrtul hõ̱ lạime.
10. Isạra Kạjnum-Gunum *(Demonstrative Adverb)* do̱ ce̱t̓ko metak̓kana? Pạrtul hõ̱ lạime.
11. Be̱niṭ Ujnum Kạjnum-Gunum *(Indefinite Pronominal Adverb)* do̱ ce̱t̓ko metak̓kana? Pạrtul hõ̱ e̱mme
12. *Nitre* do̱ okaṭak̓ Kạjnum-Gunum reak̓ sabad kana?
13. *Serma serma khajna e̱mo̱k̓ hoyok̓kana.*, noa ayatre laṛ caṛakan *serma serma* do̱ okaṭak̓ Kạjnum-Gunum reak̓ sabad kana?
14. *Marań simrak̓* o̱kte̱ do̱ amdaj tin jo̱khe̱ć reak̓ o̱kte̱ kana?
15. *Huḍiń simrak̓* o̱kte̱ do̱ tin jo̱khe̱ć reak̓ o̱kte̱ kana ?
16. *Paha poho* do̱ tin jo̱khe̱ć reak̓ o̱kte̱ kana?

17. *Pirto̱ṅ po̱rto̱ṅ* do̱ tin jo̱khe̱c̓ reak̓ o̱kte̱ kana?
18. *Piạṅ payaṅ* do̱ tin jo̱khe̱c̓ reak̓ o̱kte̱ kana?
19. *Gạí aṛak̓ deladili* do̱ tin jo̱khe̱c̓ reak̓ o̱kte̱ kana?
20. *Hanasare* do̱ okaṭak̓ Kạjnum Gunum sabad kana?
21. *he̱jhe̱je̱* sabad do̱ okṭak̓ Kạjnum-Gunum kana?
22. *unạk̓ ḍher* sabad do̱ okṭak̓ Kạjnum-Gunum kana?
23. *mit̓ do̱m* sabad do̱ okaṭak̓ Kạjnum-Gunum kana?
24. *oka hạbic̓* sabad do̱ okṭak̓ Kạjnum-Kunum kana?
25. *oka oka..un un* sabad do̱ okaṭak̓ Kạjnum Gunum kana?
26. *o̱n -o̱ṇḍe̱* sabad do̱ okaṭak̓ Kạjnum-Gunum kana?
27. *Caṇḍa cạṇḍie calaoena.* Noa ayat reak̓ *caṇḍa cạṇḍi* sabad okaṭak̓ Kạjnum-Gunum kana?
28. *Hãṛãk̓ paṭak̓e calaoena.* Noa ayat reak̓ *hãṛãk̓ paṭak̓* sa bad do̱ okaṭak̓ Kạjnum-Gunum kana?
29. *Ạḍi jeleṅ ho̱r kana.* Noa ayat reak̓ *ạḍi* do̱ okaṭak̓ Kạjnum-Gunum sabad kana?
30. *Tinạk̓em jo̱m, unạk̓iṅ e̱mama.* Noa ayat reak̓ *unạk̓* do okaṭak̓ Kạjnum-Gunum kana
31. *Oka hạbic̓em calak̓a?* Noa ayat reak̓ *oka hạbic̓* do̱ okaṭak̓ Kạjnum-Gunum reak̓ sabad kana?
32. *Tis hõ baṅ* do̱ okaṭak̓ Kạjnum-Gunum kana?

10

KẠJNUM
(VERB)

KẠJNUM – Noa sabadte cẹť bujhạuk̇kana? Kạjnum reak̇ mọtlọb dọ kạmi *(action).* Beakọrọn reak̇ ạn lekate jãhã lekanak̇ kạmige Kạjnum mẹnọgọk̇kana. Cahem *rak̇eťkan, landaeťkan, sahẹťeťkan, gitiċkan, sieťkan, gẹťakan, cahem duṛup̣kan, cahem jọmeťkan, manwa sẹ misin họtẹte kạmik̇kan;* noako sanam kạmi Beakọrọn reak̇ ạn sẹ pạrsi lekate Kạjnum *(Verb)* kana.

rọṛ, landa, gitiċ, duṛup̣, ẹḍhẹ, phanda, dạṛ, calak̇, dal, ńẹl, hẹċ idi, ạgu, lại, ir, aṛe, benao, ńir, sap̣, ńẹpẹl, dadal, jọjọm, ṭhẹp̣, ṭhẹṭhẹp̣, ẹr, ạulạu, unum, họrọk̇ eman-eman. Metak̇me; okaṭak̇ sabadte jãhãnak̇ kạmi hoyok̇ sẹ kạk̇mi baḍaeok̇kan, onage Kạjnum dọ.

Santali pạrsi reak̇ miťṭẹn nońkan gun menak̇a, ọnẹ oka dọ eṭak̇ pạrsire bạnuk̇. Ar ona dọ noage je sanam lekan sabadge Kạjnum reak̇ hõe kạmi daṛeak̇a sẹy kạmikana. Ar adọm jọkhẹċ dọ Ńunum rupre hõe kạmieťkana, jeleka :–

(i) *dạṛ* – Setak̇re *dạdạṛ* dọ họṛmọ lạgiť ran kana. (Ńunum- *Noun*)

(ii) *khok̇* – *Khok̇* ańjọmọk̇kana. (Ńunum-*Noun*)

(iii) *khok̇* – *Khok̇te* họṛmọ bạṛijok̇kana. (*Khok̇* dọ họṛmọe bạṛija.) (Ńunum-*Noun*)

Santalire Ńunum hõ Kạjnum reak̇e kạmieťkana, pạrtul :–

(i) *sakam* - *Sarjọm* sakamok̇kana.

(ii) *baha* - Sarjọm *bahak̇kana.*

Noṇḍe *sakam* ar *baha*re oton-taenom *-ok̇* ar *–k̇* Kạjnum Tayom Joṛao *(Suffix)* lagaokate Kạjnum reak̇e kạmiet̕kana. Menkhan noṇḍe disạ dohoe jạruṛkana je mit̕ṭen Kạjnum khon barea se pea Kạjnum benao daṛeak̇a. Ar ona Kạjnum sabad talare *-p* ar *-k̇* lagaokate hoyok̇kana ar adom jokhec̕ do ona reak̇ge pạhil akhor *(one syllable)* dohṛakate ayatre beoharok̇kana se noṅka hõ hoyok̇kana, sabad reak̇ pạhil Hạṭiṅõk̇ Harop *(Consonant)* são Behạṭiṅõk̇ Harop *(Vowel)* *-wante* bar dhao dohṛakate hõ beoharok̇kana Noa bujhạu lạgit̕ pạrtulbo ṅela :–

dal ⟶ **dadal**

(i) *dalkedeae;*

(ii) *dadalkanae.*

p - (iii) *dapalkanako.*

k̇ - (iv) *dak̇palkanako*

Santali reak̇ Kạjnumre asokaete Kuṛại Tala Joṛao, Ujnum Tayom Joṛao *(Pronoun Suffix) -ṅ, -m, -e, -kin, -ko, -me, -le, -bo*), Bekạmi Tayom Joṛao *(Passive Suffix -ok̇, -k̇, -ok̇, -kan, -ogok̇, -ok̇ (-k̇)kan tahẽkan, -en, -len, -len tahẽkan, -kok̇, -joṅ, -joṅkan, -joṅkan tahẽkan, -an, -an tahẽkan, -kok̇kan, -kok̇kan tahẽkan, -akan, -akan tahẽkan, -akawan, -akawan tahẽkan* eman) lagaok̇kana.

Santalire aema lekan Tayom Joṛao, Tala Joṛao lagaok̇kana. Onage noṇḍe mit̕ bar pạrtul emogok̇kana :-

Tinre Kạmiạ *(Subject)* jivianak̇ tahenkhan, tobe Kạjnum sãote Hoṛ Ujnum *(Personal Pronoun)* reak̇ Tayom Joṛao *(Suffix)* lagaok̇kana ar ona do Kạjnum Tayom Joṛao *(Verb Suffix) -re* hijuk̇a, jeleka :–

calak̇ - calak̇am, calak̇ạṅ, calak̇ape, calak̇ạkin, calak̇ako, calak̇ạkin, calak̇alaṅ emanko. Metak̇me Hoṛ Ujnum reak̇ Joṛao *(Suffix) – -m, -ṅ, -e, -pe, -ape, -ạkin, -ako, -ạliṅ, -aben, -alaṅ, -ko* lagaoena.

Kạmiạ *(Subject)* Họṛ Ujnum reak̇ jivianak̇ tahẹnkhan, tọbẹ onage hẹċkate dohṛak̇a ar Kạjnum lahare hijuk̇a. Mẹnkhan Họṛ Ujnum reak̇ khaṭọ rup tahẽna, pạrtul :–

iń + iń + calak̇a = ińiń calak̇a. (Noa dọ kuṛại baṅ tahẹnkhange hoyok̇a.) Judi tesar họṛ (*Third Person)* mit̕ lekha reak̇ Ujnum Tayọm Joṛao *(Pronoun Suffix)* Kạjnumre joṛao tahẽlen khan, tọbẹ ona dọ Kạmiạ *(Subject)* reak̇e kạmia, jeleka :–

calak̇ae. Nọṇḍẹ -*e* dọ kạmiạ reak̇e kạmiet̕kana. Ayatre Kuṛại *(Object)* tahẹnkhan, tọbẹ kuṛạire Ujnum Tayọm Joṛao dọ lagaok̇a. Nạmuna – *Ram dọ dakae jọma.* (daka são *(-e)* menak̇a.

Santalire Kạjnum lahare Họṛ Ujnum hijuk̇kana ar adọm jọkhẹċ dọ ona Ujnum reak̇ kạṭiċ rupge Kạjnumre joṛao milạukate hijuk̇kana, jeleka :–

ińiń calak̇a. (Santalire Ujnum são ona reak̇ge khaṭọ rup arhõ joṛao midok̇kana.)

(i) sẹ noṅka – *iń calak̇a.*

(ii) sẹ noṅka – *calak̇ạń.*

iii)sẹ noṅka – *hẽń calak̇a.* (Ujnum tayọm joṛao *Personominal Suffix)*

Kạjnum beste bujhạu lạgit̕ mit̕ dhao arhõ dohṛalenge. Santalire Kạjnum dọ aema lekate benaok̇kana. Ar noa rup hõ ayat jạruṛae lekate aema rup benaok̇kana. Mẹnako; Kạjnum dọ ayatren raja kanae. Ayatre Kạjnum baṅ tahẽlenkhan ayat baṅ puṛạuk̇a. Kạjnum dọ pẹ hạṭińre hạṭińkate ńẹlọgọk̇a :-

1. Jọs Kạjnum *(Transitive Verb)*

2. Bẹjọs Kạjnum (*Intransitive Verb)*

3. Gọṛọ Kạjnum *(Auxiliary Verb)*

JOS KAJNUM
(TRANSITIVE VERB)

Jos Kajnum do ona sabad kana, one okaṭak̓ do Kuṛai *(Object)* jaruṛaekan, se noa hõ men daṛeak̓a je okaṭak̓ do kuṛai jaruṛaekan. Eṭak̓ lekate bujhau lagit̓ do noa partul emogok̓kana. Mit̓ṭen sarem tuṅlekhan jãhã baṅ jãhã ṭhen bidok̓gea se jãhã baṅ jãhãnak̓ jinis josok̓gea. Okaṭak̓ josem menakat̓, ona baṅ josok̓re hõ jãhãṭak̓ jinisre bidok̓gea. Metak̓me sar do Kajnum lekae kamikana. Noa sar okare bit̓en se cet̓ jinisre bit̓ena. Okare se cet̓re bit̓ena se okoye josena. Cet̓ josena? Jãhãṭak̓ge josen se jãhãnak̓ge josen. Josenak̓ do Kuṛai *(Object)* kana. Metak̓me kamien reak̓ jo do ṅamengea.

Kajunm do jãhãṭak̓e kamieda. Kamige *(action)* Kajnum kana, ona reak̓ jo ṅamen do Kuṛai *(Object)* kana. Kajnum são *okoe (okoye)* se cet̓ kuklim kuklilekhan, oka jobab ṅamok̓kan, ona do kuṛai kana. Oka kukli hoteте jobab ṅamok̓kan, ona do Jos Kajnum *(Transitive Verb)*ko metak̓kana. Bejos Kajnum reak̓ jobab do baṅ ṅamok̓a. Jos Kajnum bujhau lagit̓ partul emogok̓kana :–

(i) Garbhu do Maheslal dorogae helec̓kedea.

Kukli – *Okoye helec̓kedea?*

Jobab – *Maheslal doroga.*

Ona iate *okoe* reak̓ jobab do – *Maheslal doroga* kana. *helec̓* do sar lekae kamikeda ar *Maheslal doroga* do josen jinis lekae kamikeda. Metak̓me Kuṛai lekage. Ona iate *helec̓* reak̓ jo do *Maheslal doroga*re purauena. Onate *helec̓* do Jos Kajnum kana.

(ii) Baṛka do hoṛoe daleda.

Kukli – *Cet̓e daleda?*

Jobab – *Hoṛo.*

Onate *dal* do Jos Kajnum kana.

(iii) *Kạnhu dọ dakae jọmeda.*

Kukli – *Cẹṫe jọmeda?*

Jobab – *Daka.*

Onate *Jọm* dọ Jọs Kạjnum kana.

Disạ dọhọ – Kuṛại sendra ńam lạgiṫ Kạjnum sãote *ọkọe (ọkọye)* sẹ *cẹṫe* sẹ *ọkọe* lạgiṫ kukli hotẹte judi jãhãnaǩ jobab ńamoǩ, ona Kạjnum dọ Jọs Kạjnumge hoyoǩa.

Cetanre ẹmakan pạrtul reaǩ *hẹlẹċ, dal, jọjọm*ko dọ Jọs Kạjnum kana. Ar ona reaǩ kuṛại dọ *Maheslal dọrọga, hoṛo* ar *daka* kana. Adọm jọkhẹċ sẹ ayatre barea kuṛại tahẹnkana. Miṫ dọ *Sọdọr Kuṛại* dosaraǩ dọ *Oko Kuṛại.* Mẹnkhan miṫ bar pạṭhuạko dọ pasẹċ noa bujhạurebon ẹstọ bẹstọǩkana je okaṭaǩ dọ Sọdọr Kuṛại *(Direct Object)* ar okaṭaǩ dọ Oko Kuṛại *(Indirect Object)* kana mẹnte. Sọdọr Kuṛại bujhạu lạgiṫ Kạjnum são *ọkọe, ọkọye, cẹṫ, cẹṫe* lagaokate kuklilenkhan oka jobab ńamoǩa, ona dọ Sọdọr Kuṛại *(Direct Object)*ko metaǩkana. Ar *ọkọe/ọkọye* lạgiṫ, *cele* lạgiṫ sãote Kạjnum joṛaokate kuklilenkhan ar oka jobab ńamoǩ, ona dọ Oko Kuṛại *(Indirect Object)*ko metaǩa. Noakin banar bujhạu lạgiṫ latarre pạrtul ẹmọgọǩkana :–

(i) *Lukhi dọ sim khodey ẹraṫkoa.*

Kukli – *Cẹṫe ẹraṫkoa?*

Jobab – *Khode.* (Sọdọr Kuṛại)

Kukli – *Ọkọe/cele lạgiṫe ẹrkeda?*

Jobab – *Sim.* (Oko Kuṛại)

(ii) *Baha dọ gidrạko sunum piṭhại emaṫkoa.*

Kukli – *Cẹṫe emaṫkoa?*

jobab – *Sunum piṭhạ.* (Sọdọr Kuṛại)

Kukli – *Ọkọye emaṫkoa?*

Jobab – *Gidrạko.* (Oko Kuṛại)

(iii) *Phulmuni dọ gidrạ lạgiṫ buru khọċ terel beley ạgukeda.*

Kukli – *Cet́e agukeda?*

Jobab – *Terel bele.* (Sodor Kuṛai)

Kukli – *Okoe lagit́e agukeda?*

jobab – *Gidrạ.* (Oko Kuṛai)

Cetanre emakan pạrtul reak̉ Kạjnum *er, em, agu* reak̉ kuṛại do – *sim, khode, gidrạ, sunum piṭhạ, terel bele* kana.

BEJOS KẠJNUM
(INTRANSITIVE VERB)

Bejos Kạjnum do onageko metak̉kana, one okaṭak̉ lạgit́ do cet́ Kuṛại hõ bạnuk̉ se baṅ ńamok̉kan, pạrtul :-

(i) Gupin do parkomrey duṛupakana.

Kukli – *Gupin do cet́e duṛupakana?*

Jobab – Jobab do bạnuk̉a.

Aema Kạjnum do noṅka hõ menak̉a, oka do banar lekate beoharok̉kana, jeleka :–

(i) Ramsiṅgại oroṅkeda – Jos Kạjnum

(ii) Ramsiṅgạ oroṅena – Bejos Kạjnum

(iii) Ṭamake rukeda – Jos Kạjnum

(iv) Ṭamak ruyena – Bejos Kạjnum

GOṚO KẠJNUM
(AUXILIARY VERB/VERB SUFFIX)

Ona Kạjnum, one oka do ayatre asol Kạjnum *(Base-word/ full verb/main verb)* são milạukate asol kạjnume goṛoaekan. Metak̉me asol Kạjnum reak̉ maney purạuet́kan. Ar okte *(Tense)* se Bekạmi Kạjnum *(Passive Voice)* bek̉naore goṛo emok̉kanak̉ge Goṛo Kạjnum do menogok̉kana, pạrtul :–

Gidrại dạṛet́kana.

Nọṇḍẹ pea jinis menaḱa – *dạṛ, -et́* ar *-kana.* Noako pẹnẹ, beakọrọn reaḱ bhasare cẹt́bo metaḱa? *dạṛ* kana mọtọte mane baṅ purạuḱkana. *dạṛ* sãote *-et́* joṛao menaḱa? Noate cẹt́ bujhạuḱkana? Nọṇḍẹ *-et́* họtẹte ọktẹy lạiet́kana. Iṅgrạjite dọ *Tense*ko metaḱa. *-et́* dọ Iṅgrạjite dọ *Tense Suffix*ko metaḱa, ọnẹ oka dọ kạmi lagatare kạmiet́kana. Kạmi dọ baṅ purạuakan reaḱe baḍae ocoet́bona. *-et́* dọ Kạjnum Tayọm Joṛao *(Verb Suffix)* hõ̱bo mẹn daṛeaḱa. Nọṇḍẹ latarre pạrtul ẹmọgọḱkana :–

dạṛ – Noa dọ asọl Kạjnum *(Main Verb)* kana.

kana – Noa dọ Gọṛọ Kạjnum *(Auxiliary Verb)* kana.

-et́ – Noa dọ ọktẹ tayọm joṛao sẹ Kạjnum Tayọm Joṛao *(Tense Suffix or Verb Suffix)*.

Santalire Kạjnum benao lạgit́ kạjnumanaḱ Tayọm Joṛao *(Verbal Suffix)* ar Ọktẹ Tayọm Joṛao *(Tense Suffix)* ar Ọktẹ Tayọm Joṛao *(Tense Suffix)* lagaokate ọktẹ reaḱe lạiet́kana, jeleka :–

Daka baṅ udugọḱkana.

uduḱ – Kạjnum *(Verb)* kana.

gọḱ – Kạjnum reaḱ bẹkạmi Tayọm Joṛao, Iṅgrạjite dọ *passive & medium suffix*ko metaḱa.

kana – Noa dọ Gọṛọ Kạjnum *(Auxiliary Verb)* kana.

Kạjnum reaḱ galmaraoḱkan iạte Santalire Kạjnum cẹt́ leka benaoakana, ona nọṇḍẹ ẹmọgọḱkana :–

1. **Sabad Benao Dhara (*The Performative Base*)**

(a) Noaṭaḱ niạm lekate oka Kạjnum emakan, metaḱme asọl Kạjnum *(Base word)* reaḱ pạhil Hạṭiṅõ̱ḱ Harọp *(Consonant)* ar ona tayọm reaḱ Bẹhạṭiṅõ̱ḱ Harọp *(Vowel)* banar dohṛakate nãwã Kạjnum benaoḱkana, jeleka :–

(i) *benao* khọn - *bebenao*

(ii) *baṅcao* khọn - *babaṅcao*

(iii) *dal* khon - *dadal*

(iv) *kuli* khon - *kukli*

(v) *roṛ* khon - *roroṛ*

(vi) *ńir* khon - *ńińir*

(b) Dosar lekanak̕ do asol Kạjnum reak̕ pạhil utạr Behạṭińõk̕ Harop tayomre -*k̕* harop hečkate sabad talare sogekate hõ nãwã Kạjnum benaok̕kana, jeleka :–

(i) *benao* khon - *bek̕nao*

(ii) *kuli* khon - *kuk̕li*

(iii) *sana* khon - *sak̕na*

(iv) *kạmi* khon - *kạk̕mi*

(v) *henosta* khon - *hek̕nosta*

(c) Tesar dhara reak̕ niạm lekate judi Kạjnum sabad reak̕ pạhil Hạṭińõk̕ Harop Ãṭ Aṛań Hạṭińõk̕ Harop *(Aspirated Consonant)* tahenkhan, tobe nãwã Kạjnum bebenaore sabad reak̕ pạhil utạr Hạṭińõk̕ Harop *(Consonant)*ge dohṛak̕a, -*h* do bań dohṛak̕a, jeleka :–

(i) *jhaṛ* khon - *jhajaṛ*

(ii) *ṭhep̕* khon - *ṭheṭep̕*

(iii) *ghanṭa* khon - *ghaganṭa*

(iv) *bhorao* khon - *bhoborao*

(d) Judi Kạjnum sabad reak̕ pạhil harop Hạṭińõk̕ Harop*(Consonant)* tahenkhan ar ona haropante Bar Haropanak̕ Mit̕ Ucrạn *(Dipthong)* hoyok̕khan, eken Bar Haropanak̕ Mit̕ Ucrạn reak̕ pạhil Behạṭińõk̕ Harop dohṛakate nãwã Kạjnum benaok̕kana. Noa Bar Haropanak̕ mit̕ ucrạn do nãwã sabadre purạu-purạu do hoyok̕kana. Noa do nãwã sabad reak̕ Dosar Akhorre *(Second Syllable)* re ńelok̕kana. Noa do Dosar Dabaṛ Aṛań *(Second Stress)* reak̕e kạmiet̕kana. Judi noṅkan sabadre -*k̕* aderlenkhan, tọbẹ Bar Harọpanak̇ Mit̉ Ucrạn *(Dipthong)* reak̇ pạhil Bẹhạṭiṅõk̇ Harọp *(Vowel)* tayọmre adẹrọk̇a. Noa niạm lekate latarre pạrtul ẹmọgọk̇kana :–

(i) *lại* khon - *lạlại*

(ii) *k̇ - lại* khọn - *lạk̇lại*

(iii) *jaora* khọn - *jajaora*

(iv) *k̇ – jaora* - *jak̇aora*

(v) *kạumạu* khọn - *kạumạmạu* (Nọṇḍẹ dọ niạm baṅ sajaok̇ Bẹhạṭiṅõk̇ Harọp tayọmre Dosar Akhọr *(Second Syllable)* reak̇ pạhil Hạṭiṅõk̇ Harọp dohṛawakana.

Disạ dọhọ – Akhọr reak̇ mọtlọb dọ – *syllable*, dabaṛ araṅ reak̇ mọtlọb dọ – *Word Stress*.

Noaṭak̇ niạm lekate sabad reak̇ pạhil Bẹhạṭiṅõk̇ Harọp tayọmre - *-k̇* hijuk̇kana; ar baṅkhan harọp dohṛak̇kana, sẹ asọkaete *-k̇* tayọmre hẹċkate purạ-puri dohṛak̇kana, jeleka :–

(i) *ẹr* khọn - *ẹk̇ẹr*

(ii) *ir* khọn - *ik̇ir*

(iii) *ạulạu* khọn - *ạk̇ạulạu*

(iv) *aosan* khọn - *ak̇aosan*

(v) *ae* khọn - *ak̇ae* (ae = amdaj)

(vi) *ạgu* khọn - *ạk̇gu*

(vii) *idi* khọn - *ik̇di*

(viii) *unum* khọn - *uk̇num*

(ix) *ọr* khọn - *ọk̇ọr*

(x) *ọl* khọn - *ọk̇ọl*

(xi) *ãṭ* khọn - *ãk̇ãṭ*

(xii) *laga* khọn - *lak̇ga*

(xiii) *dal* khọn - *dak̇dal*

(xiv) *lekha* khọn - *lek̇kha*

(xv) *sendra* khon - *sek̇ndra*

(xvi) *ẹṛẹ* khon - *ẹk̇ṛẹ*

(Cetanre emakan pạrtulrebo ńẹla arbo bujhạua je Mit̓ Akhoranak̓ *(Monosyllabic)* reak̓ pạhil Bẹhạṭińȭk̓ Harọp *(Vowel)* purạu dohṛawakan ńẹlok̓kana, sanamre dọ baṅ. Nãwã sabad reak̓ banar Bẹhạṭińȭk̓ Harọp *(Vowel)* barabạrige dabaṛakana. Ar Bar Akhọranak̓ *(Disyllabic)* ar Ḍher Akhọranak̓ *(Polysyllabic)* sabad reak̓ pạhil Bẹhạṭińȭk̓ Harọp birlạge dohṛak̓kana, metak̓me baṅ lekage.)

Noa niạm chaḍa arhȭ mit̓ṭẹn niạm menak̓a, ona niạm lekate dọ nãwã Kạjnum sabad bebenaore *-p* harọp talare hẹc̓kate hoyok̓kana. Nạmuna – *dal-dapal; racak̓-rapacak̓; rẹc̓-rẹpẹc̓; ọl-ọpọl; lạṛhại-lạpạṛhại; duṛup̓-dupuṛup̓; jak̓-japak̓; dọn-dọdọn* eman. Noa niạmre sabad judi Mit̓ Akhọranak̓ *(Monosyllabic)* kan khan ar ona pạhil harọp são pạhil Bẹhạṭińȭk̓ Harọp *(Vowel)* dohṛawakan menak̓khan, tọbẹ onare kẹcẹt̓ harọp *-k̓* pạhil akhọrre adẹrkate nãwã Kạjnum benaok̓kana, jeleka :–

(i) *dal – dadal* khọn - *dak̓dal*

(ii) *lại – lạlại* khọn - *lạk̓lại*

(iii) *jọm – jọjọm* khọn - *jọk̓jọm*

(iv) *dạṛ – dạdạṛ* khọn - *dạk̓dạṛ*

Noa niạm dharate mul Kạjnum reak̓ pạhil harọp são pạhil Bẹhạṭińȭk̓ Harọp dohṛakate *-kan* lagaok̓kana. Ar dosar akhọrre *-k̓* adẹrkate hȭ nãwã Kạjnum benaok̓kana. Noa *-kan*re *-ae* joṛaok̓kana, jeleka :–

(i) *si - sisi* - *sisikanae*

(ii) *k̓* - *sik̓sikanae*

(iii) *daka* - *dak̓kakanae*

(iv) *utu* - *uk̓tukanae*

(v) *sạbun* - *sạk̓bunkanae*

(Noare Ńunum sabadre -*k̇* harǫp adẹrkate Kạjnum benaok̇kana.)

Noa niạm lekate mul Kạjnum sabadre -*p* adẹrkate bar akhǫranak̇ Kạjnum sabad benaok̇kana. Ona nãwã Kạjnum benaoakan reak̇rege arhõ -*k̇* harǫp joṛaokate arhõ nãwã Kạjnum benaok̇kana. -*p* harǫp adẹrkate oka Kạjnum benaok̇kan, ona niạm dǫ *Reciprocal Base*ko metak̇a ar -*k̇* harǫp adẹrkate, oka Kạjnum benaok̇kana, ona dǫ *Performative Base* niạmko metak̇a :-

(i) *ńẹpẹl* khǫn - *ńẹk̇pẹl*

(ii) *rẹpẹċ* khǫn - *rẹk̇pẹċ*

(iii) *tapam* khǫn - *tak̇pam*

(iv) *lạpạṛhại* khǫn - *lạk̇pạṛhại*

(v) *rapacak̇* khǫn - *rak̇pacak̇*

Noa niạmre noae mẹnẹt̕kana je judi sabad joṛaokate benaoakan khan, mẹnẹk Joṛao Sabad *(Compound)* kan khan, ona dǫ asǫl sabad metak̇me asǫl sabad lekae kạmieda. Ona adǫm jǫkhẹċ dǫ dohṛak̇kana ar onare -*k̇* harǫp sabad reak̇ asǫl hạṭińre *(main part)* hẹċkate ucrạn ańjǫmǫk̇kana. Noa sabad reak̇ dosar akhǫr *(2nd syllable)* reak̇ pạhil harǫp dohṛak̇kana. Noakin barea sabadte benaoakan mit̕ eṭak̇ak̇re ṭehaḍkate maney oḍoket̕kana, jeleka :–

(i) *nijǫr* khǫn - *nik̇jǫjǫr. Noa do Joṛa Sabad*

(ii) *kurumuṭu* khǫn - *kurumuk̇ṭu (kuk̇rumuṭu hõ hoyok̇a).*

Noa dǫ Joṛa Sabad *(Compound word)* dǫ bań kana.

(iii) *puruchun* khǫn - *puk̇ruchun*

(iv) *dal gǫċ* khǫn - *dadal gǫgǫċ*

(v) *ńẹl gǫt̕* khǫn - *ńẹńẹl gǫgǫt̕*

(vi) *dal baṛa* khǫn - *dadal babṛa*

(vii) *ńẹl ạgu* khǫn - *ńẹl ạk̇gu*

(viii) *capat̕* jǫs khǫn - *capat̕ jǫjǫs*

jeleka :– *dak̇dalae, lek̇ńjet̕a, ak̇ńjom, (kala/kali hor ańjom), ńek̇ńel (kãrã/kãrĩ hor ńeńel), ak̇rak̇, hek̇hende, pok̇ponda, lok̇sot̕a, duk̇duruma* eman.

Noa niam dharate Kajnum reak̇ mul rup reak̇ pahil harop sãote ina tayom reak̇ Behatińõk̇ Harop dohrak̇kana ar jãhãe menjoń lagit̕ jãhãnak̇ cekae lagit̕ mente *lagit̕* tayom japak̇ ona tayom joraok̇kana, jeleka :-

(i) *Ńeńelko* senakana. *(ńel-ńeńel)*

(ii) *Kik̇rińko* kolakadea. *(kirih-kik̇rih)*

(iii) *Jojom* lagit̕ko durup̕ena. *(jom-jojom)*

(iv) *Kuk̇tuń* lagit̕ko *boloena. (kutuń-kuk̇tuń)*

(Noa Kajnumre *lagit̕* oko menak̇a.)

Noa niamre okte reak̇e badae ok̇cokana, onare mit̕ten khon jasti Kajnum songe tahenkana, jeleka :–

(i) *Horoko gek̇merkantako tahẽkana.*

(ii) *Hik̇rie* senakana.

(iii) *Lak̇laikanrege* aćgey hećena.

(iv) Alope *lak̇lai* babrawa.

(v) Kathae *khak̇tikana.*

(vi) *Tok̇darote* calaoena.

Santali reak̇ Kajnumre Kamia *(Subject),* Kurai *(Object),* okte *(Tense)* ar Sombond Tayom Jorao milauakan tahenkana. Noare Ujnum reak̇ Sombond Tayom jorao hõ tahenkana, partul :–

(i) *akhrińkedetaeae;* (ii) *idikedetaeae;* (iii) *idikedeako;* (iv) *laiaeme;* (v) *laiadeań;* (vi) rak̇ańai;(vii) *irket̕taeako;* (viii) *hoyentakoa;* (ix) *areyet̕kan tahẽkana.*

Kajnumre Khati Tayom Jorao *(Determinative Suffix - -ić,*

-*aḱ*) joṛaokate Ńunum lekae kạmieťkana, jeleka :–

ńe̱ńe̱lić, ńe̱ńe̱laḱ, raranić, raranaḱ, bebenaoić, bebenaoaḱ, seḱreńić se̱ *seḱreńko, aḱarsalaḱ, kuḱṭạmaḱ, papaṛhaoić, mamarsalaḱ, ge̱ge̱ťić, ge̱ge̱ťaḱ* emanko.

Kạjnumre Tayo̱m Japaḱ *(Postposition) -re, -re̱, -te* ar *-te̱* sãote Khạṭi Tayo̱m Joṛao *(Determinative Suffix) -aḱ* lagaokate ayatre beoharoḱkana, jeleka :–

jo̱jo̱mre ńũńũre do̱ nokokotam peṛa, gujuḱre guroḱre do̱ okorkotam oaris!

lahateaḱ, jo̱jo̱mteaḱ, haḱlateaḱ -te sãote *-aḱ* lagawakan do̱ Ńunum reaḱe kạmieda.

ẠKIL BHAŃJAO - 10

A. Ṭo̱yo̱ť kate jobab e̱mo̱ḱme :-

1. Kạjnum do̱ tinạḱ lekana?
   (a) 3 (b) 4 (c) 6 (d) 7
2. *he̱le̱ć* sabad do̱ okaṭaḱ Kạjnum kana?
   (a) Be̱jo̱s Kạjnum (b) Jo̱s Kạjnum (c) Go̱ṛo̱ Kạjnum
3. *duṛuṕ* sabad do̱ okaṭaḱ Kạjnum kana?
   (a) Be̱jo̱s Kạjnum (b) Jo̱s Kạjnum (c) Go̱ṛo̱ Kạjnum
4. *dạṛeťkana* sabad do̱ okaṭaḱ Kạjnum kana?
   a) Be̱jo̱s Kạjnum (b) Jo̱s Kạjnum (c) Go̱ṛo̱ Kạjnum
5. *babańcao* reaḱ mul Kạjnum do̱ okaṭaḱ kana?
   (a) bańcao (b) baḱańcao (c) bapańcao (d) bińcao

B. O̱lkate jobab e̱mo̱ḱme :-

1. *Setae dalkedea.* Noa ayat do̱ okaṭaḱ Kạjnum kana?
2. *bebenao, babańcao, dadal* sabad do̱ okaṭaḱ beḱnao dhara

reaḱ kana?

3. *beḱnao, kukli, kạḱmi* sabad do̠ okaṭaḱ beḱnao dhara reaḱ sabad kana?
4. *Ar dinkore ce̠t́bon jo̠ma?* Noa ayat reaḱ *ar* do̠ ce̠t́ reaḱe kạmikana?
5. *Araḱko (sare̠ċaḱ) do̠ o̠ko̠r?* Noa ayat reaḱ *araḱ* do̠ ce̠t́ reaḱe kạmikana?
6. *Ar arko do̠ko okayena?* Noa ayat reaḱ *ar arko* do̠ ce̠t́ reaḱe kạmikana?
7. *Ar bạń ro̠ṛa.* Noa ayat reaḱ *ar bạń* do̠ ce̠t́ reaḱe kạmikana?
8. *Ạgu nae are̠t́a, e̠ke̠ne ro̠ṛe̠t́a.* Noa ayat reaḱ *ar* do̠ ce̠t́ reaḱe kạmikana?
9. *Ho̠* do̠ Beako̠ro̠n reaḱ niạm lekate ce̠t́ kana?
10. *ale hõ̠, ape hõ̠.* Noa ayat reaḱ *hõ̠* do̠ ce̠t́ reaḱe kạmikana?
11. *Ado̠e me̠nkeda.* Noa ayat reaḱ *ado̠* do̠ ce̠t́ reaḱe kạmikana?
12. *Ce̠t́e̠m ńamkana ado̠?* Noa ayat *ado̠* do̠ ce̠t́ reaḱ kạmikana?
13. *Ạyup̍e̠nkhan do̠e he̠ċe̠na.* Noa ayat reaḱ *khan* do̠ ce̠t́ reaḱe kạmikana?
14. *Khane he̠ċena.* Noa ayat reaḱ *khan* ce̠t́ reaḱe kạmikana?
15. *E̠ṇḍe̠khan calaḱme.* Noa ayat reaḱ *khan* do̠ ce̠t́ reaḱe kạmikana?
16. *e̠nkhan* do̠ Beako̠ro̠n reaḱ niạm lekate ce̠t́ kana?
17. *se̠* do̠ Beako̠ro̠n reaḱ niạm lekate ce̠t́ kana?
18. *Ạuriye calaḱa.* Noa ayat reaḱ *ạuri* Beako̠ro̠n reaḱ niạm lekate do̠ ce̠t́ kana?

11

JOḱṚAO SABAD
(CONJUNCTIONS)

Joḱṛao Sabad dọ Iṅgrạjite *Conjunction*ko metaḱa. Noa sabad họtẹte miť sabad khọn eṭaḱ sabad são sẹ miťṭẹn katha khọn eṭaḱaḱ katha são sọmbọnde joṛaoeťkana, pạrtul :–

ar - Noa dọ Iṅgrạjite dọ *and*ko metaḱkana. Noa dọ Joḱṛao Sabad, Gunum, Kạjnum-Gunum ar Ujnum leka hõe kạmigea. Mẹnkhan noare Tayọm Joṛao Joṛaoaḱ tuluč hoyoḱa, jeleka :–

(i) araḱ *ar* poṇḍ, haṛam *ar* buḍhi - Joḱṛao rupre *(Conjunction)*

(ii) Họṛ *ar* Deko - Joḱṛao rupre *(Conjunction)*

(iii) *are* mẹnkeda - Joḱṛao rupre *(Conjunction)*

(iv) *ar* dinkore cẹťbon jọma? - Kạjnum Gunum rupre *(Adverb)*

(v) *ar* imạńme miť dhao - Kạjnum-Gunum rupre *(Adverb)*

(vi) *arko* dọko okaeyena? - Ujnum *(Pronoun)*

(vii) *araḱko* (sarẹčaḱ) dọ ọkọr? - Ujnum *(Pronoun)*

(viii) *ar* batarre ọmọn mọkọńẹna - Kạjnum-gunum *(Adverb)*

(ix) *ar arko* dọko okaena? - Ujnum *(Pronoun)*

(x) *ar araḱ* (sarẹčaḱ) dọ ọkọr? - Ujnum (Pronoun)

(xi) *artẹť* ḍherko hẹčena. - Kạjnum-Gunum *(Adverb)*

(xii) *ar* bạń rọṛa. - Kạjnum-Gunum *(Adverb)*

(xiii) *arhõ* imạńme. - Kạjnum-Gunum *(Adverb)*

(xiv) *ardo* bạń onkaea. - Gunum *(Adjective)*

(xv) *ardo* bạnuk̓a. - Ujnum *(Pronoun)*

(xvi) ạgu nae *areťa,* ekene roreťa.- Kạjunm *(Verb)*

(xvii) heč̓ nako *arok̓a*, dingeko koyok̓ ocoeťlea - Kạjunm *(Verb)*

hõ - Noa do Iṅgrạjite do *also, even, too* hõko metak̓a. Noa do jok̓ṛao reak̓ do bae kạmia, bickom puk̓rạu reak̓e kạmia. Noa do Kukli Ujnum são joṛaokate Beniṭ Ujnum reak̓ hõe kạmikana, pạrtul :–

(i) Am *hõń* emama.

(ii) Onko *hõ* lạiakome.

(iii) *Enhõe* calaoena.

(iv) Enre *hõko* dalkedea.

(v) Dal *hõko* dalkedea.

(vi) Sen *hõ* bae senok̓a.

(vii) Sen *hõe* senok̓a.

hõ ... hõ - Noa do barea ayate joṛaoeťkana ar noa do mana katha se baṅ reak̓ katha baḍaeok̓ barea ayate joṛaoeťkana, pạrtul :–

(i) Iń *hõ* bạń lạimea, am *hõ* bam lạiyińa.

(ii) Ale *hõ*, ape *hõ*.

(iii) Dal *hõko* dalkedea, ḍaṇḍom *hõko* ḍaṇḍomkedea.

ado - Noa do Jok̓ṛao Sabad, Kạjnum-Gunum reak̓e kạmieťa, jeleka :–

(i) *Adoe* menkeťa.

(ii) *Adom* calak̓kana.

(iii) *Adọ*e gitiċena.

(iv) Cẹťem ńamkana *adọ*.

Noare *khange* joṛaokate noṅkan katha benaok̇kana :–

"Adọ khange onka hudis baṛakate atoren họṛ ṭhen khọn barea pạiye kọe ạguketʹa; adọ onako pẹnẹ pạiye khadleketʹa; khange adọe jolak̇kana are ghaṇṭaetʹa."

Adọm jọkhẹċ dọ Kạjnum rupre hõe kạmigea, jeleka :–

Adọ cẹťem ńamkana, *adọ* cẹťiń rọṛa?

khan ar *khange* – Noa dọ *khaċ* ar *khaċge* barabạrigey kạmia ar banarge sọmangea, metak̇me banarge barabạrigea.

khan dọ Tayọm Japak̇ ar Kạjnum-Gunum reak̇e kạmieťkana. Ar *khange* dọ Kạjnum-Gunum reak̇e kạmieda, pạrtul :–

(i) Ạyup̣en*khan* dọe hẹċena. – Kạjnum-Gunum ar Tayọm Joṛao

(ii) Hẹċ*khan* hẹċ họdọk̇me. – Kạjnum-Gunum

(iii) Uniye sẹnlen*khan* iń hõń calak̇a. – Tayọm Joṛao, Kạjnum- Gunum

(iv) Nit*khan* nitge calao họdọk̇me. – Kạjnum-Gunum

(v) Uni*khan* dọ ọhọe ạgu daṛelea. – Kạjnum-Gunum

(vi) *Ẹṇḍẹkhan* calak̇me. – Tayọm Joṛao

(vii) *Khane* hẹċena. – Kạjnum-Gunum

(viii) *Baṅkhan* ọhọe daṛelea. – Tayọm Joṛao

(ix) Uniye *hẹċenkhan ẹṇḍẹkhan* ale dọle chuṭiyena – Kạjnum-Gunum

(x) Ma *ẹṇḍẹkhan* jọmme. – Kạjnum-Gunum

(xi) *Khan*geko calaoena. – Kạjnum-Gunum

ẹnkhan = ẹnkhaċ, *ẹnkhante=ẹnkhaċte* - Noa dọ Kạjnum-Gunum reak̇e kạmieťkana, pạrtul :–

(xii) *Enkhanin* calaka.

(xiii) Sari rorme *enkhante* don goroama.

(xiv) Hereltete jomlege, *enkhante* orak hortet doe joma.

jãhãtisre - Noa do Benit Ujnum kana ar Kajnum-Gunum hõ kana. Noa do banar reakgey kamia. Partul :–

(i) *Jãhãtisre* desteko calak, iń hõ laiańpe, jemon iń hõń sen dareak.

(ii) *Jãhãtinre*ye hijuk, siń se ńinda, ekalte badae ocoyińpe.

auri - Noa do Ńunum kana ar Kajnum-Gunum reak hõe kamigea, partul :–

*(i) Auri*ye calaka.

(ii) *Auritet'geń* jom legaea.

(iii) *Aurite* do alope hijuka.

(iv) Marsal *aurireko* seterena.

(v) *Aurire* jom hodpe.

(vi) *Auriakore* noabon sat hatara.

(vii) Ape *aurite* do bale bilomoka.

se - Noa do Jokrao, Topak Sabad, Tayom Japak, Pukrauak ar Kajnum reak hõe kamia, partul :–

(i) Am *se* ińiń calaka.

(ii) Dipil *se* bhariako hecena.

Noare Kajnum se mana katha *se* bań hećlenre hõ beoharoka, jeleka :–

(iii) Calaoenae ba*se*; hećakanako *se* .

(iv) Alo *se* – Pukrauak

(v) Hape *se* – Pukrauak

(vi) Jo̱me jo̱mket́a *se̱* – Puḱrạuaḱ

(vii) Ce̱t́ baṅ *se̱*; onkanaḱ do̱ bạń ńe̱lakawan tahẽ̱kana.

(viii) Do *se̱* calaḱme – Puḱrạuaḱ

(ix) Ạgui me*se̱* – Puḱrạuaḱ

(x) Chại *se̱* bam anjo̱mlet́ – Tayo̱m Japaḱ

(xi) Daḱ *se̱ḱ*kana – Kạjnum

(xii) Kũi *se̱*yena – Kạjnum

(xiii) Gaḍa *se̱*yena – Kạjnum

baṅ do̱ - Noa do̱ Joḱṛaoaḱ, Puḱrạuaḱ ar Be̱so̱do̱r Kukli reaḱ so̱do̱rre hõ̱ laṛcaṛoḱkana, pạrtul :–

(i) Digdhạḱkanạń, *baṅ do̱e* se̱nakan? – Kukli

(ii) He̱ćenae *baṅ do̱* – Kukli

(iii) Baṅ do̱ menae, *baṅ do̱e* calaoen – Joḱṛao

(iv) Bạń baḍaea, baṅ do̱ko hijuḱ *baṅ do̱* baṅ - Joḱṛao

(v) *Baṅ do̱* ho̱ṛ, *baṅ do̱* boṅga.

hõ̱ - Noa do̱ Tayo̱m Japaḱ hõ̱ kana ar Joḱṛao Sabad hõ̱ kana. *hõ̱* sãote *ba (ṅ)* joṛaokate ayate milạuet́kana, pạrtul :–

(i) Am *hõ̱* baṅ, uni *hõ̱* baṅ. *(Postposition)*

(ii) Se̱n *hõ̱* bae se̱no̱ḱa. *(Postposition)*

(iii) Ro̱ṛ *hõ̱* bạń ro̱ṛakat́a, ruhạt́ *hõ̱* bạń ruhạt́akada. *(Conjunction)*

(iv) Bae kirińjo̱ṅa, sukri *hõ̱* baṅ me̱ro̱m *hõ̱* baṅ. *(Conjunction)*

ho̱e ... ho̱e - Noa do̱ Joḱṛao Sabad kana, pạrtul :–

(i) *Ho̱e*ye calaḱa, *ho̱*eyiń jobabaea. *(Conjunction)*

(ii) *Ho̱e* mit́ ho̱ṛ ṭhene jamaṛoḱ, ho̱e mit́ ho̱ṛe kurudae. *(Conjunction) ek-ek, ek do-ek do* - Noa do Jokṛao Sabad kana, pạrtul :–

(i) *Ek doe* huṇḍạr kana, *ek doe* tạrup̣ kana. *(Conjunction)*

(ii) Gại *eke* ạguye, *eke* tahẽ ocoae. *(Conjunction)*

(iii) Okareye kombṛo ocokeťa, *ek doko* Pạhṛiạ kana, *ek doko* Jolha kana. *(Conjunction)*

co (ṅ),co (ṅ)-baṅ co (ṅ) - Noa do tok̓pag jok̓ṛawakan Iṅgrạjite do *disjunctive conjunction*-ko metak̓a.

Noa do Puk̓ṛạuak̓ *(Particle)* lekae kạmia. *coṅ* moto do sabadre Tayom Japak̓ lekae kạmieťkana, jeleka :–

(i) okoe baḍae, *hẽ coṅ baṅ coṅ.*

(ii) Ki jạni hẽge *coṅ,* hoṛo *coṅ* joṇḍra *coko* ạguakaťa.

menkhan - *menkhan* do Iṅgrạjite doko metak̓a *but*. Noa do ulṭạu jok̓ṛaoak̓ Tayom Joṛao kana. Noa do eskar sabad ar purạu ayate joṛaoeťkana, pạrtul :–

(i) Nẽotaleťkoạń *menkhan* bako hec̓lena. *(Conjunction)*

(ii) Joto hoṛe lạiaťkoa, *menkhan* iń do baṅ. *(Conjunction)*

(iii) Jãhãnak̓ge kiriń ạguime, *menkhan* mạric do alo. *(Conjunction)*

(iv) Kulạiyiń ńelledea, *menkhan* bạń sap̣ daṛeadea. *(Conjunction)*

(v) Nitok̓ do miť leka bes menak̓lea, *menkhan* tayomte do *ceť coṅ* hoyok̓.

menek - Noa do *menkhan* lekage beoharok̓a, menkhan ạḍi komge noa beohar ńelakana, pạrtul :-

(i) Calak̓e menkeda, *menek* bae senlena.

(ii) Uduk̓aeye menleťa, *menek* bae uduk̓adea.

bickom - Noa do Kạjnum-Gunum kana. Noa do Kạjnum-Gunum reak̓e kạmieťkana. Pạrtul :-

(i) *Bickom* alom rọṛa, noṅkam rọṛet̓khan nui baṅkate *bickom* nuigeń hataoea.

(ii) Nitok̓ dọ *bickom* bạń calak̓kana, tayọmteń calak̓a.

bọrọṅ, bọrọṅ cọ (ṅ), bọr cọ (ṅ) – Noa dọ Kạjnum-Gunum kana ar Kạjnum-Gunum reak̓e kạmiet̓kana. Noa ayatre puk̓rạuak̓ reak̓ hõe kạmiet̓kana, pạrtul :–

(i) Họṛ dọ ḍher dọ bako sẹnlena, *bọrọṅ* Deko dọ bạ̃ṛtigeko tahẽkana.

(ii) *Bọrcọṅ* iń dọ bạń jọma, am baṛẹ jọmme.

(iii) Iń dọ bạń calak̓a, *bọrcọṅ* iń bọdọl amge calak̓me.

(iv) *Bọrọṅ cọṅ* calak̓me, kạmim disạet̓khan.

(v) *Bọrcọṅ* iń dọ bạń jọma, ape baṛẹ jọmpe.

baṅkhan, baṅkhaċ – Noa dọ Jok̓ṛao Sabad *(Conjunction)* kana ar Gunum reak̓ hõe kạmigea, jeleka :-

(i) Ẹm *baṅkhane* cekak̓a.

(ii) Ẹm *baṅkhaċe* cekak̓a.

(iii) Am *baṅkhan* ọhọko daṛelea.

(iv) Am *baṅkhaċ* ọhọko daṛelea.

(v) Mit̓ ghạṛi *baṅkhaċe* hijuk̓a.

(vi) Onka dọ alom rọṛa, *baṅkhanlaṅ* dalmea.

(vii) Jọm *baṅkhane* cekaea.

(viii) Ma *baṅkhaċ* amge calak̓tabonme.

ẹnhõ, ẹnre hõ - Noa dọ Jok̓ṛao Sabad kana. Noa dọ mit̓ ayat khọn eṭak̓ ayat sãoe joṛaoet̓kana, jeleka :–

(i) Manakedeạń *ẹnhõ*e calaoena.

(ii) Ẹmakawadea *ẹnhõ*e kọkọekana.

(iii) Un dhao dalem jọmakat̓a, *ẹnre hõ* bam bạgiet̓a.

(iv) Jãhãtinạk̓em e̱maere hõ̱ *e̱nre hõ̱* bae tirpito̱k̓kana.

e̱nte - Noa do̱ Jok̓ṛao Sabad kana ar Tayo̱m Joṛao reak̓ hõ̱, Japak̓ reak̓ hõ̱e kạmia ar Kạjnum reak̓ hõ̱, jeleka :–

e̱nte̱t̓ - *e̱nte̱t̓* do̱ jok̓ṛao sabad kana. Noa hõ̱ *e̱nte* lekagey kạmia, jeleka :–

(i) Alom calak̓a, *e̱nte̱t̓* uni menaea.

(ii) Paesae ruạṛkat̓taea, *e̱nte̱t̓e* dharledea.

(iii) Bam ạgu daraledea bạhutte̱t̓ *e̱nte̱t̓* bape metadińkhan.

(iv) Haṭ kho̱n haṭak̓ bạń ạguleda (bam ạguạdińa), *e̱nte̱t̓* bam ro̱ṛ go̱t̓ạdińa.

onate - Noa hõ̱ barea ayate joṛaoet̓kana, pạrtul :–

(i) Katha akawat̓koale, *onate*ko he̱c̓ go̱do̱k̓a nãhãk̓.

(ii) Ruạk̓kanae, *onate* bae kạmi daṛeak̓kana.

ona iạte, onate̱ṛo̱ṅ, ona karo̱nte – Noa hõ̱ barea ayat joṛao reak̓e kạmiet̓kana, jeleka :–

(i) Ruạk̓kan tahẽ̱kạnạń, *ona iạte (te̱ṛo̱ṅ, karo̱nte)* bạń he̱c̓lena.

(ii) Ruạk̓kan tahẽ̱kạnạń, *onate̱ṛo̱ṅ* bạń he̱c̓lena.

(iii) Ruạk̓kan tahẽ̱kạnạń, *ona karo̱nte* bạń he̱c̓lena.

e̱ṇḍe̱khan, e̱ṇḍe̱khac̓; to̱be̱khan, to̱be̱khac̓ - Noa hõ̱ barea ayat joṛao reak̓e kạmiet̓kana,jeleka :-

(i) *E̱ṇḍe̱khan* amge ro̱ṛme.

(ii) Bạihạṛ kho̱ne he̱c̓ena, *to̱be̱khane* daka-utukeda. (ḍo̱bo̱k̓ joharadea)

Onkage noako hõ̱ ayate joṛaoet̓kana :–

e̱ṇḍe̱anaṅ, e̱ṇḍe̱ane̱c̓, e̱ṇḍe̱yena, e̱ṇḍe̱yenaṅ, e̱ṇḍe̱te, e̱ṇḍe̱tege, e̱ṇḍe̱ nãhĩ, e̱ṇḍe̱re, e̱ṇḍe̱rema, e̱ṇḍe̱reanaṅ, e̱ṇḍe̱te̱ṛo̱ṅ, e̱ṇḍe̱reane̱c̓, e̱ṇḍe̱reyena, e̱ṇḍe̱reyenak̓, e̱ṇḍe̱rege, e̱ṇḍe̱re se̱t̓, e̱ṇḍe̱ bapo, e̱ṇḍe̱ mo̱to̱.

hō̱ ... hō̱ - Noa hō̱ ayate joṛaoeťkana, jeleka :–

(i) E̱ke̱n So̱mae do̱ baṅ, me̱nkhan Mo̱ṅgo̱l *hō̱* calao ocoaepe.

(ii) Dhumạ eskar do̱ baṅ, me̱nkhan Co̱ro̱n *hō̱* calao ocoaepe.

(iii) E̱ke̱n gidrạko do̱ baṅ, me̱nkhan sē̱ṛã ho̱ṛ *hō̱* calak̓pe.

khạjuk, judi - Noa sabad hō̱ barea ayate joṛaoeťkana. Ona sãote *alo* sabad hō̱ mesalok̓kana. Ar noa do̱ bara bạrie kạmieťkana, jeleka :–

(i) Gapań calak̓a, *khạjuk* aloe dag.

(ii) Do̱ho̱miạń *khạjuk* ińak̓ hukum lekam calak̓.

(iii) *Judim* calak̓khan, noa idi toraeme.

(iv) *Judi* onkoko ńe̱lakaťkokhan, to̱be̱ calak̓me.

leka, ce̱ť leka, onka leka, noa leka - Noa sabad hō̱ barea ayate joṛaoeťkana, jeleka :–

(i) *Noa leka* benaome, *ce̱ť leka* ona menak̓.

(ii) Marak̓ *leka* sajaoem.

(iii) Hako *leka* utu ạikạuk̓kana.

(iv) Se̱ṅge̱l *leka* pạuṛạ ạikạuk̓kana.

(v) Bala *leka* peṛa okarem ńamkoa.

(vi) Disạime, *ce̱ť leka* tahē̱kantama.

(vii) Uduk̓aeme, *ce̱ť lekateye* kạmia.

(viii) Uduk̓aťme *leka* tearme.

(ix) Ṭhikem batlaoade *leka*keťae.

(x) *Ce̱ť leka* am, iń hō̱ *onka leka*ge.

(xi) *Ce̱ť leka*m ńe̱l oṭoleť, *onka leka* menak̓lea.

jãhã lekate, je̱mo̱n – Noa hō̱ barea ayate joṛaoeťkana ar *me̱nte* barabarie kạmieťkna. Pạrtul :–

(i) Lạiakome *jãhã lekate* aloko sorok̕.

(ii) Lạiakome *jemon* aloko sorok̕.

(iii) Bako calak̕a *mente* lạiakome.

(iv) Lạiakome aloko calak̕a *mente.*

ẠKIL BHAŃJAO - 11

A. Ṭoyot'kate jobab emok̕me :-

1. *ar* dinkore cet̕bon joma? *ar* do okaṭak̕ Jok̕ṛao Sabad kana?
   (a) Kạjnum-Gunum (b) Ujnum-Gunum (c) Ńunum-Kạjnum

2. *arko* doko okayena? *arko* doko Beakoron reak̕ niạm lekate cet̕ kana?
   (a) Kạjnum (b) Ujnum (c) Ńunum (d) Gunum

3. *Jok̕ṛao Sabad* do Iṅgrạjite cet̕ko metak̕a?
   (a) Adverb (b) Noun (c) Conjunction (d) Adjective

4. *are* menkeda. *are* do Beakoron reak̕ niạm lekate cet̕ kana?
   (a) Jok̕ṛao Sabad (b) Kạjnum-Gunum (c) Ujnum
   (d) Ńunum

5. Hoṛ *ar* Deko. *ar* do Beakoron reak̕ niạm lekate cet̕ kana?
   (a) Jok̕ṛao Sabad (b) Kạjnum-Gunum (c) Ujnum
   (d) Ńunum

B. Olkate jobab emok̕me :-

1. Puk̕ṛạuak̕ *(Particle)* reak̕ bean pạrtul selet̕ lạime.
2. Jok̕ṛao Sabad *(Conjunctions)* reak̕ bean pạrtul selet̕ lạime
3. Tayom Japak̕ *(Postposition)* reak̕ bean pạrtul selet̕ lạime.
4. Tayom Joṛao *(Suffix)* reak̕ bean pạrtul selet̕ lạime.

5. *alo* do̱ Beako̱ro̱n reak̓ niạm lekate ce̱t̓ kana?
6. *hape̱* do̱ Beako̱ro̱n reak̓ niạm lekate ce̱t̓ kana?
7. *Baṅ do̱ menae, baṅ do̱e calaoen.* Noa ayat reak̓ *baṅ do̱* do̱ ce̱t̓ reak̓e kạmikana?
8. *e̱k do̱e huṇḍạr kana, e̱k do̱e, tạrup̓ kana.* Noa ayat do̱ ce̱t̓ kana?
9. *co̱(ṅ)-baṅ co̱(ṅ)* do̱ Beako̱ro̱n reak̓ niạm lekate ce̱t̓ kana?
10. *Me̱nkhan* do̱ Beako̱ro̱n reak̓ niạm lekate ce̱t̓ kana?
11. *Me̱ne̱k* do̱ Beako̱ro̱n reak̓ niạm lekate ce̱t̓ kana?
12. *bicko̱m* do̱ Beako̱ro̱n reak̓ niạm lekate ce̱t̓ kana?
13. *bo̱ro̱ṅ* ar *bo̱ro̱ṅ co̱ṅ* do̱ Beako̱ro̱n reak̓ niạm lekate ce̱t̓ kana?
14. *Baṅkhan* ar *baṅkhaċ* do̱ Beako̱ro̱n reak̓ niạm lekate ce̱t̓ kana?
15. *e̱nre hõ̱* ar *e̱nhõ̱* do̱ Beako̱ro̱n reak̓ niạm lekate ce̱t̓ kana?
16. *khạjuk* ar *judi* do̱ Beako̱ro̱n reak̓ niạm lekate ce̱t̓ kana?
17. *ge* do̱ Beako̱ro̱n reak̓ niạm lekate ce̱t̓ kana?

12

PUḰRẠUḰ SABAD
(PARTICLES)

Noa dọ ayatre ayat puḱrạuaḱ lekae kạmieťkana, ọnẹ oka dọ noa sabad baṅ lagaolenkhan bẹpurạuaḱ leka ại̇kạuḱa.

ge - Noa dọ jãhãnaḱ kathare jọr emaḱ lạgiť beoharoḱkana Noa puḱrạuaḱ dọ sabad são joṛaoḱa. Noa dọ sabad khọn begarre dọ baṅ ọlọgọḱa, pạrtul :–

(i) Ọkọe kanam? *Iṅge.*

(ii) *Aċgeye* rọṛakaťa.

(iii) *Hẹċengeae.*

(iv) *Rọṛge* bae rọṛẹťkana.

(v) Nui *kangeae* nẹtarren guru dọ.

(vi) Unie hẹċen *khọnge* noa katha dọ aṅjọmọḱkana.

dọ - Noa purạuaḱ dọ Kạmiạ *(Subject)* sãoge hijuḱa ar adọm jọkhẹċ dọ Kuṛại *(Object)* são hõ hijuḱgea. Noa dọ jãhãn kathare jọr ẹmaḱ lạgiť hõ beoharoḱkana, jeleka :–

(i) Iṅ *dọ* baṅ, amge calaḱme. *(Subject)*

(ii) Ḍạn *dọ* ale Họṛ họpọn reaḱ maraṅ jalage. *(Subject)*

(iii) Nitoḱ *dọ* pẹ isi serma hoyoḱkana. *(Subject)*

(iv) Noko *dọ* ale leka *dọ* bako cọlọna. *(Subject & Object)*

(v) Cele oaris bạnuḱkokhan, disạmren raje ṅama dhọn *dọ*. (Kuṛại sãote)

(vi) Adom lebra hor *do* senge bako senoka onde *do*.
(Subject & Object)

(vii) Ale *do* nondele tahẽ hataroka, ape *do* lahaktabonpe.
(Subject)

(viii) Bana *doko* gockedea, khikrĩ *do*ko paskaokedea.
(Object)

co(ṅ) - Noa do bebegarak sabad kana, partul :–

(i) Okoe *coko* calak lagit.

(ii) Okoe badae *coṅ.*

(iii) Ac *coe* baeakat.

(iv) Nũkũi *coṅe* hecen.

(v) Nõkõe *coṅ* nondege menak.

(vi) Cet *coṅe* roret?

tet, tet - Noa do ayatre jor emak lagit larcaroka. Noa do jivianak ar bejivianak jinis são joraokate hõ hijuka. Noa sabad do mit lekha, bar lekha ar saṅge lekha são hõ hijukgea. Noa do Hahatiń-Ujnum *(Distributive Pronoun)* leka hõe kamia, jeleka :–

(i) *Hanatet* do baṅ, *noatetge* mõńj do.

(ii) *Unitet* do baṅ, *actetgeye* hijukma.

(iii) *Sakamtet* do baṅ, *dartetko* aguime.

(iv) Katic jhauako do mak saphaeme, menkhan *daretet* do ikakakme.

(v) *Apattet* do bale ńelledea, eken *hopontetge.*

(vi) *Sariaktet* baṅ okoka.

(vii) *Ńũroktet* do algagea, rakabok do muskilgea.

to̱, tho̱, tho̱r - Noa sabad hõ̱ jo̱r emak̓ lạgit̓ge beoharok̓kana Pạrtul :–

(i) Hẽ̱ *tho̱*, ekal ba co̱e bujhạuet̓kan.

(ii) Khange *tho̱*, dadal do̱ko cuṭ cuṭạulena.

(iii) E̱ṛe̱ alom ro̱ṛa, amren kangeae *to̱*?

(iv) Noa do̱ ran kana, ma ńũime *to̱*.

(v) Hẽ̱ *tho̱r*, iń hõ̱ onageń metaekan tahẽ̱na.

hẽ̱ - Noa do̱ ayatre Gunum, Kạjnum-Gunum ar Ńunum lekae kạmiet̓kana, jeleka :–

(i) He̱ċenae? *Hẽ̱*, he̱ċakanae. *(*Kạjnum-Gunum, *Adv.)*

(ii) Ona do̱ *hẽ̱* kangea. *(*Kạjnum-Gunum, *Adv.)*

(iii) *Hẽ̱* sạrigea. *(*Kạjnum-Gunum, *Adv.)*

(iv) *Hẽ̱* e̱nte. *(*Kạjnum-Gunum, *Adv.)*

(v) *Hẽ̱* e̱nteń ro̱ṛakat̓a edretege. *(*Kạjnum-Gunum, *Adv.)*

(vi) *Hẽ̱* co̱ṅ. *(*Ńunum, *Noun)*

(vii) *Hẽ̱*ge co̱ṅ *(*Ńunum, *Noun)*

(viii) *Hẽ̱* jạniċ. *(*Kạjnum-Gunum, *Adv.)*

(ix) *Hẽ̱* pase̱ċ. *(*Kạjnum-Gunum, *Adv.)*

(x) *Hẽ̱ma hẽ̱*ge. *(*Ńunum, *Noun)*

(xi) *Hẽ̱ke̱t̓ae.(*Kạjnum, *Verb)*

(xii) Calak̓e *hẽ̱ke̱t̓a.(*Kạjnum, *Verb)*

(xiii) Jãhãnak̓gey ro̱ṛ *hẽ̱ataeme.(*Kạjnum, *Verb)*

(ivx) Okaṭak̓bon galmaraoke̱t̓, ona do̱ *hẽ̱yena.* *(*Kạjnum, *Verb)* *hẽk̇* - Noa dọ *hẽ* reak̇ge eṭak̇ rup kana. Noa dọ Kạjnum lekagey kạmiet̓kana, pạrtul :-

(i) Amem idiakat̓a? *Hẽ,* idiakat̓ạń.

(ii) Alom *hẽga, hẽkẹt̓ae.*

hẽ hũ - Noa dọ ayatre Kạjnum lekae kạmiet̓kana, jeleka :–

(i) Enaṅ dọe *hẽ hũket̓a.*

(ii) *Hẽ hũạdińae.*

(iii) *Hẽ hũipe.*

(iv) Ạḍi suluk menak̇kinạ unkim haṛam-buḍhi dọ, *hẽk̇ak̇ hũk̇ak̇* jãhãnak̇ge koṛae mẹn kuṛi hõ inạge.

hại - Noa dọ adọm jọkhẹc̓ Bhabna Katha *(Interjection)* reak̇ hõe kạmigea ar baṅkhan jaoge *hẽ* katha *(affirmative)* sọdọr lạgit̓ge laṛcaṛok̇a, oka dọ baṅ *(negative)* kathare *hõ* beoharok̇gea, jeleka :–

(i) Hijuk̇me! *hại,* calak̇ạń.

(ii) Calak̇me *hại.*

(iii) Alom lạia, *hại.*

(iv) *Hại* tọbẹ imạńme.

(vi) *Hại-hại*, ọṇḍẹge hasoyedińkana.

(vii) *Hại* iń dọ bạń calak̇a, amge calak̇me. *(Negative)*

hi - Noa dọ *hại* lekage ayatre laṛcaṛok̇a, jeleka :-

(i) Dẹn iń hõ bape imạńa? *Hi* ẹmamale.

(ii) Ona dọpe kạmiket̓a? *Hi*, kạmitam lạgit̓ko.

(iii) Ẹ Sọmae! *Hi.*

(iv) Calak̇me *hi.*

(v) *Hi hi*, onage cọń mẹnẹt̓.

(vi) Ma sẹn hodok̇me! *Hi hi* calak̇kạnạń.

Disạ dọhọ (*Note*) – *hại ke bọṭẹ, hại ko bọṭẹ* ar *hi ke bọṭẹ dọ* nẹtarak̇ Santalire dọ baṅ beoharok̇kana ar baṅko bujhạu gọda.

Baṅ katha reak̇ puk̇rạuk̇ dọ pẹ lekana; mit̕ṭẹn dọ sadharọn *baṅ* katha sọdọr lạgit̕ hoyok̇kana, dosarak̇ dọ *jọr* emak̇ lạgit̕ hoyok̇kana ar tesarak̇ dọ *mana* katha sọdọr lạgit̕ hoyok̇kana. Onako dọ noako kana – *baṅ, ọhọ* ar *alo.*

ba, baṅ - *ba* dọ Kạmiạ-Ujnum reak̇ kạṭic̓ hĩs *(short form)* são hijuk̇kana. Ẹnhõ adọm jọkhẹc̓ purạu *baṅ* são hõ tahẹngea. Noa hõ disạ jạruṛkana je tinre sadharọn katha sọdọr lạgit̕ beohaok̇kana, tọbẹ dọ Kạjnumre dọ Sadharọn Calaoen Ọktẹ *(Simple Past)* reak̇ Kạjnum reak̇ Tayọm Joṛao *(Suffix)* dọ baṅ lagaok̇a. Noa dọ Lahate Calao Parọmen Ọktẹ *(Anterior)* reak̇ Kạjnum Tayọm Joṛao sạ eṭak̇ak̇ Ọktẹ *(Tense)* reak̓ hõ laṛcaṛ daṛeak̇a. *baṅ* dọ Kạjnum rupre hõ ayatre laṛcaṛok̇a, pạrtul :–

(i) Calaoenae? *Baṅ,* bae sẹnlena.

(ii) Lạiam sẹ *baṅ*a.

(iii) *Baṅ* ṅẹl ṅamok̇a, nọṇḍẹ khọn dọ.

(iv) Uni sọṅgẹtekhan dọ hẽge, *baṅkhan baṅtẹt̕ge bae* hijuk̇a.

(v) *Bae* emadea.

(vi) *Bae* hẹc̓ena, mẹnkhaniṅ dalea.

(vii) Oṛak̇re *bako* lạilak̇a, *baṅma* onka noṅka?

(viii) *Baṅ*a sẹ, onka dọ *baṅ* kana.

(ix) Alom *baṅạṅạ.*

(x) Ọkọr *baṅ.*

(xi) Cẹt̕ *baṅ* sẹ, ọhọm pạtiạulena.

(xii) *Baṅ* calak̇ họṛe sẹn ocokidiṅa.

(xiii) *Baṅ* ṅẹlọgọk̇ak̇ dọ ọhọ ṅẹllena.

ọhọ - Noa dọ jọr emak̇ lạgit̕ laṛcaṛok̇a. Noa tinre Kạjnum são joṛaok̇kana, tọbẹ Kạjnum reak̇ rup dọ lahate Calao Parọmen

Okte *(Anterior Past)* reak Kajnum rup lagaoka. Menkhan Bhabisot Okte reak *bań* katha sodor lagit hõ larcarokgea. *bań* ar *oho* do *-ge, -tet'* se *-let'*ge lagaokate *bań* kathare *jor* emak lagit hõe kamietkana. *oho* hõ Kajnum reake kami dareaka. *oho* do menjoń katha sodor lagit menjoń reak Okte Tayom Jorao *(Optative Tense Suffix) -ke* hõ lagaoka, partul :–

(i) *Ohoe* hećlena.

(ii) *Ohoe* gujuka.

(iii) *Ohoe* menlea.

(iv) Alom botoroka, *ohoe* cekakema.

(v) *Ohoa ohoń* em darelena.

(vi) *Ohoa* se. Onde do alo.

(vii) *Oho* toko jãhã cekamea.

(viii) *Ohotet'ge* emlena.

(ix) *Ohogem* hec darelena.

(x) Amem tahẽlenkhan, *ohotet'* honańe cekalea.

(xi) Bae *ohoea.*

(xii) *Ohobon oholetaea.*

(xiii) Tisre hõ bae *oho akawat'tińa* nin din do.

(xiv) Nit bam calaka? Bań, *ohoatińkana,* enańre do cet hõ bako menlaka.

(xv) Jãhãtege *ohoatińa.*

ũhũk ar *õhõk* - Noa do *bań* katha reak digdha sodor tuluc bhabna reak kathae sodoretkana, jeleka :–

(i) *Ũhũk*! Cet co hoyakana!

Noa do bań katha reak kathae sodoretkana, partul :–

(ii) *Ũhũk* bań calaka ar bańkhan cet co hoyoka.

Ũhũk ar *õhõk* do barabarigey kamietkana.

alo - *alo* do̱ mana katha so̱do̱r lạgit̆ laṛcaṛo̱k̆kana. Ar noa do̱ Bhạbiso̱t *(future)* Kạjnum rupre beoharok̆a. Inạ mo̱to̱ do̱ baṅ bicko̱m hukum se̱ bad̩aejo̱ṅ *(wise)* lạgit̆ hõ laṛcaṛok̆kana. *alo* sãote *-ge*, *-le̱t̆*, *-te̱t̆* se̱ *baṛe̱* lagaokate hõ hijuk̆kana, pạrtul :–

(i) *Alom* ro̱ṛa.

(ii) Bes leka to̱lme, je̱mo̱n *alo* raṛak̆.

(iii) *Aloń* se̱nlenkhan, uni tuluc̆ do̱ o̱ho̱ń ńe̱pe̱llena.

(iv) Jãhãn bạṛic̆ ghoṭna baṛe̱ *alo* hoyok̆ma.

(v) *Alo* baṛe̱ye ńũruk̆ma.

(vi) *Alo* se̱ onka do̱.

(vi) *Alogem* calak̆a.

(vii) *Alote̱t̆gem* e̱mo̱k̆a.

(viii) *Alo*ye laṅgak̆ma.

(ix) *Alo*m se̱nok̆, ona bo̱ro̱ṅ bhagea.

(x) *Alo*e ataṅma.

ńõk̆ - Noa ho̱te̱te ko̱m reak̆ katha bad̩aeok̆ lạgit̆ beoharok̆kana, pạrtul :-

(i) *Ko̱m ńõk̆gea.*

(ii) *E̱se̱l ńõk̆geae.*

tora - Calak̆ jo̱khe̱c̆ so̱ṅge̱te idi reak̆ katha bad̩aeok̆kana, pạrtul :-

(i) Idi *toraeme* so̱ṅge̱te.

(ii) Bạbu idi *toraem.*

dara - Hijuk̆ jo̱khe̱c̆ so̱ṅge̱ *tora* reak̆ katha bad̩aeok̆kana,

pạrtul:-

(i) Ạlu ạgu *daraeme.*

(ii)Dak̆ ạgu *daraeme.*

hataṛ - *hataṛ* hõ pukṛạuak̆ kana. Ayatre ac̆ mo̱to̱ do̱ ce̱t̆ mane hõ bạnuk̓a, pạrtul :-

(i) Jom *hatạrme.*

(ii) Rohoe *hatạrme;* tạṅgi *hatạriṅme.*

maṛaṅ -Noa hotẹte do jãhãnak̓ kạmi lahae reak̓ katha baḍaeok̓kana, pạrtul :-

(i) Ḍạbrạ *maṛaṅok̓abon.*

(ii) Jom *maṛaṅabo.*

(iii)Noa khẹtbon si *maṛaṅa.*

hot̓, got̓ -Noa hotẹte usạra kạmie reak̓ baḍaeok̓kana, pạrtul :-

(i) Heč̓ *got̓enae.*

(ii) Jom *hot̓kedae.*

oṭo - Noa hotẹte kạmi se sẹṭer oṭo baṛakate ruạṛok̓ reak̓ katha baḍaeok̓kana, pạrtul :-

(i) Sẹṭer *oṭokaeme.*

(ii) Dal *oṭokaeme.*

(iii) Daka em *oṭoaeme.*

(iii) Bạṭi idi *oṭokam.*

ẠKIL BHAṄJAO - 12

A. Ṭoyot̓kate jobab emok̓me :-

1. *do* do Beakoron lekate cet̓ko metak̓a?
   (a) Puk̓rạuk̓ Sabad (b) Kạjnum (c) Ṅunum (d) Ujnum
2. *Hẽ hũipe*. Noa do Beakoronre cet̓ lekae kạmiakada?
   (a) Ujnum (b) Kạjnum (c) Ṅunum (d) Kạjnum-Gunum
3. *họi* do ar noa leka hõ aṅjomok̓a?
   (a) hại (b) hui (c) hai (d) hiy

4. *Hẽ ..., ekal ba cǫe bujhạuetkan.* Khạli jaga pęręjme.
   (a) thu (b) tho (c) thǫ (d) thọ

5. ... *ǫhǫletaea.* Khạli jaga pęręjme.
   (a) Kạmi (b) Ǫhǫbon (c) Purạu (d) Jǫm

B. Ǫlkate jobab ęmǫkme :-

1. Pukṛạu Sabad reak bean ęm tuluc pạrtul ęmme.
2. *dǫ* dǫ Beakǫrǫn reak niạm lekate cęt kana?
3. *tǫ, thǫ* ar *thǫr* dǫ Beakǫrǫn reak niạm lekate cęt kana?
4. *hẽ* dǫ Beakǫrǫn reak niạm lekate cęt kana?
5. *hẽkkedae*, noa ayat reak *hẽ* dǫ cęt reake kạmikana?
6. *hạido* Beakǫrǫn lekate cęt reake kạmikana?
7. *ba* ar *baṅ* dǫ Beakǫrǫn reak niạm lekate cęt kana?
8. *ũhũk* ar *ǭhǭk* dǫ Beakǫrǫn reak niạm lekate cęt kana?
9. *ṅǭk* dǫ Beakǫrǫn reak niạm lekate cęt kana?
10. *tora* ar *dara* dǫ Beakǫrǫn reak niạm lekate cęt kana?
11. *hataṛ* dǫ Beakǫrǫn reak niạm lekate cęt kana?
12. *maṛaṅ* dǫ Beakǫrǫn reak niạm lekate cęt kana?
13. *hǫt* ar *gǫt* dǫ Beakǫrǫn reak niạm lekate cęt kana,!
14. *oṭo* dǫ Beakǫrǫn reak niạm lekate cęt kana?

13

HAHAṚA/DUK/BHABNA/ HULẠS-RẠSKẠ/BHAṚO/HASO/SARHAO *(INTERJECTION)*

Adǫm noṅkanak̓ puk̓rạuak̓ sabad menak̓a, ǫnẹ oka dǫ aṅjǫm ocoye lạgit̓ kathae hǫhǫe, aodhane reak̓, bhạbisǫtre baṅ onkae reak̓ bǫtǫr oco katha reak̓, dil-sạhẫs reak̓ katha, sarhaoe reak̓ katha, hahaṛa reak̓ katha, hulạs-rạskạ reak̓ katha, duk reak̓ katha, bhabna reak̓ katha, haso reak̓ katha ar onkage onkanak̓ katha sǫdǫr lạgit̓ hõ beoharok̓kana Noako mod khǫn adǫmak̓ dǫ sabad lahare hijuk̓kana ar adǫmak̓ dǫ ayat são joṛaok̓kana. Onako mod khǫn adǫmak̓ dǫ Kạjnum reak̓ Tayǫm Joṛao rupre hõ beoharok̓kana. Noa dǫ Hǫhǫ Katha *(Vocative Case, संबोधन कारक)* reak̓e kạmia.

ẹ - Noa dǫ Ṅutum lahare laṛcaṛok̓kana, ar jãhãe hǫṛ hudạ sẹ pǫd *(post)* eman menak̓tae, ona hudạ sẹ pǫd ṅutum lahare *ẹ* beoharok̓kana sẹ sạgại lahare hõ lagaok̓a, jeleka :–

ẹ ba; ẹ baba; ẹ gǫ; ẹ raj; ẹ Sunạ; ẹ Sunạ apat; ẹ hǫ. (Hǫṛ dạstur kana je mit̓ eṭak̓ic̓ dǫ ṅutum ṅumkate dǫ bako hǫhǫjǫṅa.)

ẹa, ea - Noa dǫ jãhãe kạṭic̓ hǫṛ hǫhǫaere Santalire beoharok̓kana, mẹnkhan noa sabad dǫ ẹkẹn koṛa gidrạ lạgit̓ge laṛcaṛok̓a, pạrtul :–

(i) *Ẹa* bạbu!

(ii) *Ẹa* Pạṇḍu!

(iii) *Ẹa* phạsiạrako!

(iv) *Ea*, onka do alom rora!

(v) Cet́ iatem *eawadińa?*

ei - Noa hõ jãhãe hor hohoae jokhećge beoharok̇a. Menkhan noa katha beohar jokhec̓ jãhãeak̓ ńutum, huda se pod são do bań beoharok̇a. Noa katha do kuri ar kora talare beoharok̇a ar barea gate talare hõ hohojońreko beoharet́kana. Menkhan apnar khon latu hor hohoaere do bań beoharok̇a, partul :–

ei, noteya beńgedme; *ei ei, note hijuk̇me se; eiańkanam, ińak̇ sagai do bam badaekana.*

e ho - Noa katha do herel-herel talare hohojońre beoharok̇kana Noa katha do herel-herel talare latu ar katic̓ talare hõ larcarok̇kangea, jeleka :–

(i) *E ho,* pera hor!

(ii) *E ho,* gorom!

(iii) *E ho,* baba!

(iv) *E ho,* note hijuk̇tabonpe!

e ho - Noa katha do maejiuko ako talareko hohojońkhan, nońkan katha doko beohara. Noa katha do adom jokhec̓ juri-paríre ac̓ jãwãeye hohoaere hõ beoharok̇kangea, jeleka :–

(i) *E ho,* hatom!

(ii) *E ho*, okatem calak̇kana?!

ia, ia ho - Noa do bhabna, duk, raska, hahara, duk-haso eman katha sodor lagit́ beoharok̇kana, partul :–

(i) *Ia ho!* Do se daktor hohowaeme.

(ii) *Ia,* do se calak̇me; *ia hoń* metamkana!

ho - Noa katha do hahara, duk, bhabna, hulas-raska, haso eman kathare beoharok̇a. Noa katha do mit́ herele hohoae jokhen beoharok̇a ar noa do mit́ umaran herel hopon talare hohojońreko beoharet́kana. Ar beńepel oprom hor talare hõ nońkan katha beoharoḱkana. Noa katha dǫ mamǫt, teńat talare hõ sẹ balat era talare hõ laṛcaṛoḱkana, jeleka :–

henda *họ*; ǫkǫe *họ*; alom *họạńạ.*

hǫ - Noa katha dǫ maejiuko talareko hǫhǫjǫṅkhan beoharoḱkana. Ar erveltẹť koṛa são katha dǫ *hǫ* reaḱe kạmikana, pạrtul :–

hape *họ*, goṅgo apat. (Hilittẹť erveltẹť koṛae hǫhǫaere beoharoḱkana. Nẹtar dǫ noṅkan katha ạḍi kǫmge aṅjǫmǫḱkana.

henda - Noa dǫ jãhãe hǫhǫaere beoharoḱkana. Noa beoharre jãhãeaḱ ńutum sẹ hudạ sẹ duk, rạskạ, bhabna, hahaṛa eman katha sǫdǫr lạgiť hõ laṛcaṛoḱkana. Noa sãote – *họ, hǫ, ya, na* joṛaokate beoharoḱkana, pạrtul :–

(i) *Henda* bạbu, cẹťem cekayeťa?

(ii) *Henda họ*, gạiye aťakantińạ, ńẹl jãhãnakadeape.

(iii) *Henda na*, okatem calaḱkana?

(iv) *Henda ya,* bam aṅjǫma?

ya - Noa dǫ jaoge henda ẹ tayǫmre hijuḱa. Noa katha dǫ rǫrǫṛiċ khǫn kạṭiċ hǫṛ hǫhǫakore ar ẹkẹn hẹrẹl hǫpǫn talare beoharoḱ lạgiť laṛcaṛoḱkana. Judi noa *ya* rǫrǫṛiċ khǫn lạṭu lạgiťe beohar lekhaċ ǫpǫman reaḱ katha hoyoḱa sẹ bẹmanǫt reaḱ katha hoyoḱa, pạrtul :–

(i) *Calaḱme ya,* hǫhǫamkanako!

(ii) *Ẹ bạbu ya,* bam *aṅjǫmẹťaya!*

(iii) Nui *dǫ ya,* oka lekan hǫṛ kan *cǫe ya?*

(iv) *Ma ya ma ya, emaeme ya!*

(v) *Dela ya!*

(vi) *Dẹ ya, ạgu gǫdme ya!*

(vi) *Henda ya, okateyam helaoḱkana ya?*

na - Noa do̠ *ya* lekage beoharok̓a; me̠nkhan kuṛi ar maejiuko talare ro̠ro̠ṛic̓ kho̠n kạṭic̓ic̓ lạgit̓ beoharok̓a, pạrtul :–

(i) *E̠ na,* hijuk̓me *na!*

(ii) *De̠ na, am na* ạguitalaṅme!

(iii) *O̠ko̠r na,* baco̠ń ńe̠lakade!

(iv) *Ma na,* bạṭiko ạguipe *na!*

(v) *Henda na,* dela hijuk̓me!

(vi) Dela *na* birtebon calak̓a sakam he̠c̓!
(hạ ar *ho̠* do̠ tayo̠m sakamre hō̠ e̠makangea.)

yọi, nọi - Noakin sabad do̠ *ya* ar *na* lekage beoharok̓a. Noa mod kho̠n *yi* do̠ he̠re̠l ho̠po̠n lạgit̓ beoharok̓a ar *ni* do̠ maejiu se̠ kuṛi-kuṛi talare beoharok̓a se̠ ho̠ho̠jo̠ṅreko beoharet̓kana. Noa do̠ raṅgao ńō̠k̓ ho̠ho̠ateko ho̠ho̠jo̠ṅa, pạrtul :–

(i) Me̠n *yọi,* ho̠r kho̠n o̠co̠go̠k̓pe, hawa gạḍi darakana!

(ii) So̠nto̠ro̠k̓pe *nọi,* bhalok̓ setae ńir baṛaekana!

hui, hui hui - Noa katha do̠ ńũt ar raṭen bir gajar kho̠n pharakok̓ se̠ aodhanko lạgit̓ beoharok̓a, pase̠c̓ jãhãnic̓ menaetane̠c̓ reak̓ kho̠bo̠r e̠mo̠k̓re, pạrtul :–

(i) *Hui,* no̠te̠re cele co̠ń ńe̠llede!

(ii) *Hui hui,* cele co̠ṅ pase̠c̓ menaea!

(iii) Ạḍi bạṛic̓e *huiadea!*

re̠ - Noa do̠ Baṅgla kho̠n hataoak̓kana ar jãhãe ho̠ṛ usạra he̠c̓ ocoye lạgit̓ ayatre laṛcaṛok̓a. Noa do̠ jaoge Tayo̠m Japak̓ *(Postposistion)* ruprege hijuk̓a. Noa do̠ aso̠kaete Santali ō̠nō̠ṛhē̠re *(poetry)* jạsti do̠ beoharok̓kana. Noa do̠ hahaṛa ar rạskạ katha so̠do̠r lạgit̓ beoharok̓kana, jeleka :–

(i) E̠ *babare̠!*

(ii) Tãhãreta nana *tarnare̠!*

eḱ, e̱ḱ -Noa hõ̱ rạskạ, bhabna, hahaṛa katha so̱do̱r lạgiť beoharoḱkana, pạrtul :-

(i) *E̱ḱ* uni! *E̱ḱ* hunkin!

(ii) Unre do̱ *eḱ,* noṅkatele se̱nlena!

(iii) *E̱ḱ* e̱n e̱ṇḍe̱!

(iv) *E̱ḱ* noko darakokana!

(v) *E̱ḱ* nitgeye jo̱skedea!

(e̱ḱ do̱ *e̱* leka hõ̱ bujhạuḱa.)

e̱ḱ e̱ḱ e̱ḱ – Iṅgrạjite noa do̱ *oh*ko metaḱkana. Jãhãnaḱ jinis ńũroḱ reaḱ se̱ jãhãnaḱ rạpudoḱ reaḱ saḍe/aṛaṅ aṅjo̱mlenkhan se̱ jãhãnaḱ acka ghoṭna hoyoḱ reaḱ saḍe aṅjo̱mo̱ḱre se̱ bujhạuḱre *e̱ḱ e̱ḱ e̱ḱ* do̱ beoharoḱa. Noa sabad do̱ Santalire hõ̱ ńe̱lo̱go̱ḱkana, pạrtul :–

(i) *E̱ḱ e̱ḱ e̱ḱ* ńũrhạyinạń, ńũrhạyinạń!

(ii) *E̱ḱ e̱ḱ e̱ḱ* rạpuťena!

(iii) *E̱ḱ e̱ḱ e̱ḱ* bhindạṛenae!

hạí, họi họi, họi, hại hại - *hại* do̱ *hẽ̱* lekagey kạmieťkana. Ar ado̱m jo̱khe̱c̓ do̱ baṅ katha so̱do̱r lạgiť hõ̱ hoyoḱkangea, pạrtul :-

(i) Calaḱgeam? *Hại,* calaḱgiạń!

(ii) Calaḱgeam? *Hại,* bạń calaḱa!

(iii) Hijuḱme; *hại,* calaḱạń.

họi hõ̱ *hẽ̱* lekagey kạmia, me̱nkhan netar do̱ ko̱mge beoharoḱkana, pạrtul :–

(i) De̱n iń hõ̱, bape imạńa? *Họi,* emamale!

(ii) Ona do̱pe kạmikeťa? *Họi* kạmitam lạgiťko!

hại, họi ar *họi họi* do̱ miť lekagey kạmia, me̱nkhan *hại hại* do̱ netar ko̱mge beohar ńe̱lo̱go̱ḱkana.

ọi, ọi ọi - Noa katha ro̱ro̱ṛic̓ ac̓ menae ṭhại babo̱tre lahae baḍae ocoedekana sẹ jãhãe họṛ jãhãnak̇ baṅ cekae sẹ andhaye lạgit̀ noṅkan katha dọ beoharok̇a, pạrtul :–

(i) *Ọi,* nọtẹre minạńa!

(ii) Mit̀ dhaoe *ọiket̀a,* adọe okaen cọṅ!

(iii) *Ọi,* cẹt̀em cekaet̀a?!

(iv) Enaṅ khọne *ọi ọi*ok̇kana, ọkọre hijuk̇kana!

ã - Noa dọ tinre jãhãe bae ańjọm ńamet̀kana sẹ jãhãn katha bạḍae sanaedekhac̀ tọbẹ noa *ã* katha mit̀ bar dhaoe dohṛaet̀kana, pạrtul :–

Dẹn ạguime! *Ã*, cẹt̀em mẹnkeda?

ẹh ẹ̃k̇, ẹhẹ̃k̇ ẹhẹ̃k̇! ọ̃họ̃k̇, ọ̃họ̃k̇, ũhũk̇, ũhũk̇ ũhũk̇ - Noa dọ jãhãn katha baṅ batao reak̇ sẹ apọti sọdọr lạgit̀ beoharok̇kana, pạrtul :-

(i) *Ẹhẹ̃k̇,* baṅ ṭhikem batlaoet̀kana!

(ii) *Ũhũk̇,* bạń disạyet̀a!

(iii) *Ọ̃họ̃k̇,* bam bạḍaea, ẹṇḍẹkhan am dọ!

(iv) *Ũhũk̇ ũhũk̇,* ona katha dọ alom rọṛa!

(vi) *Ũhũket̀ge* dọe, bae ganok̇kan dọ!

(vii) *Ũhũk̇, ũhũk̇,* bạń sẹnatama!

(viii) *Ọ̃họ̃k̇, ọ̃họ̃k̇ ọ̃họ̃k̇,* ọhọ hoe daṛelena!

ạikạ sẹ *ạikhạ* - Noa dọ cetaona katha sọdọr lạgit̀ beoharok̇kana apọti katha sọdọr lạgit̀ hõ laṛcaṛok̇gea, pạrtul :-

(i) Ạḍi ṭakań khọrọcakat̀a, *ạikạ* nịạ dhao dọ khup̀ jutakana!

(ii) Sọṅgẹteń calak̇a, alo *ạikạm* bạgiạ́ṇạ!

(iii) Dẹc̀ dọ dẹjọk̇me, *ạikạ* noa ḍạr dọ lẹbṛẹc̀gea!

(iv) Sẹn dọń sẹnọk̇gea, bạń ńamlekhan *ạikạ* alom ruhạḍińạ!

(v) Ma sabeme, *ạikhại* gẹgẹrgea!

iạ ạikạ, iạ ạikhạ - Noa họtẹte katha disạ ocoye lạgit̀ sẹ cetaoe lạgit̕ beoharok̕kana, pạrtul :-

(i) *Iạ ạikạ* din hilạk̕ hijuk̕me!

(ii) *Iạ ạikạ* alom raga, adọń idimea; baṅkhan dọ baṅ!

(iii) *Iạ ạikhạ* ọhọń sẹnlena!

hãhã, hãhãk̕ - Noa kathate cetonok̕ reak̕ kathae lạiet̕kana sẹ thirok̕ lạgit̕ sẹ baṅ onkae reak̕ kathae sọdọret̕kana. Noa dọ *hã* ar *hẽ̱* lekan katha kangea sẹ ona barabạrigey kạmiet̕kana, pạrtul :-

(i) *Hãhã,* inạk̕kak̕me! Jạsti dọ baṅ!

(ii) *Hãhã,* alom dalea!

(iii) Ọkọe hõ̱ bako *hãhãk̕lak̕a*!

(iv) *Hãhãk̕* tuluċgekin dalkedea!

(v) *Hãhãk̕* hõ̱ bae mẹnlak̕a, thoṛagan hõ̱!

ahak̕ – Noa dọ *hãhã, ẽ̱hẽ̱k̕* ar *ũhũk̕* lekage beoharok̕a, pạrtul :-

(i) *Ahak̕,* alom dalea!

(ii) *Ahak̕,* ọntẹ dọ baṅ kana!

aha!, aha aha!- Noa họtẹte hulạs-rạskạ katha sọdọr lạgit̕ beoharok̕kana, pạrtul :-

(i) *Aha aha,* nõ̱k̕õ̱etale phạṛi jel!

(ii) *Aha,* thoṛań bacọlket̕a, baṅkhanịń jọskea họnaṅ!

ahaha!, haha! - Noa katha họtẹte hõ̱ apọti sẹ cetaona katha sọdọr lạgit̕ *aha* beoharok̕kana, pạrtul :-

(i) *Ahaha,* ọntẹ dọ alom calak̕a!

(ii) *Aha haha,* onka dọ alom rọṛa!

mẹn - Noa katha họtẹte dọ disạ oco, jigạs sẹ husiạrok̕ lạgit̕ katha sọdọr lạgit̕ laṛcaṛok̕kana. Noa dọ cetaona *(warning)* lạgit̕ laṛcaṛok̕kana, pạrtul :-

(i) *Mẹn,* sọntọrọk̕pe!

(ii) *Mẹn,* alope lại baṛaea!

(iii) *Mẹn* mẹn, ape sẹċe dạṛeťkana!

mẹn baba; *mẹn* ba; *mẹn* gọ; *mẹn* ya; *mẹn* na; *mẹn* yọi; *mẹn* họ; *mẹn* bạhu; *mẹn* mại eman.

ẹhẹ, ẹhẹ ẹhẹ, ẹhẹge, ẹhẹ rẹ - Noa katha dọ husiạroǩ reaǩ katha, apọti reaǩ katha sọdọr lạgiť beoharoǩa. Cigạriạ katha sọdọr lạgiť hõ laṛcaṛoǩkana, pạrtul :-

(i) *Ẹhẹ,* okatem calaǩkana?!

(ii) *Ẹhẹ,* cẹťem cekaeťa; ńẹleťmegeạń!

(iii) *Ẹhẹge,* alo ọntẹ dọ!

(iv) *Ẹhẹ ẹhẹ,* cẹťem idieťtalea?!

(v) *Ẹhẹre,* cẹťkom kạumạu baṛaeťa?

Adọmaǩ noṅkan puǩrạuaǩko menaǩa, ọnẹ oka dọ hahaṛa sẹ bhaṛo kathako sọdọreťkana, ọnẹ oka dọ *baba* são lahare ẹ ar tayọmre dọ *-re* lagaoǩkan, adọmaǩ dọ *ayo* são *-ge, gọ* sẹ *baba* são *gọ* lagaokate hahaṛa, bhaṛoǩ reaǩ katha lạiạgoǩkan, pạrtul :-

(i) *Ayọ gọ!* Ạḍi lạṭu hakoko saṗakade!

(ii) *Ẹ baba!* Ạḍi utạr rọkọċe oarakaťko!

(iii) *Ẹ babare!* Ạḍi lạṭui gẹťakan!

(iv) *Babare!* Unạǩ hamalaǩ dọ bạń tul daṛeaǩa!

(v) *Ayọ, ayọ, ayo gọ!* Ạḍi ãṭ hasoyediṅkana!

(vi) *Ẹ babare!* Baṅ jutiń ạikạueťa!

(vii) *Baba rẹ!* Cẹť hoyakantapea!?

(viii) *Ẹ baba rẹ!* Un maraṅ hako dọ bạń ńẹlakaťkoa!

(ix) *Ayo!* Nitge nọṇḍẹye tahẽkana!

(x) *Ayoge!* Bam aṅjọmeťtiṅạ?

ạige - Noa katha họtẹte bhaṛoǩ katha sọdọr lạgiť beoharoǩkana, pạrtul :-

(i) *Ạige,* nọtẹ dọ reaṛgeye họeyet́a!

(ii) *Ạige,* nui hoṛ dọ oka leka cọe rọṛẹt́a!

ạiyo - Noa dọ *ayo* khọn bọdọlọḱ sabad kana, ar *ạige* rupre hõ beoharoḱa, pạrtul :-

(i) *Ạiyo,* enaṅre haṇḍẹń ńẹlleťmea, tinre nọṇḍẹ dọm hẹc̓ena!?

(ii) *Ạiyo,* bam bọtọrọḱkana!?

ạijo - Noa reaḱ eṭaḱ rup dọ *ạiyo* kana. Noa dọ bhaṛo katha sọdọr lạgit́ beoharoḱa, pạrtul :-

(i) *Ạijo,* okayena?!

(ii) *Ạijo,* bejaeye aťen dọ!

ạjjo, ajjo – Noakin dọ *ạijo* leka beoharoḱkana Nẹbẹtar dọ ạḍi kọm, baṅ lekage beoharoḱkana.

durrẹ - Hahaṛa sẹ baṅ ọhmaḱ ghoṭna hoyoḱre noṅkanaḱ dọ laṛcaṛoḱkana, pạrtul :-

Durrẹ, cẹt́ cọṅ ạḍi cọṭ jol rakap̓ gọťena!
(*Durrẹ* dọ, durẹ leka hõ aṅjọmoḱa.)

ẹh́, ẹh́ ẹh́, ẹh́re - Noa dọ hahaṛa/duk/rạskạ/bhaṛo eman lekan katha sọdọr lạgit́ beoharoḱkana. Noa dọ asọkaete ayo hoṛko beohareťkana.

Noa dọ ḍihạtren Baṅgaliko jạsti dọko beohareťkana. Noako sabadte cigạri/siṛạg reaḱ kathako sọdọr lạgit́ beoharoḱkana, pạrtul :-

(i) *Ẹh́,* ạḍi jut ńẹloḱkana noa dọ!

(ii) *Ẹh́,* ac̓ eskartegeye dhẹjket́a!

(iii) *Ẹh́,* jọrọạdińa!

(iv) *Ẹh́ ẹh́,* hasoyedińa!

(v) *Eh̆ eh̆,* cet̆ leka ńelok̆kana!?

(vi) *Eh̆ eh̆,* ne nãhãk̆e daleńa!

(vii) *Eh̆re,* ạḍi garteń tạkic̆ena!

eh̆ - Noa do *eh̆* leka ucrạnok̆a. Noa kathate haso ar hahaṛa/bhaṛok̆ eman reak̆ katha sodor lạgit̆ ayo hoṛgeko beohara, pạrtul :-

Eh̆, bạṛic̆geye losot̆ket̆a!

ehe hehe he, eh̆ hehe hehe - Noa katha hotete cigạri/siṛạg/hirkhạ katha sodor lạgit̆ beoharok̆kana, pạrtul :-

(i) *Ehe hehe he,* goṭae losot̆akana!

(ii) *Eh̆ hehe hehe,* noṇḍe do alope ạguyea, goṭae mạilạwa kana!

e ehe! ehe he! ehe hehe! - Noa sabad hotete hirkhạ/siṛạg reak̆ katha se haso reak̆ katha sodor lạgit̆ beoharok̆kana, pạrtul :-

(i) *Ehe he,* noṇḍe hasoyediṅkana!

(ii) *Ehe he,* nui hoṛ do tobe ạḍi bhabna baḍhaoentaea!

(iii) *Eh̆ ehe,* goṭa hoṛmo bogete hasoyediṅa!

oh̆ho, oh̆re, oh̆ hoho ho - Noa do haso, bhabna ar ikạ koe lạgit̆ beoharok̆kana, pạrtul :-

(i) *Oh̆ ho,* thoṛa bạń josleda!

(ii) *Oh̆ ho,* noṅkan hoṛ kanae!

(iii) *Oh̆re,*katha dobon kharap̆ket̆a!

(iv) *Oh̆re* durre, cet̆ lekam ńelok̆kan!

(v) *Oh̆ hoho ho,* ạḍi hasoyediṅkana, *oh̆! oh̆!*

ọh̆, ọh̆ ọh̆, ọh̆ ọh̆ọ - Noa sabad hotete do gidrạko dulạṛ, cerec̆ se thir ocoko lạgit̆ beoharok̆a. Gidrạ sãote eṅgattet̆ hõ bhabna sodor lạgit̆ noa sabad do beoharok̆a, pạrtul :-

(i) *Ọh̆* beṭa, alom laga!

(ii) *Ọh̉* sona, alom alom laga!

(iii) *Ọh̉ ọh̉,* ale chọna (sona) dọ bae laga!

(iv) *Ọh̉ ọhọ,* ale bạbu dọ bae laga (raga)!

o̱h̉! o̱h̉ o̱h̉! o̱h̉ o̱ho̱! - Noa sabad ho̱te̱te kastao/hirkhạ/haso katha so̱do̱r lạgiť beoharoǩkana pạrtul :-

(i) *O̱h̉,* hạni toraṅ paskaokedea!

(ii) *O̱h̉,* ạḍiń laṅgaṭakana kicriċ lạgiť!

(iii) *O̱h̉,* go̱ċ giḍiyenae!

(iv) *O̱h̉ o̱h̉,* noaṅ hiṛińketa̓!

(v) *O̱h̉ o̱ho̱,* thoṛa bạń jo̱sledea!

(vi) *O̱h̉ o̱ho̱ ho̱ho̱,* neyiń bạṛija me̱nte!

uh̉! uh̉re! - Noa sabad ho̱te̱te hirkhạ/ạṛis/haso/duk/bhabna ar jãhãnaǩ hoyoǩ reaǩ aṛaṅ saḍe tayo̱m hoyoǩaǩ ghoṭna baḍae lahae ar cetaoǩ katha so̱do̱r lạgiť beoharoǩkana, pạrtul :-

(i) *Uh̉,* ne̱ń bajaokoǩa!

(ii) *Uh̉,* khub bhageaǩko ńamketa̓!

(iii) *Uh̉,* abon no̱ṇḍe̱bon tahe̱nkhan ho̱naṅ, dhoragebon te̱nkoǩa!

(iv) *Uh̉re,* katha do̱bon bạṛiċketa̓!

(v) *Uh̉re,* uni do̱bon kạhil ocokedea!

uhu! uhu uhu! u huhu! u huhu huhu! uh̉ huhuhu! - Noa katha ho̱te̱te do̱ kastao reaǩ katha so̱do̱r lạgiť beoharoǩkana,pạrtul :-

(i) *Uhu,* thoṛa bạń sap̉ledea!

(ii) *Uhu uhu,* thoṛa bạń sap̉ledea!

(iii) *U huhu,* thoṛa-thoṛa bạń sap̉ ńamledea!

(iv) *U huhu huhu,* thoṛa-thoṛa lạgiťiń paskaokedea!

(v) *Uh̉ huhu,* thoṛagan bạń sap̉ ńamledea!

i, iḣ, iḣ iḣ - Noa sabad hoṭeṭe haso/duk/hirkhạ reaḱ katha sodor lạgiť noṅkanaḱ sabad hõ beoharoḱkana *i* do ạḍi komge beoharre ńelogoḱkana, pạrtul :-

(i) *I*, ạṛisgey ńeloḱkana.

(ii) *Iḣ,* hirkhạge soḱkana!

(iii) *Iḣ,* bogete rabaṅkana!

(iv) *Iḣ,* jạnumiń roḱena họ!

(v) *Iḣ iḣ iḣ,* goṭa hoṛmo laṭkaoakawadea!

is, is is - Noa sabad hoṭeṭe acka hirkhạ sodor lạgiť beoharoḱkana se haso lại sodor lạgiť beoharoḱkana, pạrtul :-

(i) *Is,* jạnumiń roḱena!

(ii) *Is,* hirkhạge soḱkana!

(iii) *Is,* ạṛisediṅkanam!

(iv) *Is is,* alom lintińạ, ạḍi ãṭ hasoyediṅkana!

ạigu - Noa sabad hoṭeṭe hõ acka haso reaḱ katha sodor lạgiť beoharoḱkana Noa do *ayo go* lekage beoharoḱa, pạrtul :-

Ạigu, ackań bereť goťena, ḍạṇḍa hĩṛĩć marte hasokidińa.

aege - Noa sabad hoṭeṭe bhaṛo/hahaṛa/botor katha sodoroḱkana. Ar noa do *ayoge* reaḱ dosar rup kana, pạrtul :-

(i) *Aege,* tiạr goťena!

(ii) *Aege,* botor goť ocokidińam!

(iii) *Aege,* unạḱ hoṛom arjaokeda!

ạu, ạu ạu - Noa sabad hoṭeṭe botor/haso/bhaṛo/hahaṛa katha sodor lạgiť noa do ayo hoṛ hoṭeṭe beoharoḱkana, pạrtul :-

(i) *Ạu* de na, ceť katha coe metalaṅkana!

(ii) *Ạu,* noṇḍe na haso goťkidińa!

(iii) *Ạu,* dela na, cele coń lebeťkede!

(iv) *Ạu ạu,* nọṇḍẹ naṅ tọhọt' hasoyena na!

ọ, ọh̐ - Noa sabad hotẹte bujhạutẹt'/edre/daya sọdọr lạgit' beoharok'kana, pạrtul :-

(i) *Ọ,* bachatiń ona kana!

(ii) *Ọ,* sạri ona dọlaṅ hiṛińkeda, *ọh̐*!

(iii) *Ọ,* onam mẹnẹt'a!

(iv) *Ọ,* hapẹ nãhãk'laṅ thapamea!

(v) *Ọ,* acha ranlaṅ kiriṅaea!

họ - Noa dọ hẹrẹl ar ayo họṛ talare katha disạ ocoe lạgit' laṛcaṛok'kana, pạrtul :-

(i) *Họ,* bạń disạyet'a!

(ii) *Họ,* bạń jọmlet'a!

ọ hae, ọ hae hae - Noa sabad hotẹte hahaṛa/duk/haso reak' bhao sọdọr lạgit' beoharok'kana, pạrtul :-

(i) *Ọ hae,* gọc'kedeae!

(ii) *Ọ hae*, bogete hasoyediṅkana!

(iii) *Ọ hae,* cẹt'iń cekaea!

(iv) *Ọ hae,* nui gidrạ dọ dayageye ńẹlọk'kana!

(v) *Ọ hae,* nui kanaye!

(vi) *Ọ hae hae,* unạk'e kọsṭọk'kana!

(vii) *Ọ hae,* dayage parkọmreye saṭaoena!

(viii) Ọ hae hae, nunạk' sud dọ bạń bạḍaelak'a!

hae, hae hae, haere, haere hae, haere haere - Noa sabad hotẹte ạḍi bhabna/haso/duk/kọsṭọ sọdọr lạgit' Santal sọmajre ạḍi jạsti beoharok'kana, pạrtul :-

(i) *Hae,* cẹt'iń cekaea!

(ii) *Hae* am dọ, cẹt'em cekayet'a!?

(iii) *Hae* hopontiń, cedak̕em bągiat̕lea!

(iv) *Hae hae,* hoete ąḍitet̕e loksanket̕a!

(v) *Hae hae,* jalapurire, *hae hae* nukin manewa, *hae hae* busą̃ṛakankin!

(vi) *Hae hae,* busą̃ṛakankin, oh̕ oh̕!

(vii) *Haere,* iń do ohoń senlena!

(viii) *Haere,* iń do abhagią hoṛ!

(ix) *Haere haere,* toa daretiń do!

(x) *Haere hae,* tinreń cekaea!

(xi) *Haere hae,* ąḍitet̕iń kosṭok̕kana!

jare jare - Noa katha do ayo hoṛ hotete ąḍi duk/bhabna ar rak̕-homor jokhec̕ko beohara, menkhan nebetar noa katha ąḍi komge ańjomok̕kana, pąrtul :-

jare jare, ado ohoń ńamlea!

durre, durre dure, durhak̕, dur kharak̕, dhurhak̕, dur karak̕, dur karahak̕ - Noako sabad hotete do bhaṛo/hahaṛa/duk/kosṭo/ hirkhą katha sodor lągit̕ beoharok̕kana,pąrtul :-

(i) *Durre,* ąḍi bąṛic̕iń botorena!

(ii) *Durre,* unąk̕ko hec̕akana!

(iii) *Dure durre,* ohobon sambṛao daṛelea!

(iv) *Dhurhak̕*, kiriń daraemań hiṛińket̕!

(v) *Dur karak̕,* cedak̕ noarepe duṛup̕akana!

(vi) *Dur karahak̕,* cedak̕ nonḍe dope duṛup̕akana.

(vii) *Dur kharak̕,* unąk̕ sorpe hec̕ got̕ena.

dir, dirre, dirhak̕, dir karak̕,dhir, *dhirre* - Noa do *dur, durre, durhak̕, dur kharak̕, dhurhak̕, dhirhak̕ dur karak̕, dur karahak̕* leka beoharok̕a. Pąrtul :-

(i) *Dirre,* ąḍi bąṛic̕iń botorena!

(ii) *Dirrẹ,* unạk̔ko hẹc̔akana!

(iii) *Dire dirrẹ,* ọhọbon sambṛao daṛelea!

(iv) *Dhirhak̔,* pạńci kirińmań hiṛińket̔!

(v) *Dhir karak̔,* cedak̔ noare dọpe duṛup̔akana!

(vi) *Dhirrẹ,* cedak̔ adọ bam hijuk̔kana!

(vii) *Dhir,* cẹt̔em cekaeda ọṇḍẹ dọ?!

mor! morhak̔! morrẹ! mor jala! - Noako sabad họtẹt cintạ/ kastao sọdọr lạgit̔ beoharok̔kana, pạrtul :-

(i) *Morrẹ,* inạk̔ ńindạ dọ cedak̔em hijuk̔kana?!

(ii) *Morem,* sẹnlenkhan boge hoekok̔a!

(iii) *Morhak̔,* cak̔ cọm hẹc̔en!

(iv) *Mor jala,* uni aloe sẹnlenkhan!

dhiṭ, dhiṭ hak̔, *dhuṭ*, *dhuṭ hak̔* - Noako sabad họtẹte dọ hirkhạ/ ạṛis/ọkta/bẹkusi katha sọdọr lạgit̔ beoharok̔kana, pạrtul :-

(i) *Dhuṭ,* onka dọ alom rọṛa!

(ii) *Dhuṭ, ọṇḍẹ* dọ ọhọń sẹnlena!

(iii) *Dhiṭ,* cak̔ cọń noṅkaket̔!

(iv) *Dhuṭ hak̔,* cedak̔ cọń rọṛ kạiket̔!

(v) *Dhiṭ hak̔,* cedak̔ cọń sẹnen!

ah̔, ah̔ ah̔, aha, a haha, a haha haha! - Noa sabad họtẹte dọ kusi-rạskạ/hahaṛa katha sọdọr lạgit̔ beoharok̔kana, pạrtul :-

(i) *A haha,* tinạk̔ rosaṛe họeyeda!

(ii) *Ah̔,* nit utạr besiń bujhạuet̔a!

(iii) *Aha,* nọtẹ khọn ạdi mõ̱ńje họet̔a!

(iv) *Ah̔ ah̔,* reaṛ ạdi mõ̱ńjiń ạikạuet̔a!

(v) *Ah̔ haha haha,* noṅkan rạṛ dọ ạdi mõ̱ńjiń bujhạuet̔a!

hạlạ, hạlạre - Noa sabad hộtẹte sabasi/sarhao katha sọdọr lạgit̔ beoharok̕kana,pạrtul :-

(i) *Hạlạ,* joskeťạń!

(ii) *Hạlạ,* teheń doko sap̕kedea!

(iii) *Hạlạ* bhại, tire com hec̕akan!

(iv) *Hạlạre,* teheń dope jitạuena!

bah̕, bah̕ bah̕, bah̕ware, baohare - Noa sabad hotete rạskạ subori eman reak̕ katha sodor lạgiť beoharok̕kana, pạrtul :-

(i) *Bah̕,* am do ạḍi bhage koṛa kanam!

(ii) *Bah̕ bah̕,* baohare nui koṛa doe uṭrạuakana!

(iii) *Baohare,* nui leka do bape khacaṛok̕kana!

do - Noa sabad do hukum se menjoń katha sodor lạgiť Kạjnum lahare hijuk̕a ar Kạjnum tayomre hõ hec̕ daṛeak̕a, pạrtul :-

(i) *Do* calak̕pe!

(ii) *Do* ya, idi oṭokam!

(iii) *Do* na, hirikom!

(iv) *Do* se, sap̕kotabonme!

de, den, dini, dinkin, denko - Noa sabad hotete udgạu, utkuť se kạmi ocoe lạgiť katha sodorre beoharok̕a. Noate mana reak̕ hõ lạiạgok̕a; inạkate hukum reak̕ hõ, jor emak̕ lạgiť hõ laṛcaṛok̕a, pạrtul :-

(i) *De* lạime; *de* se emok̕me!

(ii) *De* họ, thamakur emok̕tabonme!

(iii) *Debo* joma! *Den* daka! *den* ya ạguime!

(iv) *Dinitiń* kaṭkom! *Dinkin* kạḍa laga ạgukinme!

(v) *Denko* hako ạgukom!

se - Noa sabad hotete jor jobor utkuť reak̕ katha lạgiť laṛcaṛok̕kana, pạrtul :-

(i) De̱ *se̱* e̱mo̱k̓me!

(ii) Dela *se̱!* Alo *se̱pe* raga!

(iii) Ma *se̱* amge, ro̱ṛtalaṅme!

(iv) Ce̱t̓ baṅ *se̱* noṅkan sebel utu do̱ tis hõ̱ bạń cakha ạikạuakat̓a!

(v) Baṅ *se̱,* onka do̱ bako ro̱ṛa!

(vi) Dạṛe dạṛkeda *se̱,* riạk̓-riạk̓e dạṛkeda!

ma - Noa sabad do̱ utkut̓, hukum se̱ hoe ocoe lạgit̓ge laṛcaṛok̓kana, pạrtul :-

(i) *Ma* ạbukok̓me! *Ma* duṛup̓me!

(ii) *Ma* se̱ hijuk̓me! *Ma* e̱nte hijuk̓me!

(iii) Iń *ma* bạń ańjo̱makat̓!

(iv) Hẽ̱ *ma* hẽ̱ge.

me̱ - Noa sabad do̱ uskur katha lạgit̓ge beoharok̓kana. Ar noa do̱ sabad laharege hijuk̓a, pạrtul :-

(i) *Me̱* o̱co̱go̱k̓me! *Me̱ ya* hijuk̓me!

(ii) *Me̱* se̱ oḍokok̓pe! *Me̱* na!

(iii) *Me̱bon* calak̓a! *Me̱* dela!

(iv) *Me̱* dela, nitbon calak̓a!

dela, delaṅ, delabo(n) - Noa katha se̱ sabad ho̱te̱te calak̓/hijuk̓ uskur katha *delalaṅ* lạgit̓ beoharok̓. *delọi delọi* do̱ maejiu ho̱te̱te beoha-rok̓kana. *dela* do̱ Kạjnum sãote oko kuṛại sãote boeharok̓a, pạrtul :-

(i) Bako *delawadea!* (oko kuṛại)

(ii) *Dela* hijuk̓me!

(iii) *Delaṅ* ado̱bon calak̓a.

(iv) Me̱ *delabon* mohṇḍalenge.

(v) E̱ maraṅ bạhu, *delọi* hijuk̉ben!

mela, melaṅ, melalaṅ, melabo(n), meli, meila, meilaṅ -Noa sabad do̱ *dela* sabad lekae kạmiet̉kana. *meila* ar *meilaṅ* do̱ aso̱kaete maejiuko beohara, pạrtul :-

(i) *Mela* calak̉me, kho̱jakat̉meako.

(ii) *Melam* calak̉gea! *Melaṅlaṅ* calak̉gea!

(iii) *Meila* hijuk̉me! *Meila* yọi, hijuk̉me!

(iv) *Meila* nọi! *Meila* se̱ taṛam taṛamme!

(v) *Meila* usạrate, pase̱ darakokan.

Santal so̱majre ạsul janwar se̱ cẽ̱ṛẽ̱ noṅkan ho̱ho̱, hirkhạ/ ạṛis reak̉ katha so̱do̱r lạgit̉ beoharok̉kana, jeleka :-

(i) *Sạċ,* no̱te̱geko kocoṛ ạguet̉kana!

(ii) *Sạċ sạċre,* sạċ nạṭin mara sim!

(iii) *Titi, titi* (tete, tete)!

(iv) *Curu curu!* (Noa do̱ kạṭiċ sim ho̱po̱n ho̱ho̱ako lạgit̉ko beohara.)

(v) *Tại tại!* (Marak̉/Parwa lạgit̉ beoharok̉a.)

(vi) *He̱ṛo̱k (he̱ḍo̱k)!* (Me̱ro̱m lagakore.)

(vii) *Ḍorrae ḍorrae!* (Me̱ro̱m ho̱ho̱akore.)

(viii) *Ḍrrrrae!* (Me̱ro̱m ho̱ho̱akore.)

(ix) *Ḍrrrroṅ!* (Me̱ro̱m ho̱ho̱akore.)

(x) *He̱ṛo̱ ghurạ!* (Me̱ro̱m/bhiḍi laga ạcurkore.)

(xi) *He̱ḍo̱ ghurạ!* (Me̱ro̱m/bhiḍi laga ạcurkore.)

(xii) *He̱ṛo̱ he̱ṛo̱!* (Me̱ro̱m/bhiḍi laga ạcurkore.)

(xiv) *He̱ḍo̱ he̱ḍo̱!* (Me̱ro̱m/bhiḍi laga ạcurkore.)

(xv) *Ḍorhet̉ ḍorhet̉!* (Me̱ro̱m/bhiḍi laga ạcurkore.)

(xvi) *He̱ṛo̱k he̱ḍo̱k!* (Sukri laga o̱co̱k̉kore.)

(xvii) *Ḍuruh ḍuruh!* (Sukri ho̱ho̱akore.)

(xviii) *He̱ḍo̱ he̱ḍo̱!* (Sukri lagakore.)

(xix) *Ao ao!* (Gąi-ḍaṅgra ho̱ho̱akore.)

(xx) *Seť!* (Gąi-ḍaṅgra mõ̱ńjte teṅgo ocoko lągiť.)

(xxi) *Kuṇḍruċ kuṇḍruċ!* (Kąṭiċ sukri ho̱po̱n ho̱ho̱akore.)

(xxii) *Kuṇḍuċ kuṇḍuċ!* (Kąṭiċ sukri ho̱po̱n ho̱ho̱akore.)

(xxiii) *hum!* (Gąi-ḍaṅgra thir ocokore.)

(xxiv) *Hijąk!* (Gąi-ḍaṅgra lagakore.)

(xxv) *Hiją!* (Siąǩ jo̱khe̱ċ se̱ be̱ siąǩ jo̱khe̱ċ gąi-ḍaṅgra lagakore.)

(xxvi) *Ąisą/ąs!* (Gąi-ḍaṅgra laga ącurkore.)

Noako noṅkako beohara :-

(i) *Hijąk, hiją ghur, ąisą!* Bam ańjo̱ma, hape̱ nãhãǩ se̱n ocoąńme, ado̱laṅ batraoeťmea.

(ii) *Ao ao!* (Kaḍako ho̱ho̱akore.)

(iii) *Seť!* (Kaḍako mõ̱ńjteko teṅgo ocokore.)

(iv) *Hum!* (Kaḍako thir ocokore.)

(v) *Hijąk!* (Kaḍako lagako se̱ ḍąhrąukore.)

(vi) *Hijąk ghur!* (Kaḍako ąḍhrao ącurkore.)

(vii) *Ąs/ąisą/ąisąk!* (Kaḍako ḍahrao ącurkore.)

Siąǩ jo̱khe̱ċ noako kathako beohareťkana :-

ągą, ągą ągą, ągą bheṛ, bheṛe cala bheṛ, hijąk, hiją.

Noako do̱ maṇḍa se̱ e̱n jo̱khe̱ċko beohareťkana :-

ąs, ąisą, ąisąk (Maṇḍa lagae jo̱khe̱ċ.)

Noako do̱ kaḍa-ḍaṅgra ącurko jo̱khe̱ċko ro̱ṛa :-

ąisą ghur, ąs ghur, ṭhae ghur, ąisą ąs ąs ghur, ghur ghur thãye ghur, hijąk ąs ṭhãe ghur ghur, hum, har hum eman.

E̱tọm nakha ạcurko jọkhẹċ dọko rọṛa :-
dạhin.

Sagaṛ laga jọkhẹċ noṅkako rọṛa :-
hat̤, hum

Sagaṛ joṛao jọkhẹċ noṅkako rọṛa :-
set' lag, dhọ dhọr

Sagaṛ laga jọkhẹċ dọ noṅkako rọṛa :-
hirjạt, hạrjạt

Kaḍate siạk̓ jọkhẹċ dọ noṅkako rọṛa :-
ạgạ ạgạ, ạs t̤hãe, ghur ghur, ạisạ ạisạ

Bhiḍi, mẹrọm, sukri lạgit' dọ noṅka hõko rọṛa :-
bhet'! bhet'! bhet'!

Setako lạgit' dọ noṅkako rọṛa :-

(i) *Lẹṅ lẹṅ!* (Họhọakore.)

(ii) *Lẹlẹ lẹlẹ* (Họhọakore.)

Seta lagakore :-
hạṛire, hạṛiċ, hạṛik!

Seta họpọn họhọakore :-
(i) *Kur kur!*

(ii) *Kur kutu kutu!*

Pusi lagakore :-
pusiċ!

Pusi họhọakore :-
gunu gunu!

ẠKIL BHAŃJAO - 13

A. Ṭo̱yo̱t'kate jobab e̱mo̱k̓me :-

1. Babako ho̱ho̱jo̱ṅre do̱ *họ* sabadko beohara, Ona jagare ayo ko do̱ ce̱t̓ sabadko beohara?

   (a) họ (b) ho̱ (c) hu (d) he̱

2. Sukri do̱ ce̱t̓ lekako lagakoa?

   (a) ḍuruṅ ḍuruṅ (b) he̱ḍo̱ he̱ḍo̱ (c) ạs ạs (d) hijạk ghur

3. Seta do̱ ce̱t̓ lekako ho̱ho̱akoa?

   (a) ae ae (b) lẹṅ lẹṅ (c) gunu gunu (d) bhiṛạ ạs

4. Gại-ḍaṅgra do̱ ce̱t̓ leka ho̱ho̱ateko thir ocokoa?

   (a) hum (b) hijạk (c) ạisạ (d) ghurạ

5. Pusi do̱ ce̱t̓ lekako ho̱ho̱akoa?

   (a) gunu gunu (b) lẹṅ lẹṅ (c) ạs ạs (d) hijạ

B. O̱lkate jobab e̱mo̱k̓me :-

1. *e̱ ba!* do̱ Beako̱ro̱n reak̓ niạm lekate ce̱t̓ kana?
2. *ẹi* do̱ Beako̱ro̱n reak̓ niạm lekate ce̱t̓ kana?
3. *họ* do̱ Beako̱ro̱n reak̓ niạm lekate ce̱t̓ kana?
4. *iạ họ* do̱ Beako̱ro̱n reak̓ niạm lekate ce̱t̓ kana?
5. *henda* do̱ Beako̱ro̱n reak̓ niạm lekate ce̱t̓ kana?
6. *ya* ar *na* do̱ Beako̱ro̱n reak̓ niạm lekate ce̱t̓ kana?
7. *yọi* ar *nọi* do̱ Beako̱ro̱n reak̓ niạm lekate ce̱t̓ kana?
8. *e̱ babare̱* do̱ Beako̱ro̱n reak̓ niạm lekate ce̱t̓ kana
9. *e̱k̓ e̱k̓* do̱ Beako̱ro̱n reak̓ niạm lekate ce̱t̓ kana?
10. *ọi ọi* do̱ Beako̱ro̱n reak̓ niạm lekate cet̓ kana?

11. *aha, aha dọ* Beakọrọn reak̕ niạm lekate *cẹt̕ kana?*
12. *ẹhẹ ẹhẹ* dọ Beakọrọn reak̕ niạm lekate cẹt̕ kana?
13. *ạige, aiyo, ạijo* dọ Beakọrọn reak̕ niạm lekate cẹt̕ kana?
14. *ẹṅ ẹṅ* dọ Beakọrọn reak̕ niạm lekate cẹt̕ kana?
15. *ọṅ ọṅ /ọṅ/ọṅọhọ* dọ Beakọrọn reak̕ niạm lekate cẹt̕ kana?
16. *uhu uhu/u uhu/u uhu uhu* dọ Beakọrọn reak̕ niạm lekate cẹt̕ kana?
17. *is is* dọ Beakọrọn reak̕ niạm lekate cẹt̕ kana?
18. *iṅ iṅ* dọ Beakọrọn reak̕ niạm lekate cẹt̕ kana?
19. *aege* dọ Beakọrọn reak̕ niạm lekate cẹt̕ kana.
20. *ạu ạu* dọ Beakọrọn reak̕ niạm lekate cẹt̕ kana?
21. *ọ hae* dọ Beakọrọn reak̕ niạm lekate cẹt̕ kana?
22. *hae hae* dọ Beakọrọn reak̕ niạm lekate cẹt̕ kana?
23. *durẹ durẹk̕* dọ Beakọrọn reak̕ niạm lekate cẹt̕ kana?
24. *dirhak̕* dọ Beakọrọn reak̕ niạm lekate cẹt̕ kana?
25. *dhirrẹ* dọ Beakọrọn reak̕ niạm lekate cẹt̕ kana?
26. *morrẹ* dọ Beakọrọn reak̕ niạm lekate cẹt̕ kana?
27. *dhiṭ* dọ Beakọrọn reak̕ niạm lekate cẹt̕ kana?
28. *aṅ aṅ* dọ Beakọrọn reak̕ niạm lekate cẹt̕ kana?
29. *do* dọ Beakọrọn reak̕ niạm lekate cẹt̕ kana ?
30. *dẹ* dọ Beakọrọn reak̕ niạm lekate cẹt̕ kana?
31. *ma* dọ Beakọrọn reak̕ niạm lekate cẹt̕ kana?
32. *melaṅ* dọ Beakọrọn reak̕ niạm lekate cẹt̕ kana?
33. *tại tại* dọ Beakọrọn reak̕ niạm lekate cẹt̕ kana?
34. *sạċ* dọ Beakọrọn reak̕ niạm lekate cẹt̕ kana?

35. *se̱t̕* do̱ Beako̱ro̱n reak̕ niạm lekate ce̱t̕ kana?
36. *hum* do̱ Beako̱ro̱n reak̕ niạm lekate ce̱t̕ kana?
37. *hijạk ghur* do̱ Beako̱ro̱n reak̕ niạm lekate ce̱t̕ kana?
38. *ạgạ, ạgạ ạgạ* do̱ Beako̱ro̱n reak̕ niạm lekate ce̱t̕ kana?
39. *ạisạ, ạisạk* do̱ Beako̱ro̱n reak̕ niạm lekate ce̱t̕ kana?
40. *kur kur* do̱ Beako̱ro̱n reak̕ niạm lekate ce̱t̕ kana?
41. *lẹh̕ lẹh̕* do̱ Beako̱ro̱n reak̕ niạm lekate ce̱t̕ kana?
42. *kur kutu kutu* do̱ Beako̱ro̱n reak̕ niạm lekate ce̱t̕ kana
43. *pusiċ* do̱ Beako̱ro̱n reak̕ niạm lekate ce̱t̕ kana?
44. Haharạ *(Interjection)* reak̕ bean o̱lme ar pạrtul hõ̱ lạime.
45. Ho̱ho̱ Katha *(Vocative Case)* reak̕ bean pạrtul se̱le̱t̕ lạime.

14

JIRẠUK̓ CINHẠ AR LẠṬU AKHO̱R REAK̓ LAṚCAṚ *(PUNCTUATION AND THE USE OF CAPITAL LETTERS)*

Tinre abobo ro̱ṛeda, to̱be̱ abo do̱ aboak̓ o̱nto̱r katha so̱do̱r lạgit̓ jãhã baṅ jãhã ṭhenbo thirok̓kana. Me̱nkhan, tinre abobo o̱le̱t̓kana, to̱be̱ apnarak̓ o̱lo̱k̓re jirạuk̓ cinhạ *(punctuation mark)* reak̓bo laṛcaṛet̓kana je̱mo̱n o̱ṇḍe̱gebon thirok̓, okare do̱ aboak̓ pạrsi reak̓ mane bujhạuk̓ lạgit̓ ona cinhạ reak̓ jạruṛ paṛaok̓kana.

Jirạuk̓ cinhạ babo̱tre nahak̓ jug reak̓ hudis do̱ noa kana je jirạuk̓ cinhạ reak̓ laṛcaṛ do̱ o̱ṇḍe̱ge hoyok̓ma, okare do̱ katha so̱do̱r lạgit̓ bujhạu ar sapha-sạphi bujhạu lạgit̓ jạruṛok̓kan.

Santali lạgit̓ noako jirạuk̓ cinhạkobo beohar daṛeak̓a :-

- Lạṭu Haro̱p Cinhạ *(Capital Letter)*
- Purạu Thirok̓ Cinhạ *(Full Stop)* = (.)
- Ko̱mṅõk̓ Thirok̓ Cinhạ *(Semi Colon)* = (;)
- Ko̱m Thirok̓ Cinhạ *(Comma)* = (,)
- Udug Cinhạ *(Colon)* = (:)
- Hahaṛa Udug Cinhạ *(Exclamation)* = (!)
- Rạskạ ar Hahaṛa Se̱le̱t̓ Kukli Cinhạ *(Exclamation with Question Mark)* = (!?)
- Kukli Cinhạ *(Question Mark)* = (?)
- Katha Udug Cinhạ *(Quotation Mark)* = (“ ”) se̱ (‘ ’)

□ Gar/ḍes Cinhạ *(Dash)* = (–)

□ Jok̓ṛao Cinhạ *(Hyphen)* = (-)

□ Berkeṭ Cinhạ *(Bracket)* = [ ], { }, ( )

LẠṬU HAROP CINHẠ
(CAPITAL LETTER)

Lạṭu harop/sabad reak̓ pạhil akhor do noako obosthare beoharok̓a :-

□ Ayat reak̓ pạhil akhor – *Dela paṛhaok̓bon ceda.*

□ Hoṛak̓ ńutum ologok̓re – *Sidạ, Kạnhu, Cand, Bhaero* eman.

□ Pạris ologok̓re – *Murmu, Ṭuḍu, Kisku, Soren eman.*

□ Jãhã disạm, rajosṭi, nagraha ar atoko reak̓ ńutumre – *Dilli, Jharkhaṇḍ, Ḍumkạ, Sahebgõńj, Baḍhet* eman.

□ Pạrsi reak̓ ńutum ologok̓re – *Santali, Hindi, Baṅgla, Iṅgrạji* eman.

□ Jãhãe hoṛak̓ ńutum lahare lagaok̓ Gunumre *(Adjective)* - *Manotan (Man), Somaj Dorodiạ/Susạriạ eman.*

□ Dhorom reak̓ ńutum ologok̓re - *Hindu, Muslạ, Sikh, Isại eman.*

□ Porobko reak̓ ńutumre - *Baha, Sohrae, Erok̓, Janthaṛ eman.*

□ Jãhã Bạisi se hudạ reak̓ khaṭo rup ologok̓re – *A.I.S.W.A.C.S, DC, SDO*

□ Nagamre ghaṭaoakan ghoṭna reak̓ ńutum – *Santal Hul, Jharkhaṇḍ Laṛaona, Bạńjhi Kãṇḍ eman.*

□ Rajạri dolko reak̓ ńutumre - *J.M.M., B.J.P, S.P., AJSU*

□ Din-mạhnạko reak̓ ńutumre – *Som, Moṅgol, Cạt, Bạisạk eman.*

PURẠU THIROḰ CINHẠ
(FULL STOP)

Purạu thiroḱ cinhạ dọ noako ọbọsthare beoharoḱa :- thiroḱ

- Mela Katha *(Statement)*, Hukum *(Command)* ar Oko Kukli *(Indirect Question)* mucạtre – *Uni dọe Kạnhu kana.* (Mela Katha); *Alom kạumạua.* (Hukum); *Unie metadińạ je ińaḱ ńutum dọ cẹt' kana.* (Oko kukli).
- Bạisi, ńutum sẹ hudạ reaḱ khaṭọ rup ọlọgọḱre - *J.M.M., Dr., Ph.D*
- Jãhãe họṛaḱ ńutum khaṭọte ọlọgọḱre – *P.O. Bọḍiń, A. Murmu, R. Hãsdaḱ*
- Sọmọe, din/tạrik, mạhnạ ar bọchọr udugoḱre – *5.00 baje setaḱ, 30.6.1855*

KỌM ŃÕḰ THIROḰ CINHẠ
(SEMI-COLON)

- Judi barea Bẹṭehaḍ Gọṛọ *(Independent Clause)* talare jãhãn joḱṛao sabad (mẹnkhan, ar jẹmọn) bań tahẹnkhan tọbẹ ona banar talare gọṛọ ayat *(clause)* begar lạgit' kọm ńõḱ thiroḱ cinhạ beoharoḱa – *Do calaḱme; cedaḱ bae hijuḱkana?*
- Kọm ńõḱ thiroḱ cinhạ dọ kọm thiroḱ ar purạu thiroḱ cinhạ talare lagaoḱa - *Kuṛiko dọko sereńeda; koṛako dọko ruieda.*

KỌM THIROḰ CINHẠ
(COMMA)

Ayatre barea khọn jạsti ayat talare thoṛa thiroḱ hoyoḱkhan kọm thiroḱ cinhạ lagaoḱa :–

- *Judi iń Mạńjhi haṛamiń tahẹnkhan, jọtọ họṛakiń kạmikea.*
- Barea ayatre judi barea khọn jạsti sabad hudạ sẹ sabad hudạ

hĩs hẹc̓lenkhan tobe kom thirok̓ cinhạ lagaok̓a - *Tinre abo do reṅgec̓bo tahenkana, unre abo do cet̓ hõ babo ceka daṛeak̓kana.*

- Okare sabad bar dhao dohṛak̓ ar bhaore jor emak̓khan, tobe onḍe do kom thirok̓ cinhạ lagaok̓a - *Hape, hape, aṅjomlem.*
- Judi ayatre jahan sabad hudạ reak̓ hĩs se ayat kuṭrạ hẹc̓lenkhan, tobe kom thirok̓ cinhạ laṛcaṛok̓a - *Sidạ-Kạnhu bidạlren birbanṭa, kạdre bololen birbanṭa Gạrbhu Desmạṅjhi, nitok̓ okorko?*
- Kukli katha *(Question tag)* asol ayat hạṭiń khon begar lạgit̓ kom thirok̓ cinhạ laṛcaṛok̓kana - *Cạmpại hopon Haṛma Desmạṅjhi do, Siliṅgi atoe bandhaoleda.*
- Hoho kathako *(Words of address)* ayat khon begar lạgit̓ kom thirok̓ cinhạ laṛcaṛok̓kana – *Bạjun họ! Mase parkom teń got̓kak̓me.*

UDUG CINHẠ
(COLON)

- Udug cinhạ do jãhãn lisṭi ehob lạgit̓ laṛcaṛok̓kana – *Iń do noako jinis jạruṛạṅkana : Pạṅci, dhuti, gamcha ar mit̓ṭen jarge palaṭ.*
- Adom jokhec̓ jãhãn lisṭi etohopre udug cinhạ (:) phẹḍre (-) khayot̓/gar/ḍes *(dash)* cinhạ hõ lagao daṛeak̓a – *Noko hoṛ hoho darawakome : Sagen, Marsal, Ebhen ar Arel.*
- Ạnupat *(proportion)* lại lạgit̓ hõ udug cinhạ lagaok̓kana – *8:4:4:2*

HAHAṚA UDUG CINHẠ
(EXCLAMATION MARK)

Suk-duk se hahaṛa, hirkhạ, ạris, bhabna, edre, rạskạ udug lạgit̓ Hahaṛa Udug Cinhạ (!) do laṛcaṛok̓kana :–

- *Ạḍi rạskạ Marań Dại sẹṭẹrok̇kana!; Ẹh̃! Ạḍi marańe ghaoakan!; Chi! Ạḍi mạilạm ńẹlọk̇kana, ḍạbrạk̇me!; Alom hukạia! Sanam hukạlań caba gọṭ̇katama!; Iń samań khọn ọcọk̇me! Ạṛisgeń ńẹlẹṭ̇mea!; Thirok̇am sẹ bań!*
- Jãhãe jiọnre rạskạ/dulạṛ ạsirbad emae khan (!) cinhạ lagaok̇a - *P. O. Boḍiń, Tire-Jugey Bahaok̇ma!*
- Cigạri katha sọdọr lạgiṭ̇ (!) cinhạ laṛcaṛok̇a - *Bhageakanae! Bae lọhọmlena!*

RẠSKẠ HAHẠṚA SẸLẸṬ̇ KUKLI UDUG CINHẠ *(EXCLAMATION WITH QUESTION MARK)*

Jãhãnak̇ kathare Hahaṛa, Rạskạ sẹlẹṭ̇ kukli sọdọr lạgiṭ̇ (!?) cinhạ laṛcaṛok̇a – *Unie pasena!? As dọ bań cọ ạikạuk̇kan tahẽ̱kan.*

KUKLI CINHẠ *(QUESTION MARK)*

- Kukli katha mucạṭ̇re kukli cinhạ dọ lagaok̇a - *Unie metadińạ, "Celeama?"*
- Kukli joṛao *(Question tag)* mucạṭ̇re kukli cinhạ lagaok̇a - *Unie końkagea, hẽ̱ sẹ bań?*
- Onkan ayatre ọnẹ okaṭak̇ dọ jãhã lekan kukli, digdhạ, bẹṭhikạn katha sọdọr reak̇ menak̇khan, ọṇḍẹ dọ kukli cinhạ laṛcaṛok̇a - *Sidạ-Kạnhuṭạkin dọ pasẹċ ạḍi ḍher họṛkin ạyurlẹṭ̇koa?*
- Judi miṭ̇ṭẹn ayatre aema kukliko tahẹnkhan, tọbẹ ona ayat reak̇ mucạṭ̇re kukli cinhạ lagaok̇a - *Lạṛhại ṭhen ọkọe calak̇a? Am?*

KATHA UDUG CINHẠ
(INVERTED COMMA)

- Katha udug cinhạ do rorọṛićak̓ *(speaker)* asol katha noa cinhạ hotete bondkate ol sodorok̓a. Noa do mit̓ dhao (' ') se bar dhao (" ") leka hõ ol daṛeak̓a – *Sidạ-Kạnhutạkinkin menleda, "Hul-hul, nitok̓ do aboak̓ raj hećena".*

- Judi rororiće bodollenkhan ona katha nãwãte se judạ thạrre *(separately)* dohok̓a - *"Iń do huḍiń dak̓lo bertegeń ruạṛ hijuk̓a", Rạskại menkeda.*

- Kạhni, onol, õnõṛhẽ, khobor kagoc eman reak̓ ńutum katha do udug cinhạ bhitrire dohok̓a - *Santali beste bujhạu lạgit̓, "Santali Pạrsi reak̓ Aṛań ar Urgạn Gorhon" paṛhaome.*

ḌES CINHẠ
(DASH)

- Ayat reak̓ kathare akoṭ janam ocoe lạgit̓ ḍes do laṛcaṛok̓a - *Ińiń meneda - menet̓kạnạń - somaj lạgit̓ sanamkobo dandok̓a.*

- Ayatre adom katha okoe lạgit̓ se noa udug lạgit̓ lạiạgok̓ lạgit̓ je katha do atragea - *Hola kulhi dupuṛupre - do bae seṭerlena.*

- Ayatre esto-bestok̓ katha sodor lạgit̓ ḍes do laṛcaṛok̓a :– *I – i – iń do bạń dosakada.*

JOṚAO CINHẠ
(HYPHEN)

- Judi ayat reak̓ mucạt̓ sabad bań purạukhan, tobe dosar thạrre purạuk̓khan, tobe ona bepurạu sabad tayom joṛao cinhạ *(hyphen (-)* emogok̓kana,

- Sabadre judi mit̓ẹn khọn jąsti akhọr *(syllable)* tahẹnkhan, akhọr hąṭiṅ lągit̓ (-) cinhą dọ laṛcaṛok̇kana – *simsąṇḍi – simsąṇḍi, kurumuṭu - ku-ru-mu-ṭu*
- Ayat reak̇ thąr mucąt̓ reak̇ jãhãn sabad reak̇ mit̓ akhọr ọl sẹ ẹkẹn mit̓ akhọr aṛak̇kate joṛao cinhą tis hõ baṅ ọl jąruṛkana – *Samaṅ - sama-ṅ,* judi ądige jąruṛkhan ona sabad dọ – *samaṅ* leka ọl daṛeak̇a.
- Judi bar sabad mit̓ ṭhen joṛao reak̇ dọrkar tahẹnkhan - *loṭadak̇, tarwaṛe-dak̇, ṭikiṭ-oṛak̇* eman.

BẸRKẸṬ CINHĄKO
(BRACKETS)

- *Reference* metak̇me jãhãn katha reak̇ sąbud ẹm reak̇ tahẹnkhan bẹrkẹṭ reak̇ laṛcaṛ hoyok̇kana - *P.O. Bọḍiṅ dọ Santali harọp lągit̓ ẹ, ẹ, ọ,* ar *ọ reak̇ jąruṛe ąṭkarleda - ar ona reak̇ bibrọn dọ (Materials for A Santali Grammar, page-12re) hõe ẹmakana.*
- Judi jãhãe ọnọlią, sasapṛaoić ayatre ać sẹć khọn thoṛae joṛaoet̓ sẹ bọdọlet̓khan tọbẹ ona dọ bẹrkẹṭ bhitrirey dọhọea - *Nui họṛ (ọkọe dọ disąm ląṛhąirey mãyãm gohalen) dọ ądi dilgąriąi tahẽkana.*
- Judi ayat bhitri reak̇ jãhãṭak̇ sabad reak̇ mane beste ląi sapha reak̇ tahẹnkhan, ona reak̇ mane dọ bẹrkẹṭ bhitrire dọhọk̇a - *Nui kaṭjibą (kumãyã họṛ) dọ ọkọe hõ bae ńẹl ṭhikkoa.*

ĄKIL BHAŃJAO - 14

A. Ṭọyọt̓kate jobab ẹmọk̇me :-

1. *All India Santal Welfare and Cultural Society* reak̇ khaṭọ rup dọ cẹt̓ hoyok̇a?

(a) aiswa (b) aiswacs (c) A.I.S.W.A.C.S
(d) A.I.S.W.C.S

2. *Kuṛiko dǫko sereńeda koṛako dǫko ruieda.* Noa ayat talare okaṭaḱ jirạuḱ cinhạ lagaoḱa?
   (a) . (b) ; (c) ? (d) ,

3. *Bạjun hǫ mase parkǫm teń gǫt́kaḱme.* Noa ayat talare okaṭaḱ jirạuḱ cinhạ lagaoḱa? (a) , (b) ; (c) ! (d) ?

4. *Lạṛhại ṭhen ǫkǫe calaḱa am.* Noa ayat talare okaṭaḱ jirạuḱ cinhạ lagaoḱa? (a) . (b) ; (c) ? (d) ,

5. *Santali beste bujhạu lạgit́ Santali Pạrsi reaḱ Aṛań ar Urgạn Gǫṛhǫn paṛhaome.* Noa ayat talare okaṭaḱ jirạuḱ cinhạ lagaoḱa? (a) ? (b) " " (c) ! (d) ,

B. Ǫlkate jobab ẹmǫḱme :-

1. Jirạuḱ cinhạ dǫ cẹt́ kana? Pạrtul ẹm tuluć ǫlme.
2. Jirạuḱ cinhạ dǫ tinạḱ lekana? Jǫtǫ reaḱ ńutum lạime.
3. *jmm* dǫ pạṭi reaḱ ńutum kana. Ǫlǫḱ dhara lekate cẹt́ noa dǫ suhigea? Bań suhi khan suhieme.
4. *Uni dǫe Kạnhu kana.* Noa ayat mucạt́re okaṭaḱ jirạuḱ cinhạ lagaoḱa?
5. *Do calaḱme cedaḱ bae hijuḱkana*
   Noa ayatre okakore ar cẹt́-cẹt́ jirạuḱ cinhạ lagaoḱa?
6. *Cele kanako,* noa ayat mucạt́re okaṭaḱ jirạuḱ cinhạ lagaoḱa?

15

MIṪ SABAD REAḰ AEMA MANE *(HOMOGRAPHS)*

(Abbreviations : noun (n.); an adjective (adj.); a verb (v.); m. may stand for Medium (or Passive), or for masculine. f. for feminine; v.a.d. means a verb constructed with indirect object in the Active; v.m.d., the same in the Medium; anim. means animate, inanim. inanimate; Perform. stands for Performative, Intent. for Intentional.)

1. aha - *(int. of pleasure and of regret.)*
   Aha! bạṛiċ jute hǫekeťa nǫtẹ khǫn.
   aha - *(v.a.m. Bewitch by an evil eye), cast a spell on persons, crops, threshing-floor, grain and implements of the hunt, etc.)*

   Ahakidiṅako, ona iạteṅ uchlạukeťa.

2. aḱ - *(inanimate determinative suffix)*
   Iṅaḱ oṛaḱ.
   aḱ - *(verbal suffix)*
   Daḱaḱme.
   aḱ - *(v.a.m.-Bow)*
   Ghũṛạ̃ aḱ.

3. alaṅ - *(pers. pr. i. p. dual inclusive; v.a.m. we two, you and I; make become a pair).*
   Alaṅkaťlaṅako.
   alaṅ - *(n. The tongue, the front-brim of a winnowing fan (*haṭaḱ*) .*

Alaṅ ọbọrentaea.
Dạṭạunikate alaṅ hataroḱme.

4. amọl - *(n., v. - Indigestion, dyspesia, acidity of the stomach; get do., eructate through the acidity of the stomach.)*
Amọl ạuri cabaḱtae dhạbić ọhọe pharnaolena.
amọl - *(n., v.a.m. - Possession, charge, order; time, life time, time of day)*
Noa khẹt dọ ińaḱ amọlre menaḱa.

5. andaḱ - *(n., v.a.m. what is prepared by the* andaḱ *roasting process; dry by roasting.)*
Họlọṅko andaḱakada jẹmọn piṭhạ alo kẹṭẹjọḱ.
andaḱ - *(v.a.m. worry, harass, torment, disturb.)*
Matkọm lekako andaḱkidińa.

6. aṕ - *(v.a.m. wash (the face).*
Mẽṭhã aṕkaeme.
aṕ - *(v.m. Alight, perch (birds, insects).*
Parwa dọ sạṛimreye aṕena.

7. aṛaḱ - *(v.a.m. Release, set free, liberate, let go, untie, loose, give up.)*
Gạiko aṛaḱkeťkoa.
aṛaḱ - *(n., v.a.m. vegetables, potherbs (leaves, herbs etc. that are eaten).*
Teheń dọ mungạ aṛaḱ utuipe.

8. aṭal - *(n., v.a.m. Layer, fold, row, storey.)*
Miť aṭal aṭẹťte dọ rokoṛge bujhạuḱa.
aṭal - *(adj. Double, folded, with double flowers.)*
Aṭal kusmbi baha dọ ạḍi mõńj ńẹlọḱa.

9. baske - *(adj., v.a.m. Stale, fusty.)*
Jel utu, hako utu urgumge sebela, baskelen khan sọṛọm dọ cabaḱa.
Baske - *(n., A Santal sept.)*

Mạńjhiko do̠ko Baske pạris kana.

10. bạ̣i - *(n., v.m. wit, convulsions, cramps, an involuntary state or movement of the body over which one has no control (in epilepsy, insanity, delirium, etc.)*
Ho̠ṛ ho̠po̠n do̠ ạḍi lekan bạ̣i ruạ reak' baḍae menak'takoa.
bạ̣i - *(adv., Slowly, softly, gently, gradually.)*
Bạ̣i macha taṛamme, bạń tiạk'et'mea.

11. be̠re̠l - *(adj. fresh, raw, green, unripe, uncooked.)*
Noa do̠ be̠re̠l ul kana.
be̠re̠l - *(v.a.m. Settle, take up one's abode, dwell.)*
Raje be̠re̠le̠t'koa noa jaegare, onateko atoyet'a.

12. bir - *(adj., v.m. forest, jungle).*
Santal Pargana do̠ bir burute sajao disạm kana.
bir - *(n., v.m. Hero, brave man, warrior.)*
Gạrbhu De̠s Mạńjhi do̠ ạḍi maraṅ bir ho̠ṛe̠ tahẽ̠kana.

13. bis - *(n., num. Twenty, a score.)*
Bis ṭaka menak'khan pańcate e̠m hataṛạńme.
bis - *(n., Poison, venom.)*
Ayaṅ biń bis do̠ ạḍi tạpisa.

14. boṅga - *(n., A spirit, godling, demon.)*
Ho̠ṛ ho̠po̠nren do̠ ạḍi lekan boṅga menak'koa.
boṅga - *(n., A month, lunar month.)*
Darae boṅga nãhãk' peṛa ho̠ṛko hijuk'a.
boṅga - *(n., A (house) spirit i.e. wife.)*
Nui do̠ phalnaren oṛak' boṅga.

15. bo̠ho̠k' - *(n., The head (lit. and fig.)*
Noa pạilạ bo̠ho̠k're do̠ ạḍi lekan bud menak'a.
bo̠ho̠k' - *(v.a.m., Turn one's head (in certain direction)*
Cando rakap' se̠c'e bo̠ho̠k'akat'a.

16. bol - *(n. v.a.d. Strength, power, authority.)*
Bae bol daṛeadea.
bol - *(n. A ball.)*
Netar bol eneč do ạḍi ãṭ cạltiakana.
bol - *(v.n.m. Enter, go in.)*
Oṛak̓te bolme.

17. bhorna - *(v.a.m. Load, burden; to load.)*
Bhorna hoeyena, ma delabon.
bhorna - *(v.a.m. Give property in payment of debt.)*
Gại kaḍako jotoe bhornaket̓koa.

18. da - *(n., v.m. Tuber, bulb.)*
Sasaṅ dare ạsit̓ena, dayena.
da - *(n., Elder brother.)*
E maraṅ da!

19. dak̓ - *(n., v.a.m. water, rain.)*
Serma dak̓ bhorsa noa khet do.
dak̓ - *(v.a.m.)*
Piṇḍạ do otre dak̓a.

20. dos - *(n., v.a.m. Guilt, fault, crime, offence.)*
Uniak̓ cet̓ dos hõ bạnuk̓taea.
dos - *(num., n. Ten)*
Dos ṭaka imạṅme.

21. dhorao - *(v.a. Seize, catch hold of, take notice of, cognisance of.)*
Ran do baṅ lagaok̓a, boṅga bam dhoraolekhan.
dhorao - *(v.a.m. Engage, set to, commence, reaccustom, resume, give.)*
Seṅgel dhoraome.

22. ḍabra - *(n., A large low-lying rice-field.)*
ḍabra khet reak̓ phosol do judạk̓gea, ona iạte ḍabra-ḍabra khetge bek̓nao sanakoa.

ḍabra - *(v.m. Be submerge, be filled up with water, become a pool (always preceded by* daǩ*).*
Noa khe̱t do̱ daǩ ḍabrayena, ro̱ǩho̱e do̱ o̱ho̱ ganlena.

23. ḍak - *(n., Post (for letters, the mails)*
ḍakte ciṭhi he̱ċena.
ḍak - *(n., Call, summons)*
Ḍak hoeyena, delabon daka jo̱m.

24. ḍaṇḍo̱m - *(n., v.a.m. wine, mulet.)*
Do̱sakadam, onate ḍaṇḍo̱m e̱mo̱ǩ hoyoǩtama.
ḍaṇḍo̱m - *(n., v.a.d. Handle of an axe.)*
Noa ṭe̱ṅgo̱ċ ḍaṇḍo̱maǩme.

25. ḍubạ - *(n., v.a.m. Inundation, flood, deluge.)*
Ḍubạte ho̱ṛko ạtuyena.
ḍubạ - *(n., A small oil vessel)*
Ḍubạ sunumte sunum ạguime.

26. ḍhae - *(n., Habit, propensity, proneness, condition.)*
Am do̱ mại, sikhạunage bam aṅjo̱ma, am hõ hape̱n inạ ḍhaege calaǩtama.
ḍhae - *(v.a. Beat so that it gives a bang; to bang)*
Oṛaǩ ho̱ṛte̱ťe ḍhaekedea.

27. ḍhe̱re̱ ḍhe̱re̱ - *(adv. Staringly)*
ḍhe̱re̱ ḍhe̱re̱ye be̱ṅge̱ťakaťa.
ḍhe̱re̱ ḍhe̱re̱ - *(v.m. Become over-full (so that one does not care to move)*
Jo̱m ḍhe̱re̱ ḍhe̱re̱akanae, alope kuli baṛayea.
ḍhe̱re̱ ḍhe̱re̱ - *(adv. whirring (the sound of the spinning-wheel).*
Carkha ḍhe̱re̱-ḍhe̱re̱ saḍekana, taǩkokanae.

28. gad gad - *(adj. In crowds, numbers, flocks, very many; v.n. flock together.)*
Gad gad peṛako he̱ċena.

gad gad - *(adv. Roaringly, splashingly (water falling, flowing, also about the sound of old women passing water).*
Gad gad dak̓ ạtuk̓kana, gaḍa pe̱re̱jo̱k̓kana.

29. gad gadao - *(v.m. flock together, crowd, throng.)*
Gad gadao calaoenako pata ńe̱l.
gad gadao - *(v.m. flow, rush with a noise (water).*
Gad gadao ańje̱t̓ena, ma siok̓pe.

30. gańjo̱n - *(n., v.a.m. Ill-treatment; find fault with, censure, ill-treat, make life miserable.)*
Nui he̱re̱l ṭhen ạḍi gańjo̱nić jo̱me̱t̓kana, e̱ke̱n gidrạ mãyãteń tahe̱nkana.
gańjo̱n - *(n. v.a. Noise (of drums, etc.)*
Teheń ńindạ khub gańjo̱nko lagaoket̓a.
gańjo̱n - *(n., kind of Santal song and dance form).*
Ne̱ hạli Gańjo̱n e̱ne̱ć-sereń do̱ at̓ idik̓kana.

31. go̱l - *(n., v.a. A whistle; to whistle.)*
Kombṛo hoṛ go̱lteko ho̱ho̱ ńapama.
go̱l - *(adv. (as second part of a verb). quickly, suddenly, at once.)*
Ro̱ṛ go̱lket̓ae.

32. go̱ṅ - *(v.a. Reply, answer, respond by an inarticulate sound indicating that one has heard a call.)*
Ho̱ho̱ket̓ạń, bae go̱ṅlak̓a.
go̱ṅ - *(v.a. Bestow, give in marriage (a girl).*
Ho̱po̱nerate go̱ṅkedea.

33. go̱t̓ - *(adv. only used suffixed to verb. quickly, speedily, suddenly, at once; recently.)*
He̱ć go̱t̓enae.
go̱t̓ - *(v.a.m. Pluck, gather (fruit, beans, etc.)*
Kaṇṭhaṛe go̱t̓ke̱t̓a.

34. haḍgar - *(n., Hyena crcuta, and H. striata); fig. old in the country, not to be taken by the nose. There are two kinds, one called simply* haḍgar, *and the* dhạcri haḍgar.)
Deko sạu mare haḍgar, ro̱ho̱ṛ jaṅ hõ̱ko to̱go̱ja.
haḍgar - *(adj. Big and bony, lean (buffaloes); v.m. Become lean and bony (i.e., eat much and not strong for work).*
Nukin do̱ baṅ jut kaḍam kiriṅkeťkinạ, hape̱nkin haḍgaroǩa.

35. hal - *(n. State, condition, circumstances, state of affairs, matter; v.m. Get into a state, etc.)*
Uniaǩ halem baḍaea?
hal - *(n. Moisture (of the ground); v.m. Become moist.)*
Noa o̱tre khub hal menaǩa.

36. he̱ċ - *(v.a. Pluck leaves.)*
Sarjo̱m sakam he̱ċ ạguipe.
he̱ċ - *(v.m. Come, arrive (*hijuǩ*); v.a.d. Come to, visit.)*
Oṛaǩrege miť basna daǩ ar goṛa umul, inạ baṛe̱ he̱ċaǩpe.

37. ho̱n - *(A rat, especially the house rat.)*
Ho̱nko kakratkana, biṅ dho̱rageye bo̱lo̱akana.
ho̱n - *(n. A son, child.)*
Ho̱n ho̱po̱n cele hõ̱ bạnuǩkotaea.
ho̱n - *(dem. element. There yonder (showing) mostly used followed by other demonstratives commencing with* ho̱n.*)*
Ho̱n ho̱na ạguime.

38. ho̱ra - *(n., Part, division, strip of land, section; v.a.m. Do in parts; leave out, pass over a part.)*
Miť ho̱rae ir purạukeťa.
ho̱ra - *(adv. (only used as second part in compounds). Away, up, all.)*
Dayage, uniren gidrạ do̱ko go̱ċ ho̱raentaea!

39. ho̱ť - *(only used added to a verbal base, the sufixes being those of the principal verb).*
Me̱ro̱m laċe ho̱ťke̱ťa.

hoť - *(v.a.m. Tear off, strip off (by running the hand up the stalk).*
Mungạ aṛak̓ hoť ạguime.

40. iạ - *(indef. pr. So and so (used as a substitute for another word, which the speaker either does not wish to use, or does not remember at the moment; the word wanted is generally named afterwards); v.a.m. Do so and so (word not mentioned).*
Iạ, do se calak̓me, haṇḍe lạiakom.
iạ - *(interj., (used about equivalent to* e ho*).*
Iạ, do se calak̓me.

41. isi - *(n., A plough-beam, the beam of a plough to which the yoke is attached.)*
Nahel isi rạpuťakana, jut ocoń calak̓kana.
isi - *(num. A score, twenty.)*
Noa pạńci do miť isi ṭakako damak̓kana.

42. jala - *(n., v.a.m Troubles, distress, suffering, affliction, torment, want, difficulty, adversity.)*
Jala do soṅgere menak̓a.
jala - *(n., Anxity, soliciture.)*
Ạsulok̓ reak̓ jala ạuriye bujhạua.
jala - *(n., A sea, lake.)*
Dak̓ teṅgoakana, jala leka ńelok̓kana.

43. jao - *(n., Barley, Hordeum vulgare.)*
Jao sạtu do ạḍi sebela.
jao - *(indef. Pr. Every; adv. Always, constantly.)*
Jao hilạk̓ iskul calak̓me.

44. jawa - *(v.a.m. Soak, steep, saturate, puddle.)*
Hasako jawaea deal benao lạgiť.
jawa - *(n., adj. Twins, twin)*
Jawa gidrạkin hoeakana phalnaren.

45. jãt - *(adj., v.a.m. Heavy, oppresive; press, weigh down; be heavy, oppress.)*
Ạḍi jãt mọkọrdọmarele paṛaoena.
jãt - *(n., A bow set for killing animals.)*
Jãtko oḍaoakaťa tạrup̀ gọje lạgiť.
jãt - *(n. Time, trip (bringing charcoal, firewood, etc.).*
Tinạǩ jãtpe ạgukeťa kuilạ.
jãt - *(n., v.a. Security, pledge; show as security.)*
Jãt mẹnkate kaḍae uduǩakawadea.

46. jạlại - *(n., v.a.m. A nail (of iron).*
Sạṛim reaǩ bata rạpuťakana, jạlại kẹṭẹċ gọťkam.
jạlại - *(n., especially made by* ciṭmiṅ *rats in the field.)*
Laha laha daǩ din, goḍo dọ piṇḍhạ ar baṅkhan ghuṭureko jạlại baṛakaǩa.

47. jel - *(n., flesh, meat)*
Jel mọtọ miť sẹċre dọhọepe, ar jaṅ dọ miť sẹċre.
jel - *(n., A deer,)*
Buru sendrare jelko gọċkedea.

48. jẹrẹť - *(v.a.m. Set fire to, kindle, light, ọurn.)*
Divhe jẹrẹdme.
jẹrẹť - *(v.m. Stick together, grow together.)*
Mẽť jẹrẹťentaea.

49. joṛa - *(n., v.a. A pair; make a pair, tie two together.)*
Bar joṛa ḍaṅgra menaǩkotiṅa.
joṛa - *(n., v.a. A kind of rope or halter with which animals are tied; tie up with do.)*
Nui kaḍa dọ ạḍie dạṛeťa, joṛate tọlkaeme.

50. jọjọm - *(v. perform. Eat; adj. Eating.)*
Am dọ daka jọjọm hõ bam baḍaekana.
jọjọm - *(v. perform. right (opp. to left.)*
Ọṇḍem tiạǩlekhan dọ jọjọm sẹċ calaǩme.

51. jo̲k̓ - *(v.a.m. Sweep, starch the thread or warp in weaving.)*
    Mõ̲ńjte raca jo̲k̓ saphaeme.
    jo̲k̓ - *(adj. verbal suffix -k̓; fruits etc.)*
    Noa do̲ ạḍi jo̲k̓ dare kana.

52. kaḍa - *(n., A buffalo (male).*
    Tinạk̓ kaḍa menak̓kotapea?
    kaḍa - *(v.m. Crawl, move on all fours (children before they learn to walk, also grown-ups).*
    Gidrạ do̲e kaḍa baṛaekana.

53. karo̲n - *(n. Cause, reason, ground, occasion).*
    Karo̲n udugme, cedak̓em ro̲ṛe̲t̓kana?
    karo̲n - *(n., v.m. Disease, affliction, malady.)*
    Ce̲t̓ bato̲l co̲m jo̲makat̓te noa karo̲n do̲ sirjạuena.

54. kaso - *(n., v.a.m. fold, plait, frill; to fold (several times) tie fast.)*
    Kasoe aṛak̓akat̓a, bidlại bidlạiye taṛamet̓a.
    kaso - *(v.a. Pare off, reduce, cut off.)*
    Noa sagaṛ do̲ maraṅena, kaso huḍińpe.

55. kaṭ - *(n., v.a.m. wood, timber.)*
    Sarjo̲m kaṭge bogea.
    kaṭ - *(n., v.a.m. A measure equal to one maund, ie., 40 seers (measured not weighed).*
    Mit̓ kaṭ do̲ pon suli.
    kaṭ - *(v.a.m. Act, effect, do, be as good as, cure.)*
    Noa ran do̲ eraḍo̲m sunum lekae kaṭa.
    kaṭ - *(v.m. Become stiff, congeal.)*
    Rabaṅtele kaṭena.

56. kạli - *(adj. f., the same as kala, q. v., applied to females (deaf).*
    Uni maejiu do̲e kạligea.
    kạli - *(n. A verse (of a song.)*
    Mit̓ kạlibon sereńlege.

kạli - *(n. The Hindu goddess Kali.)*
Kạli dọ Hindukoren mit' kuṛi boṅga kanae.
kạli - *(n., adj., v.a.m. Ink, black spot)*
Kọlọmre kạli cabaena.
kạli - *(n. Area, extent (in measure).*
Tinạk' kaṭha kạli hoeyena?

57. kạsi - *(n., v.a.m. A castrated animal (especially a castrated goat.)*
Nui dọe kạsi mẹrọm kana.
kạsi - *(n. A species of grass.)*
Kạsi gẹlẹ reak' jọnọk'ko benaoa.

58. kitạ - *(n. The nearly stemless date tree, Phoenix acaulis, Roxb. Mats are woven of its leaves.)*
Kitạ gaskete kaḍale gasaokoa.
kitạ - *(n. Plot, parcel, piece (here especially about fields.)*
Mit' kitạ khẹt bạnuk'takoa.

59. kọlọm - *(n. A reed, reed-pen, pencil.)*
Amak' kọlọm imạńme.
kọlọm - *(n., v.a. Cutting, graft.)*
Noa dọ kọlọm ul kana.

60. kuṛi - *(n. A girl, a young woman, daughter, v.m. Become do., grow to maturity.)*
Nui dọe kuṛi gidrạ kana.
kuṛi - *(n. A score, twenty.)*
Kuṛi ṭaka imạńme.

61. laṛ - *(n, The fibre between the tree and bark.)*
Noa cihũṭ laṛ dọ haṛamena, baṅ laṛok'a.
laṛ - *(n. A row of a necklace, a string of beads, etc.)*
Pẹ laṛ sikṛi malae họrọk'akat'a.

62. lạp' - *(n., v.m. A flame; flicker, flare up.)*
Noa oṛak' dọ ọhọ lọlena, hana oṛak' reak' sẹṅgẹl lạp' ucạṛena.

lạp̓ - *(v.a. flutter the wings.)*
Gidi kuṛit̓ lạp̓leanẹc̓ko uḍạu daṛeak̓a.

63. loṛyot̓ - *(adj., v.a.m. Staring, gaping, gazing, stupid, silly; gape, gae, stare, be nonplussed.)*
Loṛyot̓e duṛup̓ baṛaekana, nui loṛyot̓ dọ buddi hõ bạnuk̓taea.
loṛyot̓ - *(v.a.m. Swallow, go down.)*
Cẹt̓em loṛyot̓ket̓a?

64. mạli - *(n. A gardener, florist; v.a.m Appoint, become do.)*
Mạli dọ bagwanre ạḍi mõńj-mõńj bahae rọhọeakada.
mạli - *(n. A small earthenware cup, used with oil and a wick for lighting.)*
Mạlire sunum dulme ar divhe jẹrẹdme.
mạli - *(v.a.m. To cup.)*
Ḍaṇḍa hasoyedekana, mạliyepe.
mạli - *(n. A manufacturer of fireworks.)*
Baplare mạliko ạguakadea.
mạli - *(v.a., v.m.d. Act, proceed, practice.)*
Ọṇḍẹ duṛup̓kate cẹt̓ cọko mạliyet̓kan.

65. mạn - *(n. Land held by a village official in connexion with his office.)*
Mạńjhi babawak̓ ḍhertẹt̓ dọ mạn jumi kantaea, ac̓ak̓ dọ thoṛagea.
mạn - *(v.a. Honour, entertain.)*
Peṛae hẹc̓lena, khubiń mạnkedea, dakako, utuko, hạṇḍiko khubiń emadea.

66. mela - *(n., v.a.m. A fair; hold a fair.)*
Dela Hińjlạ mela ńẹlbon calak̓a.
mela - *(n. Small-pox.)*
Ona atore mela duk bọlọakana.
mela - *(adj., adv. General, not specifying, open to all; generally, not naming a person's name or relationship.)*

Sạgại chaḍakate melate ho̱ho̱jo̱ṅ do̱ baṅ juta.
mela - *(v.a.m. Do in a general way, without religious observances, happen without people knowing curcumstances (always added to another word, denoting what is done or happening).*
Holanok̉ phalna do̱le jo̱m melakedea.
mela - *(adj. wide, large and open (area).*
Mela ṭạṇḍite gại idikope.
mela - *(intj. Come, come along (about equal to* dela, *q. v.)*
Mela calak̉me.

67. mera - *(n. Malted grain from which the liquor (beer) has been extracted; (fig.) the reason, meaning, the real matter.)*
Mera giḍikak̉pe, sukri emakope.
Noa do̱ ce̱t̉ hạṇḍi, mera bale ńamet̉a.
mera - *(n., adj. Of no significance, somebody.)*
Phalna merae tahẽ̱kana.

68. me̱n - (*intj. to warn, caution or admonish. Mind, take care, beware, look out. Often followed by another interjection.)*
Me̱n so̱nto̱rok̉pe.
me̱n - *(v.a., v.m.d. Say, utter, tell, purpose, intend; think, be of opinion, wish.)*
Ho̱ṛko me̱na, nui do̱ bae bhagea.

69. misi - *(n. A powder (composed of yellow myrobalan, gall-nut, vitriol, etc.)*
Misi ḍaṭa do̱ ńũr go̱do̱k̉a.
misi - *(n. Hair on the upper lip (just appearing.)*
Misi goco o̱mo̱nentaea, juạnok̉kanae.

70. moka - *(n., v.a.m. The forearm from elbow to wrist or to finger tips, a cubit, the length from elbow to tip of middle finger; to measure with the forearm.)*
Dare kho̱ne ńũrhạyente moka rạput̉entaea.
Ṭaka reak̉ mõ̱ṛẽ̱ mokako e̱mo̱k̉a.

moka - *(v.m. To cant, pitch (about the movement of a cart-wheel that has been worn, so that it is no longer round.)*
Sagaṛ mokak̓kana, eṭak̓ pạṭibon lagaoa.

71. morna - *(n. Death)*
Harna hilok̓, morna hilok̓ peṛa do̱ lạite hõ lạiakope.
morna - *(adj., v.m., equal to* mora, *q. v. (deprecatory).*
Am morna do̱, o̱ho̱m kạmi daṛelea.

72. mo̱ṭ - *(n., v.a.m. The gross total, total; to total, add up.)*
Mo̱ṭ nunạk̓ ṭaka hoeyena.
Mo̱ṭkate ạguime khạṛạite hoṛo bin̩ḍạ.
mo̱ṭ - *(n. A bundle, load; v.a. Make into a bundle, tie up.)*
Apan ạpin mo̱ṭ dipilpe.
mo̱ṭ - *(adv., v.a. forcibly, by force, of necessity; use force, force oneself on, thrust oneself on; v.m.d. Carry forcibly away, run away with.)*
Mo̱ṭgeń hijuk̓kana.
Mo̱ṭgeye duṛup̓ so̱ge̱yena jorok̓ lạgit̓.

73. muṇḍrạ - *(n. The distance from the elbow joint to the root of the middle finger with fist closed, used as a measure.)*
Bar moka mit̓ muṇḍrạ hoeyena, pe̱ moka do̱ bań.
muṇḍrạ - *(adj., v.a.m, equal to* muṇḍgo̱c̓, *q. v.* M. dare, *a lopped tree.)*
Muṇḍrạ ḍańgra.
Tejo sakamko jo̱m muṇḍrạket̓a.
Apat mocareye se̱ńge̱lade tayo̱mko muṇḍrạkedea.

74. muṭ - *(n. A fist, a fistful, handful.)*
Mit̓ muṭ caole emaeme.
muṭ - *(n. A handful of seed.)*
Ruhnire mit̓ muṭ baṛe̱ apho̱rme, bã̱ṛti bam daṛeak̓khan.
muṭ - *(n., v.a. Handle (of weapon, not of implements, hilt (of sword); seize, clutch.)*
Tarwaṛe muṭ,

Caṇḍbo̱l muṭkedete gạiye o̱r bereťkedea.
Ṭheṅgae muṭkeťa dadal lạgiť.

75. na - *(a postpos. particle used in calling or addressing a girl who stands in the relationship of a younger sister or of a daughter of the speaker or is a friend of equal age.)*
No̱ṭe̱ na hijuḱme.
na - *(inani. dem. element and pr.)*
Hẽ̱ nae ro̱ṛe̱ťa.
na - *(a particle signifying negation or uncertainly. Nor, or, neither...nor. Postposition.)*
Daka na utu, ce̱ť hõ̱ bako emaťlea.
na - *(a negative or private prefix (in borrowed Aryan words.)*
Na khạ̃yạ̃ na dạ̃yạ̃ kạmikanale.

76. nal - *(n. Horse-shoe, bullock-shoe, toe or heel-plate (of shoes).*
Nalko to̱lakaťtaea sado̱m.
nal - *(adj. Prepared, old (land that has been long under cultivation, opp.* khạ̃ṛti*); v.a. Occupy, take possession of (land).*
Nal jumi do̱ thoṛagetiṅa.
No̱ṇḍe̱ kho̱n alegele nalawakaťa.
nal - *(n. Tube, pipe.)*
Kũire nalko bạisạuakaťa.

77. nas - *(n. The under-side of the knee, part between the thigh and the calf of the leg (in humans); the hock (in animals); v.a. Tie the hock.)*
Nasreko maḱkedete bae taṛam daṛeaḱkana.
Gạị bae duhạu ocoaḱkana, nas to̱lepe.
nas - *(v.a.m. Ruin, destroy, waste, annihilate, spoil.)*
Ạḍi bhage jinise naskeťa.

78. nase - *(adj., adv. Untrue, false, in vain.)*

Sạri sẹ nase kana.
nase - *(adj., adv. A little, very little; slightly.)*
Nasegeye daḱketa.

79. nạpit - *(n. A barber. The same as* lạpit.*)*
Nạpit ṭhen goco họyọḱiń sẹnlenge.
nạpit - *(adj., adv. (postpositional). As much as, enough for, suitable to, in proportion to; proper, due, suitable.)*
Biḱ nạpit emaeme.

80. nẹ - *(dem. element and pr. This (inanimate, pointing to what is near and singling out).*
Nẹ uḍi.
Nẹkin khạclạḱ.
Nẹko khẹt dọ khub bhage hoṛoakana.
nẹ - *(intj., v.a., v.a.d. Take it, please; to offer; offer to.)*
Nẹ hataome.
nẹ - *(dem. pr. (animate). Such like, one like the speaker.)*
Nẹ hoṛ dọ bae bẹṅgẹtama.
nẹ - *(dem. adv. Just, about to, presently, a short while ago.)*
Nẹ nãhãḱe tioḱketa.

81. nọtẹ - *(dem. adv. Hither, to this place, to this part, in this direction.)*
Nọtẹ hijuḱme.
nọtẹ - *(v.a.m. Draw to this side.)*
Ọntẹn họṛko nọtẹketḱoa.

82. Ọl - *(adj. Musty, mouldy, fusty (the condition induced in moist vegetable matter when air is excluded); v.a.m Become musty, etc., fade.)*
Noa hoṛo dọ cakere ọlena.
ọl bele dọ bań sebela.
ọl - *(v.m. Lie down (for the night.)*
Teheń dọ niạkoregebon ọl aṅgaḱa.

83. pãk - *(n. Alluvial deposit, silt.)*
Pukhri aṅjẹt́ena, pãkbon rakaba khẹtte idi lạgit́.
pãk - *(n., v.a. Twist, round, turn; to twist, twine, turn, pervert.)*
Mit́ pãk babẹr pãkme.

84. pala - *(n. Power.)*
Ạimại palarem paṛaolenkhanem bujhạua.
pala - *(n. Hoar-frost. Seen in places in Assam where Santals have settled.)*
Pala ńũrakana, jaṅga kan kanaok̓kana.
pala - *(n., v.m. fresh leaves or shoots (that cattle or, in some cases, people, will eat.)*
Kạḍru sọsọ pala ạguakope.

85. palọn - *(adj., v.a.m. forbidden, contra-indicated (food); observe diet, prohibit, forbid.)*
Kaḍa bheḍa jel dọ am lạgit́ palọngea.
palọn - *(n. Scarcity, famine (used as second word in compounds).*
Lukhi palọn serma dọ ạḍi cas hoeyena.

86. paṭ - *(n. A wedge (for tightening); v.a.d. fix a wedge in.)*
Nahel paṭ
Nahel paṭak̓me.
paṭ - *(n. Sinew, gristle, catgut.)*
Noa paṭ dọ alope joṛa mesala.
paṭ - *(n. Half-full, of a bottle.)*
Mit́ paṭ dak̓ ạguime.
paṭ - *(n. The Deccani hemp, Hibiscus cannabinus, willd.; also called* paṭ jặṛĩ, paṭ mesta *and* paṭ sọn.*)*
Ale sẹć paṭ dọ bako casa.
paṭ - *(Throne; the administration of a zemindary.)*
Nui dọ raj paṭe calaoet́kana.
paṭ - *(n., v.a. A lesson; read, learn.)*

Teheń do okaṭak̕ paṭ reak̕ paṛhao hoyok̕a?

87. paṭa - *(n. A plank, board, slab; an oil-press.)*
Paṭare dhubi kicric̕ko soboda.
paṭa - *(n., v.a. A lease, title-deed, a deed of lease; to give do.)*
Mạńjhik̕ko do paṭa tahentakoa.
paṭa - *(adj., v.m. Coarse, thick (hair), hard, tough, strong; be do., grow strong.)*
Marań paṭa up̕ kantaea, bana up̕ leka.

88. paṭao - *(v.a.m. Irrigate, water.)*
Band khonak̕ dak̕te khetko paṭaoket̕a.
paṭao - *(v.a.m. Consolidate, make hard, plaster, over-run, fill with.)*
Soṛokko paṭaoket̕a.

89. pạk - *(n. A messenger, runner (sent by anyone in authority).*
Rajren pạk peadae hec̕lena.
pạk - *(n. A sword or stick play.)*
Pạk don do bại bạite mạutạ idik̕kana.

90. pạsi - *(n., v.a.m. A snare, loop, noose, an iron staple; ensnare, hang by a noose; be snared.)*
Potam pạsiń oḍaoakat̕a, bań doe pạsik̕ bań do bań.
pạsi - *(n. A Hindu caste that draws toddy.)*
Pạsiko hec̕akana, tạṛiko tol lạgit̕.

91. pạṭi - *(n.The outside (third) parts of a solid wheel, a strip of land, cloth, a mat.)*
Kanta sagaṛ reak̕ pạṭi haṛamena.
Goḍa reak̕ mit̕ pạṭire gundlile erakat̕a.
pạṭi - *(v.a.m. Pierce, prick, sting, puncture.)*
Sisińe pạṭikidińa.

92. pạṭkạ - *(n. A long narrow strip of cloth, about one span broad and many cubits long.)*

Rajaǩ pạṭkạm dạhṛi cabakea?
pạṭkạ - *(the same as* paḍga, *q. v.)*
Nui haṛam pạṭkạre do̱ alope raebaṛạṇ́ạ.

93. pe̱ṭe̱c̓ - *(n. Light or blighted grain, only husk without grain; v.m. Get unfilled grain.)*
Ro̱ko ńũkeťa, e̱ke̱n pe̱ṭe̱c̓le samṭaokeťa.
pe̱ṭe̱c̓ - *(v.a.m. Break off with the fingers, nip off, snip off.)*
Dạṭạuni pe̱ṭe̱c̓ ạguime.

94. poho - *(n. A locust, Pachytylus cinerascens.)*
Pohoko ãṛgolen serma goḍa casko jo̱m cabakeťa.
poho - *(v.m. Be half-boiled, hard (rice, millets), to sell up, but not be completely cooked.)*
Daka pohoakana, ạuri isinoǩa.

95. porodhol - *(n., v.m. A man whose hair is white; the white hair of age; become white haired.)*
De̱ baba, apege tho̱ poṇḍ dạhṛi hiṅgu thạilạǩ do̱ haṭ bahate porodholpe bahayentabona, noa bicạr do̱ ce̱ť leka kana, ro̱ṛpe.
porodhol - *(adj., v.m. white (flowers); bloom white.)*
Gaḍa aṛe aṛete tilại baha poṇḍge porodhol bahawakana.

96. purus - *(n. Generation.)*
Bar pe̱ purus kho̱n no̱ṇḍe̱ menaǩlea.
purus - *(n., v.a. The height of a man standing erect with arms and fingers extended above his head, a fathom; to measure the depth of water for ditch, etc.) with one's body; stretch oneself upto one's full height.)*
Kũire miť purus daǩ menaǩa.
purus - *(n. Husband)*
Tiri purus kanalin̓.

97. pus - *(n. The ninth solar month of the Hindus (middle of December to middle of January), the full moon of which is near pushya, three stars in Cancer.)*

Pusreye dak̓lekhane pas pusa.
pus - *(v.a.. Miss, not hit (the small stick, in* (ir eneč̓).
Pusket̓ae, gočenae.

98. puṭi - *(v.m. Shrink, contract (after having been wet).*
Baber puṭiyena.
puṭi - *(v.m. Swell, bloat, puff up, be distended.)*
Puṭik̓ dhạbič̓ jojomtegeye tahena.

99. phel - *(v.a.m. Reject, not let pass; fail.)*
Biḍạureko phelkedea.
phel - *(adj. who has missed being maried (mature girls).*
Phelgeae, noṅkateye buḍhik̓a.

100. rata - *(adj., v.m. full-grown, mature; become do.)*
Noa atore do khub rata kuṛi-koṛa menak̓koa.
rata - *(v.m. Become black.)*
Itạ joṇḍra dhũạ̃te ratayena.

101. rataṅ - *(n., frost, hoar-frost, rime, snow.)*
Nahak̓ rataṅ do baṅ ńũruk̓kana, sedae do Aghãṛ-Pus cando ạḍi ãṭ ńũruk̓kan tahẽkana, setak̓ jokheč̓ ohom taṛam daṛelea, rataṅte jaṅga do kạṭhuạ utạrok̓a.
rataṅ - *(adj., v.m. Lean, meagre, who does not grow at; become do. (people, animals)*
Nui rataṅ kaḍa do tis hõ bae moṭak̓a.

102. raṭen - *(n., the same as* aṭen, *q. v.)*
Raṭen jhạuạ leka katham gajaṛkhanem ạikạu ńama.
raṭen - *(adj., v.m. Impenetrable, impassable (thicket); become do.)*
Noa hor do raṭengea, ohom parom daṛelena.

103. rại - *(n., v.a.m. Decision, judgement, order, rule, opinion, custom, counsel; to decide, regulate, make a rule.)*
Disom hoṛ rạiko bandhaoakat̓a.
rại - *(n., A kind of mustard.)*

Rại tuṛi dọ baṛgereko casa.

104. rạs - *(n., v.a. A heap; to heap.)*
Rạs hoṛo reak' dọ bale ạkriṅa.
rạs - *(n. Look, appearance, figure, kind.)*
Nukin gại dọ mit' rạsgekin ṅẹlok'kana.
rạs - *(n., v.m. Luck, ortune, success; to become manifold, be multiplied, productive, abundant.)*
Sedae dọ khub rạs tahẽkana, nahak' dọ rạs bạnuk'a.

105. rạu rạu - *(v.a.m. Make a noise, a row, vociferate; adv. Noisily.)*
Rạu rạuko andoṛet'a.
rạu rạu - *(adv., v.m. Blazing up; to blaze up for a moment.)*
Pạtạulak'ko tiṅgiakat'a, rạu rạu jolok'kana.

106. rel - *(n., v.a. A rail, railway, railroad; make do.)*
Relteko calak'kana.
rel - *(v.a. To clean in a winnowing-fan, to winnow.)*
Caole rel saphaeme.

107. rela - *(v.a.m. To twist, twine.)*
Parkọm baber khub relaepe.
rela - *(v.a.m. Make, become even, smooth (road, by many people passing.)*
Noa hoṛ dọko relawakat'a hijuk' sẹnok'te.

108. reta - *(v.a. To saw or cut (by drawing the cutting implement backwards and forwards), play on a fiddle.)*
Kicriće reta topak'ket'a, ọrte baṅ cirạk'kante.
reta - *(n., v.a. Introduction, humming a tune in music; to hum or trill a tune, sing the scale.)*
Sereń dọ retawak'pe, ẹkẹn sereń dọ baṅ jutok'a.
reta - *(v.a.m. Press together (preparatory to tying); scrape off (ears of the Palmyra-palm.)*
Bata retaepe urij lạgit'.

109. rẹsẹť - *(v.a. To crush, squash.)*
Goṅghań lẹbẹť rẹsẹťkedea.
rẹsẹť - *(v.a.d., v.m.d. Brew beer.)*
Abo hõ miť goṭẹč rẹsẹťabonpe.
rẹsẹť - *(adj. Tender, juicy; v.m. Become do., fat; become mature (girl).*
Noa jel dọ khub rẹsẹť sebelkana.
rẹsẹť - *(postp. Then only, in that case.)*
Gọg rẹsẹťem ạikạua hamal dọ.

110. sẹ - *(conj. disjunctive. Or.)*
Am sẹ ińiń calaǩa?
sẹ - *(postpos. particle, used to add emphasis, incitement, encouragement.)*
Cẹť baṅ sẹ, onkanaǩ dọ bạń ńẹlakawan tahẽkana.
sẹ - *(v.m. To boil over, foam, well up, froth.)*
Daka sẹǩkana.

111. sẹlẹť - *(post. Together with, along with, in company with, including, with concerning.)*
Iń sẹlẹť dọ bae rọṛlaǩa.
sẹlẹť - *(v.a.m. To include, mix up in, or with, to take along, implicate; adj. Included, mixed up, implicated.)*
Am hõe sẹlẹťkeťmea.
Noa kạmire dọ bạń sẹlẹdoǩa.

112. sidhạ - *(n. Provisions, victuals, ration (foodstuff not cooked).*
Kạmiko sidhạ emakope pẹ bela reaǩ.
sidhạ - *(adj., v.a.m. Straight, direct, honest, straightforward; to make, become straight, etc.)*
Sidhạte calaǩme, haṇḍẹ họrem ńama.

113. sikạ - *(n., v.a.m A mark burnt on the left forearm.)*
Phalna dọ leṅga tire sikạ menaǩtaea.
sikạ - *(n. A four-anna bit (of silver)*

Mõṛẽ sikạko ḍaṇḍo̱mkedea.

114. sikwạr - *(n. A sling made of strong cord in which to hang or carry things; v.a.d. Provide with the sling.)*
Sikwạr benaome sunum ṭhili akae lạgiť.
Kohṇḍa sikwạraḱpe alo ńũruḱ lạgiť.
sikwạr - *(v.a.m. To give, get a fissure, crack (earthenware vessel at bottom).*
Daka daḱte noa ṭukuċko sikwạrkeťa.

115. sil - *(n., v.a. A stone, hone; to rub and sharpen on a hone.)*
Silre holaťko lase̱ra.
sil - *(n. Nature, quality, benevolence, humanity, politeness, generosity.)*
Kuṛi ho̱po̱nko apnaraḱ sil do̱ aloko adma.

116. siń - *(v.a.m. To close, shut (as a door, box, etc.)*
Silpiń sińkaḱme.
siń - *(The day (from sunrise to sunset), daylight; v.m. To become day.)*
Siń bhorre kạmi cabaepe.
Sińke̱ siń, sińke̱ ńindạ miť lekae daḱeťa, hatạḱte are̱ċ leka.

117. sir - *(n. A vein, artery, blood-vessel, tendon, nerve, sinew, rib (vein of leaf), edge; muscle (when felt hard and standing somewhat out).*
Ho̱ṭo̱ḱ sir hasoyedińkana.
sir - *(adj., v.m. Superior, better, more proficient; to be, become do.)*
Nui koṛa do̱ jo̱to̱ kho̱ne sirgea kạmire.

118. sirbạ - *(adj., v.m. Rough, that cannot be planed smooth (wood); to be do., to peel off the skin of a finger, run a splinter into the hand, tear a nail to the quick.)*
Noa kaṭ do̱ sirbạgea, cikạ̃ṛ bań lagoḱkana.
sirbạ - *(v.a.m. To cause trouble, bring in disturbing matter (in judging).*

Jo̱to̱le jut́laḱa, nui phalnageye sirbạket́a.

119. siṛi - *(n., A ladder, a flight of steps or stairs.)*
Koṭhate de̱jok̀ lạgit́ siṛiko benaoa.
siṛi - *(v.a.m. To inquire, ascertain, find out, search.)*
Ape atokore jãhãe ạṛko ạkriń khaċ ma se̱ siṛiwạńme.
Bạhu siṛialeme ale koṛa lạgit́.

120. Sitạ - *(n. Sita, the wife of Rama, mentioned in Santal traditions; in Santali the name is mostly given as Chitạ.)*
Sitạ do̱ Ramren bạhui tahẽ̱kana.
sitạ - *(n. A grain of boiled rice.)*
Ninạḱ gan sitạte̱t́e e̱moḱa, ar daḱte̱t́ do̱ aema.

121. sit́ - *(v.a.m. To pluck, gather.)*
Aṛaḱ sit́ko se̱nakana.
sit́ - *(v.a.m. To finish, run out, run short, be exhausted.)*
Khe̱tle benao sit́ket́a.

122. so̱ - *(n., num. A hundred.)*
So̱ ṭaka e̱moḱme, baṅkhan bale gatemea.
so̱ - *(n., v.m. Smell, odour, stench; to smell, emit a smell; v.a. impers. To smell.)*
He̱ṛe̱m so̱ no̱te̱ kho̱n hijuḱana.
Seage so̱ kana, biń tanaḱe go̱ċakana.
so̱ - *(n. The Black Plum tree.)*
So̱ bele tioḱ ạguipe.

123. so̱ho̱r - *(n. A city, town (large).*
Kolkata do̱ ạḍi maraṅ so̱ho̱r kana.
so̱ho̱r - *(n., v.a.d. A cross-border on cloth; to make border.)*
Noa kicriċ reaḱ araḱ so̱ho̱r menaḱa.
so̱ho̱r - *(v.a.m. To throw forward, hurl, dart, rush head throw (a shuttle), fall forward, push forward, move forward, advance.)*
Ṭạrup̀ bo̱rlo̱me so̱ho̱radea.

124. sǫk' - *(v.a.m. To clean rice or other grain winally.)*
Caole bagaṛgea sǫk' machaeme.
sǫk' - *(v.a. To suspend a plough from the yoke while on the bullocks' neck.)*
Kulhire nahel sǫk' dǫ barǫngea.

125. sǫṅ - *(v.a.m. To measure, survey.)*
Pạite hoṛom sǫṅketa', tinạk' mǫnem sǫṅketa'?
sǫṅ - *(n., adj. Companion, partisan.)*
Nui dǫ iṅren sǫṅ kanae.
Sǫṅ hǫṛko hẹc'ena, aleren dǫ bae hẹc'lena.
sǫṅ - *(postp., v.a.m. Along with, together with, in company with; to take along with oneself.)*
Iṅ sǫṅren kanae.
Alerenko sǫṅkedea peṛa hǫṛǫk' lạgit'.
sǫṅ - *(v.m. To be equal to.)*
Uni tuluc' ǫhǫṅ sǫṅlena.

126. sui - *(n. A needle.)*
Suite rǫgme.
sui - *(v.m. To come up like needles, sprout, spire.)*
Hoṛo aphǫr suiakana.

127. tãhã - *(adv. Likewise, too.)*
Am hõ tãhã ǫṇḍẹm tahẽkana.
tãhã - *(adv. Certainly, there.)*
Suṇḍi salre tãhãm tahẽkana, arem mẹneta' oṛak'regem tahẽkana.
tãhã - *(indef. pr. and adv. (correlative of* jãhã, *inanimate).*
Jãhã ạyup' tãhãm aṅgayena.

128. tak - *(n. Opportunity.)*
Takiṅ ṅamlekhaniṅ calak'a.
tak - *(n. Thread, strand.)*
Pẹ tak sutạme pãkakata'.

129. tic' - *(v.a.m. To stretch out. distend, extend.)*

Phalna dọ parkọmreye tiċakana.
tiċ - *(v.m. To belong to, be equal, of the same kind, be counted as, be comprised under, come in under the species, be like, similar to.)*
Hoṛte hõ bae tijok̕kana, Dekote hõ baṅ, cele jạt kan coe.
Dakate hõ baṅ tijok̕kana, dak̕ mạṇḍite hõ baṅ, tite hõ baṅ jọmọk̕kana, cukṛuċte hõ baṅ.

130. tikin - *(postp. The same as* -tekin*).*
Phalnatikinkin hẹċena.
tikin - *(n., dual. The hands.)*
Tikin nọtẹtam.
tikin - *(n., adv. Noon, midday; at noon; v.a.m. To keep until, to become noon, reach the meridian.)*
Tikin jọkhẹċ hijuk̕me.
Tikinreye hẹċena.
Tikin tikin oṭak̕reko tahẹna.

131. topot̕ - *(n., v.a. The exit of a subterranean passage, egress; to make do.)*
Topot̕ ẹsẹdpe, baṅkhanko dạṛa.
topot̕ - *(n., v.m. A pimple, acne (appearing on the face of a boy or girl reaching maturity); to get do.)*
Topot̕ ọmọnentaea, harayenae.
topot̕ - *(n. A kind of insect living in the ground; their bite is very painful.)*
Ọtreń gitiċakan tahẽkana, topot̕ko gẹrkidińa siḍiċ siḍiċ.
topot̕ - *(n. A cock-fight; v.m.n. To fight like cocks, to fight.)*
Sikhạr disomre sim topot̕ reak̕ akhṛa menak̕takoa, Robibar hilok̕ko topot̕ ocokoa.

132. tora - *(postp. (when added to a verb). Along (with, when going, going along).*
Idi toraeme.
Peṛae hiri toraket̕koa.
tora - *(adverbial postp. Just after, immediately after, as*

soon as.)
Hẹċ tora lạiaeme.
Rọṛ torageye hẹċena.
tora - *(postp., added to a personal or certain demonstrative pronouns, also to* ọkọń *or* ọkọe. *Off, off and away, just (like, now).*
Jọmken, ńũken, hą̃i torae calaoena.
Nũk̓ũi torae calaoena.

133. toṛ - *(n. A squirrel.)*
Toṛ dọko kạṭiċ janwar kana.
toṛ - *(v.a. To sting.)*
Phalna dọ dumurko toṛkedea.

134. toṛao - *(v.a.m. To break, manage, finish, accomplish, demolish, spend.)*
Ale dọ hurut̓ khuṇṭut̓le toṛaoakat̓a, sedaeren họṛ kanale.
toṛao - *(v.a. To pause to indicate that a fresh start is to be made (dancing, drumming, singing).*
Tumdak̓ko toṛaoket̓a.

135. tot̓ - *(v.a.m. To bring or come out, tear out, extract, pick.)*
Gạchiko tot̓et̓kana.
tot̓ - *(v.a. To peck (Vowls).*
Sim eṅgae tot̓kidińa.

136. tuli - *(n. Bottom, foundation.)*
Tuli dọ dhirigea.
Baksa reak̓ tulitẹt̓reń ńamkeda.
tuli - *(adj., v.a.m. full, rich, well-to-do; to stand, settle; remain full, be filled; to become well-to-do, rise.)*
Gạḍa dọ tulige menak̓a.
Netar dọko tuliyena.

137. ṭạku - *(n. A spindle, the spinning axle of a spinning-wheel.)*
Ṭạkure sutạmko badhaoa takoe jọkhẹċ.
ṭạku - *(v.m. To be stunted, backward in shooting forth ears.)*

Gelek̓ jokheće huḍurketťe adom horo do ṭạkuyena.
ṭạku - *(n. The erectile spies of a porcupine.)*
Jhĩk ṭạku reak̓ kolomko benaoa.

138. ṭher - *(adj. Hot-tempered, passionate, ill-tempered; v.a. To boast, brag, bluster.)*
Ạḍi ṭher hoṛ kanae.
Onka do alom ṭhera, baṅkhanem thapa ocok̓a.
ṭher - *(v.a. To peal (about the sound of a stroke of lightning), to strike; n. A stroke of lightning.)*
Ṭherteye goćena.
Bar pe dhaoe ṭherketa̓, ạḍile botorena.

139. up̓ - *(v.a.m. To eject, throw out, tip out; pour out (solids); spill.)*
Noṇḍe hasa ubme.
Ḍopkate dak̓ up̓ goťkak̓me.
up̓ - *(n. Hair, wool; v.m. Become hairy, get hair.)*
Bohok̓ up̓ko ãṛgoketa̓.
Bana up̓ko tolakoa bhạlki ruạre.

ẠKIL BHAŃJAO - 15

A. Ṭoyot'kate jobab emok̓me :-

1. Khạli jaega peṛejme. *Noa do ... ul kana.*
   (a) berel (b) berel (c) biril (d) berel
2. Khạli jaega peṛejme. *Sarjom sakam ... ạguipe.*
   (a) heć (b) heć (c) hić (d) hoć.
3. Khạli jaega peṛejme. *Am do daka ... hõ bam baḍaekana.*
   (a) jojom (b) jojom (c) jujum (d) jojom
4. Khạli jaega peṛejme. *Noa do ... ul kana.*

(a) kolom (b) ko̱lo̱m (c) kulum (d) kolum

5. Khạli jaega pe̱re̱jme. … bele do̱ baṅ sebela.

(a) ol (b) o̱l (c) ọl (d) ẹl

B. O̱lkate jobab e̱mo̱k'me :-

1. Noakin sabad ayatre beoharkate begarte̱t' lạime - *be̱re̱l, be̱re̱l.*
2. Noakin sabad ayatre beoharkate begarte̱t' lạime - *karo̱n, karo̱n.*
3. Noakin sabad ayatre beoharkate begarte̱t' lạime - *jo̱jo̱m, jo̱jo̱m.*
4. Noakin sabad ayatre beoharkate begarte̱t' lạime - *amo̱l, amo̱l.*
5. Noakin sabad ayatre beoharkate begarte̱t' lạime - *aṗ, aṗ.*

16

AŃJO̠MRE MIṪ, MANE JUDẠ
(HOMONYMS

1. baṛe - *(n. The banyan tree.)*
   Capakiạ baṛe latarre, kuṛikomako duṅguṫ duṅgudoḱ.
   baṛe̠ - *(opt. particle. Please, do. O that (may)*
   Uni do̠ baṅ, am baṛe̠ hijuḱme.

2. bhor - *(adv. The whole, as long as, as much as.)*
   Teheń do̠ din bhorle kạmikeda.
   bho̠r - *(n., v.a.d. Blessing; bless.)*
   Iso̠raḱ bho̠r ape sãote tahe̠nma.

3. ceṫ- *(v.a.m. Learn; v.a.d. Teach, v.m.d. Learn.)*
   Seḱreńe ceṫkeṫa.
   ce̠ṫ - *(interrog. pron. (inanim). what (with* hõ̠ *or* ge *and a negation following it functions as an indefinite pron. meaning anything, nothing; with* co̠ṅ, *something or other).*
   Noa do̠ ce̠ṫ kana?
   Ce̠ṫ co̠ṅko ro̠ṛeṫa?

4. do - *(int. used in calling on people, v.a.d. Call on, urge (v.* do dela*).*
   Do ya calaḱme.
   do̠ - *(an expletive postpositional particle, affixed to all parts of speech. As for, with respect to, regarding, with reference to, concerning. Generally not translated or translatable.)*
   Iń do̠ baṅ, amge.
   Ḍaṅgra do̠e go̠ċena.
   Sukri do̠ko tuńkedea.

Nitok̓ dobon gitiċa.

5. doho - *(v.a.m. Place, put, put down keep, retain.)*
Khạclạk̓ dohoeme.
Ḍoho - *(n., v.m. Tumour, growth, knob, excescence, hump (on back of camels, etc.); become, get do.)*
Gahnare sasaṅe rit̓et̓ tahẽkana, onate ḍoho janam daraakawadea.

6. era - *(n., v.a.m. A female, wife, lady, mistress.)*
Nui doe okoeren era kana?
er(a) - *(v.a.m. Sow, scatter, strew.)*
Joṇḍra do ạurile era.

7. goḍo - *(n. A rat.)*
Ạḍi lekan goḍo menak̓koa.
godo-godo - *(adv., v.a.m. with a splashing sound (water falling); make a splashing sound (especially when passing water.)*
Gaḍare dak̓ godo-godo ạtu paromok̓kana.

8. gol - *(n., v.a. A whistle; to whistle.)*
Kombṛo hoṛ do golteko hoho ńapama.
gol - *(adv. (as second part of a verb). quickly, suddenly, at once.)*
Roṛ golket̓ae.
gọl - *(n., v.a. Goal in match)*
Okoeṭak̓ ṭim hõ bako gọl daṛeada, barabạriyenako.

9. heṛak̓ - *(adj. Variegated, specled (colour of fowls); v.m. Be do.)*
Jaherre do heṛak̓ simko dãṛẽkoa.
heṛak̓ - *(adj. Leaf which chipped out, cut out, pared, trimmed, pruned; worn away.)*
Noa do heṛak̓ sakam kana.

10. ho̱ - *(interj. O! Used by women.)*
Henda ho̱, ado̱ ale se̱c̓ bape hijuǩa?
họ - *(interj. Ọ! Used by men.)*
Johar họ!

11. hoe - *(v.a. finish, bring to an end; bring to one's bearings, suo̱due; v.m. Become, be; come to pass, happen; come into existence; be born; be sufficient; serve (a purpose); come to and end, be finished.)*
Kạmile hoekeťa.
ho̱e - *(n. wind, air, climate; v.a. Blow.)*
Ce̱ť ho̱e hõ baṅ aṭkaroǩkana, ạḍi ãṭ udgạrkana.

12. hoyoǩ - *(Middle form of* hoe, *q.v. (as frequently written, instead of* hoeoǩ)*; adj. fertile, rich (soil, crops).*
Noa do̱ ạḍi hoyoǩ khe̱t kantalea.
ho̱yo̱ǩ - *(v.a.m. Shave.)*
Setaǩre gocoń ho̱yo̱ǩa.

13. hoṛo - *(n. The rice plant, Oryza sativa, L.; paddy, unhusked rice; v.m. Grow (paddy), get grain (paddy).*
Nes hoṛo cas do̱ ạḍi mõ̱ńj hoyakana.
ho̱ṛo̱-ho̱ṛo̱ - *(adv. Man by man, each one, individually.)*
Ho̱ṛo̱-ho̱ṛo̱ babar go̱ṭe̱c̓ko emaťlea.

14. jo̱(ko) - *(n., plural of* jo̱. *fruits.)*
Noa birre do̱ ạḍi lekan jo̱ko jo̱akana.
jo̱ko̱ - *(adj., v.m. frinkled, shrivelled; wither, crumple, together, shrivel.)*
Nui do̱ ạḍi jo̱ko̱ buḍhi kanae.

15. joroǩ - *(v.m. warm oneself at a fire)*
Rabaṅeťmea, joroǩme.
jo̱ro̱(ǩ) - *(v.a.m. Dip, drop, trickle, leak.)*
Sạṛim kho̱n daǩ jo̱ro̱ǩkana.

16. kẹṛ kẹṛ - *(adv., slogan used during* Dọṅ *and* Lagṛẽ *dance.)*
Sogoe koṛa do pajhẹṛ kẹṛ kẹṛko hohokeda.
keṛ keṛ - *(adj., Stiff, hard, starched; make, become do.)*
Setoṅte hasa do rohoṛ keṛ keṛena.

17. kol - *(v.a.m. Send, despatch.)*
Ciṭhi kolme.
kọl - *(n. The Indian cuckoo)*
Kọl cẽṛẽ do ạḍi mõńjko sereńa.
kol - *(n. Machinery, engine.)*
Dak̓ kol bạṛiċakantalea.

18. lo - *(v.a.m. Draw (water, etc.), fetch, take out (food etc) by dipping a ladle or vessel into, lade out.)*
Dak̓ lo ber hoyena.
Daka loạńpe.
lo - *(v.a.m. Burn, scald, be in anguish, ache.)*
Kicriċe lo ocokeťa.

19. ọl - *(adj. Musty, mouldy. v.a.m. Become musty. v.m. Lie down (for the night)*
Ọl hoṛo.
Ọl bele do baṅ sebela.
Teheń ńindạ do nọṇḍegele ọl aṅgak̓a.
ol - *(n., v.a.m. Mark, figure, writing; make (long) marks, figures, draw, delineate, write.)*
Goṭa duạrre atnak̓ sakam lohoť dak̓te holoṅateko ola.
Mťṭeċ ciṭhiye olkeťa.

20. oco(k̓) - *(casuative and permissive verbal suffix, with direct casuative)*
Em ocok̓kanae.
ocok̓ - *(v.a.m. Move away, remove; v.a.d. Remove to make place for.)*
Ghãs ocok̓ saphaeme.

21. se - *(n. A louse; v.a. To infect with lice.)*
Bo̱ho̱k̕re bogete se menak̕kotaea, go̱se̱c̕kaepe.
Kạḍa bogeteko se akadea.
se̱ - *(conj. disjunctive. Or.)*
Am se̱ ińiń calak̕a?
se̱ - *(postpos. particle, used to add emphasis, incitement, encouragement.)*
Alo se̱.
Hape̱ se̱,
Jo̱mle jo̱mket̕a se̱.
se̱ - *(v.m. To boil over, foam, well up, froth.)*
Daka se̱k̕kana.
Ạḍi jho̱mo̱re dak̕leda, gaḍa se̱yena.

22. sọl - *(n. a fish, found in river.)*
Sọl hako do̱ gaḍareko ńamok̕a.
so̱l - *(n., A plant found in pond, light, used to make boat.)*
So̱l reak̕ lạukạ do̱ ạḍi rawalgea.

23. tho - *(n., v.a.m. Spittle, saliva; to spit, expectorate.)*
Tho ro̱ho̱ṛentaea, dak̕ tetaṅte.
tho̱ - *(postpos. particle, the same as* to̱, *q. v.* Hijuk̕me tho̱.
Ro̱ṛket̕am tho̱.

ẠKIL BHAŃJAO - 16

A. Ṭo̱yo̱t'kate jobab e̱mo̱k̓me :-

1. *Iso̱rak̓ ... ape sãote tahe̱nma.* Khạli jaega pe̱re̱jme.
   (a) bhor (b) bho̱r (c) bhur (d) bhọr

2. *Am ... hijuk̓me.* Khạli jaega pe̱re̱jme.
   (a) baṛe (b) baṛe̱ (c) baṛi (d) bere

3. *Kicriċe ... ocokeda.* Khạli jaega pe̱re̱jme.
   (a) lo̱ (b) lo (c) lu (d) lọ

4. *Bo̱ho̱k̓re ... menak̓kotaea.* Khạli jaega pe̱re̱jme.
   (a) se̱ (b) si (c) se (d) sa

5. *Setak̓re gocoń ...* Khạli jaega pe̱re̱jme.
   (a) hoyok̓a (b) ho̱yo̱k̓a (c) huyuk̓a (d) ho̱yok̓a

B. O̱lkate jobab e̱mo̱k̓me :-

1. *o̱co̱k̓* sabadte ayat benaome.
2. Jahe̱rre do̱ ce̱t̓ lekan simko dãṛẽ̱koa -*he̱ṛak̓* se̱ *heṛak̓.*
3. Noako sabadte ayat benaome - *kol, ko̱l, kọl.*
4. Noakin sabadte ayat benaome - *era, e̱ra.*
5. Noakin sabadte ayat benaome - *hoe, ho̱e.*

JỌTỌ PAṬ REAK̇ RỌṚ RUẠṚ

ẠKIL BHAŃJAO - 1

A.

1. (c) 2.(c) 3. (d) 4.(d) 5.(d) 6.(a) 7.(c) 8.(c)
9.(c) 10.(a) 11.(b) 12.(b) 13.(c) 14.(b) 15.(a)

ẠKIL BHAŃJAO - 2

A.

1. (c) 2. (d) 3. (b) 4. (c) 5. (b) 6. (b) 7. (c) 8. (c)
9. (b) 10. (b) 11. (c) 12. (c)

ẠKIL BHAŃJAO - 3

A.

1. (c) 2. (b) 3.(a) 4. (b) 5. (b) 6. (a) 7. (c) 8. (b)
9. (a) 10. (b)

ẠKIL BHAŃJAO - 4

A.

1. (b) 2. (a) 3. (b) 4. (b) 5. (c) 6. (b) 7. (b) 8. (b)
9. (c) 10. (a)

ẠKIL BHAŃJAO - 5

A.

1. (c) 2. (b) 3. (a) 4. (a) 5. (b)

ẠKIL BHAŃJAO - 6

A.

1. (b) 2. (a) 3. (b) 4. (b) 5. (c)

ẠKIL BHAŃJAO - 7

A.

1. (b) 2. (a) 3. (b) 4. (a) 5. (d) 6. (b) 7. (d) 8. (d)

9. (b) 10. (d) 11. (b) 12. (c) 13. (a)

ẠKIL BHAŃJAO - 8

A.

1. (a) 2. (a) 3. (a) 4. (b) 5. (a)

ẠKIL BHAŃJAO - 9

A.

1.(b) 2. (a) 3. (a) 4. (b) 5. (a)

ẠKIL BHAŃJAO - 10

A.

1. (a) 2. (b) 3. (a) 4. (c) 5. (a)

ẠKIL BHAŃJAO - 11

A.

1. (a) 2. (b) 3. (c) 4. (a) 5. (a)

ẠKIL BHAŃJAO - 12

A.

1. (a) 2. (b) 3. (a) 4. (c) 5. (b)

ẠKIL BHAŃJAO - 13

A.

1. (b) 2. (b) 3. (b) 4. (a) 5. (a)

ẠKIL BHAŃJAO - 14

A.

1. (c) 2. (b) 3. (c) 4. (c) 5. (b)

ẠKIL BHAŃJAO - 15

A.

1. (b) 2. (b) 3. (a) 4. (b) 5. (c)

ẠKIL BHAŃJAO - 16

A.

1. (b) 2. (b) 3. (a) 4. (c) 5. (b)